STYLE

Studies in English Language

A Course Book in English Grammar, 2nd Edition —
        Dennis Freeborn
From Old English to Standard English — Dennis Freeborn
Style: Text Analysis and Linguistic Criticism — Dennis Freeborn
Varieties of English, 2nd Edition — Dennis Freeborn with Peter
        French and David Langford
Analysing Talk — David Langford
English Language Project Work — Christine McDonald

Series Standing Order

If you would like to receive future titles in this series as they are published, you can make use of our standing order facility. To place a standing order please contact your bookseller or, in case of difficulty, write to us at the address below with your name and address and the name of the series. Please state with which title you wish to begin your standing order. (If you live outside the United Kingdom we may not have the rights for your area, in which case we will forward your order to the publisher concerned.)

Customer Services Department, Macmillan Distribution Ltd
Houndmills, Basingstoke, Hampshire RG21 6XS, England

STYLE

TEXT ANALYSIS AND LINGUISTIC CRITICISM

Dennis Freeborn

MACMILLAN

© Dennis Freeborn 1996

First published 1996 by
MACMILLAN PRESS LTD
Houndmills, Basingstoke, Hampshire RG21 6XS
and London
Companies and representatives
throughout the world

ISBN 0–333–46876–7 hardcover
ISBN 0–333–46877–5 paperback

A catalogue record for this book is available
from the British Library

10   9   8   7   6   5   4   3   2   1
05   04   03   02   01   00   99   98   97   96

Typeset in Great Britain by
Aarontype Limited
Easton, Bristol

Printed and bound in
Great Britain by
Antony Rowe Ltd
Chippenham, Wiltshire

Contents

Symbols   xvi

Acknowledgements   xix

Introduction   xxi

1 **WHAT IS STYLE?**   1
   1.1   Dictionary definitions of style   1
   1.2   Style in literary criticism and reviews of books   2
        1.2.1   'The common pursuit of true judgement'   2
        1.2.2   On Robert Browning's *Dramatic Monologues*   3
        1.2.3   On W. B. Yeats's verse   3
   1.3   Raymond Queneau's *Exercises in Style*   4
        1.3.1   Samples from *Exercises in Style*   4
            'Different types of speech' – Asides   4
            'Different types of written prose' – Official letter   5
            'Different styles of poetry' – Sonnet   5
            'Character sketches through language' – Ignorance   5
            'Experiments with grammatical & rhetorical forms' –
            Reported speech   5
            'Jargon' – Botanical   5
            'Odds & ends' – Permutations   6
            Commentary on 'Botanical'   6
            Commentary on 'Permutations'   6

2 **WORDS**   8
   2.1   Choice of words – 'rules of good writing'   8
        2.1.1   The Fowler brothers and the King's English –
            practical rules for good writing   8
            Rule 1 – familiar and far-fetched words   9
            Rule 2 – Concrete and abstract   9

	Rule 3 – Single words and circumlocutions	10
	Rule 4 – Short and long words	10
	Rule 5 – Saxon, Romance and Latinate words in modern English	10
	(A) Old English and Old Norse words	10
	(B) Romance words	11
	(C) Latin words in English	11
	(D) The core vocabulary	12
	(E) Latinate words	12
2.2	Choice of words in speaking and writing – formal and informal	12
2.2.1	Two versions of a proverb	12
2.2.2	Pronunciation of words derived from French	14
2.3	A claim for Latin	15
2.4	Thomas Hardy's – *The Woodlanders* – formal words	16

3   NEW WORDS FOR OLD   **20**

3.1	*Riddley Walker* by Russell Hoban	20
3.1.1	Commentary, first sentence	20
3.1.1.1	Words, grammar and spelling	21
3.1.1.2	Sentences and punctuation	22
3.1.1.3	Foregrounding	23
3.1.2	*Riddley Walker* – first paragraph	24
3.1.3	Commentary – rest of first paragraph	24
3.1.4	More about the language of *Riddley Walker*	24
3.1.4.1	The end of our civilisation	24
3.1.4.2	Vocabulary	25
3.1.4.3	Editing and rewriting	26
3.2	*A Clockwork Orange* by Anthony Burgess	28
3.2.1	Commentary	29
3.3	*Finnegans Wake* by James Joyce	30
3.3.1	Commentary	31

4   WORDS AND GRAMMAR IN PROSE TEXTS 1   **33**

4.1	George Orwell on good writing	33
4.1.1	Active and passive verb phrases	33
4.1.2	Orwell's use of the passive in *Animal Farm*	35
4.1.2.1	Passive and active voice	35
4.1.2.2	Deletion of the agent	35
4.1.2.3	Focus of information – theme in the clause	36
4.1.2.4	Focus of information – end-weighting, or right-branching	37
4.2	Orwell's vocabulary and the Fowlers' rules	39
4.2.1	Commentary	39
4.3	Academic writing and nominalisation	40
4.3.1	Commentary on academic writing	42
4.4	More on NPs and PrepPs	45
4.4.1	Commentary	46

5 WORDS AND GRAMMAR IN PROSE TEXTS II   47
  5.1 Style and grammar in William Faulkner's *The Bear*   47
    5.1.1 Punctuation, structure and style (i)   48
    5.1.1.1 Commentary   48
      Interior monologue   48
      Punctuation   48
      Sentence structure   49
      Clause structures   49
    5.1.2 Punctuation, structure and style (ii)   50
    5.1.2.1 Commentary   51
    5.1.2.2 Deconstructing the meaning   52
    5.1.3 Vocabulary   53
  5.2 Style and grammar in James Joyce's *Eveline*   54
    5.2.1 Commentary   55
    5.2.1.1 Vocabulary   55
    5.2.1.2 Structure   56

6 TRADITIONAL RHETORIC   58
  6.1 The medieval Art of Rhetoric   58
  6.2 Tropes and figures   61
    6.2.1 Tropes   62
    6.2.1.1 Simile (or similitudo)   62
    6.2.1.2 Metaphor   63
      Personification   64
      Tenor and vehicle   64
    6.2.1.3 Metonymy and synecdoche   65
    6.2.1.4 Other tropes   65
      Climax   65
      Hyperbole   65
      Irony   66
      Litotes   66
      Oxymoron   66
    6.2.2 Figures   66
    6.2.2.1 References to rhetorical figures in *Tristram Shandy*   66
      Aposiopesis   66
      Pun, or paronomasia   67
      Exclamation   67
      Apostrophe   68
    6.2.2.2 Other rhetorical figures   68
      Antithesis   68
      Parenthesis   68
      Periphrasis   69
      Chiasmus or antimetabole   69
      Onomatopeia   69
      Parison   70
  6.3 Rhetoric and style   71

7 RHETORICAL STYLE 72
  7.1 Structure and rhetoric in Dr Johnson's prose 72
    7.1.1 Letter to Lord Bute 72
      7.1.1.1 Commentary 73
        Clauses 73
        Negatives 73
        Passives 74
        Parallelism and balance 74
    7.1.2 Letter to Boswell 75
      7.1.2.1 Commentary 75
        Style 75
        Vocabulary 76
    7.1.3 *The Rambler* and rhetorical style (i) 76
      7.1.3.1 Commentary 77
        Vocabulary 77
        Rhetoric and patterning 77
        Nominalisation, verbs and structure 78
    7.1.4 *The Rambler* and rhetorical style (ii) 80
      7.1.4.1 Commentary 80
        Structure 80
        Rhetorical patterning 82
        Vocabulary 83

8 WRITING WITHOUT STYLE 84
  8.1 Roland Barthes's *Writing Degree Zero* and Albert Camus's *The Outsider* 84
    8.1.1 Commentary on *The Outsider* 86
  8.2 Vikram Seth's *A Suitable Boy* 87
    8.2.1 Commentary on *A Suitable Boy* 87
  8.3 George Orwell's *Animal Farm* 89
    8.3.1 Commentary on *Animal Farm* 90
      8.3.1.1 'Grammatically simple sentences' 90
      8.3.1.2 The vocabulary 91
        Unpretentious and sophisticated vocabulary 92
        Clichés 92

**9 WORDS AND GRAMMAR IN PROSE TEXTS III –
TWO NINETEENTH-CENTURY CLASSICS** 93
  9.1 Fenimore Cooper – *The Last of the Mohicans* (i) 93
    9.1.1 First paragraph 94
      9.1.1.1 Commentary – first rewritten version, first paragraph 95
      9.1.1.2 Commentary – second rewritten version,
        first paragraph 96
    9.1.2 Second paragraph 97
      9.1.2.1 Commentary 98
        Second paragraph – formal vocabulary 98
        Second paragraph – nominalisations 98
        Second paragraph – post-modifying phrases
        and clauses 99

9.2 *The Last of the Mohicans* (ii)   99
9.3 Sir Walter Scott *The Bride of Lammermoor* (i)   100
    9.3.1   Commentary on vocabulary   101
    9.3.2   Commentary on grammatical structure − first sentence   102
       9.3.2.1   Rewriting the first sentence   103
    9.3.3   Commentary on grammatical structure − second sentence   103
9.4 *The Bride of Lammermoor* (ii)   104

10 **WORDS AND GRAMMAR IN VERSE**   105
    10.1 'The real language of men'   105
       10.1.1   Commentary   106
          10.1.1.1   The vocabulary   106
          10.1.1.2   The order of the words   106
    10.2 Poetic diction and word order   107
       10.2.1   Thomas Gray's 'On the Death of Richard West'   107
       10.2.2   Commentary   108
          10.2.2.1   Poetic diction − the vocabulary   109
          10.2.2.2   The order of words − the grammar   109
       10.2.3   George Crabbe's 'Peter Grimes'   111
       10.2.4   Samuel Johnson's 'London'   112
          10.2.4.1   Commentary   113
       10.2.5   'Propriety' in language use   114
       10.2.6   John Milton's *Paradise Lost*   116
          10.2.6.1   The opening sentence of *Paradise Lost*   117
               Reference and meaning   117
               Vocabulary   117
               Structure   118
               Rhetoric   118
               The verse   119
          10.2.6.2   'Latinate' vocabulary   120
          10.2.6.3   Poetic rhetoric   122
               Commentary   122
    10.3 'Linguistic creativity' in Gerard Manley Hopkins's poetry   122
       10.3.1   Words and grammar in 'Harry Ploughman'   122
          10.3.1.1   Words   123
          10.3.1.2   Deviance in grammar   124
               Rhythm and sound   125

11 **PROSE TRANSLATIONS**   126
    11.1 *The Swiss Family Robinson*   126
       11.1.1   Commentary   126
          11.1.1.1   Words   127
          11.1.1.2   Phrases   129
               Discussion   129
          11.1.1.3   Sentence structure   130
               Discussion   131

II.2	Translations of the Bible	133
	II.2.1 From the Sermon on the Mount	133
	II.2.1.1 Vocabulary	134
	II.2.1.2 Structure	134
	II.2.2 St John's Gospel – 'In the beginning...'	135
	Vocabulary	135
	Structure	136
	II.2.2.1 Commentary – vocabulary	137
	II.2.2.2 Commentary – structure	137
	II.2.3 Peter's denial	137

12 RHYME, RHYTHM AND SOUND I – PATTERNS OF STRESS AND RHYTHM — 139

12.1	Patterns of stress and rhythm in everyday speech	139
	12.1.1 Stress patterns in words	139
	12.1.2 Stress patterns in sequences of words	140
	12.1.2.1 Falling and rising rhythm	140
	12.1.3 Equal-timed stress – isochrony	141
	12.1.4 Reading a poem	142
	12.1.4.1 Commentary	142
12.2	Patterns of stress and rhythm in verse	143
	12.2.1 Nursery rhymes	143
	12.2.2 Alliterative verse, stress-timed	145
	12.2.3 Metrical verse	147
	12.2.4 Alliterative metrical verse	149
	12.2.4.1 Commentary on the York *Pentecost Play* verse	149
	Metre	149
	Rhyme	149
	Alliteration	149
	12.2.5 Rhythm and metre	150
	12.2.5.1 The metrical foot	151

13 RHYME, RHYTHM AND SOUND II – HEIGHTENING AND FOREGROUNDING — 152

13.1	Foregrounding rhythm	152
13.2	Foregrounding the final syllables of lines – rhyme	153
13.3	Foregrounding consonants and vowels – alliteration, assonance, consonance	156
13.4	Gerard Manley Hopkins's 'Harry Ploughman'	157
	13.4.1 Rhythm and metrical patterns	157
	13.4.2 Alliteration	162
	13.4.3 Assonance and rhyme	162
13.5	Gerard Manley Hopkins' 'Pied Beauty'	163
13.6	Sound and rhythm in Dylan Thomas's *Under Milk Wood*	164

14	**RHYME, RHYTHM AND SOUND III**	**166**
14.1	Free verse	166
	14.1.1 Commentary	166
14.2	Doggerel	167
	14.2.1 Commentary	168
	Rhyme	168
	Rhythm and metre	168
	Content	168
14.3	'Energetic rhythms and grisly rhymes'	169
	14.3.1 'Energetic rhythms'?	169
	14.3.1.1 Commentary	169
	14.3.2 'Grisly rhyme'?	170
	14.3.2.1 Commentary	170
14.4	'Thumping'	171
	14.4.1 Commentary	172
	14.4.1.1. W. B .Yeats	173
	14.4.1.2 W. E. Henley	173
	14.4.1.3 G. K. Chesterton	173
	14.4.1.4 Rudyard Kipling	174
14.5	Verse and music – Edith Sitwell's 'Façade'	174
	14.5.1 The words set to music	175
	14.5.1.1 'Waltz'	175
	14.5.1.2 'Fox Trot'	176
14.6	Games with words – 'concrete poetry'	177
	14.6.1 Commentary	179
14.7	Six poems	180
15	**POETIC PROSE**	**183**
	Prose and verse	**183**
15.1	Poetry and rhetoric in *The Old Curiosity Shop* – 'The death of Little Nell'	183
	15.1.1 Why *little* Nell?	183
	15.1.2 Verse rhythms in prose	185
	15.1.3 Prose or verse?	187
	15.1.4 The vocabulary	188
	15.1.5 Structure, rhetoric and style	189
	15.1.5.1 Grammatical structure	189
	15.1.5.2 Rhetoric – parallelism	190
15.2	Mock-elevated style in *Pickwick Papers*	190
	15.2.1 Commentary	192
	15.2.1.1 Vocabulary	192
	15.2.1.2 Grammatical structure	192
15.3	Satire in *Dombey and Son*	192
15.4	Poetry and rhetoric in *The Rainbow*	193
	15.4.1 Is the extract poetic?	194

	15.4.1.1	Rhythm, metre and sound	194
		Metrical rhythm	194
		Repetition and parallelism	194
		Assonance, alliteration and vowel harmony	195
	15.4.1.2	Vocabulary – lexical words	195
	15.4.1.3	Grammatical structure	195

16 VERSE TRANSLATION — **197**

16.1	Homer's *Iliad*		197
	16.1.1	Opening lines of Book III	198
		16.1.1.1 Commentary	199
		Alexander Pope's translation	200
		Richard Lattimore's translation	202
		Christopher Logue's translation	202
	16.1.2	Extract from Book XIX	202

17 FIRST PERSON NARRATIVE — **206**

17.1	*The Catcher in the Rye* and *David Copperfield*		206
	17.1.1	Discussion – structure and vocabulary	207
		17.1.1.1 *The Catcher in the Rye*	207
		Structure	207
		Vocabulary	207
		17.1.1.2 *David Copperfield*	207
		Structure	207
		Vocabulary	208
17.2	Joseph Conrad's *Heart of Darkness*		208
	17.2.1	Classification of participants	212
	17.2.2	Vocabulary	212
	17.2.3	Themes and imagery	212
	17.2.4	Negatives	213
	17.2.5	Participant-process analysis	213
		17.2.5.1 Processes involving Marlow	213
		17.2.5.2 Processes involving the African men	213
	17.2.6	Clause structure: transitive/intransitive; focus of information	213
	17.2.7	Foregrounded features of style	214
	17.2.8	Narration and the spoken voice	215
		17.2.8.1 Minor sentences	216
		17.2.8.2 Introductory words and initial *and* or *but*	216
		17.2.8.3 Use of 1st and 2nd person	216
		17.2.8.4 Questions and exclamations	216
		17.2.8.5 Reduction in informal speech	216
		17.2.8.6 Informal vocabulary	217
	17.2.9	Linguistic description and literary criticism	217

18	**THE SPOKEN VOICE**	**218**
18.1	Dialogue	218
	18.1.1 Direct speech and free direct speech	218
	18.1.2 Indirect, or reported speech	219
	18.1.2.1 Declarative clauses	220
	18.1.2.2 Interrogative clauses	221
	18.1.3 Free indirect speech	221
	18.1.4 Speech acts referred to in the narrative	223
18.2	Dialectal speech in novels	224
	18.2.1 Discussion	225
	18.2.2 Commentary	226
	18.2.2 Scottish dialectal speech in *The Bride of Lammermoor*	228
18.3	The spoken voice in letters	231
18.4	The unspoken voice – interior monologue	232
	18.4.1 James Joyce's *Ulysses*	232
	18.4.1.1 Leopold Bloom	232
	18.4.1.2 Molly Bloom	233
	18.4.1.3 Stephen Dedalus	233
19	**ORIGINAL AND SIMPLIFIED TEXTS**	**235**
19.1	Robert Louis Stevenson's *Treasure Island*	235
	19.1.1 Omission and changing of words	237
	19.1.2 Grammatical structure – sentence level	238
	19.1.3 Grammatical structure – clause level	239
	19.1.4 The dialogue	241
	19.1.5 Is a change of words a change of meaning?	241
19.2	Charles Dickens's *David Copperfield*	241
19.3	Shakespeare's *Macbeth* 'made easy'	245
	19.3.1 Commentary	246
	19.3.1.1 Changes in the meanings of words	246
	19.3.1.2 Shakespeare's use of language	247
20	**PARODY AND PASTICHE**	**249**
	Part 1 – Parody	249
20.1	Guide-books	249
20.2	Guide-book to Woolbridge and the West Leys	250
	20.2.1 Vocabulary	251
	20.2.1.1 Connotation and collocation	251
	20.2.1.2 Descriptive and evaluative adjectives	251
	20.2.1.3 NPs with modifiers	251
	20.2.1.4 Nouns in semantic sets	251
	20.2.1.5 Unmodified nouns	252
	20.2.1.6 Abstract nouns and 'literariness'	252
	20.2.1.7 Relational and actional verbs	253
	20.2.1.8 Adverbs	254

20.2.2 Grammar   254
    20.2.2.1 Complexity of structure – parallelism   254
    20.2.2.2 Complexity of structure – formal style   255
    20.2.2.3 The spoken voice   256
    20.2.2.4 'Old-fashioned' style?   256
20.3 Guide-book to Llaregyb – a parody   256
  20.3.1 Vocabulary   256
    20.3.1.1   Adjective modifiers in NPs   256
    20.3.1.2 Other vocabulary   257
      NPs with modifiers   257
      Nouns in semantic sets   258
      Abstract nouns   258
      Verbs   258
      Adverbs   258
  20.3.2 Grammar   258
    20.3.2.1 Parallelism and lists   258
    20.3.2.2 Formal style   259
20.4 Stella Gibbons's *Cold Comfort Farm*   259
  20.4.1 Commentary   260
  Part 2 – Pastiche   262
20.5 Medieval fantasy   263
  20.5.1. Commentary   263

21 STYLES OF NEWS REPORTING   265
Preliminary – political reporting and ideology   265
21.1 Tabloid and broadsheet newspapers   265
  21.1.1 Readability   267
    21.1.1.1 Vocabulary – long and short words   267
    21.1.1.2 Structure   268
      Tabloid leader   268
      Broadsheet leader   269
21.2 Tabloid reporting style   270
  21.2.1 Commentary   271
    21.2.1.1 Naming   271
    21.2.1.2 Colloquial vocabulary   271
21.3 Tabloid vocabulary   271
  21.3.1 'Gnome-napped'   271
    21.3.1.1 Commentary   272
  21.3.2 'Posh kids'   273
21.4 Broadsheet and tabloid vocabulary   273
  21.4.1 'Curried eggs'   273
21.4 Choices of vocabulary – what connotations imply   275
  21.4.1 Degrees of violence   275
    21.4.1.1 Commentary   275
  21.4.2 Classifying participants   276
    21.4.2.1 Commentary   278
21.5 Grammar, vocabulary and style   279

21.5.1	Commentary − vocabulary		280
	21.5.1.1	Word-classes and length of words	280
		Tabloid	280
		Broadsheet	281
	21.5.1.2	Core and non-core vocabulary	281
		Tabloid	281
		Broadsheet	281
21.5.2	Commentary − structure		282
	Tabloid		282
	Broadsheet		282

Bibliography 283

Index of texts quoted and used for stylistic analysis 284

General index 297

Symbols

Symbols and abbreviations are used because they save time and space in describing grammatical features.

Word-classes (parts of speech)

n	noun
v	verb
adj	adjective
adv	adverb
pn	pronoun
p	preposition
cj	conjunction
scj	subordinating conjunction
ccj	coordinating conjunction

Classes of phrase

NP	noun phrase
VP	verb phrase
AdjP	adjective phrase
AdvP	adverb phrase
PrepP	prepositional phrase
PossP	possessive phrase

Classes of clause (form)

NCl	noun clause
PrepCl	prepositional clause
AdvCl	adverbial clause
NonfCl	nonfinite clause

Classes of clause (function)

MCl	main clause
SCl	subordinate clause
RelCl	relative clause
AppCl	appositive clause (in apposition)

Elements of NP structure

Use lower-case letters:

d	determiner
m	modifier (= pre-modifier)
h	head word
q	qualifier (= post-modifier)

Elements of clause structure

Use upper-case letters (capitals):

S	subject
P	predicator
C	complement
A	adverbial

Kinds of complement:

O	object (complement) or Co
Od	direct object
Oi	indirect object
Ci	intensive (complement)
Ca	adverbial (complement)
pt	adverb particle (complement)

Bracketing of grammatical structures

( )	to mark phrases
[ ]	to mark clauses
⟨ ⟩	to mark coordinated elements (words, phrases or clauses)

Languages from which words have derived

OE	Old English
ON	Old Norse
OF	Old French
ME	Middle English
EMnE	Early Modern English
MnE	Modern English
Fr	French
L *or* Lat	Latin
f.	= from

Phonetic transcription

Square brackets are also used with symbols of the International Phonetic Alphabet to indicate the pronunciation of spoken words and sounds, e.g. [æ], [ʃ].

Other symbols

The sign ∅ is used to mark the deletion (or ellipsis) of a word that is 'understood', e.g. *The letter ∅ I wrote yesterday* ... from *The letter **that** I wrote yesterday* ....

Acknowledgements

The author is grateful to Geoffrey Egginton for producing the musical examples on pages 175 and 176.

The author and publishers wish to thank the following for permission to use copyright material: Calder Publications Ltd on behalf of the Calder Educational Trust for material from Raymond Queneau, *Exercises in Style*, trans. Barbara Wright, Calder Publications Ltd, © Editions Gallimard 1947, translation © Barbara Wright 1958, 1979. Carcanet Press Ltd for Edwin Morgan, 'Summer Haiku', 'Bee's Nest', 'Siesta of a Hungarian Snake' and 'I am the resurrection and the life' from *Collected Poems*; and for William Carlos Williams, 'Between Walls' and 'This is Just to Say' from *Collected Poems*. Curtis Brown, London, on behalf of the Estate of Stella Gibbons for material from Stella Gibbons, *Cold Comfort Farm*, © Stella Gibbons 1932. Faber & Faber Ltd for extracted material from W. H. Auden, 'O where are you going' from 'Five Songs' from *Collected Poems*; for Christopher Logue, *The Husbands*, 1994; and for Christopher Logue, *War Music*, 1981.

The *Guardian* for extracts from John Mullin, 'PC who hit boy wins job reprieve', *Guardian*, 23 July 1994; and for a review by James Wood, 'A Suitable Boy', *Guardian*, 13 March 1993, © The Guardian. Mirror Syndication International for extracts from 'Fowl! Farmers' anger at Currie's egg crack', *Daily Mirror*, 5 December 1988; for Vince Wilson, 'Cup Fans Riot', *Sunday Mirror*, 8 January 1978; and for 'Gnome-napped', *Daily Mirror*, 10 August 1988. A. M. Heath & Co. Ltd on behalf of the author for material from George Orwell, *Animal Farm*, © estate of the later Sonia Brownell Orwell and Martin Secker and Warburg Ltd. David Higham Associates Ltd on behalf of the author for material from Russell Hoban, *Riddley Walker*, Jonathan Cape, 1980; and on behalf of the estate of the author for extracted material from Edith Sitwell, 'Some Notes on My Poetry' and Edith Sitwell, 'Waltz' and 'Fox Trot' from *Collected Poems*, Sinclair Stevenson. Newspaper Publishing plc for extracts from Nick Cohen, 'Currie provokes storm with salmonella claim', *Independent*, 5 December 1988; and for 'Slap case PC reprimanded but allowed to keep job', *Independent*, 23 July 1994. Oxford University Press for dictionary entries from the *Oxford English Dictionary*, 2nd edition. Laurence Pollinger Ltd on behalf of the Estate of

Frieda Lawrence Ravagli for material from D. H. Lawrence, *The Rainbow*, and D. H. Lawrence 'Whatever Man Makes' from *The Complete Poems of D. H. Lawrence*. Random House UK Ltd for material from William Faulkner, 'The Bear' from *Go Down Moses*, Chatto & Windus, 1942. Reed Books for material from Anthony Burgess, *The Clockwork Orange*, William Heinemann. Rex Features for material from Mark Wood, 'Thanks a Bundle', *The Sun*, 22 July 1994; and for 'Posh kids are forced to sweep the streets', *The Sun*. Vernon Scannell for 'Jailbird'. Solo Syndication Ltd for material from Gordon Greig, 'Edwina egg row boils over', *Daily Mail*, 5 December 1988. A. P. Watt Ltd on behalf of the Royal Literary Fund for material from G. K. Chesterton, 'The Rolling English Road' and 'The Donkey'; on behalf of the National Trust for Places of Historic Interest or Natural Beauty for material from Rudyard Kipling, 'Cities, Thrones and Powers' and 'Boots'; and on behalf of Michael Yeats for material from W. B. Yeats, 'Three Songs to the Same Tune' and 'Girl's Song'.

Every effort has been made to trace all the copyright-holders, but if any have been inadvertently overlooked the publishers will be pleased to make the necessary arrangement at the first opportunity.

Introduction

This book is a continuation of the last chapter of *A Course Book in English Grammar* (2nd edition 1995) and its Postscript:

> The analysis of these texts shows how important grammatical and lexical choices are in affecting the style of speech and writing. If we can recognise and specify these choices, we can then use this knowledge in the formal study of style, called *stylistics*. We study grammar not just for its own sake (though some of us do enjoy it), but in order to apply what we have learned in an interesting and useful way. We should also become more aware of the choices of vocabulary and grammar that are open to us when we write and talk.

Literary criticism and linguistic criticism

We respond to different styles of writing intuitively at first, and may try to describe them subjectively as *terse*, *brittle*, *flowing*, *transparent* and so on – the method of much literary criticism and book-reviewing. This is discussed in chapter 1. The approach to style from a linguistic point of view tries to be objective. We ask the question 'How do I know?' if a subjective description of style is made, and apply our understanding of the forms and functions of vocabulary and grammar in a way that (we hope) may be verified by others.

My intention is to provide a resource book that need not be followed in sequence, though there is in the first chapters an attempted logical development in the study of the vocabulary of texts first, and then the grammar. Of course the two are inseparable in their stylistic effects, and the following chapters look at a variety of genres that seem to me to provide interesting ways of studying style, drawing upon insights from the choices of words or structures as seems appropriate. You may therefore find some repetition in the definition of particular features of style, from chapter to chapter.

Rhetoric

Traditional rhetoric is important for its historical place in literary criticism. Only a few of the classical tropes and figures listed in such profusion in older books of rhetoric have survived into modern criticism, but chapter 6 refers briefly, with illustrations, to a larger number.

Readability

A modern word-processing application will provide 'readability statistics' for a selected text, based upon the average number of sentences per paragraph, words per sentence and characters per word. The text must, of course, be spelt and punctuated according to the conventions of correctness of Standard English. These averages then provide a level of 'reading ease', from *very easy*, through *easy, fairly easy, standard, fairly difficult* and *difficult*, to *very difficult*. The computer is a mechanical tool, and takes no account of the meanings of words, and so must not be relied on. However, its assessment of readability is interesting to discuss and you may agree or disagree with the grading. So for this reason, the readability grade is printed after many of the texts.

Commentary and Data Book

We arrive at a lot of the conclusions about how vocabulary and structure contribute to the style of a text by preparing data beforehand. Words have to be listed, and their derivations and definitions looked up separately. The structure of a text has to be analysed and diagrammed. Once this is done, only some of the data proves to be relevant to the stylistic question being asked. It would have increased the size of the book too much to have included all the preliminary data, so only a little is included to illustrate the method.

However, teachers and lecturers will find it useful to be able to provide their students with the raw data sometimes, so that they can do some first-hand analysis, particularly on texts which are not followed by a commentary. This is a very time-consuming and routine kind of occupation, even with the help of the *Oxford English Dictionary* on CD-ROM. So the author has provided a supplementary *Commentary and Data Book* in typescript, available to teachers and lecturers. For details write to: Dennis Freeborn, PO Box 82, Easingwold, York YO6 3YY.

I. What is style?

1.1 Dictionary definitions of style

This book is about styles of writing, that is, different ways of using our common language by which we identify one writer, or one kind of writing, from another. It would be useful to look at some dictionary definitions to start with, which you can then refer back to if you want to remind yourself of some of the uses of the word *style*.

The following extracts from the New Edition of the *Oxford English Dictionary* (1991) contain those definitions of *style* which you are likely to find relevant in studying written and spoken language. Some of the quotations which illustrate the different meanings have been printed also. Obsolete meanings are not included. The numbers before each paragraph indicate the different sections of the entry on *style* in the *OED*. The original meaning of the word, with its earliest recorded occurrence, was:

I. Stylus, pin, stalk.
1a. An instrument made of metal, bone, etc., having one end sharp-pointed for incising letters on a wax tablet, and the other flat and broad for smoothing the tablet and erasing what is written: = stylus
   1387 *John of Trevisa* Seinte Barnabe his body was founde in a den...with þe gospel of Mathew þat he hadde i-write wiþ his owne **stile**.

Activity 1.1

Read the extracts through and consider their differences. Notice how the original meaning of the word has developed and changed.

II. Writing; manner of writing (hence also of speaking).
13a. The manner of expression characteristic of a particular writer (hence of an orator), or of a literary group or period; a writer's mode of expression considered in regard to clearness, effectiveness, beauty, and the like.
13b. Used for: A good, choice or fine style.
13c. Proverbial phrase. *the style is the man.*
   1624 *R. Burton* It is most true, *stylus virum arguit*, our stile bewrayes vs.
   1753 *G. Buffon* Le style est l'homme même.

14. In generalized sense: Those features of literary composition which belong to form and expression rather than to the substance of the thought or matter expressed. Often used for: *Good or fine style.*
    1713 *Steele* The Rules of Method, and the Propriety of Thought and Stile.
    1749 *Chesterfield* Style is the dress of thoughts.
15. A manner of discourse, or tone of speaking, adopted in addressing others or in ordinary conversation.
    1667–8 *Pepys Diary* 23 Feb., But here talking, he did discourse in this stile: 'We', and 'We' all along, 'will not give any money'.

III. Manner, fashion.
21b. In generalized sense. Often used for: Beauty or loftiness of style.

Notice that some of these definitions make a distinction between the **form** or **manner** or **mode of expression** and the **content, message,** or **substance of thought**. The idea that 'style is the dress of thoughts' has been disputed, on the grounds that thought and expression are inseparable.

1.2   Style in literary criticism and reviews of books

The study of English Literature is principally concerned with *evaluation*, *appreciation* and *personal response*. The aims of the English Literature syllabus of one Examinations and Assessment Board are:

> to present the subject as a discipline that is humane (concerned with values), historical (setting literary works within the context of their age) and communicative (concerned, that is, with the integrity of language as a means of enabling human beings to convey their thoughts and feelings one to another).

> (Northern Examinations and Assessment Board syllabus for 1994)

In assessing the value of a piece of writing, whether it is good of its kind or not, it is essential that we produce some evidence for our judgement. Among other things, we evaluate its style. One common practice of reviewers and students of literature we can call **subjective** or **impressionistic** – an appeal to the impression that the writing makes on the reviewer by finding descriptive words and phrases which attempt to match or reproduce this impression. This is not the method used in this book, which tries to find and use **objective** criteria in describing the style of a piece of writing. But before attempting to do this, let us look at a few examples of the way in which judgements on a variety of different texts are made within the academic study of English Literature and by literary reviewers of books.

1.2.1   *'The common pursuit of true judgement'*

F. R. Leavis (1895–1978) was a Cambridge academic and literary critic who had a great influence, from the 1930s onwards, on the way that English Literature has been taught in universities and schools. He believed that the business of students of literature and literary critics was 'the common pursuit of true judgement'. This point of view has come down into classrooms, for example in lessons where pupils are asked to judge which of two poems or passages of prose is 'the better'.

But though you will find plenty of positive judgements in F. R. Leavis's criticism, there is little analysis of the language of authors. For example, in *D. H. Lawrence: Novelist* (1955), chapter 3, on *The Rainbow*, he quotes two paragraphs from the beginning of the novel. Leavis is establishing his judgement that Lawrence (1885–1930) belongs to 'the same tradition of art' as the nineteenth-century novelist George Eliot (1819–80) by first of all saying that 'George Eliot doesn't write this kind of prose'. He continues:

> Lawrence is not indulging in descriptive 'lyricism', or writing poetically in order to generate atmosphere. Words here are used in the way, not of eloquence, but of creative poetry (a wholly different way, that is, from that of *O may I join the choir invisible**): they establish as an actual presence – create as part of the substance of the book – something that is essential to Lawrence's theme. The kind of intense apprehension of the unity of life that they evidence is as decidedly not in George Eliot's genius as it is *of* Lawrence's.
>
> **'O may I join the choir invisible' is a poem by George Eliot.

Students of literature are left to infer from the text what it is that produces an *intense apprehension of the unity of life*. A stylistic study of the text is an attempt to find out *how* this effect is produced. (You can read the extract from *The Rainbow* in section 15.4, where its style is discussed.)

I.2.2   *On Robert Browning's* Dramatic Monologues

The following paragraph is *part* of a review of an edition of Browning's verse:

> No reader of poetry could scan more than a few lines of any of them without knowing that they are by Robert Browning. The energetic rhythms and hectic vocabulary, as much as the finely calibrated moral scales in which each assertion is weighed, are unmistakeable; even the lapses – the occasional grisly rhyme and the jovial embellishments – give the game away.
>
> (Robert Winder 'Browning's "Dramatic Monologues"',
> *Folio Society quarterly magazine Summer*, 1991, pp. 4, 8)

The phrases *energetic rhythms, hectic vocabulary, grisly rhyme, jovial embellishments* and, elsewhere, *the capriciousness of Browning's grammar* are used to describe Browning's style. But how do you recognise and agree on aspects of a writer's work that are called *energetic, hectic, grisly, jovial* or *capricious*? What are the specific features of the language – vocabulary, syntax, phonology – by which *energy* or *capriciousness* can be recognised? Notice also that some of these features (*grisly rhyme* and *jovial embellishments*) are called *lapses*, that is, they fall short of some notional standards of verse writing.

Some of Browning's verse is discussed in section 14.3.

I.2.3   *On W. B. Yeats's verse*

> It was his stubbornly Anglo-Irish ear that saved him from thumping like Henley or Chesterton or Kipling.
>
> (Peter Levi, 'W. B. Yeats', *Folio Society quarterly magazine*, Summer 1989, p. 29)

3

This asserts a generalisation about four writers – the verse of Henley, Chesterton and Kipling is said to 'thump', while Yeats's does not because 'his Anglo-Irish ear' is 'stubborn'. Examples of each poet's verse are discussed in section 14.4.

1.3   Raymond Queneau's *Exercises in Style*

Exercices de Style (1947) by the French author, Raymond Queneau, tells the same fragment of a story in 99 different styles. It was translated into English in 1958 as *Exercises in Style*. His first 'exercise', called *Notation*, is written like a set of notes for a story – an outline of what happens.

1   *Notation*

In the S bus, in the rush hour. A chap of about 26, felt hat with a cord instead of a ribbon, neck too long, as if someone's been having a tug-of-war with it. People getting off. The chap in question gets annoyed with one of the men standing next to him. He accuses him of jostling him every time anyone goes past. A snivelling tone which is meant to be aggressive. When he sees a vacant seat he throws himself on to it.

Two hours later, I meet him in the Cour de Rome, in front of the gare Saint-Lazare. He's with a friend who's saying: 'You ought to get an extra button put on your overcoat.' He shows him where (at the lapels) and why.

Exercises in Style would seem to be an obvious choice for inclusion in a book on style, but the story is so banal (*commonplace* or *trite*) that it is hard for someone studying literary criticism to see how it can be '*humane (concerned with values)*', or '*communicative (concerned, that is, with the integrity of language as a means of enabling human beings to convey their thoughts and feelings one to another)*', in the terms of the A Level syllabus quoted in section 1.2. The 99 versions of the story are probably best described as *games with language*.

The translator, Barbara Wright, has analysed the variations into roughly seven groups. Here are extracts from an example of each kind. The titles are an essential part of each 'exercise', and give a vital clue to how we should read them.

Activity 1.2

Explain how the texts of the exercises match their titles.

1.3.1   *Samples from* Exercises in Style

'*Different types of speech*' – Asides

The bus arrived bulging with passengers. Only hope I don't miss it, oh good, there's still just room for me. One of them queer sort of mug he's got with that enormous neck was wearing a soft felt hat with a sort of little plait round it instead of a ribbon just showing off that is and suddenly started hey what's got into him to vituperate his neighbour...

'Different types of written prose' – **Official letter**

I beg to advise you of the following facts of which I happened to be the equally impartial and horrified witness.

Today, at roughly twelve noon, I was present on the platform of a bus which was proceeding up the rue de Courcelles in the direction of the Place Champerret. The aforementioned bus was fully laden — more than fully laden, I might even venture to say, since the conductor had accepted an overload of several candidates, without valid reason . . .

'Different styles of poetry' – **Sonnet**

Glabrous was his dial and plaited was his bonnet,
And he, a puny colt – (how sad the neck he bore,
And long) – was now intent on his quotidian chore–
The bus arriving full, of somehow getting on it . . .

'Character sketches through language' – **Ignorance**

Personally, I don't know what they want of me. Yes, I got on an S bus about midday. Were there a lot of people? Of course there were, at that hour. A young man with a felt hat? It's quite possible. Personally I don't give a damn. A kind of plaited cord? Round his hat? I'll agree that's a bit peculiar, but it doesn't strike me personally as anything else. A plaited cord . . . He had words with another man? There's nothing unusual about that.

'Experiments with grammatical and rhetorical forms' – **Reported speech**

Dr Queneau said that it had happened at midday. Some passengers had got into the bus. They had been squashed tightly together. On his head a young man had been wearing a hat which had been encircled by a plait and not by a ribbon. He had had a long neck. He had complained to the man standing next to him about the continual jostling which the latter had been inflicting on him. As soon as he had noticed a vacant seat, said Dr Queneau, the young man had rushed off towards it and sat down upon it.

'Jargon' – **Botanical**

Activity 1.3

List all the words that are part of the vocabulary of botany — the study of plants. Some are literal, some metaphorical, and others are puns, or slang and colloquial usages. (Remember that the narrative about the incident on the S bus underlies every exercise.)

After nearly taking root myself under a heliotrope, I managed to graft myself on to a vernal speedwell where hips and haws were squashed indiscriminately and where there was an overpowering axillary scent. There I ran to earth a young blade or garden pansy whose stalk had run to seed and whose nut, cabbage or pumpkin was surmounted by a capsule encircled by snakeweed. This corny, creeping sucker, transpiring at the palms, nettled a common elder who started to tread his daisies and give him the edge of his bristly ox-tongue, so the sensitive plant stalked off and parked himself.

'Odds and ends' – Permutations

This group of exercises in style is the furthest removed from traditional literary texts of any in the book. The first is *Permutations by groups of 2 letters*, and the text is,

> Ed on to ay rd wa id sm yo da he nt ar re at
> pl rm fo an of us sb aw is ou ay ma ng ho nw
> ne se wa ck oo st ng lo dw an wa ho ea sw ng
> ri at ah th wi la ap ro it dt un sa he me.

Activity I.4 _____

Given the title, *Permutations by groups of 2 letters*, can you work out the meaning and purpose of the exercise?

Commentary on 'Botanical'

All the following listed words belong to the semantic set which we could call 'botanical', or have something to do, in one of their senses, with plants or gardens:

taking root	axillary	nut	sucker	sensitive plant
heliotrope	scent	cabbage	transpiring	stalk(ed)
to graft	(ran to) earth	pumpkin	palms	park
vernal	(a young) blade	capsule	nettle(d)	
speedwell	garden pansy	snakeweed	common elder	
hips and haws	stalk	corny	daisies	
squash(ed)	run to seed	creeping	bristly ox-tongue	

Commentary on 'Permutations'

To *permute* is *to subject to permutation; to alter the order of; to re-arrange in a different order*. This is the original text of the exercise,

> one day towards midday on the rear platform of an S bus I saw a young man whose neck was too long and who was wearing a hat with a plait round the same.

and this is how you produce 'permutations by groups of two letters':

1. Divide the text into groups of two letters, without any punctuation:

    > on ed ay to wa rd sm id da yo nt he re ar pl at fo rm of an sb us Is aw ay ou ng ma nw ho se ne ck wa st oo lo ng an dw ho wa sw ea ri ng ah at wi th ap la it ro un dt he sa me

2. Permute the order of each pair of two letters, so that every second pair (boxed for illustration) changes places with the pair of letters before it. The beginning,

    > on ⌐ed⌐ ay ⌐to⌐ wa ⌐rd⌐ sm ⌐id⌐ da ⌐yo⌐ nt ⌐he⌐ re ⌐ar⌐ pl ⌐at⌐ . . .

then becomes,

ed on to ay rd wa id sm yo da he nt ar re at ...

which is the first line of the exercise,

Ed on to ay rd wa id sm yo da he nt ar re at...

which you then complete in the same way.

Activity 1.5

What was the original text of the next exercise in this group?

Permutations by groups of 3 letters

Den sud est lyh edt art ran oha his gue ghb
nei cla our ngt imi hew hat urp asp lyt ose din
rea his gon sev toe tim ery yon ean tin ego
ut oro

There are brief commentaries on section 1.3 in the *Commentary & Data Book*.

2. Words

Oh wondrous power of words, how sweet they are
According to the meaning which they bring!

(William Wordsworth, *The Prelude*, Book 7, lines 121–2)

2.1 Choice of words – 'rules of good writing'

2.1.1 *The Fowler brothers and the King's English – practical rules for good writing*

Two brothers, H. W. and F. G. Fowler, published a book called *The King's English* in 1906 as a guide to good writing. H. W. Fowler's *A Dictionary of Modern English Usage* was published later in 1926, and is still in print in a revised edition. Both books are **prescriptive**, that is, they make positive recommendations about usage and pronunciation based on the authors' judgement and preferences. People still 'look it up in Fowler' if they want to check 'correct' usage.

In *The King's English* the Fowler brothers list some practical rules for choosing **words**, 'roughly in order of merit':

1   Prefer the familiar word to the far-fetched.
2   Prefer the concrete word (or rather expression) to the abstract.
3   Prefer the single word to the circumlocution.
4   Prefer the short word to the long.
5   Prefer the Saxon word to the Romance.

Activity 2.1

Before reading any further, discuss your first reactions to these rules. Take any paragraph from a book that is handy, and apply the rules to its style. Substitute different words to see if you can improve the writing or not.

Rule 1 – Familiar and far-fetched words

The criterion by which we classify words as *familiar* or *far-fetched* must be subjective and personal. We have to make an intelligent guess about how well-known a word is to those who are listening to us or reading what we are writing, even though we ourselves may know it well. For example, the Fowlers assume that their readers know what *circumlocution* means in their third rule above. It is not an everyday word, and it is also *abstract* (rule 2), *long* (rule 4), and derived from *Latin* (rule 5). *Circum* meant *around*, *locutio* meant *speech* – hence 'a roundabout way of speaking'. It is, however, a *single* word (rule 3). So are the Fowlers keeping rule 1 or not in their own proposals?

Activity 2.2

Select a paragraph from any text in a book, newspaper or journal, and list words which are not familiar to you . If you do this in pairs or groups, you can discover whether you all agree on which words are familiar and which are far-fetched.

Rule 2 – Concrete and abstract

Concrete nouns are those which refer to things in the world, physical entities that can be touched, seen, heard, tasted or smelt, like *cup*, *desk*, *fence*, *scent*, *air*. **Abstract nouns** refer to things constructed or thought in the mind, emotions, ideas, or attributes of objects, like *analysis*, *fear*, *psychology*, *height*. The terms are **semantic**, that is, they refer to the meaning of a noun. Like most categories of language, they are useful but not always clear-cut. But the Fowlers present rule 2 rather oddly by amending *word* to *expression*, commenting that 'abstract expression and the excessive use of nouns are almost the same thing'. So their examples are not of uses of concrete and abstract nouns, and what they call 'excessive use of nouns' turns out to be complex **prepositional phrases** (PrepPs). A PrepP consists of a **preposition** (p) followed by a **noun phrase** (NP), e.g. *over the moon*, *down the chimney*, *in the morning*, *of an hour*, etc.

One of their examples is,

No year passes now without evidence of the truth of the statement that...

The noun *evidence* in the PrepP *without evidence* is **post-modified** by the PrepP *of the truth* to form the complex PrepP *without evidence of the truth*. Similarly, *truth* is post-modified by *of the statement* to form the more complex PrepP *without evidence of the truth of the statement*.

This is what the Fowlers mean by 'excessive use of nouns', which they then refer to as an 'abstract expression'. Their preferred version is,

No year passes now	without evidence	of the truth	of the statement	that...

Every year shows again how true it is that...

Activity 2.3

Is this version more 'concrete' than the first?

Rule 3 – Single words and circumlocutions
The meaning of *circumlocution* has already been discussed under rule 1.

Activity 2.4

(i) Is a single word necessarily prefereable to a phrase? For example, is *roundabout way of speaking* a circumlocution for *circumlocution*? Discuss the use and necessity of technical terms and jargon.

(ii) H. W. Fowler in *Modern English Usage* gives examples of circumlocution or *periphrasis*. The first of each of the following expressions is the 'roundabout way', the second is what Fowler prefers. What is your opinion?

    a In Paris there reigns a complete absence of really reliable news.
       There is no reliable news in Paris
    b the year's penultimate month
       November
    c The answer is negative.
       No.
    d was made the recipient of
       received

(iii) Select a short text and look for examples of cicumlocution/periphrasis/a roundabout way of writing.

Rule 4 – Short and long words
It seems reasonable to use the shorter of two words with the same meaning, not so much to save time or space, but because short words tend to be the more familiar ones. But there are plenty of long words of five syllables which are well-known, like *unnecessary, congratulated, administration* (taken from the front page of the *Sun* newspaper), and short one-syllable or two-syllable words which are not, like *gavel, gelid, gault* and *gemmule* (taken at random from one page of the *Concise Oxford Dictionary*).

Rule 5 – Saxon, Romance and Latinate words in modern English

(A) *Old English and Old Norse words*
We now refer to **Old English** (OE) rather than *Saxon* when describing early English. The **common core** of the language, some 50,000 or 60,000 words, derives mostly from the English of a thousand years ago, spoken by the descendants of the Angles and Saxons who invaded and settled in Britain from the fifth century onwards, and brought the language with them. These words also tend to be short and familiar in modern English (MnE), like æppel, *apple*; cu, *cow*; hlaford, *lord*.

📖 There is a selection of common words derived from OE in the *Commentary & Data Book*.

As a result of later raiding and settlement in northern and eastern England by the Vikings (Danes and Norwegians) which began in the late eighth century, many words of **Old Norse** were adopted. Viking Old Norse was similar to Old English (we believe that speakers of the two languages could understand each other). Consequently, there are many MnE words whose source is both OE and ON, for example, earm (OE), armr (ON), *arm*; land (OE), land (ON), *land*.

📖 There is a selection of common words derived from both OE and ON in the *Commentary &* Data Book.

Scots and northern English dialect words can often be traced back to an ON source, e.g. *kirk*, *dyke*, while the Standard English words come from OE, *church*, *ditch*. There are also a lot of MnE words of ON derivation which have survived while the OE word has been lost, for example ON *egg* and *sky*.

📖 There is a selection of common words derived from ON in the *Commentary & Data Book*.

Both OE and ON belonged to the Germanic family of languages, so we refer to the **Germanic core** of modern English vocabulary.

(B) *Romance words*
Romance words are those which have been taken into English from the **Romance languages**. The word *Romance* is here used in its earliest meaning, related to the word *Roman*. Old French **Romanz** was the **vernacular** version of Latin spoken in France at the time of the Roman Empire which has since changed and developed into modern French. The word *Romance* is now used to describe all those other languages which developed from local forms of Latin, like Spanish, Portuguese, Italian and Romanian.

A very large number of Romance words were borrowed from **French** in the centuries immediately following the conquest of England by the French-speaking Normans in 1066. If you have studied French, you will be able to recognise many MnE words which must have come from Old French (OF), although they are fully **assimilated** into English, that is, their pronunciation (and sometimes spelling) conform to English rules of speaking, for example, boeuf, *beef*; fruit, *fruit*; rivière, *river*.

📖 There is a selection of common words derived from OF in the *Commentary & Data Book*.

Compare the use of Latin in the Roman Empire two thousand years ago as an official language for purposes of government with the use of English throughout the British Empire from the eighteenth to the twentieth centuries. This has led to the growth of many different Englishes in use throughout the world today, just as different Romance languages developed from Latin, though the Englishes have not yet had time to develop into different languages.

(C) *Latin words in English*
The language of the great period of Roman literature at the time of the Emperor Augustus (d. 14 AD) is preserved as **classical Latin.** The everyday Latin spoken in the different regions of the Roman Empire gradually changed, and eventually

diverged into the different modern Romance languages. Classical Latin remained the language of the Church and of scholarship for hundreds of years. For example, the scientist Isaac Newton wrote his major works on mathematics in Latin at the end of the seventeenth century. The influence and prestige of Latin, especially during the 'Revival of Learning' (the **Renaissance**) in the sixteenth century and after, was so great that writers 'Englished' hundreds of words which were taken directly from Latin. Borrowing from Latin (and Greek) has gone on ever since, e.g. *television* from *tele-* (Greek for *far*) and *-vision* (from the Latin for *see*).

There are, however, many words in MnE which were taken from Latin both in the OE period (roughly up to *c.*1150) and the **Middle English** (ME) period (from *c.*1150 to *c.*1450), long before the Renaissance. They have been assimilated like the OF words, and are usually short and familiar. You would probably be surprised to learn that the following words were originally Latin, and came into the language in OE or ME times; *belt*, balteus; *mat*, matta; *school*, schola.

📖 There is a selection of common words derived from Latin in OE in the *Commentary & Data Book.*

(D) *The core vocabulary*
Most of the common, everyday words that form the **core vocabulary** of English are therefore derived from Old English, or from Old French and Latin words that had been completely assimilated into the language 600 or more years ago.

(E) *Latinate words*
The term **Latinate** is used to describe words that were introduced directly from Latin by scholars and writers from the late fifteenth century onwards, especially during the sixteenth and seventeenth centuries. The words were coined either to provide a word for which there was no suitable English equivalent, or because it was thought that a word of Latin origin carried much more prestige than a native word. Such 'Latinate' words are not always long and **polysyllabic** (having many syllables), e.g. *drama* (1515), although many are, e.g. *exasperate* (1534).

📖 There is a selection of 'Latinate' words in the *Commentary & Data Book.*

The term *Latinate* is also used to describe the structure of English writing which shows the influence of Latin grammar on the writer's style.

2.2 Choice of words in speaking and writing – formal and informal

2.2.1 *Two versions of a proverb*

As a result of these historical changes and developments in the vocabulary of MnE, we often have a choice between words of Old English, French or Latin derivation when we speak or write. These words are **synonyms**, that is, they have more or less the same meaning. But we use them in different contexts, to speak or write formally or informally, and this affects the **style** or defines the **register** of our language in use.

A simple example is the change of style between the old proverb,

Birds of a feather flock together

in which all the words derive from Old English – *birdas, of, an, feþer, flocc, togædre* – and a version in formal style,

Ornithological creatures of identical plumage congregate in close proximity

in which the derivation of the lexical words is as follows (the dates from the *Oxford English Dictionary* are of the first known use of the word in a written source):

ornithological	1802 from *ornithology* (1655), from modern Latin (16th C) *ornithologia*, from Greek.
creature	1300 from French *créature*, from Latin *creatura*.
identical	1633 from medieval Latin *identicus*.
plumage	1481 from French *plumage* from Latin.
congregate	1400 from Latin *congregatus*.
close	1325 from French *clos*, from Latin.
proximity	1480 from French *proximité* from Latin.

The sources of these words show why the Fowlers' rule 5 encourages us to use 'Saxon' words rather than Romance (French) or Latin. The Old English **core vocabulary** consists of common, familiar words usually of one or two syllables. On the other hand, there are also many one-syllable or two-syllable words in the core vocabulary which were taken from French or Latin into Old and Middle English up to the early fourteenth century. They have also become fully assimilated, so the Fowlers' rule is probably impossible to observe in fact. *Creature* and *close* in the rewritten proverb would probably be accepted as common and familiar words in the core vocabulary. Both words were adopted from Old French by the early fourteenth century:

1300 He fordestend tuin **creature** to serue him in þat hali ture.
1325 Wyth yȝen open & mouth ful **clos**.

Activity 2.5

Discuss the differences, if any, between the following synonyms and when they might be used.

from OE	*from OF*	*from Latin*
folk	people	persons
go	depart	progress
home	residence	domicile
kingly	royal	regal
loving	amiable	affectionate
wise	sensible	sagacious

Activity 2.6

(i) Discuss how you pronounce the word *village*. Are there any differences between your pronunciation and that of others?

(ii) Now discuss the different pronunciations of *garage* that you have heard.

(iii) Have both the words been fully assimilated?

(iv) Look up the dates when *village* and *garage* were first recorded in English. Does this explain the answer to (iii)?

(v) Which of the following French words in the vocabulary of English is fully assimilated – that is, pronounced according to the normal rules of English spelling and pronunciation?

(vi) If you know how to pronounce French, compare the French pronunciation of a word with typical English ways of saying it. There may be several pronunciations in English. How do you explain this?

alliance	cliché	envelope	naïve	rôtisserie
amateur	collage	figure	orange	royal
art	connoisseur	fines herbes	papier mâché	saint
ballet	courgette	foyer	pigeon	sausage
baton	crime	haute couture	poison	sermon
beef (f. boeuf)	de luxe	hors d'oeuvre	prison	souvenir
biscuit	debris	impasse	rage	surprise
brochure	début	innocent	repertoire	surveillance
bureau	déjà vu	liaison	reservoir	tête-à-tête
café	double	lingerie	restaurant	turquoise
champagne	élite	menu	reveillé	valet
chant	ensemble	morale	revue	vinegar

The choice of words of OE, French or Latin derivation has a marked effect on the style of our writing. Of course, when we write, most of us do not usually choose a particular word knowing that it is from OE, French, Latin or some other language, but because it seems the right word for the situation – in general terms, whether it is relatively formal or informal.

2.2.2 *Pronunciation of words derived from French*

The earliest recorded written use of *village* is from Chaucer's *Pardoner's Tale*,

1386 Henne oure a myle, withinne a greet **village**.

while that of *garage* is, for the noun (in inverted commas, to show that it is a new word),

1902 *Daily Mail* 11 Jan. 6/7 The new '**garage**' founded by Mr. Harrington Moore, hon. secretary of the Automobile Club. The '**garage**', which is situated at the City end of Queen Victoria-street, has accommodation for eighty cars.

and for the verb,

> 1906 *Daily Chron.* 26 May 3/7 They will **garage** your car, wash it, clean it, adjust it, repair it, keep it always at 'concert pitch'.

Clearly, *village* is a fully assimilated English word, while the various pronunciations of *garage* range from the fully assimilated ['gærɪdʒ] to a French-like [gə'rɑːʒ] – the choice probably being related to social class. The pronunciation of the words of French origin listed in section 2.2.1 ranges similarly from those fully assimilated (e.g. *alliance, champagne, crime, orange, saint, vinegar* etc.) to those spoken with a French or pseudo-French accent (e.g. *brochure, cliché, début, ensemble, hors d'oeuvres,* etc.). Some have more than one pronunciation, e.g.

de luxe	də lyks	dɪ lʌks
envelope	ɒnvələup	ɛnvələup
foyer	fwaɪje	fɔɪjə *or* fɔɪje
lingerie	læ̃ʒəri	lɪŋgəri
restaurant	rɛstərɑ̃	rɛstərɒnt
valet	væle	vælɪt

2.3 A claim for Latin

Here is a letter to the editor of a national newspaper. The writer was supporting the teaching of Latin in schools, which had been the subject of a previous letter:

> The campaign for the retention of Latin in schools is emphatically not special pleading for a minority cause. It is basic to the intellectual and spiritual sanity of the nation. It is an irony not lost, I am sure, that two words right at the centre of the issue, *education* and *curriculum,* are both Latin. But then English is drenched in Latin. It is the prime source of the language. Most of the words I have just used have a Latin derivative....

(Letter in the *Independent,* 14 November 1987, p. 14)

The writer claims that Latin is the prime source of the language, and that most of the words in his letter are from Latin. In fact (excluding the proper nouns), 59 words come from Old English, 22 from French and 5 from Latin. However, it would be wrong to reject the writer's claim simply on these figures. We must distinguish between **grammatical words** (pronouns, prepositions, conjunctions, determiners, auxiliary verbs) and **lexical words** (nouns, verbs, adjectives, adverbs). Lexical words have meanings which refer to the world and our experience of it. Grammatical words hold together the structure of sentences. There are thousands of lexical words, but relatively few grammatical words, which are used over and over again, so that there may be several occurrences (**tokens**) of one word (**type**).

Almost all grammatical words are derived from Old English, so that it would be difficult to write a paragraph with most of the words from Latin because you must use grammatical words. Of all the words in the letter, both grammatical and lexical, 67% are from OE, 27% from French and 6% from Latin.

On the other hand, it would be less difficult to write a letter with most of the lexical words from Latin. But are most of the writer's lexical words from Latin? There are10 tokens (9 types) from OE (that is, out of 10 words, 9 are different), 22 tokens (19 types) from French and 5 tokens/types from Latin. That is, out of 37 lexical words, 27% are from OE, 60% from French, and 13% from Latin. Although French is a Romance language (see the Fowlers' rule 5) and therefore ultimately derived from Latin, this does not support the writer's argument, because he is advocating the teaching of classical Latin, not Romance languages derived from it.

📖 A complete list of the words can be found in the *Commentary & Data Book*.

Furthermore, it is quite easy to rewrite the letter, making sure that as many of the lexical words as possible are from Old English, and avoiding those less familiar and more formal words which derive from French or Latin. The style changes and the meaning is also modified (it is difficult, for example, to find a word of OE origin for *irony*) but this version is close enough to the original:

> The **fight** for **keeping** Latin in schools is **clearly** not special pleading for **the good of a few.** It is **needed for the health** of the nation**'s mind and soul.** Everyone **must know that** two words right at the **heart** of the issue, *education* and *curriculum*, are both Latin. But then English is drenched in Latin.

Because his final sentence would have to be written as

> Most of the words I have just written **come** from Old English.

the revised version would make nonsense of the argument. Even if we took into account the fact that Old French derived directly from Latin, the writer's claim about Latin as the 'prime source' of English is not convincingly demonstrated in the vocabulary of his letter. On the other hand, there are styles of writing in which the choice of Latinate words has a marked effect.

2.4 Thomas Hardy's *The Woodlanders* – formal words

It is soon obvious to anyone reading a novel by Thomas Hardy (1840–1928) that from time to time he uses words and phrases which are not common and familiar. These examples are from *The Woodlanders* (1887):

- the forsaken coach-road running almost in a **meridional** line from Bristol to the south shore of England
- the **physiognomy** of a deserted highway expresses solitude to a degree that is not reached by mere dales or downs
- But he made no reply and without further pause plunged towards the **umbrageous** nook
- their visitor made it his business to stop opposite the casements of each cottage that he came to, with a **demeanour** which showed that he was **endeavouring to conjecture**, from the persons and things he observed within, the whereabouts of somebody or other who **resided** here.

These quotations could be rewritten,

- the forsaken coach-road running almost in a line **south** from Bristol to the south shore of England
- the **look** of a deserted highway expresses solitude to a degree that is not reached by mere dales or downs
- But he made no reply and without further pause plunged towards the **shady** nook
- their visitor made it his business to stop opposite the casements of each cottage that he came to, with a **manner** which showed that he was **trying to guess**, from the persons and things he observed within, the whereabouts of somebody or other who **lived** here.

The derivations of the selected words with the date of their earliest recorded forms, from the *OED*, are:

Hardy's words:		**Replaced by**	
meridional	Fr 1386	south	OE
physiognomy	Fr 1390	look (*n*)	OE
umbrageous	Fr 1587	shady	OE
demeanour	Fr 1494	manner	Fr 1275
endeavour	Fr c. 1400	try	Fr c. 1330
conjecture (*v*)	Fr 1618	guess	ME 1330
resided	Fr 1456	lived	OE

Activity 2.7

(i) Does the substitution of these words make any significant difference to Hardy's meaning?

(ii) Read the following six extracts from the novel and the derivations and meanings of the following words, listed after the extracts: *fundamental, physiological, conventionalism, gradations, member, concluded, perambulation, commodious, edifice, lucubrations, propinquity, recalcitration, immoderate, risibility, engendered.*

(iii) Rewrite the extracts, substituting more familiar words for those in bold type.

- As with so many right hands born to manual labour, there was nothing in its **fundamental** shape to bear out the **physiological conventionalism** that **gradations** of birth show themselves primarily in the form of this **member**.
- Having now **concluded** her **perambulation** of this now uselessly **commodious edifice**, Grace began to feel that she had come a long journey since the morning;
- 'Do you keep up your **lucubrations** at Little Hintock?' the lady went on.
- Grace was indeed quite unconscious of Fitzpiers's **propinquity**.

- From this hour, there was no serious **recalcitration** on her part.
- She burst into an **immoderate** fit of laughter... her shoulders suddenly shook as the scene returned upon her; and the tears of her **risibility** mingled with the remnants of those **engendered** by her grief.

Word		Earliest recorded occurrence and derivation
fundamental	1449	ME f. French *fondamental* or Late Latin *fundamentalis*
physiological	1610	relating to the material universe or to natural science, physical f. *physiology* (1564). f. French *physiologie* or Latin *physiologia* f. Gk *phusiologia*
conventionalism	1833	adherence to or regard for what is conventional (in conduct, thought, or art). f. *conventional* (1583) f. French *conventionnel* or Late Latin *conventionalis*.
gradations	1549	stages of transition or advance. f. Latin *gradatio* f. *gradus* step.
member	1290	any part or organ of the body, esp. a limb. f. ME f. OF *membre* f. Latin *membrum* limb.
concluded	1388	bring or come to an end. f. ME f. Latin *concludere* (as *com-, claudere* shut).
perambulation	1485	action of walking through, over, or about (streets, the country, etc.). f. Latin *perambulare perambulat-* (as *per-, ambulare* walk).
commodious	1420	roomy and comfortable, (*archaic*) convenient. f. French *commodieux* or f. med. Latin *commodiosus* f. Latin *commodus*.
edifice	1386	a building, esp. a large imposing one. ME f. OF f. Latin *aedificium* f. *aedis* dwelling+ *-ficium* f. *facere* make.
lucubrations	1595	(*literary*) nocturnal study or meditation. Literary writings, esp. of a pedantic or elaborate character. f. *lucubrate*; f. Latin *lucubratio* (as lucubrate).
propinquity	1374	nearness in space; proximity, close kinship, similarity. ME f. OF *propinquité* or Latin *propinquitas* f. *propinquus* near f. *prope* near to.
recalcitration	1658	the action of recalcitrating, or kicking against something. f. Latin. *recalcitrare* to kick out.
immoderate	1398	excessive; lacking moderation. ME f. Latin *immoderatus*.
risibility	1620	the faculty of laughing; laughter; a disposition to laugh. f. Late Latin *risibilitas*.
engendered	1325	give rise to; bring about (a feeling etc.). ME f. OF *engendrer* f. Latin *ingenerare*.

Activity 2.8

(i) Rewrite the following extracts from the novel, substituting common words for any which you judge to be formal or unfamiliar. Discuss any problems you found in doing this.

(ii) Look up the derivation of the words.

(iii) Is the hypothesis of the previous section supported − *that words classified as 'formal' tend to be those which were taken into English from the late fourteenth century onwards?*

- In years she was no more than nineteen or twenty, but the necessity of taking thought at a too early period of life had forced the provisional curves of her childhood's face to a premature finality.
- ... like Trafalgar line-of-battle ships, with which venerable hulks, indeed, these vehicles evidenced a constructive spirit curiously in harmony.

- It was still dark, but she began moving about the house in those automatic initiatory acts and touches which represents among housewives the installation of another day.
- Here Creedle threw grieved remembrances into physical form by resigning his head to obliquity and letting his eyes water.
- In the hollow shades of the roof could be seen dangling and etiolated arms of ivy...
- The intersection of his temporal orbit with Mrs Charmond's for a day or two in the past had created a sentimental interest in her at the time, but it had been so evanescent that in the ordinary onward roll of affairs he would scarce ever have recalled it again.

📖 A list of the words and their derivations is in the *Commentary & Data Book*.

English is known to have an abundant stock of words, and we have many to choose from with similar meanings – **synonyms**. Words with similar meanings, however, may have very different **connotations** or associated meanings, and choosing the right word can present problems. It is well-known that in an examination, for example, it is better not to use slang words, whose use is normally confined to familiar speech within a group. For the examination we use **formal** words and for our friends we use **informal** words. The examination is a formal occasion, and we learn to associate different sets of words with different occasions.The choice of words affects the style of everything written or spoken, so the topic will continue to be relevant in the following chapters.

3. New words for old

POLONIUS   What do you read, my Lord?
HAMLET   Words, words, words.

3.1 *Riddley Walker* by Russell Hoban

A novel called *Riddley Walker* was written by Russell Hoban and published in 1980. Russell Hoban has written other novels and children's books, but the language of Riddley Walker was quite different from anything that he had previously produced.

Activity 3.1

(i) Read the opening paragraph of the novel printed below, and before you go to read the Commmentary, discuss your first impressions, who the 1st person 'I' seems to be and what happens in this paragraph.

(ii) Comment on any features of the words, grammar, spelling and punctuation that seem unusual to you.

(iii) Discuss any difficulties you have in reading and understanding the text.

On my naming day when I come 12 I to gone front spear and kilt a wyld boar he parbly ben the las wyld pig on the Bundel Downs any how there hadnt ben none for a long time befor him nor I aint looking to see none agen. He dint make the groun shake nor nothing like that when he come on to my spear he wernt all that big plus he lookit poorly. He done the reqwyrt he ternt and stood and clattert his teef and made his rush and there we were then. Him on 1 end of the spear kicking his life out and me on the other end watching him dy. I said, 'Your tern now my tern later.' The other spears gone in then and he wer dead and the steam coming up off him in the rain and we all yelt, 'Offert!'

3.1.1 Commentary – first sentence

In the first few lines it is clear that the normal vocabulary and grammar, spelling and punctuation of written English today are not being used. The style of the

opening paragraph is consistently followed for the rest of the novel, so if we look in detail at the different ways in which conventions are being broken in this paragraph, we shall be better prepared to read the whole novel, and then to discuss the important questions: why does Russell Hoban write like this? what effect does this style produce in us as readers? what does the novel <u>mean</u>?
Here is a detailed analysis of the language of the first sentence,

> On my naming day when I come 12 I to gone front spear and kilt a wyld boar he parbly ben the las wyld pig on the Bundel Downs any how there hadnt ben none for a long time befor him nor I aint looking to see none agen.

3.1.1.1   WORDS, GRAMMAR AND SPELLING

- *naming day* – is an immediate puzzle, because it is not a phrase which clearly relates to any anniversaries that we normally keep – it might be simply the narrator's twelfth birthday, but what immediately follows suggests some kind of 'coming of age', he 'to gone front spear'. We have to postpone a full understanding.
- *I come 12* – the word *come* is a nonstandard form of the past tense of the verb *come*, used often in present-day dialects, but Standard English (StE) requires *came*. It is also probably short for *became*. The effect of 'hearing' a speaker of dialectal nonstandard English, in the conventions of writing fiction, is to suggest someone who is perhaps uneducated, or from some rural or urban 'lower class' environment.
- The use of figures in *12* rather than the word *twelve* breaks a convention you have been taught to follow in your own writing.
- *to gone* – another puzzle at first until you say it aloud. Is it perhaps *took on*, meaning *I took on the job of*? If so, we shall have to remember to listen to the <u>sound</u> of the words, and not simply rely on looking at them for their meaning. But why should Riddley Walker's spelling match his pronunciation? What has happened to the standard spelling of English which we have all been taught?

  * The phrase *I to gone* is from the hardback version of the novel. In paperback, it is printed as *I gone* – StE *I went*, like *come* for *came*, a nonstandard form of the past tense.

- *kilt* – for *killed* – we would pronounce the past tense suffix spelt -ed in *killed* as [d] because it follows a **voiced** sound [l]. The narrator presumably says [kɪlt], further evidence of a different pronunciation from any present-day English dialectal accent.
- *wyld* – for *wild* – there is no difference in pronunciation, but it looks different, and so continues to make the text look 'strange'.
- *parbly* – must be *probably*, and reflects the narrator's pronunciation.
- *ben* – for *been*, indicates pronunciation, and is at the same time a nonstandard form of the past tense of *be*. We would say *was* in StE.
- *las* – for *last* – spelt as pronounced when the final [t] is **unreleased**.

Questions begin to form at the back of our minds: are we to imagine the narrator actually speaking the story (as in, for example, J. D. Salinger's *The*

Catcher in the Rye), or has the writing of his language changed to reflect pronunciation more directly than it does today? But why should it? It certainly does not look and sound like a new Standard English. When does this story take place? Is it in the past or in the future? It cannot be present-day. And so on.

In fact, at the end of chapter 1 we read, *Thats why I finely come to writing all this down . . .* , and at the beginning of chapter 7, *This what Im writing down now . . .* , so the author's intention is to suggest a new written form of English which appears to be based on its pronunciation.

- ***any how*** is written as two words. Perhaps the writing system used by the narrator points to a fresh start, the conventions which we follow having been forgotten?
- ***hadnt ben none*** – the **double** or **multiple negative**, today a sign of dialectal, nonstandard usage, though historically the normal negative in English.
- ***befor*** – spelt without the final ⟨e⟩, pronunciation unaffected but the word looking odd.
- ***nor I aint looking to see none*** – makes a second multiple negative construction; *nor I aint* is also marked for some people as a nonstandard spoken form of *I'm not*.
- ***agen*** – spelt according to a normal pronunciation of *again*, the second syllable being **reduced** from the diphthong [eɪ] to [ɛ].

In the first sentence, therefore, we have found the following kinds of nonstandard spelling, punctuation, word-forms and grammar:

(a) nonstandard spellings which do not seem to mark differences in pronunciation – *wyld, any how, befor,*
(b) nonstandard spellings which mark pronunciations similar to our own in normal speech – *las, agen,*
(c) nonstandard spellings which also indicate a modified or dialectal pronunciation – *to gone, kilt, parbly,*
(d) nonstandard word-forms and grammar – *come, ben, aint* and the *multiple negative,*
(e) words with different connotations of meaning – *naming day, looking to see.*

3.1.1.2 SENTENCES AND PUNCTUATION

The division of a written text into sentences is to some extent a matter of choice and style, but it is clear that if you wrote a sentence for an English assignment like the first one of *Riddley Walker*, it would be returned with a lot of red ink corrections on it. We would probably agree that there should be three sentences, and also that some commas would help in marking the clauses and phrases,

> On my naming day, when I come 12, I to gone front spear and kilt a wyld boar. He parbly ben the las wyld pig on the Bundel Downs. Any how, there hadnt ben none for a long time befor him, nor I aint looking to see none agen.

If you read the whole novel, you will find that the only commas used in the text occur after phrases like *he said, . . .* which introduce direct speech. There are no commas within sentences to mark embedded clauses and phrases. Also, Riddley Walker's text does not use the apostrophe – *hadnt* for *hadn't* and *aint* for *ain't*.

3.1.1.3 FOREGROUNDING

The first sentence of Riddley Walker is typical of the whole of the novel in its unconventional spelling and punctuation, which serve to reinforce and represent the much more important fact that Riddley's world is very different from the contemporary England of today. He is only twelve years old, but he takes on 'front spear' on a hunting expedition. Spears and wild boars in England? And the boar is a rarity too, having being hunted almost to extinction perhaps.

The effect of the unconventional presentation of the text is to **foreground** differences in language – to make them prominent – and so to reinforce the total contrast between the state of civilisation now and in Riddley's times. To print the first sentence in present-day English is to lose much of the effect of the original. Compare the two side by side:

On my naming day when I come 12	On my naming day when I (be)came twelve
I to gone front spear and kilt a wyld boar	I took on front spear and killed a wild boar.
he parbly ben the las wyld pig on the	He probably was the last wild pig on the
Bundel Downs	Bundel Downs.
any how there hadnt ben	Anyhow, there hadn't been
none for a long time befor him	any for a long time before him,
nor I aint looking to see none agen.	and I'm not expecting to see any again

3.1.2 Riddley Walker – *first paragraph*

Activity 3.2

Study the rest of the first paragraph from *Riddley Walker*, and list the nonstandard features in the way that has been demonstrated in the Commentary on the first sentence. Are there any new features which we did not find in the first sentence?

Riddley Walker *text*	*Standard English version*
He dint make the groun shake nor nothing	He didn't make the ground shake or anything
like that when he come on to my spear	like that when he came onto my spear.
he wernt all that big plus he lookit poorly.	He wasn't all that big; also he looked poorly.
He done the reqwyrt he ternt and	He did the required (thing) – he turned and
stood and clattert his teef and made his rush	stood and clattered his teeth and made his rush
and there we were then.	and there we were then,
Him on 1 end of the spear kicking his life out	him on one end of the spear, kicking his life out,
and me on the other end watching him dy.	and me on the other end watching him die.
I said, 'Your tern now my tern later.'	I said, 'Your turn now, my turn later.'
The other spears gone in then and he wer dead	The other spears went in then and he was dead,
and the steam coming up off him in the rain	and the steam coming up off him in the rain,
and we all yelt, 'Offert!'	and we all yelled, 'Offered!'

3.1.3   Commentary – rest of first paragraph

(a)   Nonstandard spellings which do not seem to mark differences in pronunciation – *wernt, dy, tern, wer.*

(b)   Nonstandard spellings which mark pronunciations similar to our own in normal speech – *dint, groun.* These spellings indicate the **elision** of the consonant [d] in our informal speech: [dɪdnt] ⇒ [dɪnt] and [graʊnd] ⇒ [graʊn], which have become the norm in Riddley's.

(c)   Nonstandard spellings which also indicate a modified or dialectal pronunciation – *lookit, reqwyrt, ternt, clattert, teef, yelt, 'Offert!'* The pronunciation of *teef* is not uncommon in children and some dialects today: [tiːθ] ⇒ [tiːf]. We pronounce the past tense of *look* as [lʊkt]; Riddley pronounces the suffix as a full syllable [ɪt]. The other words are all verbs, past tenses or past participles, spelt with *-ed* in StE and pronounced [d] today.

(d)   Nonstandard word-forms and grammar – *nor nothing, come, wernt, plus, done, gone, wer.*

(e)   Words with new meanings/connotations – *plus, done the reqwyrt, offert!*

3.1.4   More about the language of Riddley Walker

3.1.4.1   THE END OF OUR CIVILISATION

It becomes clear as you read the novel that it is set in the future after a nuclear war in 1997 destroyed our civilisation. Memories of this have survived in the form of legends called the Eusa Story, about the 'clevverness what made us crookit' which split the 'Littl Shynin Man the Addom' in a cataclysmic explosion they call 'the 1 Big 1', whose centre was Canterbury. There was no 'year count' for a long time afterwards:

> He said, 'We dont know jus how far that count ever got becaws Bad Time put an end to it... After Bad Time dint no 1 write down no year count for a long time... Since we startit counting its come to 2347 o.c. which means Our Count.'

Here is one reference to *Bad Time*:

> Evere thing wuz blak & rottin. Ded peapl & pigs eatin them & thay pigs dyd. Dog paks after peapl & peapl after dogs tu eat them the saym. Smoak goin up from bernin evere wayr.

There is a memory of some of the things people had in the *Good Time*, 'time back way back', like aircraft and television:

> Thay had boats in the ayr & picters on the win & ever thing lyk that.

The irony of the story is that Riddley's generation are seeking out the secret of the '1 Littl 1' by combining 'yellerboy stoan' (sulphur), 'Saul and Peter' (saltpetre) and 'chard coal' (charcoal). The '1 Littl 1' is therefore gunpowder, and the cycle of violence is starting all over again.

3.1.4.2 VOCABULARY

The story is set in Kent, in the south-east of England, where old place names have been remembered, but changed in the handing-down by word of mouth, like so many of the words that Riddley uses and writes down, for example:

Cambry	*Canterbury*	Good Mercy	*Godmersham*
Ram Gut	*Ramsgate*	Fork Stoan	*Folkestone*
Horny Boy	*Herne Bay*	Do It Over	*Dover*
Widders Bel	*Whitstable*	Sams Itch	*Sandwich*
Fathers Ham	*Faversham*	Brabbas Horn	*Brabourne*

The changes are plausible. Compare, for example, the Anglo-Saxon and contemporary names of towns such as;

Æglesford	*Aylesford*	Folcanstan	*Folkestone*
Bedcanford	*Bedford*	Heopwinesfleot	*Ebbsfleet*
Brycgstow	*Bristol*	Hwitcirice	*Whitchurch*
Cantwaraburg	*Canterbury*	Suthriganaweorc	*Southwark*
Dofras	*Dover*	Weogornaceaster	*Worcester*

This change in the spelling and pronunciation of words is not confined to place names, but appears in many other words and phrases which are in common use today. For example; *comping station* for *compensation*, *gallack seas* for *galaxies*, *Mincery* for *Ministry*. In the world created by Russell Hoban this is made plausible when we are told,

> Bint no writing for 100s and 100s of years til it begun agen. All them other storys tol by mouf they ben put to and took from and changit so much thru the years theyre all bits and blips and all mixt up.

Hoban has devised a form of spelling which <u>looks</u> as if it has been reconstructed again from speech. His readers today are relating the text to familiar Standard English spelling, vocabulary and grammar, and the clash between the two systems produces a remarkable effect of 'authenticity'. The linguistic ingenuity is, of course, meant for contemporary readers. One example is how today's phrase 'helping the police with their enquiries', which implies the arrest of a suspect and his interrogation, is used by Hoban to mean 'torture':

> When Goodparley made some of the hevvys **help the qwirys** on others of them they wer ready for the bringdown...

Activity 3.3

(i) What contemporary word or phrase do you think is represented by the spelling of the following words or phrases in Ridley's language?

(ii) Rewrite in Standard English the complete sentences printed below in which they occur. If you say the phrases aloud it will help you to decipher them.

1.	suching waytion	7.	Ardship of Cambry
2.	some poasyam	8.	axel rating the Inner G
3.	soar vivers	9.	strapping the lates
4.	tryl narrer & spare the mending	10.	regenneril guvner man
5.	deacon termination	11.	goach the wayt
6.	stablisht men	12.	pour the ounts of judgd men

1. I thot a littl on our **suching waytion** and I done what I cud to dark it down a littl.
2. 'How dyou do that kynd of gethering what youre going to do? Do you all set down and pul datter or dyou jus think to gether or what?'
   He said, 'We do **some poasyum**.'
   I said, 'Whats poasyum?'
   He said, 'It aint jus poasyum you all ways say *some* **poasyum**.'
3. Them what wer lef in the towns them what wer the **soar vivers** of the barming they torchert Eusa then.
4. 'I know itwl take **tryl narrer and spare the mending** but may be this time wewl do it.'
5. Granser he wer what they callit a knowing man he knowit herbs and roots and mixters he done **deacon terminations** he done healing and curing plus he knowit dreams and syns.
6. Orfing said, 'Trufax it is. This heres going to be the parper **stablisht men** story is it.'
7. He said, 'Wel Im the **Ardship of Cambry** enn I.'
8. 'If we go to Fork Stoan weare keaping the circel which thatwl be **axel rating the Inner G** you know.'
9. 'How it looks to Erny and me and **strapping the lates** from what littl dater weve got we pirntow the other siders mus have plenny of yellerboy and theywl be senning out mor farring seakert tryers.'
10. All the seanyer members of the form in front plus the **regenneril guvner man** from the Ram his name wer Riser Partman.
11. '...it wer a farring seakert tryer from other side and looking to **goach the wayt** he wer looking to bargam a seakert gready mint for the Nos. of the mixter.'
12. Erny said, 'Wel Rightway whats it going to be? Be you going to put on your wig and hold the bailey and **pour the ounts of judgd men** or you going to let wester day go down and ter morrer come up?'

  Suggested answers can be found in the *Commentary & Data Book*.

Russell Hoban also puts into Riddley's narrative unfamiliar words which are not just re-spellings of present-day words, such as *girzel, kincher, sturgling, zanting*. You can only infer their meanings from the context in which they occur. He also uses familiar words in new ways, for example *I wer roading*, meaning *I was travelling*, from the noun *road*; *to word* meaning *to write down*; *b*eartht, meaning *born*, from the noun *birth*. You can find some in the sentences printed above also.

3.1.4.3   EDITING AND REWRITING
Although changing the text also changes the meaning to some extent, it is a worthwhile linguistic exercise for students who are looking closely at Hoban's use of language in *Riddley Walker*. Rewriting a part of it in Standard English is one way of ensuring that this is done. It is not an easy book to read, and you tend to skim and skip over the hard bits the first time, in order to get the overall impression of the narrative.

Here are two more extracts, the first continuing from the second paragraph of the opening, and the second providing some further information about Riddley's world.

Activity 3.4

(i) Read the extracts, and choose a section or sections for close study.

(ii) Rewrite these sections in Standard English and comment on the changes you make.

(iii) Make a detailed examination of the language, as demonstrated earlier, and mention any new or different features that you discover.

(iv) Comment further on the differences between Hoban's text and your Standard English version — does rewriting really make a difference?

Extract 1

The woal thing fealt jus that littl bit stupid. Us running that boar thru that las littl scrump of woodling with the forms all roun. Cows mooing sheap baaing cocks crowing and us foraging our las boar in a thin grey girzel on the day I come a man.

The Bernt Arse pack ben follering jus out of bow shot. When the shout gone up ther ears all prickt up. Ther leader he wer a big black and red spottit dog he come forit a littl like he ben going to make a speach or some thing til 1 or 2 bloaks uppit bow then he slumpt back agen and kep his farness follering us back. I took noatis of that leader tho. He wernt close a nuff for me to see his eyes but I thot his eye ben on me.

Coming back with the boar on a poal we come a long by the rivver it wer hevvyer woodit in there. Thru the girzel you cud see blue smoak hanging in be twean the black trees and the stumps pink and red where they ben loppt off. Aulder trees in there and chard coal berners in amongst them working ther harts. You cud see 1 of them in there with his red jumper what they all ways wear. Making chard coal for the iron reddy at Widders Dump. Every 1 made the Bad Luck go a way syn when we past him.

Extract 2 – Other clues to Riddley Walker's world: from a story, 'Why the Dog Wont Show Its Eyes'

Time back way way back befor peopl got clevver thay had the 1st knowing. They los it when they got the clevverness and now the clevverness is gone as wel....

... Every morning they were counting every thing to see if any thing ben took off in the nite. How many goats how many cows how many measurs weat and barly. Cudnt stop ther counting which wer clevverness and making mor the same. They said, 'Them as counts counts moren them as dont count.'

Counting counting they wer all the time. They had iron then and big fire they had towns of parpety. They had machines et numbers up. They fed them numbers and they fraction out the Power of things. They had the Nos. of the rain bow and the Power of the air all workit out with counting which is how they got boats in the air and picters on the wind. Counting clevverness is what it wer.

When they had all them things and marvelsome they cudnt sleap realy they dint have no res. They wer stressing ther self and straining all the time with counting. They said, 'What good is nite its only dark time it aint no good for nothing only them as want to sly and sneak and take our parpety a way.' They los out of memberment who nite wer. They jus wantit day time all the time and they wer going to do it with the Master Chaynjis.

They had the Nos. of the sun and moon all fraction out and fed to the machines. They said, 'Wewl put all the Nos. in to 1 Big 1 and that wil be the No. of the Master Chaynjis.' They bilt the Power Ring thats where you see the Ring Ditch now. They put in the 1 Big 1 and woosht it roun there came a flash of lite then bigger nor the woal worl and it ternt the nite to day. Then every thing gone black. Nothing only nite for years on end. Playgs kilt peopl off and naminals nor there wernt nothing growit in the groun. Man and woman starveling in the blackness looking for the dog to eat it and the dog out looking to eat them the same. Finely there come day agen then nite and day regler but never like it ben befor. Day beartht crookit out of crookit nite and sickness in them boath.

Now man and woman go afeart by nite afeart by day. The dog all lorn and wishful it keaps howling for the nites whatre gone for ever. It wont show its eyes no mor it wont show the man and woman no 1st knowing. Come Ful of the Moon the sad ness gets too much the dog goes mad. It follers on the man and womans track and arga warga if it catches them.

The fires col

My storys tol

📖 The extracts are discussed in the *Commentary & Data Book*.

3.2 *A Clockwork Orange* by Anthony Burgess

Russell Hoban invents some new words in *Riddley Walker*, but most belong to present-day English, athough spelt differently in order to produce the effect of a changed pronunciation of partly remembered words. Many of them have shifted in their meanings, but their origins are, mostly, clear enough.

Another contemporary novelist, Anthony Burgess, wrote *A Clockwork Orange*, which became notorious for a film which was based on it because of its depiction of violence. The novel is told in the 1st person by a young delinquent whose vocabulary includes a significant number of unfamiliar coined words. In the following extract he is describing how he underwent psychiatric treatment called 'aversion therapy'. Some of the words have been left blank:

Activity 3.5

(i) Identify the probable/possible word-class of the missing words in the text (noun, verb, adjective or adverb), and then try to match them with the original coined words, which are listed underneath in alphabetical order.

(ii) Discuss the evidence (or lack of evidence) for assigning a meaning and a place in the text to each word.

(iii) Complete the text. Is it possible to be certain about each word? If not, why not?

(iv) Which of these words do you think the author had himself made up? Check in a dictionary.

'First-class,' ...1... out this Dr. Brodsky. 'You're doing really well. Just one more and then we're finished.'

What it was now was the ...2... 1939-45 War again, and it was a very blobby and liny and crackly film you could ...3... had been made by the Germans. It opened with German eagles and the Nazi flag with that like crooked cross that all ...4... at school love to draw, and then there were very haughty and ...5... like German officers walking through streets that were all dust and bomb-holes and broken buildings. Then you were allowed to ...6... ...7... being shot against walls, officers giving the orders, and also horrible ...8... ...9... left lying in gutters, all like cages of bare ribs and white thin ...10... Then there were ...11... being dragged off ...12... though not on the sound-track, my brothers, the only sound being music, and being ...13... while they were being dragged off. Then I noticed, in all my pain and sickness, what music it was that like crackled and boomed on the sound-track, and it was

Ludwig van, the last movement of the Fifth Symphony, and I ...14... like ...15... at that. 'Stop!' I ...16... 'Stop, you ...17... disgusting sods. It's a sin, that's what it is, a filthy unforgivable sin, you...18... !'

bezoomny	lewdies (2)	plotts
bratchnies	malchicks	starry
creeched (3)	nadmenny	tolchooked
creeching	nagoy	viddy(2)
grahzny	nogas	

The only words which appear in the *OED* are *creech* (with an entirely different and irrelevant meaning *a kind of stony or gravelly soil*), *starry* and *vide* for *viddy*.

starry adj. (starrier, starriest) covered with stars, resembling a star; visionary; enthusiastic but impractical, euphoric.

vide [Latin *vide*, imp. sing. of *videre* to see.] See, refer to, consult; a direction to the reader to refer to some other heading, passage, or work (or to a table, diagram, etc.) for fuller or further information. Frequently abbreviated as *vid*.

📖 The completed extract can be found in the *Commentary & Data Book*.

3.2.1 *Commentary*

Allocating these words to their right places in the text is, of course, more difficult than trying to infer their meaning when we read the novel. We use a different process of guesswork. We have to ask ourselves what kind of word fits the place in the text – what is its **function?** – and then see which word(s) might fit, using their **form** as one criterion, and perhaps using their similarity to an existing word to guide us to their meaning. For example, words ending in ⟨-s⟩ might be **plural nouns** – *bratchnies, lewdies, malchicks, nogas, plotts*. Words with the suffix ⟨-ed⟩ might be either the **past tense** forms or the **past participles** of verbs – *creeched, tolchooked*. This is confirmed for *creeched* because the **present participle** form *creeching* with the suffix ⟨-ing⟩ also occurs.

Five of the remaining words end with the very common suffix ⟨-y⟩, *bezoomny, grahzny, nadmenny, starry, viddy,* so their function is less definite, because more than one word-class ends in ⟨-y⟩ – **adjectives** like *gloomy, lazy, many, merry, giddy*; **nouns** like *enemy, daisy, penny, berry, melody*, and a few **verbs** like *bury, embody*. There are no examples in this short extract with the common **adverb** suffix ⟨-ly⟩, however. *Nagoy* is difficult to place; there are relatively few English words ending in ⟨-oy⟩ (*boy, coy, joy, toy* for example) and none in ⟨goy⟩. The word *starry* is not a coinage, but it is used, like many of the words in *A Clockwork Orange,* with a new meaning. *Viddy* is an example of a coined word whose meaning (*see*) may be guessed from its resemblance to *video*, and known either from *video recorder*, or from a knowledge of Latin – *video* means *I see*.

The fact that we can read the words aloud shows that they conform to normal sound-patterns, what is technically called the **phonotactics** of English – that is, there are no combinations of vowel or consonant which cannot already be found in English.

By inventing a new vocabulary for his principal character, Anthony Burgess is using the fact that people in different groups or communities make use of known words with changed meanings, or else invent words, in order to mark their belonging to a particular group, and to keep outsiders away – what the character Dr Brodsky calls 'the dialect of the tribe'. A clue to the form and spelling of Burgess's new words is in a comment by one of the doctors, 'most of the roots are Slav'.

The extract continues:

> 'Stop it, stop it, stop it,' I kept on creeching out. 'Turn it off you grahzny bastards, for I can stand no more.' It was the next day, brothers, and I had truly done my best morning and afternoon to play it their way and sit like a horrorshow smiling cooperative malchick in the chair of torture while they flashed nasty bits of ultra-violence on the screen, my glazzies clipped open to viddy all, my plott and rookers and nogas fixed to the chair so I could not get away. What I was being made to viddy now was not really a vesch I would have thought to be too bad before, it being only three or four malchicks crasting in a shop and filling their carmans with cutter, at the same time fillying about with the creeching starry ptitsa running the shop, tolchooking her and letting the red red krovvy flow. But the throb and like crash crash crash in my gulliver and the wanting to be sick and the terrible dry rasping thirstiness in my rot, all were worse than yesterday. 'Oh, I've had enough' I cried. 'It's not fair, you vonny sods,' and I tried to struggle out of the chair but it was not possible, me being as good as stuck to it.
>
> 'First-class,' creeched out this Dr. Brodsky...

Activity 3.6

Here is a list of the coined words, or existing words used with a new sense, in the extract.

(i) Make a selection and discuss their form and the evidence for their probable meanings.

(ii) Can you give them a meaning using current English words?

(iii) Comment on the function of the word *like* in the character's speech, e.g.
   *the throb and **like** crash crash crash in my gulliver*
   *the Nazi flag with that **like** crooked cross*
   *what music it was that **like** crackled and boomed on the sound-track*

carmans	fillying	krovvy	ptitsa	tolchooking
crasting	glazzies	malchick(s)	rookers	vesch
creeched/creeching (2)	grahzny	nogas	rot	viddy (2)
cutter	gulliver	plott	starry	vonny

It is not the practice of many writers to use new words like Hoban and Burgess in *Riddley Walker* and *A Clockwork Orange* (the technical term for a newly coined word is **neologism**), but there is one notable exception.

3.3   *Finnegans Wake* by James Joyce

Joyce virtually created his own vocabulary in this novel published in 1939. It is presented in the form of a dream, so that the language is distorted and given a dream-like shape. Many words are derived from the way Humpty Dumpty, in Lewis Carroll's *Through the Looking-Glass* (1872), made up **portmanteau words**, words created from the blended sounds of two distinct words and combining the meanings of both:

> Well, 'slithy' means 'lithe and slimy'... You see it's like a portmanteau – there are two meanings packed up into one word.
> 'Mimsy' is 'flimsy and miserable' (there's another portmanteau for you).

Meanings of words shift and combine, with ambiguity created by lots of puns.

Activity 3.7

See what you make of the following extracts from *Finnegans Wake*. You are listening to a guide taking you round the Wellington Museum in Dublin. You need to read it aloud and listen to the sound and rhythm as well as trying to work out what the words mean.

> This is the way to the museyroom. Mind your hats goan in! Now yiz are in the Willingdone Museyroom. This is a Prooshious gunn. This is a ffrinch. Tip. This is the flag of the Prooshious, the Cap and Soracer. This is the bullet that byng the flag of the Prooshious. This is the ffrinch that fire on the Bull that bang the flag of the Prooshious. Saloos the Crossgunn! Up with your pike and fork! Tip. Bullsfoot! Fine! This is the triplewon hat of Lipoleum. Tip. Lipoleumhat. This is the Willingdone on his same white harse, the Cokenhape. This is the big Sraughter Willingdone, grand and magentic in his goldtin spurs and his ironed dux and his quarterbrass woodyshoes and his magnate's gharters and his bangkok's best and goliar's goloshes and his pulluponeasyan wartrews. This is his big wide harse.

> (*Finnegans Wake*, p. 8)

3.3.1 Commentary

An academic industry has developed, researching into the meaning of *Finnegans Wake* and publishing annotated guides to the text. Here are some of the connotations and related words, historical people and events that are hinted at. They are only suggestions, and you will probably find others. A question mark ? means 'I don't know what to make of this'.

museyroom	museum + room
goan in	going in (dialectal pronunciation?)
yiz	you (dialectal)
Willingdone	Duke of Wellington (commanded the British and Prussian armies that defeated the French Emperor Napoleon at the Battle of Waterloo in 1815)
Prooshious	Prussian + precious
gunn	gun
ffrinch	French
Tip	? Is this 'a small present of money for a service rendered or expected'? What the guide receives, or wants?

Cap and Soracer	cup and saucer
byng	Admiral Byng had been executed (shot) in 1757. Wellington also had a General Byng with him at Waterloo.
Saloos	salute + echo of the Battle of Salo in 1796
Crossgunn	There is a Crossgun Bridge in Dublin.
pike and fork	knife and fork +
	1. The Irish leader De Valera commenting on the Easter Rebellion of 1916 in Dublin said, 'If only you'd come out with knives and forks'.
	2. 'To put down your knife and fork' is recorded as slang for 'to die'.
triplewon hat	A 'hat trick' is the taking of three wickets by the same bowler with three successive balls in cricket, or the scoring of three goals, points, etc. in other sports.
Lipoleum	Napoleon – the Greek for *fat* is *lipos* – ?linoleum?
Cokenhape	Wellington's horse was called Copenhagen.
Sraughter Willingdone	Sir Arthur Wellington
magentic	majestic + magnetic. There was a Battle of Magenta in 1859.
goldtin spurs	There was a Battle of Guldensporenslag (Golden Spurs) in 1302.
ironed dux	Wellington was called 'the Iron Duke'; *dux* is Latin for *leader*. There is also a reference to duck trousers worn by Wellington – trousers made of a linen or cotton fabric used for outer clothing (white ducks).
quarterbrass	Battle of Quatre Bras, a French defeat in 1814.
woodyshoes	There was an Orange toast to William III – 'brass money and wooden shoes'.
magnate's gharters	Magna Carta; garters
bangkok's best	?
goliar's goloshes	French *goliard*, a minstrel or jester + Goliath.
pulluponeasyan wartrews	1. easy to pull on + Peloponnesian Wars 431–404 BC.
	2. *trews* for *trousers* + Waterloo

Notice the echo of the rhythm of 'This is the house that Jack built', with alliteration in the first two lines,

> This is the bullet that byng the flag of the Prooshious.
> This is the ffrinch that fire on the Bull that bang the flag of the Prooshious...
> This is the triplewon hat of Lipoleum...
> This is the Willingdone on his same white harse, the Cokenhape.
> This is the big Sraughter Willingdone, grand and magentic...
> This is his big wide harse .

and the deliberate weaving into the text of names of battles.

Joyce is playing a complex language game with both words and general knowledge.

4. Words and grammar in prose texts I

> Proper words in proper places, make the true definition of a style.
> (Jonathan Swift, *Letter to a Young Gentleman in Holy Orders*, 1721)

Jonathan Swift defines a style as 'proper words in proper places'. Words alone do not make up language, or communicate to others, except in restricted texts consisting simply of lists. The 'proper places' for words implies that there is an ordering of words which we recognise as making sense. The rules which underlie correct and acceptable **word order** make up the **grammar** or **syntax** of the language. And just as different words have different meanings and connotations, so differences in the choices we make from the rules of the grammar affect the meaning and style of what we say.

4.1 George Orwell on good writing

George Orwell (1903–50), the author of *1984* and *Animal Farm*, often made comments on language use and style in his writings. In his essay 'Politics and the English Language', published in 1946, he repeats the Fowlers' rules for good writing (see section 2.1.1), and adds another one:

> Never use the passive where you can use the active.

4.1.1 Active and passive verb phrases

The sentence,

> Orwell tells us that we should never use the passive where we could use the active.

contains three **verb phrases** (VPs), *tells, should . . . use* and *could use* which function as the **predicator** (P) in each clause and which are all in the **active voice.** They are part of active clauses. The VP functioning as predicator has a **subject** (S) whose meaning or **semantic role** is as **actor** or **agent** (the one who is doing or causing the action), and an **object** (O) with the semantic role of **affected** (the one on which the verb acts):

       S   P O
(a)   Orwell tells us

       S P   O
(b)   we should (never) use the passive

       S P   O
(c)   we could use the active

Those clauses could all be written using the **passive voice**:

       S P   Ca
(d)   We are told by Orwell

       S   P   Ca
(e)   The passive should never be used by us

       S   P   Ca
(f)   The active could be used by us

The active sentence has been 'transformed':

(i)   The subjects *Orwell, we, we* become **prepositional phrases** (PrepPs) *by Orwell, by us,* with the preposition *by,* which function as **adverbial complements** (Ca) in the clause. Their function as actor or agent remains <u>unchanged</u>, so we say that *by Orwell* and *by us* function as **agentive phrases**.

(ii)   The object NPs *us, the passive, the active* become the subjects of their clauses. *We* and *us* change to *us* and *we* respectively as a result of another rule of English grammar about the form of pronouns.

(iii) The verb is used in its **past participle** form, *told, used,* and the verb *be* is introduced in its appropriate form, *are, be.*

The description seems complicated, but everyone uses actives and passives all the time without having to think about how to construct them in talking and writing. They affect the way we present information, and whether or not we know, or want to reveal, who did something.

Putting the three passive clauses into a sentence, we get:

    We are told by Orwell that the passive should never be used where the active could be.

Activity 4.1

A number of words in clauses (d), (e) and (f) have been **deleted** from this sentence containing passive clauses.

(i) Rewrite the sentence to include the detailed items.

(ii) Discuss why this version would not normally be spoken or written.

(iii) Discuss the differences of meaning or emphasis between the active and passive versions, and when we would be likely to use the alternatives.

4.1.2 *Orwell's use of the passive in* Animal Farm

The following text consists of an extract from Orwell's novel *Animal Farm* (published in 1945). It was chosen because it contains a number of passive clauses, but it is typical of Orwell's style throughout the novel, and many other examples can be found.

Text 1

All orders were now issued through Squealer or one of the other pigs. Napoleon himself was not seen in public as often as once a fortnight. When he did appear, he was attended not only by his retinue of dogs but by a black cockerel who marched in front of him and acted as a kind of trumpeter, letting out a loud 'cock-a-doodle-doo' before Napoleon spoke.

4.1.2.1 PASSIVE AND ACTIVE VOICE

There are three sentences in text 1, each containing a passive verb phrase:

1(a) All orders **were** now **issued** through Squealer or one of the other pigs.
1(b) Napoleon himself **was not seen** in public as often as once a fortnight.
1(c) When he did appear, he **was attended** not only by his retinue of dogs but by a black cockerel who marched in front of him and acted as a kind of trumpeter, letting out a loud 'cock-a-doodle-doo' before Napoleon spoke.

Remembering that Orwell recommended the use of the active rather than the passive, why is there a passive verb in each of those three sentences? If we rewrite the extract using only active verbs, we get:

1(d) X now **issued** all orders through Squealer or one of the other pigs.
1(e) X **did not see** Napoleon himself in public as often as once a fortnight.
1(f) When he did appear, not only his retinue of dogs but a black cockerel who marched in front of him and acted as a kind of trumpeter, letting out a loud 'cock-a-doodle-doo' before Napoleon spoke, **attended** him.

4.1.2.2 DELETION OF THE AGENT

X was used for the subject of 1(d) and 1(e) because the agent is not named in a PrepP beginning with *by* in the original passive forms 1(a) and 1(b). We are not told explicitly *who issued the orders* in 1(a), or *who did not see Napoleon* in 1(b), and this is a normal feature of language use. Clause 1(a) is part of the narrative describing a series of Napoleon's actions as dictator, so we already know he is the actor/agent. It would be repetitive, and not good style, to begin every clause with 'Napoleon', followed by what he did. Using the passive is therefore a grammatical resource of style, to be used when the actor is already known, and so need not be named.

In clause 1(b), the actor of the 'seeing' of Napoleon is not a specific person, but all the animals in general, so this information would add little or nothing to the narrative, and can be easily inferred by a reader.

Both these clauses are therefore examples of **agent deletion** when the actor/agent is clearly understood from the context.

4.1.2.3 FOCUS OF INFORMATION – THEME IN THE CLAUSE

In an unmarked active clause, ~~the~~ first, 'left-most' item is the subject, and therefore also the main **focus of information** or **theme** of the clause; for example, in the following sentences from *Animal Farm*, the subject comes first and is therefore also the theme (S-theme).

> *S-theme*   *P*   *O*
> **The animals** watched them

> *S-theme*   *P*   *O*
> **Two of the men** had produced a crowbar and a sledge hammer.

> *S-theme*   *P*   *A*
> **The pigeons** swirled into the air

In these active clauses, the S-themes are also **actors**, the ones who are doing something. In the following passive clauses, the subject is the theme still, but no longer the actor as in clauses 1(a) and 1(b):

> *S-theme*   *P*   *A*
> **All orders** were now issued through Squealer

> *S-theme*   *P*   *A*
> **Napoleon** himself   was not seen in public

If the clauses had been in the active voice , the focus of information would have been different,

> *S-theme*   *A*   *P*   *O*   *A*
> **Napoleon**   now issued all orders through Squealer

> *S-theme*   *P*   *O*   *A*
> **The animals** did not see Napoleon himself in public

Other elements in a clause, especially **adverbials**, can be brought to the front and made the theme, either to focus attention on them, or to provide continuity and coherence in the text, for example,

> *A-theme*   *S*   *P*   *A*
> **Meanwhile** the timber was being carted away at high speed.

> *A-theme*   *S*   *P*
> **The very next morning** the attack came.

> *A-theme*   *S*   *P*   *P*   *Od*
> **Boldly enough** the animals sallied forth to meet them

Activity 4.2

The following sentences are from *Animal Farm*, chapter VIII, which describes the battle between the men and the animals. The theme of each clause is marked.

(i) Rewrite any passive clauses as active.

(ii) Re-order the clauses where necessary so that the subject is the theme.

(iii) Discuss the difference these changes of theme make to the focus of information and style of each clause.

1. **A cow, three sheep, and two geese** were killed, and
2. **nearly everyone** was wounded.
3. **At eleven o'clock** Squealer came out to make another announcement.
4. **At the beginning** the retiring age had been fixed for horses and pigs at twelve.
5. **A corner of the large pasture** was to be fenced off and turned into a grazing-ground for superannuated animals.
6. **In the general rejoicings** the unfortunate affair of the bank-notes was forgotten.
7. **At about half past nine** Napoleon was distinctly seen to emerge from the back door.
8. **Three of them** had their heads broken by blows from Boxer's hoofs.
9. **For the time being,** the young pigs were given their instruction by Napoleon himself in the farmhouse kitchen.
10. **A stump of hay and part of the potato crop** were sold off, and the contract for eggs was increased to six hundred a week.

4.1.2.4   FOCUS OF INFORMATION – END-WEIGHTING, OR RIGHT-BRANCHING

In sentence 1(c) in section 4.1.2.1, the main clause (MCl) is in the passive voice, its predicator being the passive verb phrase (VP) *was attended*:

> When he did appear, **he was attended** not only by his retinue of dogs but by a black cockerel who marched in front of him and acted as a kind of trumpeter, letting out a loud 'cock-a-doodle-doo' before Napoleon spoke.

We can transform this sentence into its corresponding active version,

> When he did appear, not only his retinue of dogs but a black cockerel who marched in front of him and acted as a kind of trumpeter, letting out a loud 'cock-a-doodle-doo' before Napoleon spoke, **attended him**

which has the structure:

AdvCl		[[When he did appear]
MCl		
	Subject	not only his retinue of dogs
		but a black cockerel
		RelCl [who marched in front of him] and
		RelCl [∅ acted as a kind of trumpeter,
		NonfCl [letting out a loud 'cock-a-doodle-doo'
		AdvCl [before Napoleon spoke]]],
	Predicator	attended
	Object	him

The subject is complex. It has two head nouns, *retinue* and *cockerel*, coordinated together, and contains four embedded clauses which modify, or depend upon, the second head noun *cockerel* – two relative clauses (RelCl), a nonfinite clause (NonfCl) and an adverbial clause (AdvCl). As a result, the sentence is **front-weighted**, and we have to carry in our mind the unravelling of the subject while we wait for the verb to come up, and this makes understanding more difficult.

Using the passive lets us identify the subject and verb *he was attended* first, and then we can take in the meaning of the complex agentive with its embedded clauses, without having to wait for the main verb. It is easier for a reader or listener to process Orwell's original sentence with **end-weighting** of its information, and so it is recognised as better style. The sentence begins with an adverbial clause (AdvCl) with *he* as subject, (referring back to *Napoleon*) – *When he did appear*. This is another good reason for beginning the complex main clause (MCl) which follows with *he*, by using the passive,

> *AdvCl*   *MCl*
> When **he** did appear, **he** was attended by...

The two pronouns *he* are close together and there is no problem in identifying who they refer to.

Activity 4.3

(i) Identify and discuss Orwell's use of the passive in the following extracts. Refer to agent deletion, theme and end-weighting if appropriate.

(ii) Are all the uses of the passive justified in terms of style or focus of information?

(iii) Can you discover any aspects of the uses of the passive which have not yet been discussed?

Text 2

2(a) Napoleon was now never spoken of simply as 'Napoleon'.

2(b) He was always referred to in formal style as 'our Leader, Comrade Napoleon'.

3(a) Meanwhile, through the agency of Whymper, Napoleon was engaged in complicated negotiations with Frederick and Pilkington.

3(b) The pile of timber was still unsold.

4(a) Sentinels were placed at all the approaches to the farm.

4(b) In addition, four pigeons were sent to Foxwood with a conciliatory message, which it was hoped might re-establish good relations with Pilkington.

5   The animals could not face the terrible explosions and the stinging pellets, and in spite of the efforts of Napoleon and Boxer to rally them, they were soon driven back.

Activity 4.4

Discuss the usefulness of Orwell's 'rules of good writing': *Never use the passive where you can use the active.*

📖 Activities 4.1–4.4 are discussed in the *Commentary & Data Book*.

4.2 Orwell's vocabulary and the Fowlers' rules

Activity 4.5

Orwell advocated the Fowlers' 'rules for good writing' (see section 2.1). Look up the derivation of the words in texts 1 and 2 and discuss the extent to which Orwell follows the 'rules', that is, uses short words derived from Old English and concrete expressions without circumlocutions.

    The words are listed by derivation in the *Commentary & Data Book*.

4.2.1 *Commentary*

If the two very short texts from Orwell's *Animal Farm* are typical of the style of the whole book, then about 11% of his vocabulary was derived from Latin, 46 % from OE or ON, 42% from French, with the odd 1%, the word *comrade*, derived from Spanish. However, we have to ask the question 'So what?' Orwell has always been admired for the clarity and direct simplicity of his style. Clearly, 11% of Latin-derived words in Orwell's prose does not create difficulties of under-standing. It depends on <u>which</u> words are chosen, and many words derived from Latin are now common and familiar, e.g. *addition, agency, animals, formal*, etc.

Orwell himself quoted as an example of clear, simple prose this passage from the Old Testament book Ecclesiastes in its translation in the 1611 King James Bible,

> I returned, and saw under the sun, that the race is not to the swift, nor the battle to the strong, neither yet bread to the wise, nor yet riches to men of understanding, nor yet favour to men of skill; but time and chance happeneth to them all.
>
> Readability – very easy.

and then made up his own version designed to be a parody of formal, bureaucratic English,

> Objective consideration of contemporary phenomena compels the conclusion that success or failure in competitive activities exhibits no tendency to be commensurate with innate capacity, but that a considerable element of the unpredictable must invariably be taken into account.
>
> Readability – very difficult.

It is a **parody** (see chapter 20), because it exaggerates and takes to an extreme the features of certain kinds of writing, both 'official' and 'academic'. These features are not just a matter of using formal vocabulary, however, but of the predominant use of certain grammatical constructions.

We can repeat the investigation into Orwell's style, and whether or not he keeps the 'rules', by looking at the following complete paragraph from *Animal Farm*, chapter X. The figures for the derivations of the 104 lexical word types in the paragraph are:

OE	OF	16th and 17th C words from French or Latin
73 = 70%	16 = 15.5%	15 = 14.5%

Activity 4.6

(i) Are there any passive clauses? Can they be made active?

(ii) Use your own judgement to identify any words that you think are not short and from Old English, then look up their derivations.

(iii) Do the 14.5% of the lexical words that are derived from Latin or French in the sixteenth or seventeenth centuries make a stylistic difference to the text? Can you substitute words derived from OE or OF?

The complete vocabulary of the paragraph is listed in the *Commentary & Data Book*.

Text 3

And yet the animals never gave up hope. More, they never lost, even for an instant, the sense of honour and privilege in being members of Animal Farm. They were still the only farm in the whole county – in all England! – owned and operated by animals. Not one of them, not even the youngest, not even the newcomers who had been brought from farms ten or twenty miles away, ever ceased to marvel at that. And when they heard the gun booming, and saw the green flag fluttering at the masthead, their hearts swelled with imperishable pride, and the talk always turned towards the old heroic days, the expulsion of Jones, the writing of the Seven Commandments, the great battles in which the human invaders had been defeated. None of the old dreams had been abandoned. The Republic of the Animals which Major had foretold, when the green fields of England should be untrodden by human feet, was still believed in. Some day it was coming: it might not be soon, it might not be within the lifetime of any animal now living, but still it was coming. Even the tune of 'Beasts of England' was perhaps hummed secretly here and there: at any rate, it was a fact that every animal on the farm knew it, though no one would have dared to sing it aloud. It might be that their lives were hard and that not all of their hopes had been fulfilled; but they were conscious that they were not as other animals. If they went hungry, it was not from feeding tyrannical human beings; if they worked hard, at least they worked for themselves. No creature among them went upon two legs. No creature called any other creature 'Master'. All animals were equal.

Readability – fairly easy.

4.3 Academic writing and nominalisation

Formal academic writing tends to use a characteristic style which caters for other academics rather than the general public. There is a high frequency of **nominalisations** and a tendency to use the **passive voice** in VPs. Passives and noun phrases which are nominalisations of verbs both have grammatical properties that tend to hide the **actor** of a process, the person or thing responsible for the action. In a nominalisation, an active process, something which happens, can be turned into a 'thing'. This affects the style, because using nominalisations creates a large number of noun phrases (NPs) and prepositional phrases (PrepPs). Here is Orwell's parody with the NPs and PrepPs that are nominalisations printed in boxes, to show the kinds of embedded structure that are typical:

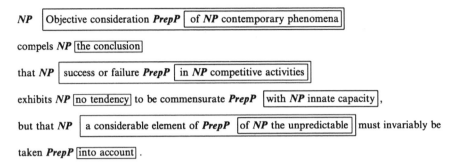

A *nominalisation* is therefore *a noun created from a verb*. The word is also used to refer to the process by which a verb is *nominalised*. Words in Orwell's parody which are nominalisations include:

Nouns		Verbs
consideration (1386 f. Fr)	⇔	consider (1375 f. Fr)
conclusion (1382 f. Fr)	⇔	conclude (1386 f. Latin)
success (1537 f. Latin)	⇔	succeed (1375 f. OF or Latin)
failure (1641)	⇔	fail (*c.* 1225 f. OF)
competitive (1829 f. Latin)	⇔	compete (1620 f. Latin)
activities (1549 f. Fr)	⇔	act (1594 f. Latin)
tendency (1628 f. Latin)	⇔	tend (*c.* 1300 f. attend, OF)
Adjective used as a noun:		
(the) unpredictable (1857)	⇔	(not) predict (1671 f. Latin)
f. predictable *adj* (1857)	⇔	predicted (1546 f. Latin)

Here is the opening paragraph of an American text-book.

Activity 4.7

(i) Read the text and identify all the NPs, PrepPs and passive verbs in the text

(ii) How many of the NPs are nominalisations of underlying actions/processes? Can you identify the actors of these actions/processes?

(iii) Rewrite the text using verbs for the nouns which represent processes, restoring the actors to the text, and avoiding the passive, as far as seems reasonable to the sense.

The aim of this study is to work out an empirical method of conversational analysis capable of recovering the social assumptions that underlie the verbal communication process by focusing on actors' use of speech to interact, i.e., to create and maintain a particular definition of a social situation. The basic theoretical position that sets this work apart from other work in sociolinguistics is that, in the analysis of face-to-face encounters, the sorts of things that social anthropologists and sociologists refer to by such terms as role, status, social identities, and social relationships will be treated as communicative symbols. They are signaled in the act of speaking and have a function in the communication process akin to that of syntax in the communication of referential meaning. Just as grammatical knowledge enables the speaker to distinguish potentially meaningful sentences from non-sentences, knowledge of the social values associated with the activities, social categories, and social relationships implied in the message is necessary in order to understand the situated meaning of a message, i.e., its interpretation in a particular context.

(John J. Gumperz and Eleanor Herasimchuk,
The Conversational Analysis of Social Meaning: A Study of Classroom Interaction)

Readability – difficult.

4.3.1 *Commentary on academic writing*

NPs and PrepPs form a large proportion of the text and a marked feature of this style is the relatively small number of verbs, because so many of the active processes implied in the meaning are written as nouns in nominalised phrases.

📖 A table showing the NPs and PrepPs is in the *Commentary & Data Book*

In this text, there are only seven main verbs in main clauses (MCls) – *is, is, will be treated, are signaled, have, enables, is* – of which four are the simple linking verbs *is* or *have*. The other two are both in the passive voice, *will be treated* and *are signaled*. The other ten verbs are either in a nonfinite form (infinitives, present or past participles) or the verbs of relative clauses (RelCls).

This is shown more clearly in the following version of the text:

NPs and PrepPs	Verbs		
	Nonfinite	*RelCl|NCl*	*MCl*
The aim of this study ⇒			*is*
to ⇒	**work out**		
an empirical method of conversational analysis capable of ⇒	**recovering**		
the social of assumptions that ⇒		**underlie**	
the verbal communication process by ⇒	**focusing**		
on actors' use of speech to ⇒	**interact**		
i.e., to ⇒	**create**		

and (to) ⇒	**maintain**
a particular definition of a social situation.	

The basic theoretical position that ⇒		**sets**
this work apart from other work in sociolinguistics ⇒		**is**
that, in the analysis of face-to-face encounters, the sorts of things that social anthropologists and sociologists ⇒		**refer to**
by such terms as role, status, social identities, and social relationships ⇒		**will be treated**
as communicative symbols.		

They ⇒	**are signaled**
in the act of speaking and ⇒	**have**
a function in the communication process akin to that of syntax in the communication of referential meaning.	

Just as grammatical knowledge ⇒		**enables**
the speaker to ⇒	**distinguish**	
potentially meaningful sentences from non-sentences,		
knowledge of the social values ⇒	**associated**	
with the activities, social categories, and social relationships ⇒	**implied**	
in the message ⇒		**is**
necessary in order to ⇒	**understand**	
the situated meaning of a message, i.e., its interpretation in a particular context.		

The greater part of the text consists of NPs and PrepPs, creating a style in which nothing seems to happen, while the complexity of the structure creates difficulties for readers. Verbs are traditionally known as 'doing words', especially when in the active voice. There is not one in the text which 'does' anything in the ordinary sense of the word.

In the development of the English language many verbs have been created from nouns, and nouns from verbs. Which came first, verb or noun, is not relevant in our study of style, and if we make a list of the nouns and verbs in the text, we can see that most could be used in either form:

nouns	verbs	nouns	verbs
act	(to) act	process (2)	(to) process
activities	(to) act	relationships	(to) relate
aim	(to) aim	sentences	?
analysis (2)	(to) analyse	situation	?(to) situate
assumptions	(to) assume	sociolinguistics	?
categories	(to) categorise	sorts	?(to) sort
communication	(to) communicate	speaker	(to) speak
context	(to) contextualise	speaking	(to) speak
definition	(to) define	speech	(to) speak
function	(to) function	study	(to) study
interpretation	(to) interpret	symbols	(to) symbolize
knowledge (2)	(to) know	syntax	?
meaning (2)	(to) mean	terms	?
message (2)	?	use	(to) use
method	?	value	(to) value/evaluate
non-sentences	?	work (2)	(to) work
position	(to) position		

This shows that we often have a choice of verb or noun available to express our meaning. Here is another version of the text in which **verbs** are substituted for *nouns* in the original, and in which there are no passive verbs.

Activity 4.8

(i) Is the rewritten version in fact any clearer?

(ii) Can you justify the usage and style of the original?

Original text

The *aim* of this *study* **is to work out** an empirical method of *conversational analysis capable* of **recovering** the social *assumptions* that **underlie** the verbal *communication process* by **focusing** on actors' *use of* speech to **interact**, i.e., to **create** and **maintain** a *particular definition* of a social situation.

The basic theoretical *position* that **sets** this work apart from other *work* in sociolinguistics **is** that, in the *analysis of* face-to-face *encounters*, the sorts of things that social anthropologists and sociologists **refer to** by such terms as role, status, social identities, and social relationships **will be treated** as *communicative* symbols.

Rewritten text

In this book we **aim** to **study** how to **work out** an empirical method by which we **can analyse** how people **converse** together. We **hope to be able to recover** what it is that people **assume** when they **communicate** by **talking** together. We **shall focus** on how speakers **use** speech to **interact** – that **is**, how they **create** and **maintain** what they **define** as the meaning of a social situation.

We **hold** basic theoretical opinions different from others who **work** in sociolinguistics. These theories **mean** that when we **analyse** the speech of people who **talk** face-to-face, we **treat** the sorts of things that social anthropologists and sociologists **refer to** by such terms as role, status, social identities, and social relationships as symbols by which people **communicate** with each other.

They **are signaled** in the *act of speaking* and **have a** *function* in the *communication process* akin to that of syntax in the *communication of* referential meaning. Just as grammatical *knowledge* **enables** the speaker to **distinguish** potentially meaningful sentences from non-sentences, *knowledge* of the social values **associated** with the activities, social categories, and social relationships **implied** in the *message* **is** necessary in order to **understand** the **situated** meaning of a message, i.e., its *interpretation* in a particular context.

People **signal** these symbols when they **speak**. The symbols **function** when we **communicate** in a way akin to that in which syntax **works** to **convey** referential meaning. **Knowing** grammar **enables** us to **distinguish** sentences with potential meaning from non-sentences. Similarly, it **is** necessary to **know** what social values speakers **associate** with the activities, social categories and social relationships that they **imply** when they **talk**, in order that we **can understand** the 'situated meaning' of a message, i.e., how we **should interpret** it in a particular context.

There are not many passive forms in the original text, though they often form a significant stylistic feature of this kind of writing. They can be transformed into the active, though supplying the actors of the verb as its grammatical subject can sometimes be awkward because they are often general references to *people* or *speakers*, etc.

Passive verbs in original text

The basic theoretical position that sets this work apart from other work in sociolinguistics is that, in the analysis of face-to-face encounters, the sorts of things that social anthropologists and sociologists refer to by such terms as role, status, social identities, and social relationships **will be treated** as communicative symbols.

They **are signaled** in the act of speaking...

...knowledge of the social values **associated with** the activities, social categories, and social relationships **implied in** the message is necessary...

Active verbs in rewritten text

These theories mean that when we analyse the speech of people who talk face-to-face, we **treat** the sorts of things that social anthropologists and sociologists refer to by such terms as role, status, social identities, and social relationships as symbols by which people communicate with each other.

People **signal** these symbols when they speak. Similarly, it is necessary to know what social values speakers **associate** with the activities, social categories and relationships that they **imply** when they talk,...

Activity 4.9

Rewrite Orwell's parody by substituting active verbs for nominalisations and passive verbs wherever this can be done and seems appropriate.

A rewritten version is in the *Commentary and Data Book*

4.4 More on NPs and PrepPs

A series of NPs and PrepPs does not necessarily lead to a style similar to the academic writing discussed in section 4.3. The grammatical feature exploited in the following extract from *Small World* by David Lodge (1984) is **post-modification** of the head nouns of NPs. These post-modifiers (or **qualifiers**) are themselves either NPs or PrepPs, or else nonfinite or relative clauses (NonfCls or RelCls).

Activity 4.10

Try to work out the structure of the grammatical object in the subordinate adverbial clause (AdvCl) following *as he sipped . . .*, before going on to read the commentary.

'There's something I must ask you, Fulvia,' said Morris Zapp, as he sipped Scotch on the rocks poured from a crystal decanter brought on a silver tray by a black-uniformed, white-aproned maid to the first floor drawing-room of the magnificent eighteenth century house just off the Villa Napoleone.

4.4.1   Commentary

The text is easy to read and understand. One thing follows another,

			NP	Scotch on the rocks
NonfCl	poured	*PrepP* from	NP	a crystal decanter
NonfCl	brought	*PrepP* on	NP	a silver tray
		PrepP by	NP	a black-uniformed, white-aproned maid
		PrepP to	NP	the first floor drawing-room
		PrepP of	NP	the magnificent eighteenth century house
		PrepP just off	NP	the Villa Napoleone

but each item is dependent upon the preceding item. The PrepP *just off the Villa Napoleone* qualifies *house*, and so is part of the NP,

> the magnificent eighteenth century house [just off the Villa Napoleone]

which is the complement of the preposition *of*,

> of [the [magnificent eighteenth century house [just off the Villa Napoleone]]]

which in turn qualifies *drawing-room*,

> the first floor drawing-room

> of [the   magnificent eighteenth century house [just off the Villa Napoleone]]

and so on. The fact that you can qualify any NP or PrepP means that this is a **recursive** process, like 'The House that Jack built', which can go on and on.

Activity 4.11

Write a similar sentence of your own invention using a string of post-modifying NPs and PrepPs and then show how it is structured. Is there a maximum length? If so, what is it? If not, why not?

5. Words and grammar in prose texts II

5.1 Style and grammar in William Faulkner's *The Bear*

The novels and short stories of the American writer William Faulkner
(1897–1962) are set in Mississippi in the South of the USA, and create a whole
world of families and characters in stories that range in their date of setting from
before the American Civil War, which ended in 1865, to the mid-twentieth
century. *The Bear* (1942) is a short novel whose main character is referred to
throughout simply as *he*, so the whole tale is told from his **point of view**. His name
is Isaac McCaslin (Ike), born in 1867 and brought up by his father and uncle.

The narrative part of the story tells of the young Ike's experiences as a hunter in
the 1870s and 1880s, beginning at the age of ten. Much of the land was still forest,

> He was sixteen. For six years he had been a man's hunter. For six years now he had heard the
> best of all talking. It was of the wilderness, the big woods...

The story moves backwards and forwards in time tracing the events of his life.
The injustice of both slavery and the theft of the land from the American Indians
weighs on his mind. He remembers how he was in the store owned by his family,

> the square, galleried, wooden building squatting like a portent above the fields whose
> labourers it still held in thrall '65 or no...

reading through the ledgers to try to trace family events in the past,

> the older ledgers clumsy and archaic in size and shape, on the yellowed pages of which were
> recorded in the faded hand of his father Theophilus and his uncle Amodeus during the two
> decades before the Civil War, the manumission* in title at least of Carothers McCaslin's slaves:

> * *manumission = setting free*

Carothers McCaslin was his grandfather, a legendary figure, who half built but
did not finish the enormous family house – the 'barn-like edifice' – referred to in
the following extract, in which Ike is reading about the treatment of the family's
slaves.

5.1.1   *Punctuation, structure and style (i)*

Activity 5.1 _____

(i)   What is unusual about the punctuation of this extract?

(ii)   Can you identify the sentences?

To him it was as though the ledgers in their scarred cracked leather bindings were being lifted down one by one in their fading sequence and spread open on the desk or perhaps upon some apocryphal Bench or even Altar or perhaps before the Throne Itself for a last perusal and contemplation and refreshment of the All-knowledgeable before the yellowed pages and the brown thin ink in which was recorded the injustice and a little at least of its amelioration and restitution faded back for ever into the anonymous communal original dust

the yellowed pages scrawled in fading ink by the hand first of his grandfather and then of his father and uncle, bachelors up to and past fifty and then sixty, the one who ran the plantation and the farming of it and the other who did the housework and the cooking and continued to do it even after his twin married and the boy himself was born

5.1.1.1   COMMENTARY

Interior monologue

The paragraphs are not punctuated, so there are no conventionally indicated sentences, but each paragraph is one long clause-complex. The introductory,

To him it was as though the ledgers in their scarred cracked leather bindings **were being lifted down** one by one...

tells us not what McCaslin is actually doing, but what he imagines – the injustice of slavery is being recorded at the Last Judgement, when the ledgers would be placed *upon some apocryphal Bench or even Altar or perhaps before the Throne Itself for a last perusal and contemplation and refreshment of the All-knowledgeable.*

He contemplates the contents of the ledgers in an **interior monologue** (see section 18.4 for further discussion), in which the unbroken flow of memory is partly achieved through the lack of punctuation marks. This is not the most important stylistic feature of the text, but a means to an end.

Activity 5.2 _____

Try to punctuate the text as you have been taught to use full stops, commas and other marks. What problems do you find?

Punctuation

We can add three or four commas and a full stop to the first paragraph. The second paragraph already has two commas, so we add a capital letter at the beginning and a full stop at the end. The text remains complex and difficult, not because of its lack of punctuation, but because of its structure.

Activity 5.3

Sentence structure

The first paragraph can be analysed into five clauses, the main clause consisting only of the introductory *To him it was*. The two coordinated *as though* clauses of similarity and the *before* clause of time contain all the meaning.

> [*MCl* To him it was
> [*AdvCl* as though the ledgers in their scarred cracked leather bindings (were being lifted down one by one in their fading sequence **and**
> [*AdvCl 2* ∅ spread open on the desk, or perhaps upon some apocryphal Bench or even Altar, or perhaps before the Throne Itself) for a last perusal and contemplation and refreshment of the All-knowledgeable,
> [*AdvCl* before the yellowed pages and the brown thin ink ... [**RelCl*] ... faded back for ever into the anonymous communal original dust
> [**RelCl* in which was recorded the injustice and a little at least of its amelioration and restitution].

The second paragraph has no main verb. McCaslin thinks of *the yellowed pages* and what they contain, which is related in two very long succeeding paragraphs, equally complex and unpunctuated. The effect is to make a reader share McCaslin's memories. There seems to be no narrator or implied author to get in the way. If it began *the yellowed pages were scrawled in fading ink*, the effect would be different, because when reading Faulkner's paragraph, we are all the time expecting a main verb, which never arrives – literally a 'stream of consciousness' in McCaslin's mind.

> [*Verbless Cl* the yellowed pages [*q* scrawled in fading ink by the hand first of his grandfather and then of his father and uncle, bachelors up to and past fifty and then sixty, the one [*RelCl* who ran the plantation and the farming of it] and the other [*RelCl* who did the housework and the cooking] and [*RelCl* ∅ continued to do it [*AdvCl* even after his twin married]] and [*AdvCl* ∅ the boy himself was born]]].

The clauses are long and complex, and the style is marked by the grammatical features that produce this complexity.

Activity 5.4

Clause structures

The structure of a clause is described in terms of its constituent **phrases** and their functions within the clause. NPs and PrepPs are particularly open to complexity, through pre- and post-modification of the head nouns, and through **coordination** and **apposition**. A diagram of some of the phrases will show this:

1. **S**
   d   h   q
         p   d   m   m   m   h
   the ledgers in their scarred cracked leather bindings   3 pre-modifiers (m)
   NP   **PrepP**
         A   **A**
2. Ø spread open ⟨on the desk, **or** perhaps upon some apocryphal Bench **or** even
     A   **A**
3. (*upon some*) Altar, **or** perhaps before the Throne Itself⟩   4 coordinated PrepPs
4. for a last ⟨perusal **and** contemplation **and** refreshment⟩   3 coordinated head nouns
   of the All-knowledgeable,
5. the yellowed pages scrawled in fading ink
   by the hand ⟨first of his grandfather **and** then of his ⟨father **and** uncle⟩⟩,   coordination
   bachelors ⟨up to **and** past fifty **and** then sixty⟩,   coordination
   ⟨the one   apposition and coordination
   who ran ⟨the plantation **and** the farming of it⟩   ⇓
   and the other
   ⟨who did ⟨the housework **and** the cooking⟩
   and (*who*) continued to do it
   even ⟨after his twin married **and** (*after*) the boy himself was born⟩⟩⟩

5.1.2 *Punctuation, structure and style (ii)*

Activity 5.5

(i) Read the longer paragraph that follows the two we have just looked at.

(ii) Identify the main clauses that carry the principal events that McCaslin is remembering, and write them out as a shorter text, using conventional punctuation and omitting subordinate clauses and long post-modifying (qualifying) phrases, except those that you think are essential to the continuity of the basic narrative.

the two brothers who as soon as their father was buried moved out of the tremendously-conceived, the almost barn-like edifice which he had not even completed, into a one-room log cabin which the two of them built themselves and added other rooms to while they lived in it, refusing to allow any slave to touch any timber of it other than the actual raising into place the logs which two men alone could not handle, and domiciled all the slaves in the big house some of the windows of which were still merely boarded up with odds and ends of plank or with the skins of bear and deer nailed over the empty frames: each sundown the brother who superintended the farming would parade the negroes as a first sergeant dismisses a company, and herd them willynilly, man woman and child, without question protest or recourse, into the tremendous abortive edifice scarcely yet out of embryo, as if even old Carothers McCaslin had paused aghast at the concrete indication of his own vanity's boundless conceiving: he would call his mental roll and herd them in and with a hand-wrought nail as long as a flenching-knife and suspended from a short deer-hide thong attached to the door-jamb for that purpose, he would nail to the door of that house which lacked half its windows and had no hinged back door at all, so that presently and for fifty years afterward, when the boy himself was big to hear and remember it, there was in the land a sort of folk-tale: of the countryside all night long full of skulking McCaslin slaves dodging the moonlit roads and the Patrol-riders to visit other plantations, and of the unspoken gentlemen's agreement between the two white men and the two dozen black ones that, after the white man had counted them and driven the home-made nail into the front door at sundown, neither of the white men would go around behind the house and look at the back door, provided that all the negroes were behind the front one when the brother who drove it drew out the nail again at daybreak

(The computer cannot provide a Readability grade because it relies on full stops to mark sentences.)

5.1.2.1 COMMENTARY

Here is a shortened version of the main paragraph, using Faulkner's words, but with conventional punctuation. Asterisks mark the places where **subordinate clauses** have been left out.

> The two brothers * moved out of the tremendously-conceived, the almost barn-like edifice * into a one-room log cabin * and domiciled all the slaves in the big house * . Each sundown the brother who superintended the farming would parade the negroes * , and herd them * into the tremendous abortive edifice * . He would call his mental roll and herd them in and with a hand-wrought nail * he would nail to the door of that house * . So that presently and for fifty years afterward * , there was in the land a sort of folk-tale: of the countryside all night long full of skulking McCaslin slaves, * and of the unspoken gentlemen's agreement between the two white men and the two dozen black ones, that * neither of the white men would go around behind the house and look at the back door * .
>
> Readability – easy.

The new text is much easier to read, partly because it is punctuated into sentences, but mostly because its structures are less complex. It has 139 words, 39% of the original 357. Notice the importance of the relative pronoun *who* at the beginning of the original paragraph – *the two brothers who* .... Again there is no main verb for the subject NP *the two brothers*, with the same effect as in the preceding paragraph of delaying any 'resolution', rather like an incomplete cadence in music.

If we set out the original text in two columns, labelling the clauses, the relationship of the main *narrative* clauses to the subordinate *descriptive* clauses will be clearer:

Narrative clauses	*Descriptive clauses*
[*MCl* the two brothers [***RelCl*** (who) ⇒ moved out of the tremendously-conceived, the almost barn-like edifice ⇒ into a one-room log cabin ⇒	[*AdvCl* as soon as their father was buried]
	[*RelCl* which he had not even completed],
	[*RelCl* which the two of them ⟨built themselves and added other rooms to⟩ [*AdvCl* while they lived in it], [*NonfCl* refusing to allow any slave to touch any timber of it other than the actual raising into place the logs [*RelCl* which two men alone could not handle]],
and [*RelCl* (who) domiciled all the slaves in the big house ⇒	[*RelCl* some of the windows of which were still merely boarded up with odds and ends of plank or with the skins of bear and deer [*q* nailed over the empty frames]]:
[*MCl* each sundown the brother [*RelCl* who superindented the farming] would parade the negroes] ⇒	

and [*MCl* herd them	⇒	[*AdvCl* as a first sergeant dismisses a company], willynilly, man woman and child, without question protest or recourse,
into the tremendous abortive edifice	⇒	[*q* scarcely yet out of embryo], [*AdvCl* as if even old Carothers McCaslin had paused aghast at the concrete indication of his own vanity's boundless conceiving]:

[*MCl* he would call his mental roll] and
[*MCl* herd them in]

and [*MCl* with a hand-wrought nail	⇒	[*q* as long as a flenching-knife] and [*q´* suspended from a short deer-hide thong [*q* attached to the door-jamb for that purpose],
he would nail to the door of that house	⇒	[*RelCl* which lacked half its windows] and [*RelCl* (*which*) had no hinged back door at all]
[[*AdvCl* so that presently and for fifty years afterward,	⇒	[*AdvCl* when the boy himself was big to hear and remember it],

MCl there was in the land a sort of folk-tale:

of [*Verbless Cl* the countryside all night long full of skulking McCaslin slaves]	⇒	[*NonfCl* dodging the moonlit roads and the Patrol-riders [*NonfCl* to visit other plantations],
and of [*Verbless Cl* the unspoken gentlemen's agreement between the two white men and the two dozen black ones that,	⇒	[*AdvCl* after the white man had counted them] and [*AdvCl* (*after he had*) driven the home-made nail into the front door at sundown],
[*NCl* reported neither of the white men would go around behind the house] and [look at the back door,	⇒	provided that [*NCl* all the negroes were behind the front one [*AdvCl* when the brother [*RelCl* who drove it] drew out the nail again at daybreak]]]

📖 Further discussion of 5.1.1 and 5.1.2 is in the *Commentary & Data Book*.

5.1.2.2 DECONSTRUCTING THE MEANING

Faulkner uses complex grammatical structures with their lack of conventional punctuation for more than one reason. In addition to taking us into the mind of McCaslin while he recalls his past life, a great deal of information can be packed into them. If we reduce some of the text to a series of basic **propositions** (simple clauses) by 'deconstructing' the surface grammar of the second paragraph, you can see how this is done:

> the yellowed pages scrawled in fading ink by the hand first of his grandfather and then of his father and uncle, bachelors up to and past fifty and then sixty, the one who ran the plantation and the farming of it and the other who did the housework and the cooking and continued to do it even after his twin married and the boy himself was born

Deconstructed text

	Participant 1	Process	Participant 2	Attribute	Circumstance
1.	the pages	were		yellow	
2.	the hand of his grandfather	scrawled	the pages		first
3.	the hand of his father	scrawled	the pages		then
4.	the hand of his uncle	scrawled	the pages		then
5.	the ink	was		fading	

	6.	his father	was		a bachelor	up to fifty
	7.	his father	was		a bachelor	past fifty
	8.	his uncle	was		a bachelor	up to fifty
	9.	his uncle	was		a bachelor	past fifty
	10.	his father	was		a bachelor	up to sixty
	11.	his father	was		a bachelor	past sixty
	12.	his uncle	was		a bachelor	up to sixty
	13.	his uncle	was		a bachelor	past sixty
	14.	the one	ran	the plantation		
	15.	the one	farmed	the plantation		
	16.	the other	did	the housework		
	17.	the other	did	the cooking		
	18.	the other	continued to do	the housework		
	19.	the other	continued to do	the cooking		
	20.	AFTER his twin	married			
	21.	AFTER the boy	was born			

These propositions represent twenty-one separate facts that the text compresses by means of grammatical processes like modification, subordination and coordination. This **deconstruction** of the paragraph shows its underlying **semantic** structure – how the **meaning** is conveyed.

Activity 5.6

Select a part of the third paragraph and reduce it to simple propositions, each of which contains one piece of information.

📖 The deconstructed text is in the *Commentary & Data Book*.

5.1.3 VOCABULARY

It is clear that the complexity of the structure in Faulkner's text is complemented by the formality of some of the words that occur from time to time. I suggest that the lexical words in the following phrases 'heighten' the overall stylistic effect of the extract, and contrast with the core vocabulary lexical words that make up most of it, such as *the two brothers, father, buried, barn, log cabin, built, rooms, lived* etc.

fading sequence
some apocryphal Bench
a last perusal and contemplation and refreshment of the All-knowledgeable
its amelioration and restitution
the anonymous communal original dust
the tremendously-conceived, the almost barn-like edifice
domiciled all the slaves
superintended the farming
without question protest or recourse
the tremendous abortive edifice scarcely yet out of embryo
had paused aghast
the concrete indication of his own vanity's boundless conceiving

Activity 5.7

Is it possible to rewrite these expressions using simpler core vocabulary?

📕 The lexical words are listed in the *Commentary & Data Book* with derivations and dates of adoption.

5.2 Style and grammar in James Joyce's *Eveline*

James Joyce's first published volume of short stories was called *Dubliners* (published in 1914). Its syle is in marked contrast to the many constrasting styles that Joyce deliberately adopted in *A Portrait of the Artist as a Young Man*, *Ulysses* (see section 18.4.1) and *Finnegans Wake* (see section 3.3), the novels that followed. In a letter of 5 May 1906, at the time of the writing of some of the stories, he referred to it as having a style of 'scrupulous meanness'.None of the stories flatters the Dublin characters in them, and there are themes of frustration, degradation and paralysis that run through each portrayal. The story of *Eveline* is of a young woman's inability to leave home to marry the man she has agreed to emigrate with. Some extracts, including the opening and final paragraphs, are printed below.

Activity 5.8

Can you identify any stylistic features of Joyce's writing that support his description of the style – one of 'scrupulous meanness'?

She sat at the window watching the evening invade the avenue. Her head was leaned against the window curtains, and in her nostrils was the odour of dusty cretonne. She was tired....

She had consented to go away, to leave her home. Was that wise? She tried to weigh each side of the question. In her home anyway she had shelter and food; she had those whom she had known all her life about her. Of course she had to work hard, both in the house and at business. What would they say of her in the Stores when they found out that she had run away with a fellow? Say she was a fool, perhaps; and her place would be filled up by advertisement. Miss Gavan would be glad. She had always had an edge on her, specially whenever there were people listening.

'Miss Hill, don't you see these ladies are waiting?'

'Look lively, Miss Hill, please.'

She would not cry many tears at leaving the Stores....

She was about to explore another life with Frank. Frank was very kind, manly, open-hearted. She was to go away with him by the night-boat to be his wife and to live with him in Buenos Ayres, where he had a home waiting for her...Frank would save her. He would give her life, perhaps love, too. But she wanted to live. Why should she be unhappy? She had a right to happiness. Frank would take her in his arms, fold her in his arms. He would save her.

She stood among the swaying crowd in the station at the North Wall. He held her hand and she knew that he was speaking to her, saying something about the passage over and over again. The station was full of soldiers with brown baggages. Through the wide doors of the sheds she caught a glimpse of the black mass of the boat, lying in beside the quay wall, with illumined portholes. She answered nothing. She felt her cheek pale and cold and, out of a maze of distress, she prayed to God to direct her, to show her what was her duty. The boat blew a long mournful whistle into the mist. If she went, tomorrow she would be on the sea with Frank, steaming towards Buenos Ayres. Their passage had been booked. Could she still draw back after all he had done for her? Her distress awoke a nausea in her body and she kept moving her lips in silent fervent prayer.

A bell clanged upon her heart. She felt him seize her hand:

'Come!'

All the seas of the world tumbled about her heart. He was drawing her into them; he would drown her. She gripped with both hands at the iron railing.

'Come!'

No! No! No! It was impossible. Her hands clutched the iron in frenzy. Amid the seas she sent a cry of anguish.

'Eveline! Evvy!'

He rushed beyond the barrier and called to her to follow. He was shouted at to go on, but he still called to her. She set her white face to him, passive, like a helpless animal. Her eyes gave him no sign of love or farewell or recognition.

5.2.1 Commentary

The phrase 'scrupulous meanness' is a subjective, impressionistic description of style, and needs to be assessed in linguistic terms that can be verified and agreed. In this context, Joyce's *scrupulous* means 'minutely exact or careful; strictly attentive even to the smallest details; characterized by punctilious exactness', and *meanness* is 'poverty of style, execution, or design; want of grandeur or nobility'. Such a style is meant to match the 'want of nobility' of the principal characters in the stories.

The story is told from Eveline's **point of view** – that is, although the narrative is in the 3rd person, *she, he, they*, almost everything is either taking place in her mind, or a description of her actions only. She is unable to decide whether to make the change and go with Frank, or to stay at home. The 'meanness' of style matches the restricted nature of her experience and imagination.

5.2.1.1 VOCABULARY

In contrast to Faulkner's range of words, Joyce employs core vocabulary words that Eveline would use, including colloquialisms like *she always had an edge on her*. There are only a few words that might be classified as 'literary' or non-core, but of these, only *recognition* and *cretonne* were adopted later than the early sixteenth century, and the fabric *cretonne* would be an everyday word for Eveline in her role as housekeeper.

anguish	OF 13th C	*illumined*	Fr 14th C	*odour*	OF early 14th C
cretonne	Fr 19th C	*nausea*	Lat 16th C	*recognition*	Lat 16th C
fervent	Fr early 15th C				

The complete vocabulary is listed by word-class in the *Commentary & Data Book*.

5.2.1.2 STRUCTURE

The traditional classification of sentence structures recognises four types:

- *Simple sentences* consisting of one clause
- *Compound sentences* consisting of two or more **coordinated** clauses
- *Complex sentences* consisting of a main clause and one or more **subordinate** clauses
- *Compound-complex sentences* consisting of two or more **coordinated** clauses and one or more **subordinate** clauses

There are 50 sentences in the extract, with the following distribution of types:

Simple sentences		31	62%
Complex		9	18%
with 2 clauses	5		
with 3 clauses	3		
with 4 clauses	1		
Compound		6	12%
with 2 clauses	6		
Compound-complex		4	8%
with 3 clauses	2		
with 4 clauses	2		

The fact that 62% of the sentences are simple, consisting of one clause, has a stylistic effect in portraying the to-ing and fro-ing of Eveline's mental turmoil, as she debates with herself whether to leave home or not, for example in these sequences:

> Was that wise?
> She tried to weight each side of the question.
> Frank would save her.
> He would give her life, perhaps love, too.
> But she wanted to live.
> Why should she be unhappy?
> She had a right to happiness.

But a text with only simple sentences (e.g., infants' reading primers) would be monotonous, and the necessary variety is obtained by the placing of compound or complex sentences. They provide rhythmic variation in the reading of the text, and the linking of narrative thoughts and events by different forms of coordination and subordination. The longer sentences provide a counter-balance to the shorter ones, for example:

> *Complex sentence, 3 clauses:*
> *AdvCl*   [[If she went],
> *MCl*   tomorrow she would be on the sea with Frank,
> *NonfCl* [steaming towards Buenos Ayres]].
>
> *Compound-complex sentence, 4 clauses:*
> *MCl*   [She felt her cheek pale and cold] and,
> *MCl*   [out of a maze of distress, she prayed to God
> *NonfCl* [to direct her],
> *NonfCl* [to show her what was her duty]].

Eveline's indecision is shown by the **questions** she asks herself,

> Was that wise?
> What would they say of her in the Stores...?
> Why should she be unhappy?
> Could she still draw back after all he had done for her?

but her assured statement *He would save her* which concludes the first section is denied by her actions at the station by the boat:

> She answered nothing.
> She gripped with both hands at the iron railing.
> Her hands clutched the iron in frenzy.

Joyce's scrupulous meanness restricts the narrative to plain factual statements, except for the single **metaphor** in,

> **All the seas of the world** tumbled about her heart. He was drawing her into them; he would **drown** her.... **Amid the seas** she sent a cry of anguish.

and the **simile** in,

> She set her white face to him, passive, **like a helpless animal**.

(Metaphor, simile and other figures of speech are discussed in the following chapter 6.)

📖 A complete structural analysis of the text is in the *Commentary & Data Book*.

6. Traditional rhetoric

6.1 The medieval Art of Rhetoric

The word rhetoric is sometimes used to describe what we have up to now been calling *style*. In the Middle Ages, Rhetoric was one of the seven 'liberal arts', the first of the three parts of a university education with Grammar and Logic – the Trivium – and so an important area of study. The meanings of *rhetoric* changed over time, and the word may now carry either favourable or unfavourable connotations, so that you can use it **pejoratively** – to express an unfavourable response to someone's style, an *artificial* rather than an *elegant* way of writing – or **positively**, to commend a style. Its various meanings have included,

- Elegant language; eloquent speech or writing (now obsolete)
- The art of using language so as to persuade or influence others
- Speech or writing expressed in terms calculated to persuade (often in depreciatory sense)
- Language characterised by artificial or ostentatious expression
- Artistic style or technique

The following illustration of its present-day pejorative use – rhetoric is *bogus*, whereas statistics are reliable – comes from a political column in a newspaper (May 1995):

> Any figure about job losses, however firmly asserted, and whomever it comes from, is bound to be bogus, **more rhetoric than statistic**.

Medieval rhetoric's reputation was maintained well into the eighteenth century. The art of Rhetoric included the studies called **Invention** (finding new ways of expressing things), **Disposition** (the art of interweaving and ordering themes) and **Elocution** (what we call *style* and the use of vocabulary and grammar).

For example, *disposition* might be 'natural', that is, beginning the story at the beginning and going on to the end, or 'artificial', such as the established ordering of an epic by beginning *in medias res* – in the middle of the story. Or you might begin with a *sententia* or general truth expressed in a sentence, like Chaucer in *The Parlement of Foules*:

> The lyf so short, the craft so long to lerne,
> Th'assay so hard, so sharp the conquerynge

Evidence for the continuing tradition of rhetorical studies can be seen in the publication of many books on rhetoric from the sixteenth century onwards, with titles like

16th century – 1588

THE

Arcadian Rhetorike:

Or

The præcepts of Rhetorike made plaine by examples, Greeke, Latin, English, Italian, French, Spanishe
By Abraham Fraunce
AT LONDON

17th century – 1663

Practical

RHETORICK

OR,

Certain little SENTENCES

varied according to the *Rules*

prescribed by ERASMUS, in

his most Excellent Book

De Copia Verborum & Rerum.

Wherein Children may be

Exercised, when they first begin

to translate *Latin*, with many

Advantages, as will appear

by the ensuing Epistle.

Framed first for the use of a

Private School, kept in the House

of Mr. *Francis Atkinson*: and

now commended to the

use of all *SCHOOLS*

BY *Joshua Pool*, Mr of Arts.

London, Printed for *T Johnson*, at the

Golden Key in *Pauls* Church yeard, 1663.

18th century – 1733

A

SYSTEM

OF

RHETORIC;

IN A

Method entirely New:

CONTAINING

All the TROPES AND FIGURES

necessary to illustrate the *Classics*,

both Poetical and Historical.

For the Use of SCHOOLS

By *JOHN STIRLING*, M.A.

LONDON:

M DCC XXIII Price 4*d*.

They are interesting evidence of how the English curriculum in schools and universities has changed since the seventeenth and eighteenth centuries.

6.2   Tropes and figures

'Figures of speech' have traditionally been classified into two types in the study of rhetoric – *tropes* and *figures*, the phrase which appears on the title page of the 1733 book, *A System of Rhetoric*. In general, a **trope** is a device that involves meaning, and a **figure** one that involves expression, but the terms are not always clearly distinguished. (The term *scheme* is sometimes used for *figure*.)

The names of the tropes and figures were taken from Greek. Some, like *metaphor*, *irony*, *parenthesis*, *onomatopeia* and *climax* are fully assimilated into English and will be familiar from literary criticism. Raymond Queneau, in his *Exercises in Style* (see section 1.3), includes the following tropes and figures as subjects of some of his exercises, most of which will be quite unknown to you:

antiphrasis	epenthesis	metathesis	polyptotes
apheresis	exclamation	onomatopeia	prosthesis
apocope	homeoptotes	paragoge	synchrisis
apostrophe	litotes	parechesis	syncope

Here are some short descriptions of the more important and familiar rhetorical terms.

6.2.1 Tropes

The most familiar tropes in literary criticism today are *simile, metaphor* and *metonymy*. Others that are commonly identified include *climax, hyperbole* and *irony*, which are also words used outside literary criticism, and the less familiar *litotes, oxymoron* and *synecdoche*.

In the following discussion of the tropes, the dictionary definition is given first. This is followed by an example taken from Joshua Pool's little book *Practical Rhetorick* (1663), which consisted of short sentences containing the trope or figure named. Each illustration is a variant of a simple sentence – *Love ruleth all things*. Only *synecdoche* was not described. Then follows a couplet from John Stirling's *A System of Rhetoric* (1733) that attempts to define each trope in rhyme.

6.2.1.1 SIMILE (OR SIMILITUDO)
A comparison of one thing with another, especially as an ornament in poetry or rhetoric.

All things in the hand of Love, are as Pygmies in the hand of Hercules.
Love is like Coeneus, is invulnerable and invincible.

(*Simile* is not listed in Stirling's *System of Rhetoric*.)

Similes may vary from a short, simple comparison, as in Milton's description of Lucifer in *Paradise Lost* (Book I, lines 589–91),

...he above the rest
In shape and gesture proudly eminent
Stood like a Tow'r;

to long, 'extended similes', which were a particular feature of epic poetry from Homer onwards (see chapter 16). You will also find them in *Paradise Lost*, for example just after the short simile just quoted, and continuing the description of Lucifer, with the two parts of the simile made explicit by the introductory words *As when*, and *so*,

> **As when** the Sun new ris'n
> Looks through the Horizontal misty Air
> Shorn of his Beams, or from behind the Moon
> In dim Eclips disastrous twilight sheds
> On half the Nations, and with fear of change
> Perplexes Monarchs. Dark'n'd **so**, yet shon
> Above them all th' Arch Angel: but his face
> Deep scars of Thunder had intrencht...

A simile is an explicit comparison of one thing to another, most often linked by *like* or *as*. Laurie Lee in *Cider with Rosie* is here describing his memories of sleeping with his mother as a three-year-old child,

> That darkness to me was **like the fruit of sloes**, heavy and ripe to the touch...I was **as snug as a mouse in a hayrick**.

 Dylan Thomas's *Under Milk Wood* has many similes, for example,

> Milk-churns stand at Coronation Corner **like** short silver policemen.
> The town ripples **like** a lake in the waking breeze.
> Night in the four-ale, quiet **as** a domino

6.2.1.2 METAPHOR

A name or descriptive term is transferred to some object different from, but analogous to, that to which it is properly applicable.

> Love is another Achilles, another Hercules: but much more strong than either.

> A *metaphor*, in place of proper Words,
> Resemblance puts; and Dress to Speech affords.

If a comparison is implicit or compressed, then simile becomes metaphor, so that the comparison of a man deeply asleep to a drowned man becomes, in *Under Milk Wood*,

> Ocky Milkman, **drowned** asleep in Cockle Street

In *Metaphors We Live By*, published in 1980, the American authors George Lakoff and Mark Johnson show that metaphor is not only 'a device of the poetic imagination and the rhetorical flourish' but 'pervasive in everyday life, not just in language but in thought and action'. Ordinary language and thought are metaphorical. For example, it is commonplace to hear politicians talk about 'the **war** against inflation' and of '**squeezing** inflation out of the system' – two metaphors rather incongruously used to oversimplify what is a complex and controversial economic and political topic.

Journalists and columnists often report economic affairs metaphorically using the vocabulary of violence and war, for example,

> Two short, **violent** bursts of selling sent the pound **crashing** to new lows yesterday in the continuing **fall-out** from last week's heavy poll defeat for the Conservatives
> The first **attack** on the pound came in late morning and after a modest lunchtime **rally** sterling was **hit** again

These commonplace metaphors are used to describe the buying and selling of money.

Personification

We know the difference between the **literal** meanings of *war* and *squeeze* and the **figurative** meanings they convey when we talk about the *war against inflation* and *squeezing it out of the system*. Inflation is **personified**, that is, turned into a *person* or *entity* – it is an *enemy* or *adversary* out there in the world, and gallant politicians *wage war* against it, *grapple* with it and call upon people to *make sacrifices* to *defeat* it – all terms in the same **semantic field** with related meanings.

In the headline POUND HEADS FOR NEW CRISIS, the pound is personified. The fact that currency dealers in international exchanges are buying and selling sterling at devalued prices is entirely hidden by the metaphorical wording of the headline. The metaphor takes over and provides an inaccurate explanation of a process in which men and women are responsible for what happens, not 'the pound'.

Dylan Thomas in *Under Milk Wood* personifies the sunrise and likens it to an energetic person:

> The sun **springs** down on the rough and tumbling town. It **runs** through the hedges of Goosegog Lane, **cuffing** the birds to sing. Spring **whips** green down Cockle Row, and the shells **ring out**.

Tenor and vehicle

In a news headline like BALKAN WAR ERUPTS ON NEW FRONT, the sudden and unexpected outbreak of war is reported in the same terms as the violent eruption of a volcano. In rhetorical terms, the **tenor** (or topic) of the metaphor is *war*, but the **vehicle** by which it is described is *volcano*.

Given that everyday thinking and talk are metaphorical, it is not surprising that metaphor is one of the commonest tropes in literary writing. Here are some more examples from *Under Milk Wood*.

Activity 6.1

Discuss the tenor and vehicle of each metaphorical expression.

- Spring **whips** green down Cockle Row, and the shells **ring out**
- Evans the Death presses hard with black gloves on **the coffin of his breast** in case his heart jumps out.
- PC Attila Rees, **ox-broad**, **barge-booted**, stamping out of Handcuff House in **a heavy beef-red huff**
- and the children (are) **shrilled** off to school.
- And in the town, the shops **squeak** open.
- Outside, the sun **springs down** on the rough and tumbling town.
- Spring this morning **foams in a flame** in Jack Black as he cobbles a high-heeled shoe for Mrs Dai Bread Two the gypsy
- the **spittingcat** kettles throb and hop on the range.

6.2.1.3 METONYMY AND SYNECDOCHE

Metonymy – a name or descriptive term is transferred to some object different from, but analogous to, that to which it is properly applicable.

Both Heaven and Earth know the power of love.

> A *Metonymy* does new Names impose,
> And Things for Things by near Relation shews.

Synecdoche – a part is named but the whole is understood, e.g. *fifty sail* for *fifty ships*, or the whole is named but a part understood, e.g. *England beat Australia at cricket*.

Rome was victorious in battle.

> *Synecdoche* the Whole for Part doth take,
> Or Part for Whole; just for the Metre's Sake.

Metonymy and synecdoche are similar tropes, because figurative words are substituted for literal words, but they are distinguished as in the dictionary definitions above. In metonymy, a word or phrase that is related or *contiguous* to the other is used, whereas the essential feature of synecdoche is the substitution of a part for the whole, or the whole for a part. The short sentence *Ships sail the sea* is literal in its meaning. In *Keels plough the deep*, *keels* is an example of synecdoche, as a keel is part of the whole ship, *the deep* is a metonymy and *plough* is a metaphorical compression of the simile *a ship sails across the sea like a plough across the earth*.

6.2.1.4 OTHER TROPES

Climax
Series arranged in order of increasing importance; the last term in such a series.

Not only brute creatures, but men; nor they only, but likewise gods, yield to the violence of Love.

> A *Climax* by gradation still ascends,
> Until the Sense with finish'd Period ends.

Hyperbole
Exaggerated or extravagant statement, used to express strong feeling or produce a strong impression, and not intended to be understood literally.

The Victories of Love are more than the Sands of the Sea, Hairs of the Head, Drops of Rain, Stars of the Skie, Leaves of the Trees, Motes in the Sun, Pellets of Hail, Drops of Dew, Hybla's Bees, the Birds of the Air, the Fishes of the Sea, Flowers of the Spring, Appels of Autumn, Summer's Flies, Summer's Ants, Blades of Grass, Ears of Corn, Boughs of the Forrest, &c.

> Hyperbole soars high, or creeps too low;
> Exceeds the Truth, Things wonderful to shew.

Irony

The intended meaning is the opposite of that expressed by the words used; usually taking the form of sarcasm or ridicule in which laudatory expressions are used to imply condemnation or contempt.

Love is weak, forsooth! and every thing overcomes it; yes, indeed.

> An *Irony*, dissembling with an Air,
> Thinks otherwise than what the Words declare.

Litotes

Ironical understatement, especially expressing an affirmative by the negative of its contrary, e.g. *not small* for *great*.

Love overcometh no small things.

> *Litotes* does more Sense than Words include,
> And often by two Negatives hath stood.

Oxymoron

The joining together of apparent contradictions, e.g. *faith unfaithful kept him falsely true*.

Who can express the great littleness, and little Greatness; the childish manliness, and manly Childishness of that blind God?

> In *Oxymoron* Contradictions meet;
> And jarring Epithets and Subjects greet.

6.2.2 Figures

There are dozens of 'figures' described and exhaustively listed in the old books of rhetoric, but this kind of detailed analysis and classification is not popular in the teaching of English or the classics today, though the terms were formerly familiar to educated people.

6.2.2.1 REFERENCES TO RHETORICAL FIGURES IN *TRISTRAM SHANDY*

The currency of terms of rhetoric in the eighteenth century can be illustrated by a few passing references in Laurence Sterne's novel *Tristram Shandy* (1759).

Aposiopesis

A rhetorical artifice, in which the speaker comes to a sudden halt, as if unable or unwilling to proceed.

Love made Jove – but we must speak nothing rashly of the gods.

> *Aposiopesis* leaves imperfect Sense;
> Yet such a silent Pause speaks Eloquence.

Tristram's Uncle Toby has just spoken an incomplete sentence,

> My sister, I dare say, does not care to let a man come so near her **** .

and the narrative goes on,

> the world stands indebted to the sudden snapping of my father's tobacco-pipe for one of the neatest examples of that ornamental figure in oratory, which Rhetoricians style the **Aposiopesis**.

Pun, or paronomasia

The use of a word in such a way as to suggest two or more meanings, or the use of two or more words of the same or nearly the same sound with different meanings, so as to produce a humorous effect; a play on words.
(Not in Pool's *Practical Rhetorick*.)

> *Paronomasia* to the Sense alludes,
> When Words but little vary'd it includes.

Uncle Toby's 'hobby-horse' is a passion for constructing miniature fortifications and re-enacting the sieges of towns in war, and his brother Mr Shandy (Tristram's father) pokes fun at Toby,

> I would not, brother Toby, continued my father, – I declare I would not have my head so full of curtins and hornworks. That I dare say you would not, quoth Dr. Slop, interrupting him, and laughing most immoderately at his **pun**....
>
> Sir, quoth my uncle Toby, addressing himeself to Dr. Slop, – the curtins my brother Shandy mentions here, have nothing to do with bedsteads, nor have the hornworks he speaks of, anything in the world to do with the hornworks of cuckoldom

Uncle Toby goes on to give a very full explanation. Briefly, a curtin is part of a rampart, and a hornwork is 'a single-fronted outwork' – both words belonging to the technical vocabulary of military fortification in the eighteenth century. The spelling *curtin* is an obsolete fom of *curtain*, and its meaning in fortification is 'the plain wall of a fortified place; the part of the wall which connects two bastions, towers, gates, or similar structures'. The pun in *hornworks* rests on the old association of a *cuckold* – 'a derisive name for the husband of an unfaithful wife' – with horns, because a cuckold was fancifully said to wear horns on his brow. The confusion of meanings leads to the pun on the two words.

The pun as a figure based on two words similar but not identical in sound can be illustrated in,

> Who **hapless** and eke **hopeless**, all in vain...
>
> (Spenser, *The Faerie Queene*)

Exclamation

An outcry; an emphatic or vehement speech or sentence.

> Oh the many and great Victories, that Love bears away from all things!

(Not in Stirling's *System of Rhetoric*.)

> O blessed health! cried my father, making an **exclamation**, as he turned over the leaves to his next chapter, thou art above all gold and treasure

Exclamation is a familiar everyday word, but was a commonly used figure in rhetoric.

Apostrophe

A figure of speech, by which a speaker or writer suddenly stops in his discourse, and turns to address pointedly some person or thing, either present or absent; an exclamatory address.

> O Love, thou little, but puissant, and imperious, god; what doest not thou overcome?

> > *Apostrophe* from greater Themes or less,
> > Doth turn aside to make a short Address.

Uncle Toby and his companion Corporal Trim are enacting a successful attack on enemy ramparts,

> But when the *chamade** was beat, and the corporal helped my uncle up it, and followed with the colours in his hand, to fix them upon the ramparts – Heaven! Earth! Sea! – but what avails **apostrophes**?

> *A *chamade* is a call for a truce or a surrender.

A rhetorical *apostrophe* (not to be confused with the punctuation mark) is like an exclamation, but specifically addressed to someone or something.

6.2.2.2 OTHER RHETORICAL FIGURES

A few other rhetorical figures that have survived in ordinary language and literary criticism are listed below, with examples from Joshua Pool's *Practical Rhetorik* where he included them in his book. They are variations on another short sentence, *Love ruleth all things*.

Antithesis

An opposition or contrast of ideas, expressed by using words which are the opposites of, or strongly contrasted with, each other; as in '*he* must *increase*, but *I* must *decrease*', 'in *newness* of *spirit*, not in the *oldness* of the *letter*'.

> The house of the wicked shall be overthrown: but the Tabernacle of the upright shall flourish. (Proverbs 14: 11)

(Not in Stirling's *System of Rhetoric*.)

Parenthesis

An explanatory or qualifying word, clause, or sentence inserted into a passage with which it has not necessarily any grammatical connexion.

> I believe, (nor is my belief vain) that the power of Love is above all things.

> > *Parenthesis* is independent Sense,
> > Clos'd in a Sentence by this ( ) double Fence.

Periphrasis

That figure of speech which consists in expressing the meaning of a word, phrase, etc., by many or several words instead of by few or one; a roundabout way of speaking, circumlocution.

> Venus Son overcomes all things.
> The Cyprian Queen's blind boy subdues all things.
> Necessity, that hard and inevitable Weapon, doth not conquer more than Love.

> > *Periphrasis* of Words doth use a train,
> > Intending one Thing only to explain.

See chapter 2, section 2.1.1, for a discussion of periphrasis, or circumlocution. Two other traditional figures are,

Chiasmus or antimetabole

A grammatical figure in which the order of words in one of two parallel clauses is inverted in the other.

> Kings are **Lords** to their **Subjects**: but **Subjects** to their **Lords**

> > *Antimetabole* puts chang'd Words again
> > By Contraries; as the Example will explain:
> > A **poem** is a speaking **Picture**; a **Picture** is a mute **Poem**

In this figure, two or more words are repeated in reverse order, for example,

> > Ah my dear God! Though I am clean forgot,
> > Let **me not love thee**, if **I love thee not**

> > > > (George Herbert, '*Affliction*')

> > **My** face in **thine** eye, **thine** in **mine** appears

> > > > (John Donne, '*The Good-Morrow*')

Chiasmus is also mentioned in section 10.2.4.1.

Onomatopeia

The formation of a name or word by an imitation of the sound associated with the thing or action.
(Not in Joshua Pool's book.)

> > *Onomatopeia* coins a Word from Sound,
> > By which alone the Meaning may be found.

Words like *cuckoo* and *tu-whit-tu-whoo* are onomatopeic because they are a reasonable approximation, in English, to the sounds of the cuckoo and owl, but genuine onomatopeia is rare. How far does *ting-ting* really imitate the sound of a bell, *cock-a-doodle-doo* the crowing of a cock, *bow-wow* the barking of a dog or *miaow* the sound of a cat? Their equivalents in Japanese, for example, are *chirin-chirin, kokekokko, wa-wa* and *nyao*.

> **Onomatopeia** has suffered some disrepute because too much has been claimed for it. Once a linguistic form and a meaning are associated with one another, it can be very difficult not to think of the two as essentially appropriate to each other. Words like *crack, growl, roar, squeak* seem to be especially suited to their meaning; but in fact, when spoken, they are not very much like the sounds they denote...
>
> (Valerie Adams, *An Introduction to Modern English Word-Formation,* 1973)

Onomatopeia belongs to a more general category of language that we call **sound symbolism**, in which certain combinations of sounds in words have similar meanings.

Activity 6.2

(i) Have the words in the following groups any meanings in common? If so, how far do you think that similarity of sound contributes to this meaning?

(ii) Can you think of any other groups of words with similar sounds that have similar or related meanings?

1. bump, clump, dump, grump, hump, lump, plump, rump, thump
2. splash, splatter, splay, splice, splinter, split, splosh, splotch, splutter
3. squab, squabble, squalid, squalor, squall, squander, squash, squat
4. squeak, squeal, squeamish, squeeze, squelch, squiggle, squint, squirm, squirt, squish
5. flap, flip, flop
6. vain, venal, venomous, vicious, vindictive, violent, vitriolic, vituperative, vociferous

Parison

In a sequence of clauses or phrases like,

> A Youth of frolicks, an old Age of Cards,
> Fair to no purpose, artful to no end,
> Young without Lovers, old without a Friend

the grammatical structure of each pair is identical and balanced, while the lexical words change. This figure was called **parison** in traditional rhetoric. It is a common feature of literary writing, and is now generally called **parallelism**, and introduced in more detail in the next chapter, section 7.1.1.1. The dictionary definition of parison is 'an even balance in the parts of a sentence'.

> The good is geason*, and short is his abode
> The bad bides long, and easie to be found
> Our life is loathsome, our sinnes a heauy lode,
> Conscience a curst iudge, remorse a priuie goade.
>
> (George Puttenham, *The Arte of English Poesie,* 1589)

*Geason (from an OE word *gæsne*) meaning *barren, unproductive; exhausted.*

Activity 6.3

Joshua Pool also used variations on another sentence, *Fortune is Unconstant*, to illustrate the rhetorical terms listed in his book *Practical Rhetorick*.

Can you pair off the tropes or figures with the sentences that are intended to illustrate them?

aposiopesis	hyperbole	oxymoron
apostrophe	irony	parenthesis
climax	litotes	periphrasis
exclamation	metaphor	simile

- Fortune is as inconstant as the Sea, every day ebbing and flowing.
- Fortune is constantly inconstant and certainly-uncertain.
- Fortune is not always constant.
- Fortune! for shame leave wronging her, by taxing her of inconstancy: Why, she is the most constant Goddess in the World, ever performs her promise, never takes what she once gives, and what would you more?
- Fortune's inconstancy is – but I will beware; lest I provoke her cruelty against me.
- I believe (nor is my belief vain) that Fortune is the most inconstant thing in the World.
- Let Fortune be a Goddess, let her be powerful, let her have Riches, Honours, Pleasures at her command; yet she is inconstant, uncertain, blind, and Mad.
- O Fortune, how can thy inconstancy throw the greatest from the highest top of Honour and Glory, to the lowest step of calamity and misery.
- O shame! that Fortune whom we forsooth call a Goddess, place in heaven, erect Altars to offer Sacrifice, should be destitute of all providence, and continue obstinately in a blind inconstancy.
- O the intolerable inconstancy of Fortune!
- The changes and turnings of Fortune are more than the Sands of the Sea, Stars of the Skie, Hairs of the Head, Drops of Rain, Pellets of Hail, Flakes of Snow, Drops of Dew, Leaves of Trees, &c.
- There is neither crumb, nor drop of sense, or reason, in those things, that are spoken against this Truth, that there is no inconstancy to be compared to the inconstancy of Fortune

📖 The correct pairing of rhetorical terms and these examples of tropes and figures may be found in the *Commentary & Data Book*.

6.3 Rhetoric and style

The terms discussed in this short survey of traditional rhetoric will not be systematically applied in analysing style in the following chapters, though many of the texts quoted will in fact contain examples of tropes and figures. The word *rhetoric* will be used in the sense of 'artistic style or technique', and chapter 7 examines some of the characteristic stylistic features of the writing of the great eighteenth-century author Dr Samuel Johnson.

7. Rhetorical style

7.1 Structure and rhetoric in Dr Johnson's prose

Dr Samuel Johnson (1709–84) is probably best known for his *Dictionary of the English Language* of 1755, which became a standard reference book for spelling and word definition. He was a prolific writer of essays, political articles and reviews, and the *Life of Samuel Johnson* by James Boswell, which was published in 1791, portrays him as one of the most eminent literary figures of his time, and a great conversationalist. In 1762 he was awarded a crown pension of £300 a year. His letter of thanks to Lord Bute is a good short introduction to Johnson's style of writing:

Activity 7.1

(i) Describe some of the features of Johnson's style.

(ii) Rewrite the letter, changing all the passive verbs into the active voice.

(iii) Identify all the negative words.

7.1.1 *Letter to Lord Bute*

To the Right Honourable the Earl of Bute
My Lord,
    When the bills were yesterday delivered to me by Mr Wedderburne, I was informed by him of the future favours which his Majesty has, by your Lordship's recommendation, been induced to intend for me. Bounty always receives part of its value from the manner in which it is bestowed; your Lordship's kindness includes every circumstance that can gratify delicacy, or enforce obligation. You have conferred your favours on a man who has neither alliance nor interest, who has not merited them by services, nor courted them by officiousness; you have spared him the shame of solicitation, and the anxiety of suspense. What has been thus elegantly given, will, I hope, not be reproachfully enjoyed; I shall endeavour to give your

Lordship the only recompense which generosity desires, – the gratification of finding that your benefits are not improperly bestowed.
I am, my Lord,
Your Lordship's most obliged,
Most obedient, and most humble servant,

SAM. JOHNSON
July 20, 1762

Readability – difficult.

7.1.1.1 COMMENTARY

Clauses

[[*AdvCl* When the bills were yesterday delivered to me by Mr Wedderburne],
MCl I was informed by him of the future favours
[*RelCl 1* which his Majesty has, by your Lordship's recommendation, been induced to intend for me]].
[*MCl* Bounty always receives part of its value from the manner
[*RelCl 2* in which it is bestowed];
[*MCl* your Lordship's kindness includes every circumstance
[*RelCl 3* that can gratify delicacy], or
[*RelCl 4* enforce obligation]].
[*MCl* You have conferred your favours on a man
[*RelCl 5* who has neither alliance nor interest],
[*RelCl 6* who has not merited them by services], nor
[*RelCl 7* courted them by officiousness];
[*MCl* you have spared him ⟨the shame of solicitation, and the anxiety of suspense⟩].
[*MCl* [*S* What has been thus elegantly given], will, [*Comment Cl* I hope], not be reproachfully enjoyed;
[*MCl* I shall endeavour to give your Lordship the only recompense
[*RelCl 8* which generosity desires], –
the gratification [*PrepCl* of finding [*NCl reported* that your benefits are not improperly bestowed]].

There are eight relative clauses, a number which makes them a significant stylistic feature.

Negatives
Johnson uses the negative form of verbs for stylistic effect,

will, I hope, *not* be reproachfully enjoyed;
the gratification of finding that your benefits are *not* improperly bestowed.

It is difficult to find an adverb that is an exact **antonym** of *reproachfully* in *will not be reproachfully enjoyed* in order to make a positive statement – perhaps *will be happily enjoyed*? *That your benefits are not improperly bestowed* has the same logical meaning as *that your benefits are properly bestowed*, but it has the effect of an understatement that seems more polite than the positive. It is a form of **double negative** in Standard English that is not proscribed, and an example of the rhetorical trope **litotes** (see section 6.2.1.4).

The other negatives reinforce the **parallelism** of their phrases,

> a man who has *neither* alliance *nor* interest,
> who has *not* merited them by services, *nor* courted them by officiousness

as well as implying deference and some self-deprecation.

Passives

The fact that seven of the verbs are in the passive voice is sufficient to mark this also as a stylistic feature,

the bills	**were** yesterday **delivered** to me
I	**was informed** by him
his Majesty has, ...	**been induced**
the manner in which it	**is bestowed**
What	**has been** thus elegantly **given**
	will ... **not be** reproachfully **enjoyed**
your benefits	**are not** improperly **bestowed**.

Not all passives are readily reversible into the active voice, but it can be done in Johnson's letter:

> When **Mr Wedderburne delivered** the bills yesterday to me, **he informed me** of the future favours which **your Lordship's recommendation has induced** his Majesty to intend for me. Bounty always receives part of its value from the manner in which **a person bestows it**; ...
> What **you have thus elegantly given**, I hope **I shall not reproachfully enjoy**. I shall endeavour to give your Lordship the only recompense which generosity desires, – the gratification of finding that **you have not improperly bestowed your benefits**.

The difference is, like so many stylistic changes that rewriting can produce, not easy to define, but the use of the passive is rather more formal in tone.

Parallelism and balance

Pairs of expressions frequently occur in Johnson's writing with the same grammatical structure but with different lexical words, such as,

	verb	*noun*
every circumstance that can	gratify	delicacy
or	enforce	obligation

They seem to act in **parallel** with each other, so the figure is called **parallelism** (called **parison** in traditional rhetoric – see section 6.2.2.2).

> a man who has **neither alliance**
> nor   interest

P	*A*
verb	*PrepP*

> who has not **merited** them by **services**
> nor **courted** them by **officiousness**

```
              NP
              d      h        q
you have spared him  the  shame  of  solicitation
and                  the  anxiety of  suspense
```

```
                   adverb        verb
What has been thus  elegantly    given,
will, I hope, not be  reproachfully enjoyed
```

The balanced pairing of structures in parallel is a prominent feature of Johnson's formal style.

7.1.2 Letter to Boswell

To show that Dr Johnson was quite capable of writing less formal prose, here is one of his many letters written to James Boswell. It shows that he would adopt a rhetorical or **high style** when he thought it appropriate.

Johnson to Boswell, 1766

Dear Sir,

Apologies are seldom of any use. We will delay till your arrival the reasons, good or bad, which have made me such a sparing and ungrateful correspondent. Be assured, for the present, that nothing has lessened either the esteem or love with which I dismissed you at Harwich. Both have been increased by all that I have been told of you by yourself or others; and when you return, you will return to an unaltered, and, I hope, unalterable friend.

All that you have to fear from me is the vexation of disappointing me. No man loves to frustrate expectations which have been formed in his favour; and the pleasure which I promise myself your journals and remarks is so great, that perhaps no degree of attention and discernment will be sufficient to afford it.

Come home, however, and take your chance. I long to see you, and to hear you; and hope that we shall not be so long separated again. Come home, and expect such a welcome as is due to him, whom a wise and noble curiosity has led, where perhaps no native of his country ever was before.

I have no news to tell you that can deserve your notice; nor would I willingly lessen the pleasure that any novelty may give you at your return. I am afraid we shall find it difficult to keep among us a mind which has been so long feasted with variety. But let us try what esteem and kindness can effect.

Readability – fairly easy.

7.1.2.1 COMMENTARY

Style

The letter has some stylistic figures, for example, the play on two words repeated with slight variation in *an **unaltered**,* and, I hope, ***unalterable*** *friend* (an example of the rhetorical figure **paronomasia** – section 6.2.2.1); the two sentences beginning *Come home*; the structure with relative clause, *due to **him**, **whom** a wise and noble curiosity has led*; the two negatives of ***no** ... news **nor** would I*. Each of these creates a balance of features that is typical of the 'Augustan' style of prose of the eighteenth century, but the letter is much less formally constructed than the prose of Johnson's literary writing.

Vocabulary

Notice also that most of the words are from the core vocabulary, or at least belong to a reasonably familiar set of formal words – *esteem, vexation, frustrate, expectations, discernment* and so on. The derivations of the 88 lexical words are,

Old English	44	50%	
Old French	26	30%	
Middle English from Latin	6	7%	i.e. **87%** are older, probably core words
French 15th–17th centuries	8	8.5%	
Latin 15th–17th centuries	4	4.5%	i.e. **13%** are later, perhaps non-core words

📖 A complete list of the lexical words is in the *Commentary & Data Book*.

7.1.3 The Rambler *and rhetorical style (i)*

In 1750 Johnson had founded *The Rambler*, a periodical which he wrote almost entirely himself. The essays and articles in *The Rambler* show Johnson at his most stylistically rhetorical. The following text is part of Samuel Johnson's article in *The Rambler* No. 38 published on 28 July 1750.

Activity 7.2

(i) Discuss the style and identify any rhetorical tropes and figures.

(ii) List the lexical words by word-class. How many nouns are abstract?

(iii) How much of the lexical vocabulary consists of core and non-core words?

(iv) Identify the verbs of the main clauses. What do you notice?

The advantages of mediocrity

Health and vigour, and a happy constitution of the corporeal frame, are of absolute necessity to the enjoyment of the comforts, and to the performance of the duties of life, and requisite in yet a greater measure to the accomplishment of any thing illustrious or distinguished; yet even these, if we can judge by their apparent consequences, are sometimes not very beneficial to those on whom they are most liberally bestowed. They that frequent the chambers of the sick, will generally find the sharpest pains, and most stubborn maladies among them whom confidence of the force of nature formerly betrayed to negligence and irregularity; and that superfluity of strength, which was at once their boast and their snare, has often, in the latter part of life, no other effect than that it continues them long in impotence and anguish.

These gifts of nature are, however, always blessings in themselves, and to be acknowledged with gratitude to him that gives them; since they are, in their regular and legitimate effects, productive of happiness, and prove pernicious only by voluntary corruption, or idle negligence. And as there is little danger of persuing them with too much ardour or anxiety, because no skill or diligence can hope to procure them, the uncertainty of their influence upon our lives is mentioned, not to depreciate their real value, but to repress the discontent and envy to which the want of them often gives occasion in those who do not enough suspect their own frailty, nor consider how much less is the calamity of not possessing great powers, than of not using them aright...

Readability – difficult.

7.1.3.1 COMMENTARY

Vocabulary

As we have seen in previous chapters, the style of a text is partly dependent upon whether the words are familiar and informal, or not, and how the derivation of the vocabulary provides a guide to this. The *Rambler* text contains 100 lexical words, 23% of which derive from French or Latin from the fifteenth to the seventeenth centuries, compared with 13% in the letter to Boswell:

Old English	32	32%	
Old French	43	43%	
Middle English from Latin	2	2%	i.e. **77%** are older, probably core words
French 15th–17th centuries	13	13%	
Latin 15th–17th centuries	10	10%	i.e. **23%** are later, perhaps non-core words

📖 A complete list of the lexical words is in the *Commentary & Data Book*.

Rhetoric and patterning

The rhetorical features of a text can often be made visually clearer by setting it out in a diagrammatic form, boxing the words, phrases or clauses in parallel or in a balanced pair:

$$\begin{bmatrix} & \text{Health} \\ \textbf{and} & \text{vigour} \\ \textbf{and} & \text{a happy constitution of the corporeal frame} \end{bmatrix}$$

ARE

of absolute necessity ⌐ to the enjoyment of the comforts **and** to the performance of the duties of life ⌐

and requisite in yet a greater measure to the accomplishment of any thing ⌐ illustrious **or** distinguished ⌐ ;

yet even these, [*if* we can judge by their apparent consequences],

ARE

sometimes not very beneficial to those [on whom they are most liberally bestowed].

They [**that** frequent the chambers of the sick], will generally find

⌐ the sharpest pains **and** most stubborn maladies ⌐

among them [**whom** confidence of the force of nature formerly betrayed to

⌐ negligence **and** irregularity ⌐];

and **that** superfluity of strength,

[**which** was at once ⌐ their boast **and** their snare ⌐]

HAS often, in the latter part of life,

no other effect than [**that** it continues them long in ⌐ impotence **and** anguish ⌐].

These gifts of nature

ARE, however, always

> blessing in themselves **and** to be acknowledged with gratitude to him [**that** gives them] ;

since they ARE, in their | regular **and** legitimate | effects, productive of happiness,

and   prove pernicious only by | voluntary corruption **or** idle negligence |

And

as   there is little danger of persuing them with too much | ardour **or** anxiety | ,

because   no | skill **or** diligence | can hope to procure them,

the uncertainty of their influence upon our lives is mentioned,

| **not** to depreciate their real value **but** to repress the discontent and envy |

[**to which** the want of them often gives occasion

     in those [**who** | do not enough suspect their own frailty **nor** consider how much less IS |

       | the calamity of not possessing great powers **than** ∅ of not using them aright |].

The first paragraph begins with a triple subject, *Health, vigour and a happy constitution*. The 'rule of three' is a well-known feature of rhetoric in speech-making. The remaining paragraphs show a patterning of balanced pairs, either single words, e.g. *skill or diligence*, phrases, e.g. *their boast and their snare*, or clauses, e.g. *do not enough suspect their own frailty nor consider how much less . . .*, all of which are figures of **parallelism**.

Nominalisation, verbs and structure
The grammatical structure can be seen more clearly if the main clauses are separated from the subordinate clauses. The verbs are printed in SMALL CAPITALS and main clause verbs are also boxed:

> *Main clauses (MCl)*
>   *Subordinate clauses*
> [*MCl 1* Health and vigour, and a happy constitution of the corporeal frame, | ARE | of absolute necessity to the enjoyment of the comforts, and to the performance of the duties of life, and requisite in yet a greater measure to the accomplishment of any thing illustrious or distinguished];
> [*MCl 2* yet even these,
>   [*AdvCl* if we CAN JUDGE by their apparent consequences],
> | ARE | sometimes not very beneficial to those
>   [*RelCl* on whom they ARE most liberally BESTOWED].
> [*MCl 3* They
>   [*RelCl* that FREQUENT the chambers of the sick],
> | WILL GENERALLY FIND | the sharpest pains, and most stubborn maladies among them
>   [*RelCl* whom confidence of the force of nature formerly BETRAYED to negligence and irregularity]; and

[*MCl 4* that superfluity of strength,
   [*RelCl* which WAS at once their boast and their snare],
  HAS often, in the latter part of life, no other effect than
   [*NCl* that it CONTINUES them long in impotence and anguish].
[*MCl 5* These gifts of nature ARE, however, always blessings in themselves], and
[*MCl 6* ($\emptyset =$ ARE) to be acknowledged with gratitude to him
  RelCl that GIVES them];
  [*AdvCl* since they ARE, in their regular and legitimate effects, productive of happiness], and
  [*AdvCl* PROVE pernicious only by voluntary corruption, or idle negligence].
And [[*AdvCl* as there IS little danger
     [*PrepCl* of PERSUING them with too much ardour or anxiety],
     [*AdvCl* because no skill or diligence CAN HOPE TO PROCURE them],
[*MCl 7* the uncertainty of their influence upon our lives IS MENTIONED ,
  [*NonfCl* not to DEPRECIATE their real value, but
  [*NonfCl* to REPRESS the discontent and envy
    [*RelCl* to which the want of them often GIVES occasion in those
     [*RelCl* who DO NOT enough SUSPECT their own frailty,
     [*RelCl* nor CONSIDER how much less is the calamity
      [*PrepCl* of NOT POSSESSING great powers], than
      [*PrepCl* of NOT USING them aright]]]]].

The argument is carried in the subordinate clauses except for the long first clause – the main clauses are 'main' only in their grammatical function, not in their content. Most of the verbs in the seven main clauses are relational – *are* (4 times) and *has* – nor are the other two – *will find, is mentioned* – actional, 'doing words'.

Many of the nouns are **nominalisations** (see section 4.3), which we have seen to be a typical feature of the style of formal, academic writing. There are several examples in Johnson's first long clause,

> Health and vigour, and a happy constitution of the corporeal frame, are of absolute necessity to the **enjoyment** of the comforts, and to the **performance** of the duties of life, and **requisite** in yet a greater measure to the **accomplishment** of any thing illustrious or distinguished

which we can rewrite using verbs rather than nouns, and replacing some expressions with core vocabulary words:

> Health and vigour and a well-knit body are absolutely necessary if we want to **enjoy** the comforts and **perform** the duties of life, and **we require** them even more if we want to **accomplish** anything illustrious or distinguished

There is a clear difference in style between the two versions. The rewritten version is more active and direct in tone. Johnson prefers nominalisations because they contribute to the formality of a style that avoids 'low and vulgar language' and 'meanness of expression' (see section 10.2.2.1).

The difficulty of the writing also lies in the grammatical structure, with its balanced coordinated clauses and, in the last clause (MCl 7), a series of successively embedded subordinate clauses to a depth of four levels.

7.1.4 The Rambler *and rhetorical style (ii)*

Activity 7.3

Read the following paragraph from another essay in *The Rambler*.

(i) What grammatical construction marks this paragraph by its frequency?

(ii) What is the rhetorical effect?

(iii) List the words that you would classify as non-core, formal vocabulary.

Rambler *No. 49, 4 September 1750 – A disquisition upon the value of fame*

The advocates for the love of fame allege in its vindication, that it is a passion natural and universal; a flame lighted by heaven, and always burning with greatest vigour in the most enlarged and elevated minds. That the desire of being praised by posterity implies a resolution to deserve their praises, and that the folly charged upon it, is only a noble and disinterested generosity, which is not felt, and therefore not understood by those who have been always accustomed to refer every thing to themselves, and whose selfishness has contracted their understandings. That the soul of man, formed for eternal life, naturally springs forward beyond the limits of corporeal existence, and rejoices to consider herself as co-operating with future ages, and as co-extended with endless duration. That the reproach urged with so much petulance, the reproach of labouring for what cannot be enjoyed, is founded on an opinion which may with great probability be doubted; for since we suppose the powers of the soul to be enlarged by its separation, why should we conclude that its knowledge of sublunary transactions is contracted or extinguished? Upon an attentive and impartial view of the argument, it will appear that the love of fame is to be regulated, rather than extinguished; and that men should be taught not to be wholly careless about their memory, but to endeavour that they may be remembered chiefly for their virtues, since no other reputation will be able to transmit any pleasure beyond the grave.

Readability – difficult

7.1.4.1 COMMENTARY

Structure

This a complex paragraph structurally, as the following diagram shows. Each of the six noun clauses following the opening *The advocates for the love of fame allege* report an allegation. Grammatically, they are **rank-shifted** clauses, because they operate as direct objects in a clause, and the normal object of a verb is a phrase. To follow the sense, you must mentally repeat 'The advocates for the love of fame allege' before each of the first six reported noun clauses beginning with *that*.

[*MCl*   The advocates for the love of fame allege in its vindication,
[*NCl 1*   **reported**
            [that] it is a passion natural and universal; a flame lighted by heaven, and always burning
            with greatest vigour in the most enlarged* and elevated* minds].
            * *enlarged = free from narrowness, liberal; elevated = dignified*
[*NCl 2*   **reported**
            [That] the desire [*q – PrepCl* of being praised by posterity] implies a resolution
            [*q – NonfCl* to deserve their praises], and

[*NCl 3* **reported**
        ⟨that⟩ the folly charged upon it, is only a noble and disinterested* generosity,
          [*RelCl* which is not felt], and
          [*RelCl* therefore not understood by those
              [*RelCl* who have been always accustomed to refer every thing to themselves], and
              [*RelCl* whose selfishness has contracted their understandings.
      * *disinterested* = *impartial, unbiased, unprejudiced*
[*NCl 4* ⟨That⟩ the soul of man, [*NonfCl* formed for eternal life], naturally springs forward beyond the limits of corporeal existence*], and
      * *corporeal existence* = *life in the body (as against the immortal life of the soul)*
[*NCl 5* (⟨∅⟩ = *that the soul of man*) rejoices to consider herself as
      [*NonfCl* co-operating with future ages], and as
      [*NonfCl* co-extended* with endless duration].
      * *co-extended* = *extending over the same space or time*
[*NCl 6* ⟨That⟩ the reproach*
      [*q* urged with so much petulance*],
      the reproach
      [*q* of labouring for [*NCl* what cannot be enjoyed],
      is founded on an opinion
      [*RelCl* which may with great probability be doubted];
      * *reproach* = *blame or censure directed against a person; petulance* = *peevishness, pettishness*

The formality of the style of this opening paragraph would have been lessened a little if Johnson had set it out differently, for example,

The advocates for the love of fame make a number of allegations in its vindication:

- Firstly, it is a passion natural and universal; a flame lighted by heaven, and always burning with greatest vigour in the most enlarged and elevated minds.
- Secondly, the desire of being praised by posterity implies a resolution to deserve their praises.
- Thirdly, the folly charged upon it, is only a noble and disinterested generosity, which is not felt, and therefore not understood by those who have been always accustomed to refer every thing to themselves, and whose selfishness has contracted their understandings.
- Fourthly, the soul of man, ... etc.

but Johnson expected his readers to be able to understand this series without any further typographical aids.

The paragraph ends with two further statements following *for*, that give reasons for the previous allegations by those who love fame – an argument that Johnson comments on in the final paragraph of this extract.

[*MCl* for
      [*AdvCl* since we suppose the powers of the soul to be enlarged by its separation],
      why should we conclude
      [*NCl* **reported** that its knowledge of sublunary* transactions is ⟨contracted or extinguished⟩]?
      * *sublunary* = *beneath the moon, therefore belonging to this world; earthly*
[*MCl*   [*Verbless Cl* Upon an attentive and impartial view of the argument],
      it will appear
      [*NCl **reported*** that the love of fame is to be ⟨regulated, rather than extinguished⟩; and
      [*NCl **reported*** that men should be taught
          [*NonfCl* not to be wholly careless about their memory], but
          [*NonfCl* to endeavour
             [*NCl **reported*** that they may be remembered chiefly for their virtues],
               [*AdvCl* since no other reputation will be able to transmit any pleasure beyond the grave]].

Rhetorical patterning

The repetitive structure of noun clauses after *allege that* provides its own rhythmic pattern. Within most of the clauses we find the balance and parallelism seen in the previous extracts from Johnson's prose writing.

The advocates for the love of fame ALLEGE in its vindication,

[that] it is

```
⎡ a passion      natural and universal                                              ⎤
⎢ a flame        lighted by heaven                                                  ⎥
⎣ and always     burning with greatest vigour in the most enlarged and elevated minds ⎦
```

[That] the desire of being praised by posterity implies a resolution to deserve their praises,

and

[that] the folly charged upon it,

is only a noble and disinterested generosity

```
⎡ which is           not  felt        ⎤
⎣ and therefore      not  understood  ⎦
```

```
⎡ by those        who have been always accustomed to refer everything to themselves ⎤
⎣ and therefore   whose selfishness has contracted their understandings              ⎦
```

That the soul of man, formed for eternal life,

naturally springs forward beyond the limits of corporeal existence,

and rejoices to consider herself

```
⎡ as co-operating with future ages and ⎤
⎣ as co-extended with endless duration  ⎦ .
```

[That]
```
⎡ the reproach urged with so much petulance           ⎤
⎣ the reproach of labouring for what cannot be enjoyed ⎦ ’
```
is founded on an opinion which may with great probability be doubted;

for since we suppose the powers of the soul to be enlarged by its separation,

why should we conclude

[that] its knowledge of sublunary transactions is contracted or extinguished ?

Upon an attentive and impartial view of the argument,

it will appear

[that] the love of fame is to be regulated rather than extinguished ;

and

[that] men should be taught

not to be wholly careless about their memory but to endeavour

they may be remembered chiefly for their virtues

since no other reputation will be able to transmit any pleasure beyond the grave.

Vocabulary

The distribution of lexical word derivations is,

Old English	29%	
Old French	50%	=**79%** core vocabulary
French, 16th and 17th C	6%	
Latin 15th–17th C	15%	=**21%** later derivations

which is a proportion very similar to that of the other *Rambler* text in section 7.1.3.1.

Activity 7.4

Check the following list of late-derived words from French and Latin against the list that you have judged to be non-core vocabulary. How many correspond?

French		*Latin*	
1420	reproach	1432	generosity
1483	accustomed	1420	transmit
1551	probability	1460	transactions
1570	attentive	1484	vindication
1593	impartial	1497	elevated
1610	petulance	1530	contracted
1612	disinterested	1545	extinguished
		1560	urged
		1604	co-operating
		1617	co-extended
		1592	sublunary
		1610	corporeal
		1630	regulated

📖 A complete list of the vocabulary, with derivations, is in the *Commentary & Data Book*.

8. Writing without style

This novel, so vast and so amiably peopled, is a long, sweet, sleepless pilgrimage to life. Rich and epical, *A Suitable Boy* is nonetheless strikingly unpretentious, almost unintellectual. Its **loose, styleless prose** is relaxed to the point of conversation. For the book pretends only to this: to allow life to move through its frame as life does in the world, with a charged aimlessness. It is almost impossible to imagine an unswayed reader.

(James Wood reviewing *A Suitable Boy* by Vikram Seth)

The reviewer describes the novelist's prose as without style – prose, presumably, that has no marked features by which it may be identified and described. This topic has been discussed at length by Roland Barthes (1915–80), a French literary critic and theorist, who proposed a theory of neutral writing, 'without style', in his book *Le Degré Zero de L'Écriture* (1953). It was translated as *Writing Degree Zero* (1967).

8.1 Roland Barthes's *Writing Degree Zero* and Albert Camus's *The Outsider*

Activity 8.1

Read the following extract from Barthes's *Writing Degree Zero*, and then the translation of the opening paragraph of Albert Camus's *L'Étranger* (1942), translated as *The Outsider* (1946).

Can you identify any consistent features of vocabulary or grammar in Camus's text which might explain or match Barthes' concept of *neutral writing, writing without style*?

In this same attempt towards disengaging literary language, here is another solution: to create a colourless writing, freed from all bondage to a pre-ordained state of language. A simile borrowed from linguistics will perhaps give a fairly accurate idea of this new phenomenon; we know that some linguists establish between the two terms of a polar opposition (such as singular–plural, preterite–present) the existence of a third term, called a neutral term or zero element: thus between the subjunctive and the imperative moods, the indicative is according to them an amodal form. Proportionally speaking, writing at the zero degree is basically in the indicative mood, or if you like, amodal; it would be accurate to say that it is a journalist's writing, if it were not precisely the case that journalism develops, in general, optative or imperative (that is, emotive) forms. The new neutral writing takes its place in the midst of all those ejaculations and judgements, without becoming involved in any of them; it consists precisely in their absence. But this absence is complete, it implies no refuge, no secret; one cannot therefore say that it is an impassive mode of writing; rather, that it is innocent. The aim here is to go beyond Literature by entrusting one's fate to a sort of basic speech, equally far from living languages and from literary language proper. This transparent form of speech, initiated by Camus's *Outsider*, achieves a style of absence which is almost an ideal absence of style; writing is then reduced to a sort of negative mood in which the social or mythical characters of a language are abolished in favour of a neutral and inert state of form...

Readability – standard.

Barthes uses a number of grammatical terms to explain his idea of a *neutral or zero element*. A *polar opposition* consists of two terms, one of which must operate at any time. They are at 'opposite poles', so for example, a noun must be *either* singular *or* plural in **number**. The **tense** of a verb must be *either* preterite (= past) *or* present.

But the category of **mood** does not have such either/or oppositions, so the notion of a *neutral term*, between polar opposites, may apply.

- The *indicative* mood of a verb is used to express facts and make statements. The verbs in these sentences and most of the book are written in the indicative mood.
- The *imperative* mood is used to make requests or give commands – ***Pass the salt, please, Come** here at once!*
- The *subjunctive* mood of a verb, used to express what is not factual, but hypothetical – the idea of possibility, obligation and so on – has almost disappeared from present-day English. It survives in sentences like *If I **were** you..., I propose that Sheila **be** nominated....*
- We generally express non-facts by using *modal* verbs like *can/could, may/ might* etc., together with *modal adverbs* like *possibly, probably*. Barthes uses the term *amodal* for a verb which is not modal.
- Expressing a wish like *God **save** the Queen, So **be** it*, uses a form of modal called *optative* mood (the Latin word *optatio* meant *a wish*).

Albert Camus, *The Outsider*

Mother died today. Or, maybe, yesterday; I can't be sure. The telegram from the Home says: *Your mother passed away. Funeral tomorrow. Deep sympathy.* Which leaves the matter doubtful; it could have been yesterday.

The Home for Aged Persons is at Marengo, some fifty miles from Algiers. With the two-o'clock bus I should get there well before nightfall. Then I can spend the night there, keeping the usual vigil beside the body, and be back here by tomorrow evening. I have fixed up with my employer for two day's leave; obviously, under the circumstances, he couldn't refuse. Still, I had an idea he looked annoyed, and I said, without thinking: 'Sorry, sir, but it's not my fault, you know.'

Afterwards it struck me I needn't have said that. I had no reason to excuse myself; it was up to him to express his sympathy and so forth. Probably he will do so the day after tomorrow, when he sees me in black. For the present, it's almost as if Mother weren't really dead. The funeral will bring it home to one, put an official seal on it, so to speak...

I took the two-o'clock bus. It was a blazing hot afternoon. I'd lunched, as usual, at Celeste's restaurant. Everyone was most kind, and Celeste said to me, 'There's no one like a mother.' When I left they came with me to the door. It was something of a rush, getting away, as at the last moment I had to call in at Emmanuel's place to borrow his black tie and mourning-band. He lost his uncle a few months ago.

I had to run to catch the bus.

Readability – easy.

'Writing without style' is described by Barthes as *colourless, neutral, basic, transparent, inert,* **metaphorical** terms to describe the impression of the 1st person narrator's speech. The vocabulary is simple. We have to assume that the translation from the French uses words which match those of the original in meaning and connotation. The sentences tend to be short, and the clauses largely in unmarked order. There are no rhetorical figures of speech or features like parallelism to draw attention to the language. Some observers would say that we 'see through' the language to the meaning directly – hence the metaphorical use of *transparent* by Barthes – but this is somewhat misleading. The speaker's style of narration conveys an impression of his character. The language is all we have, so its style must be capable of description, even if we can say little more than what it is not.

Activity 8.2

(i) Relate your impression of the narrator's character to his language.

(ii) Identify those features of the language which convey the impression of the spoken voice.

(iii) Write out a linear clause analysis of the text (or part of it).

(iv) Examine the clause and sentence structures to see if there is any marked patterning of structure.

📖 A complete linear clause analysis is in the *Commentary & Data Book.*

8.1.1 *Commentary on* The Outsider

Setting out the text clause by clause helps you to see more clearly how the grammar and simple vocabulary contribute to its apparent absence of marked stylistic features. As a 1st person narrative, it suggests the tone of a speaking voice, and so will contain some features that are familiar in speech rather than in writing, like the opening,

Mother died today. Or, maybe, yesterday; I can't be sure.

in which the alternative adverbial *Or, maybe, yesterday*, is punctuated as a sentence and conveys the break in the voice after *today*, a change of mind. We can supply the appropriate intonation mentally.

Notice also how the first three paragraphs give the impression of an immediate speaker through reference to the present – *today* – and in the present tense of *can't be sure, says, leaves,* and so on. The modal *should* in *I should get there* implies the future, *have fixed up* the present in time. At paragraph four the simple past tense is taken up and used for the rest of the novel, but the impression of a present narrator remains. This is reinforced by the colloquial forms and words that we associate with conversation like,

Or, maybe, yesterday	and so forth
Which leaves the matter doubtful	The funeral will bring it home to one
it struck me that...	so to speak
it was up to him	it was something of a rush

and the **thematic** fronting of *obviously, still, afterwards, probably, for the present.*

There is no particular pattern of clauses within the sentences, and the general lack of grammatical complexity matches the colloquial vocabulary.

8.2 Vikram Seth's *A Suitable Boy*

This novel was published in 1993. It is long (1,349 pages) and complex in its plot and the large number of characters. The reviewer quoted at the beginning of the chapter describes it as *loose* and *styleless*, and we may assume that he saw no variety or change in the style from beginning to end. Here is a narrative extract, without dialogue, from the middle of the book, the opening of section 11.8, p. 706:

When the jeep had first descended to the sands below the Fort, Dipankar Chatterji, who was one of its passengers, had been truly astonished.

The roads on the Pul Mela sands among the tents and encampments were packed with people. Many were carrying rolls of bedding and other possessions with them, including pots and pans for cooking, food supplies, and perhaps a child or two tucked under an arm or clinging onto their back. They carried cloth bags, pails and buckets, sticks, flags, pennants, and garlands of marigolds. Some were panting with heat and exhaustion, others were chatting as if they were on a picnic outing, or singing bhajans and other holy songs because their enthusiasm at finally getting a glimpse of Mother Ganga had removed in an instant the weariness of the journey.

Readability – fairly difficult.

8.2.1 *Commentary on* A Suitable Boy

The structure of the sentences is varied,

[[*AdvCl* When the jeep had first descended to the sands below the Fort], *MCl* Dipankar Chatterji, [*RelCl* who was one of its passengers], had been truly astonished].

[*MCl* The roads on the Pul Mela sands among the tents and encampments were packed with people].

[*MCl* Many were carrying rolls of bedding and other possessions with them, [*Verbless Cl* including pots and pans for cooking, food supplies, and perhaps a child or two [*NonfCl* tucked under an arm] or [*NonfCl* clinging onto their back].

[*MCl* They carried cloth bags, pails and buckets, sticks, flags, pennants, and garlands of marigolds]

[*MCl* Some were panting with heat and exhaustion], [*MCl* others were chatting [*AdvCl* as if they were on a picnic outing]], or [*MCl* Ø Ø singing bhajans and other holy songs [*AdvCl* because their enthusiasm [*PrepCl* at finally getting a glimpse of Mother Ganga] had removed in an instant the weariness of the journey]]].

and there is some complexity at phrase level, for example, post-modification,

(*NP* The roads (*q* on the Pul Mela sands (*q* among the tents and encampments)))...

and coordination,

(*NP* rolls of bedding) and (*NP* other possessions)
including (*NP* (pots and pans) for cooking), (*NP* food supplies), and perhaps (*NP* a (child or two)...)
(*NP* cloth bags), (*NP* (pails and bucket)), (*NP* sticks), (*NP* flags), (*NP* pennants), and (*NP* garlands of marigolds)

but no particular features of the grammar appear to be foregrounded.

We may contrast this 'styleless prose' with a typical extract from a short story by the American novelist Ernest Hemingway,

Inside the station café it was warm and light. The wood of the tables shone from wiping and there were baskets of pretzels on glazed paper sacks. The chairs were carved, but the seats were worn and comfortable. There was a carved wooden clock on the wall and a bar at the far end of the room. Outside the window it was snowing.

('Homage to Switzerland', in *The Short Happy Life of Francis Macomber*, 1939)

Readability – easy.

The structure in this paragraph is unvaried – a series of main clauses without subordination at sentence level – and therefore foregrounded.

[*MCl* Inside the station café it was warm and light].
[*MCl* The wood of the tables shone from wiping] and
[*MCl* there were baskets of pretzels on glazed paper sacks].
[*MCl* The chairs were carved], but
[*MCl* the seats were (worn and comfortable)].
[*MCl* There was ((a carved wooden clock on the wall) and (a bar at the far end of the room))].
[*MCl* Outside the window it was snowing].

There is coordination of two pairs of clauses with *and* or *but*. The scene is precisely observed and evoked, but the structure is stylistically marked by the absence of the variety found in the 'styleless' prose of Vikram Seth.

Activity 8.3

(i) Do you find a similar contrast between the continuation of the extract from Vikram Seth's *A Suitable Boy* and the opening paragraph of Ernest Hemingway's short story 'Wine of Wyoming'?

(ii) Are there any features of the style of *A Suitable Boy* which begin to suggest a marked style – in other words, that it is not 'styleless prose'?

...Men, women and children, old and young, dark and fair, rich and poor, brahmins and outcastes, Tamils and Kashmiris, saffron-clad sadhus and naked nagas, all jostled together on the roads along the sands. The smells of incense and marijuana and heat and noonday cooking, the sounds of children crying and loudspeakers blaring and women chanting kirtans and policemen yelling, the sight of the sun glittering on the Ganga and the sand swirling in little eddies wherever the roads were not packed with people, all combined to give Dipankar an overwhelming sense of elation. Here, he felt, he would find something of what he was looking for, or the Something that he was looking for. This was the universe in microcosm; somewhere in its turmoil lay peace.

Readability – fairly easy.

It was a hot afternoon in Wyoming; the mountains were a long way away and you could see snow on their tops, but they made no shadow, and in the valley the grain-fields were yellow, the road was dusty with cars passing and all the small wooden houses at the edge of the town were baking in the sun. There was a tree over Fontan's back porch and I sat there at a table and Madame Fontan brought up cold beer from the cellar. A motor car turned off the main road and came up the side road, and stopped beside the house. Two men got out and came in through the gate. I put the bottles under the table. Madame Fontan stood up.

Readability – very easy.

📖 An analysis of the two texts is in the *Commentary & Data Book*.

8.3 George Orwell's *Animal Farm*

We have already looked at a very limited example of the structure of George Orwell's writing in chapter 4, in relation to his 'rule' about avoiding the passive voice. One critic refers to his 'vigorous prose style', its 'clarity and conciseness', and another writes of,

his preference for grammatically simple sentences and unpretentious vocabulary

and goes on,

The prose succeeds brilliantly at balancing entertainment and argument because Orwell blends homely, even clichéd, language with sophisticated diction.

Vigour, *clarity* and *conciseness* are qualities that are felt subjectively, but *grammatically simple sentences*, *unpretentious vocabulary* and *sophisticated diction* can be more objectively defined and classified. It would be interesting to take a longer extract from *Animal Farm* to see if these descriptions can be verified, and whether Orwell's writing can be classified as another example of 'styleless prose'.

The traditional classification of sentence structures into four types, simple, compound, complex and compound-complex, was introduced in section 5.2.1.2.

Activity 8.4

(i) Read the following extract from chapter VIII of *Animal Farm* and identify the sentence types.

(ii) Does it show a preference for 'grammatically simple sentences'?

(iii) Do you find the style *vigorous*, *clear* and *concise*?

Terrified, the animals waited. It was impossible now to venture out of the shelter of the buildings. After a few minutes the men were seen to be running in all directions. Then there was a deafening roar. The pigeons swirled into the air, and all the animals, except Napoleon, flung themselves flat on their bellies and hid their faces. When they got up again, a huge cloud of black smoke was hanging where the windmill had been. Slowly the breeze drifted it away. The windmill had ceased to exist!

At this sight the animals' courage returned to them. The fear and despair they had felt a moment earlier were drowned in their rage against this vile, contemptible act. A mighty cry for vengeance went up, and without waiting for further orders they charged forth in a body and made straight for the enemy. This time they did not heed the cruel pellets that swept over them like hail. It was a savage, bitter battle. The men fired again and again, and when the animals got to close quarters, lashed out with their sticks and their heavy boots. A cow, three sheep, and two geese were killed, and nearly everyone was wounded. Even Napoleon, who was directing operations from the rear, had the tip of his tail chipped by a pellet. But the men did not go unscathed either. Three of them had their heads broken by blows from Boxer's hoofs; another was gored in the belly by a cow's horn; another had his trousers nearly torn off by Jessie and Bluebell. And when the nine dogs of Napoleon's bodyguard, whom he had instructed to make a detour under cover of the hedge, suddenly appeared on the men's flank, baying ferociously, panic overtook them. They saw that they were in danger of being surrounded. Frederick shouted to his men to get out while the going was good, and the next moment the cowardly enemy was running for dear life. The animals chased them right down to the bottom of the field, and got in some last kicks at them as they forced their way through the thorn hedge.

Readability – fairly easy.

8.3.1 *Commentary on* Animal Farm

This classification into four types does not distinguish any of the many possible varieties within each category (e.g. the variable number of coordinate and/or subordinate clauses), nor does it distinguish the different degrees of complexity of the phrases within clauses. If we assume that the critic is using *simple* in the sense, 'consisting of one clause', the reference to Orwell's prose as consisting of 'grammatically simple sentences' is not verified.

8.3.1.1 'GRAMMATICALLY SIMPLE SENTENCES'
Of the 22 sentences in the extract, only seven are simple; three are compound, eight complex and four compound-complex. Here is an example of each category:

Simple	It was a savage, bitter battle.
Compound	A cow, three sheep, and two geese were killed, and nearly everyone was wounded.
Complex	Even Napoleon, who was directing operations from the rear, had the tip of his tail chipped by a pellet.
Compound-complex	The animals chased them right down to the bottom of the field, and got in some last kicks at them as they forced their way through the thorn hedge.

But within the four categories there is a variety of sentence structures, which helps to make the paragraph a balanced unit. The rhetorical effect of this variety contributes to the sense of a 'vigorous prose style'. The simple sentences are placed in strategic positions, for example after the explosion,

Slowly the breeze drifted it away. The windmill had ceased to exist!

before the description of the battle,

> It was a savage, bitter battle.

and after the description of the animals' casualties,

> But the men did not go unscathed either.

There is no one pattern of sentence, however, which is itself repeated or foregrounded, and within a sentence, the types of clause structure also vary. For example, this complex sentence is relatively 'simple' in the ordinary meaning of the word, with two clauses, a main clause followed by a restrictive relative clause qualifying *pellets*,

> [*MCl* This time they did not heed the cruel pellets [*RelCl* that swept over them like hail]].

whereas another has four, its main clause coming last, following an adverbial *when*-clause, which is split by a non-restrictive relative clause and followed by a nonfinite clause,

> And [[*AdvCl* when the nine dogs of Napoleon's bodyguard, [*RelCl* whom he had instructed to make a detour under cover of the hedge], suddenly appeared on the men's flank, [*NonfCl* baying ferociously]], *MCl* panic overtook them].

Similarly, the variety of coordinated and/or subordinated clauses in compound and compound-complex sentences determines the movement of the prose and its style. So the characteristic of this kind of prose – its style – is the balance achieved by its structural variety. Therefore it cannot be described as 'writing without style'.

📖 A complete structural analysis of the extract is in the *Commentary & Data Book*.

8.3.1.2 THE VOCABULARY

The critic quoted at the beginning of section 8.3 refers to Orwell's 'unpretentious vocabulary' (which we can assume is the **core vocabulary** discussed in previous chapters) and then to his 'clichéd language' and 'sophisticated diction'. A *cliché* is a phrase, or collocation of two or more words, which people judge to be 'stereotyped' or 'hackneyed' – used so much that it has lost its force. The term is **pejorative** and implies a dislike of the over-used phrase. *Sophisticated* is another judgmental term, meaning *subtle, discriminating*, so we expect this kind of vocabulary to be non-core, literary, less familiar.

Presumably the critic intended to imply that these contrasting aspects of vocabulary are all present in Orwell's writing, otherwise the statement would be contradictory.

Activity 8.5

Study the vocabulary of the extract:

(i) Without using a dictionary, divide the lexical words into two groups, (I) 'unpretentious vocabulary' and (2) 'sophisticated diction'.

(ii) Then use a dictionary to look up a sample of your group I to see whether they derive from Old English (OE), Old Norse (ON) or Old French (OF) – that is, whether they were in the language by the fourteenth century.

(iii) Look up the words in your group 2 and find out the date of their first recorded occurrence in the language. Are your group 2 words all 'late entries' (fifteenth century or later, and probably from Latin or French)?

(iv) Can you find any clichés?

📖 A complete list of the lexical vocabulary of the extract, with derivations, is in the *Commentary & Data Book*.

Unpretentious and sophisticated vocabulary

According to the *Oxford English Dictionary,* sixteen lexical word types in the extract entered the language between 1413 and 1775, six from French, eight from Latin, one from Spanish and one from Irish. The late dates are not proof of 'sophisticated vocabulary', but I would expect at least some, if not all, of your group 2 words to be among them. The derivations of the lexical word types are as follows (the distribution figures are slightly simplified because a few words do not fit exactly into one category):

Old English	68	50%	
Old Norse	13	9.5%	OE + ON 59.5%
Old French	36	27%	OE + ON + OF 86.5%
French 15th C+	6	4%	
Latin 14th C+	8	6%	
Other 16th–17th C	3	2.1%	
Not known 15th–16th C	2	1.4%	Late entries 13.5%

Clichés

You cannot prove that a phrase is a cliché, only assert that it is one. I suggest that *get out while the going was good* and *running for dear life* might qualify, and that *charged forth* and *they did not heed* are both of old-fashioned usage.

9. Words and grammar in prose texts III – two nineteenth-century classics

9.1 Fenimore Cooper – *The Last of the Mohicans* (i)

The following text is an extract from *The Last of the Mohicans* (*A Narrative of 1757*), a famous tale by the American author James Fenimore Cooper (1789–1851). It was published in 1826. Film versions have been made of the story, the most recent in the early 1990s. We expect an adventure story to be fast-moving and exciting, with a style to match. Cooper's stories have plenty of action and bloodshed, and evoke the 'spirit of the wilderness', but like the early translations of *The Swiss Family Robinson* studied in chapter 11, the style is marked by a formality of expression which is no longer fashionable.

Activity 9.1

Read the extract which follows. Does it present any problems of understanding? How would you describe its style?

[*The story so far has followed the adventures of a party of travellers. They are making their way to an English fort, in frequent danger from hostile Indians. Major Duncan Heyward, an English officer, is escorting two sisters; they are guided by Hawk-eye the white scout and two Mohican Indian companions, Chingachgook the father and Uncas the son – 'the last of the Mohicans'.*]

While his auditors received a cheering assurance of the security of their place of concealment from this untutored description of the falls, they were much inclined to judge differently from Hawk-eye of its wild beauties. But they were not in a situation to suffer their thoughts to dwell on the charms of natural objects; and, as the scout had not found it necessary to cease his culinary labours while he spoke, unless to point out with a broken fork the direction of some particularly obnoxious point in the rebellious stream, they now suffered their attention to be drawn to the necessary though more vulgar consideration of their supper.

The repast, which was greatly aided by the addition of a few delicacies that Heyward had the precaution to bring with him when they left their horses, was exceedingly refreshing to the wearied party. Uncas acted as attendant to the females, performing all the little offices within his power, with a mixture of dignity and anxious grace that served to amuse Heyward, who well knew that it was an utter innovation on the Indian customs, which forbid their warriors to descend to any menial employment, especially in favour of their women. Once or twice the young chief was compelled to speak, to command the attention of those he served. In such cases, he made use of English, broken and imperfect, but sufficiently intelligible, and which he rendered so mild and musical by his deep, guttural voice, that it never failed to cause both ladies to look up in admiration and astonishment.

Readability – difficult.

Clearly, both the vocabulary and sentence structure of the extract could be described as formal or literary, far removed from colloquial spoken language.

9.1.1   *First paragraph*

If we take the first paragraph to start with, a number of words and phrases such as *auditors, security, place of concealment, untutored, were much inclined, suffer, cease his culinary labours, obnoxious, rebellious, suffered, vulgar,* belong to the category of formal vocabulary and expression.

Activity 9.2

Rewrite the text by substituting more common or familiar words from the lists of synonyms below, to replace the marked formal words and phrases. You may need to change the form of a word, e.g. *safe* rather than *safety*.

A complete list of the words, synonyms, derivations and dates of first recorded use is in the *Commentary & Data Book*

While his auditors received a cheering assurance of the security of their place of concealment from this untutored description of the falls, they were much inclined to judge differently from Hawk-eye of its wild beauties. But they were not in a situation to suffer their thoughts to dwell on the charms of natural objects; and, as the scout had not found it necessary to cease his culinary labours while he spoke, unless to point out with a broken fork the direction of some particularly obnoxious point in the rebellious stream, they now suffered their attention to be drawn to the necessary though more vulgar consideration of their supper.

Word	Synonyms
auditors	listeners, hearers, audience
security	safety, invulnerability
concealment	hiding, cover
untutored	homespun, simple, plain, artless
inclined	tended
suffer/suffered	allow(ed), permit(ted)
cease	give up, stop, quit, terminate
culinary	cooking, kitchen
labours	work (*n*), toil (*n*)

The current meaning of *obnoxious* is *offensive, repulsive, hateful, annoying, objectionable, disagreeable, odious,* none of which is acceptable in this context. Its original meaning of *vulnerable* makes sense, with Hawk-eye pointing out a place in the stream from which danger might threaten their security – hence *exposed, unprotected*.

obnoxious	vulnerable, exposed, unprotected

Rebellious is used metaphorically to describe the flow of the river, so a true synonym would not be relevant here and another descriptive term is needed:

rebellious	fast-running, swiftly flowing, rapid, turbulent
vulgar	common(place), coarse, crude, low

9.1.1.1 COMMENTARY – FIRST REWRITTEN VERSION, FIRST PARAGRAPH

Here is a version of the paragraph with some of its vocabulary simplified and made less formal.

> **First rewritten version**
> While his listeners received a cheering assurance of the safety of their place of hiding from this artless description of the falls, they tended to judge differently from Hawk-eye of its wild beauties. But they were not in a situation to allow their thoughts to dwell on the charms of natural objects; and, as the scout had not found it necessary to stop cooking while he spoke, unless to point out with a broken fork the direction of some particularly exposed point in the fast-running stream, they now allowed their attention to be drawn to the necessary though more commonplace consideration of their supper.

But this replacement of single words or short phrases only partly changes the style of the paragraph. There still remains a formality of expression in the grammar. The number of NPs and PrepPs, sometimes embedded one within the other, is a marked feature of the style. A 'Chinese box' diagram will show this – the more embedding of one box in another there is, the greater is the grammatical complexity:

[[*AdvCl* WHILE his auditors received

| *NP* a cheering assurance | *PrepP* of the safety | *PrepP* of their place | *PrepP* of hiding |

| *PrepP* from this artless description | *PrepP* of the falls |]

[*MCl* they tended to judge differently from Hawk-eye | *PreP* of its wild beauties |]

[*MCl* But they were not

| *PrepP* in a situation | *NonfCl* [to allow their thoughts to dwell |

| *PrepP* on the charms | *PrepP* of natural objects]] |

and,

[[*AdvCl* AS the scout had not found it necessary [*NonfCl* to stop cooking [*AdvCl* while he spoke]]

[*NonfCl* unless to point out | *PrepP* with a broken fork |

| *NP* the direction | *PrepP* of some particularly exposed point | *PrepP* in the fast-running stream |]

MCl they now allowed their attention to be drawn

| *PrepP* to the necessary though more commonplace consideration | *PrepP* of their supper |]

The stylistic complexity of the first paragraph is a result of the high proportion of **qualifiers** which post-modify either the noun heads of NPs, as in,

p	d	m	h	qualifier = PrepP
	a	cheering	**assurance**	(of the safety of their place of concealment)
	the		**direction**	(of some particularly exposed point in the fast-running stream)
p	**d**	**m**	**h**	*qualifier = NonfCl*
in	a		**situation**	[to allow their thoughts to dwell on the charms of natural objects]

or adjectives,

h	qualifier = NonfCl
necessary	[to stop cooking [while he spoke]]

If we were to find that this frequency of qualifying structures occurs throughout the novel, then we would define it as a stylistic feature of the grammar of the whole book.

Another feature of the style is the number of abstract nouns which are derived from, or can be transformed into verbs. The process of deriving a noun from a verb, called **nominalisation**, was introduced in section 4.3. The **deverbal nouns** in the first paragraph, with their corresponding verbs, are:

Noun		*Verb*
assurance	⇔	assure
security	⇔	secure
concealment	⇔	conceal
description	⇔	describe
thoughts	⇔	think
attention	⇔	attend
consideration	⇔	consider

Rewriting the paragraph, changing the vocabulary and modifying the grammatical structure, does not necessarily 'improve' it, but it will help us to judge the effectiveness of Cooper's original.

Activity 9.3

(i) Rewrite the first paragraph again, incorporating the changes made in the first rewritten version, and changing deverbal nouns, wherever possible, to active verbs or adjectives. If necessary, change the sentence structures and punctuation.

(ii) Discuss and justify the changes that you made.

(iii) Compare your new paragraph with the second rewritten version following.

9.1.1.2 COMMENTARY – SECOND REWRITTEN VERSION, FIRST PARAGRAPH

Second rewritten version

Hawk-eye described the falls in his homespun manner, and assured his listeners that the place where they were hiding was safe. This cheered them up, though they did not share his love of the wild beauty of the place. But as they were situated, they could not allow their thoughts to dwell on the beauties of nature. The scout had not needed to stop cooking while he spoke, except when he pointed with a broken fork to where there was a particularly exposed point in the fast-running stream. Supper being ready, they allowed Hawk-eye to draw their attention from the scenery to the need to eat, commonplace though that was.

Any simplified version of the paragraph will narrate the underlying events, after a fashion, but it is no longer in Fenimore Cooper's style and therefore will not carry the same meaning in the same way. It will not reproduce the effect of, for example, *the necessary though more vulgar consideration of their supper*, in which the author is implicitly comparing the spiritual values of contemplating natural beauty and merely satisfying bodily hunger. Much is implied in the original which is lost when simplifying it.

Furthermore, the **order** of the clauses in some sentences of Fenimore Cooper's original is marked. The unmarked position of an adverbial clause (AdvCl) is after its main clause (MCl), just as in an unmarked clause the adverbial element comes last (SPCA). In the first sentence of the paragraph, the order of the clauses is,

[[*AdvCl* while . . .] *MCl*]

which matches the meaning, because receiving Hawk-eye's assurance <u>precedes</u> their judging differently, so the 'temporal order' of events is kept. But readers have to keep the whole of the AdvCl in mind – *While his auditors received a cheering assurance of the security of their place of concealment from this untutored description of the falls* – before the MCl tells them the outcome. A rearrangement of the order of this first sentence should demonstrate this:

His auditors were much inclined to judge differently from Hawk-eye's untutored description of the wild beauties of the falls, while they received a cheering assurance of the security of their place of concealment.

This is unatisfactory. By fronting the AdvCl and making it **thematic** in the sentence, Cooper draws attention to the importance in the narrative of Hawk-eye's '*cheering assurance*'. Structurally, however, it does increase (for some readers) the difficulty of understanding.

9.1.2 *Second paragraph*

The [*repast*] , which was greatly aided by the addition of a few [*delicacies*] that Heyward had the [*precaution*] to bring with him when they left their horses, was [*exceedingly*] refreshing to the wearied party. Uncas acted as attendant to the [*females*] , performing all the little [*offices*] within his power, with a mixture of dignity and anxious grace that [*served to amuse*] Heyward, who well knew that it was an utter [*innovation*] on the Indian customs, which forbid their warriors to [*descend to*] any [*menial*] [*employment*] , especially in favour of their women. Once or twice the young chief was [*compelled*] to speak, to command the attention of those he served. In such cases, he made use of English, broken and imperfect, but [*sufficiently intelligible*] , and which he [*rendered*] so mild and musical by his deep, guttural voice, that it never failed to cause both ladies to look up in admiration and astonishment.

Activity 9.4

(i) Repeat Activity 9.2 on the second paragraph, replacing the boxed words that are less familiar with others from the core vocabulary, if possible. Use a thesaurus or dictionary to get a choice of alternatives.

(ii) List any deverbal nouns (nominalisations) with their corresponding verbs, and see if you can incorporate some of these words as verbs into your version of the paragraph.

(iii) Identify the qualifying phrases and clauses in the text, that is, NPs, PrepPs and RelCls that post-modify nouns.

(iv) Identify the post-modifying PrepPs and relative clauses in the second paragraph (see section 9.1.1.1 for a diagrammed example).

9.1.2.1 COMMENTARY

Second paragraph – formal vocabulary
Most of the vocabulary with formal connotations dates from the ME period, derived from OF and fully assimilated. None of these words comes from Old English. Most of the following suggested alternatives are derived from OE or from OF words that entered the language early. Remember however that derivation is only a guide to a word's use in formal or informal contexts; it does not determine it, and OE-derived words are not available for everything we want to say.

Original word	Alternative	Original word	Alternative
repast	meal	descend to	stoop to
delicacies	food	menial	degrading
precaution	foresight	employment	work
exceedingly	most, very	compelled	had to
females	women, ladies	sufficiently	enough
offices	tasks	intelligible	understandable
served to amuse	caused to laugh	rendered	made
innovation	change		

The sources of the original and alternative words are listed in the *Commentary & Data Book*.

Second paragraph – nominalisations

addition	⇔	add	employment	⇔	employ
precaution	⇔	*no corresponding verb*	attention	⇔	attend
attendant	⇔	attend	admiration	⇔	admire
innovation	⇔	innovate, change	astonishment	⇔	astonish

Using verbs rather than corresponding abstract nouns tends to produce a more positive style. Verbs are known as 'doing words' and turning a verb into a noun tends to change an action into a 'thing', because the grammatical functions of nouns are quite different from those of verbs, in spite of possible similarities in meaning.

The verb *be* or a similar linking verb like *make*, followed by an adjective, may function like a single verb in its meaning, and have a corresponding nominalisation, for example, *make new – renew – renewal; be attentive – attend – attention.*

Some suggestions for changing the deverbal nouns in the paragraph to verbs are,

the **addition** of a few delicacies	⇒	He **added** some delicate foods
Uncas acted as **attendant** to the females	⇒	Uncas **attended** on the women
to command the **attention** of those he served	⇒	to make sure that they **attended** to him
to look up in **admiration**	⇒	they looked up and **admired** him
and **astonishment**	⇒	he **astonished** them

If a noun you want to change has no suitable corresponding verb, then you have to paraphrase,

Heyward had the **precaution** to bring	⇒	Heyward **had made sure** to bring

Remember, however, that deverbal nouns have an important and essential role in the language, and sometimes the corresponding verb cannot easily be used instead.

Second paragraph – post-modifying phrases and clauses

Fenimore Cooper's style, from the evidence of the two paragraphs we have studied, is marked by its frequency of post-modifying qualifiers – NPs, PrepPs and RelCls – which are sometimes embedded in recursive structures. However, it is not too difficult to read, because these qualifiers generally follow each other to form 'end-weighted' constructions. Diagrams can show this visually in a way that is not shown in prose writing.

Activity 9.5

Identify the post-modifying PrepPs and relative clauses in the second paragraph (see section 9.1.1.1. for a diagrammed example).

📖 Diagrams showing the post-modification can be found in the *Commentary & Data Book*.

9.2 The Last of the Mohicans (ii)

Activity 9.6

(i) Read the further extract from *The Last of the Mohicans* which follows.

(ii) Does it show stylistic features of grammar similar to those in the extract we have just discussed?

(iii) Rewrite some of it to change the style, and describe the changes you make in terms of vocabulary and grammar.

📖 A vocabulary list and structural analysis are in the *Commentary & Data Book*.

[*They are hiding in a ruined blockhouse, and have just avoided discovery by a party of Huron Indians.*]

Hawk-eye waited until a signal from the listening Chingachgook assured him that every sound from the retiring party was completely swallowed by the distance, when he motioned to Heyward to lead forth the horses, and to assist the sisters into their saddles. The instant this was done, they issued through the broken gateway, and stealing out by a direction opposite to the one by which they had entered, they quitted the spot, the sisters casting furtive glances at the crumbling ruin, as they left the soft light of the moon, to bury themselves in the gloom of the woods. During the rapid movement from the blockhouse, and until the party was deeply buried in the forest, each individual was too much interested in the escape to hazard a word even in whispers. The scout resumed his post in the advance, though his steps, after he had thrown a safe distance between himself and his enemies, were more deliberate than in their previous march, in consequence of his utter ignorance of the localities of the surrounding woods. More than once he halted to consult his confederates, the Mohicans, pointing upward at the moon, and examining the barks of the trees with care. In these brief pauses, Heyward and the sisters listened, with sense rendered doubly acute by the danger, to detect any symptoms which might announce the proximity of their foes. Birds, beasts, and man, appeared to slumber alike, if, indeed, any of the latter were to be found in that wide tract of wilderness. But the sounds of the rivulet, feeble and murmuring as they were, relieved the guides at once from no trifling embarrassment, and toward it they immediately held their way.

Readability – fairly difficult.

9.3 Sir Walter Scott – *The Bride of Lammermoor* (i)

One reason why James Fenimore Cooper wrote adventure novels in a style that now seems dated and unsuitable for the kind of narrative of action that he was telling, was because it was fashionable and expected. It is likely that one of the most important influences on Cooper, as on other novelists of the period in Britain and the USA, was the writing of Sir Walter Scott (1771–1832), 'whose influence as a novelist was incalculable; he was avidly read and imitated throughout the 19th C'. The extracts chosen for study in this chapter are from *The Bride of Lammermoor* (1819).

Activity 9.7 _____

Study the lexical words and structure of the following paragraph.

(i) Divide the lexical words (nouns, verbs, adjectives and adverbs) into two categories, (a) informal, core vocabulary and (b) formal, non-core vocabulary. If necessary, have a third category (c) 'don't know'.

(ii) Look up the lexical words in a dictionary and note their derivations – the period when they were adopted and the language they came from. What is the correlation between a word's date of adoption and your classification of it as core or non-core?

(iii) What is distinctive about the grammatical structure?

[*The story is set in Scotland in the early eighteenth century, following the 1707 Act of Union between England and Scotland. Edgar, Master of Ravenswood and heir of an ancient family, has been displaced from his ancestral home, and is watching the progress of a hunt over his family's former land.*]

The sense that he was excluded by his situation from enjoying the silvan sport, which his rank assigned to him as a special prerogative, and the feeling that new men were now exercising it over the downs, which had been jealously reserved by his ancestors for their own amusement, while he, the heir of the domain, was fain to hold himself at a distance from their party, awakened reflections calculated to depress deeply a mind like Ravenswood's, which was naturally contemplative and melancholy. His pride, however, soon shook off this feeling of dejection, and it gave way to impatience upon finding that his volatile friend Bucklaw seemed in no hurry to return with his borrowed steed, which Ravenswood, before leaving the field, wished to see restored to the obliging owner.

Readability – very difficult.

9.3.1 *Commentary on vocabulary*

I classified the following lexical words as formal, non-core vocabulary, using my own judgement, before looking up their derivations:

ancestors	OF ancestre	ME	1297
assigned	OF asi(g)ner	ME	1340
calculated	late L calculare	EMnE	1570
contemplative	OF contemplatif	ME	1340
dejection	L dejectio	ME	1450
domain	F domaine	ME	1425
excluded	L excludere	ME	1440
exercising	OF exercice	ME	1382
fain (obliged)	OE fægen (*glad*)	OE	
impatience	OF f. L impatiens	ME	1225
jealously	OF gelos + -ly	ME	1382
melancholy (adj)	*f. noun*	EMnE	1526
melancholy (n)	OF melancolie	ME	1303
obliging	oblige	EMnE	1632
oblige	OF obliger	ME	1297
prerogative	OF prerogative	ME	1404
reflections	OF reflexion	ME	1386
reserved	OF reserver	ME	1340
restored	OF restorer	ME	1297
silvan	F sylvain	EMnE	1565
situation	F situation	EMnE	1490
steed	OE steda	OE	
volatile	F volatil	EMnE	1597

Most of these words were adopted in the Middle English period from Old French or Latin. *Silvan* and *calculated* were adopted in the sixteenth century. Only two were Old English words, *fain* and *steed*, and both of these words are now archaic.

Assuming that if a word is not a core word it must be non-core, then the remaining lexical words should be informal, non-core vocabulary:

Words derived from Old English		*Words adopted in Middle English or later*			
awakened	onwæcnan	*amusement*	OF amusement	EMnE	1611
borrowed	borgian	*depress*	OF dépresser	ME	1325
deeply	deop + -ly	*distance*	OF distance	ME	1297
downs	dun	*enjoying*	OF enjoier	ME	1380
feeling	felan	*heir*	OF eir	ME	1275
field	feld	*hurry*	imitative	EMnE	1600

Words derived from Old English		Words adopted in Middle English or later			
finding	findan	*naturally*	OF naturel + -ly	ME	1430
friend	freond	*party*	OF partie	ME	1290
gave	giefan	*rank*	OF ranc, renc	EMnE	1547
hold	healdan	*return*	OF returner	ME	1366
leaving	læfan	*sense*	L sensus	EMnE	1526
men	mann/menn	*special*	OF especial	ME	1225
mind	gemynd	*sport*	OF desporte	ME	1440
new	niwe				
owner	agen, agnian + -er				
pride	pryde				
see	seon				
seemed	ON soema				
shook	scacan				
way	weg				
wished	wyscan				

More than half do in fact turn out to derive from Old English, and are therefore most likely to be common, familiar words, but the others resemble the previous list in deriving from Old French or Latin in the Middle English period or later.

This suggests that *core* and *non-core* are not 'either/or' terms, though useful for identifying general types of vocabulary. Nor is the date of a word's adoption into English necessarily a guide to its use in formal or informal contexts, but interesting supporting evidence in quite a large number of cases.

There are only a few nouns and adjectives which have corresponding verbs, so their use does not contribute significantly to the style of the text:

feeling	⇔	feel
amusement	⇔	amuse
reflections	⇔	reflect
contemplative	⇔	contemplate

9.3.2 Commentary on grammatical structure – first sentence

The paragraph contains two sentences only, and the first is a long complex structure. If we reduce it to a simple skeleton form, we have,

S	*P*	*O*	*A*
This sense and feeling	awakened	reflections	in his mind

The subject of the sentence, however, is not a simple NP. It consists of two complex coordinated noun clauses which specify and clarify what this 'sense and feeling' were. The sentence is heavily 'front-weighted':

		1st sentence
Subject 1		[The sense
	that	[*NCL* he was excluded by his situation
	from	[*PrepCl* enjoying the silvan sport,
		[*non-restr RelCl* which his rank assigned to him as a special prerogative],

Subject 2	and	[the feeling
	that	[*NCl* new men were now exercising it over the downs],
		[*nonrestr RelCl* which had been jealously reserved by his ancestors for their own amusement]
	while	[*AdvCl* he, the heir of the domain, was fain to hold himself at a distance from their party],
Predicator		awakened
Object		reflections
		[*q = NonfCl* calculated to depress deeply a mind like Ravenswood's],
		[*nonrestr RelCl* which was naturally contemplative and melancholy].

Activity 9.8

Rewrite the first sentence with sentences containing only one or two clauses, if possible. Keep Sir Walter Scott's vocabulary as far as you can, but change the order and relationship of the clauses as much as you wish.

9.3.2.1 REWRITING THE FIRST SENTENCE

Rewriting is difficult, and we find that any change of vocabulary or structure distorts Scott's narrative style. Here is an attempt that tries to keep the vocabulary unchanged. New words are italicised:

> His situation excluded him from enjoying *hunting*, although his rank assigned him the special prerogative of the silvan sport. Although his ancestors had jealously reserved the downs for their own amusement, the new men were now exercising his prerogative there. He, the heir of the domain, was fain to hold himself at a distance from their party. He sensed and felt *these things* for his mind was naturally contemplative and melancholy. *As a result*, these awakened reflections *inevitably* depressed his mind deeply.

If we then paraphrase the text by changing both words and structure, the result is then unrecognisable as being by Sir Walter Scott:

> He was unable to go hunting, even though it was his special privilege as heir to Ravenswood, since his ancestors had jealously kept the right to amuse themselves by hunting on the downs. And he had to keep clear of those new men who had taken over that right and were hunting there. He was by nature gloomy and sad, and these thoughts and feelings depressed him a lot.

9.3.3 Commentary on grammatical structure – second sentence

The second sentence of the paragraph differs from the first in being shorter and less complex. It is 'end-weighted', as the following diagram shows. Its adverbial, coming last, consists of a complex prepositional clause containing four other dependent clauses:

		2nd sentence
		Clause 1
Subject		[His pride, however, soon
Predicator		shook off
Object		this feeling of dejection],
	and	

		Clause 2
Subject		[it
Predicator		gave way
Complement		to impatience
Adverbial	upon	[*PrepCl* finding
	that	[*NCl* his volatile friend Bucklaw seemed in no hurry
	to	[*NonfCl* return with his borrowed steed],
		[*nonrestr RelCl* which Ravenswood, . . .
	before	[*PrepCl* leaving the field], . . . wished to see restored to the obliging owner].

9.4   The Bride of Lammermoor (ii)

Activity 9.9

Discuss the vocabulary and structure of the following further narrative extract from *The Bride of Lammermoor.*

[*Sir William Ashton ('the stranger') and his daughter Lucy ('the masked damsel') have taken shelter from a storm in the Master of Ravenswood's castle, Wolf's Crag.*]
'Daughter,' said the stranger to the masked damsel, 'this is the Master of Ravenswood.' It would have been natural that the gentleman should have replied to this introduction; but there was something in the graceful form and retiring modesty of the female to whom he was thus presented, which not only prevented him from enquiring to whom, and by whom, the annunciation had been made, but which even for the time struck him absolutely mute. At this moment, the cloud which had long lowered above the height on which Wolf's Crag is situated, and which now, as it advanced, spread itself in darker and denser folds both over land and sea, hiding the distant objects and obscuring those which were nearer, turning the sea to a leaden complexion, and the heath to a darker brown, began now, by one or two distant peals, to announce the thunders with which it was fraught; while two flashes of lightning, following each other very closely, showed in the distance the grey turrets of Wolf's Crag, and, more nearly, the rolling billows of the ocean, crested suddenly with red and dazzling light.

Readability – standard.

This formal narrative style is matched by the style of speech used by the aristocratic, educated characters in the story, but contrasts with the dialogue spoken by the servants and lower class Scots characters. This is discussed in chapter 18, 'The spoken voice'.

📖 A discussion of the vocabulary and stucture is in the *Commentary & Data Book.*

10. Words and grammar in verse

10.1 'The real language of men'

The poets William Wordsworth (1770–1850) and Samuel Taylor Coleridge (1772–1835) published a volume of verse in 1798 called *Lyrical Ballads*. The style of verse which they used (in their different ways) was a deliberate reaction against that which we associate with much of the eighteenth century. Wordsworth wrote a controversial Preface to the ballads in 1800, in which he said,

> ...the proper diction for poetry in general consists altogether in language taken, with due exceptions, from the mouths of men in real life, a language which actually constitutes the natural conversation of men under the influence of natural feelings.

believing that he had in fact used the language of men in 'low and rustic life' in his poems. Coleridge did not share Wordsworth's assertion that 'rustic language' should be used as the basis for poetic language. Writing later in 1817 he quotes from a poem by Wordsworth in *Lyrical Ballads* to make his point.

Activity 10.1

Read the stanza of verse and, before reading the commentary that follows, discuss whether it uses 'the real language of men', that is, would you be likely to hear this kind of language in conversation? Consider the words (or diction) and the order of the words (the grammar).

In distant countries have I been,
And yet I have not often seen
A healthy man, a man full grown,
Weep in the public roads, alone.
But such a one, on English ground,
And in the broad highway I met;
Along the broad highway he came,
His cheeks with tears were wet:
Sturdy he seemed, though he was sad;
And in his arms a lamb he had.

10.1.1 *Commentary*

Coleridge comments in these words:

> The words here are doubtless such as are current in all ranks of life; and of course not less so in the hamlet and cottage than in the shop, manufactory, college, or palace. But is this the *order*, in which the rustic would have placed the words?

In other words, using the terms introduced in chapter 2, Coleridge says that Wordsworth uses *core vocabulary* in the stanza, but not in the usual, unmarked grammatical order.

10.1.1.1 THE VOCABULARY
Most of the words in the stanza derive from Old English, with only five exceptions (the dates are those of the first recorded occurrence in writing, from the *OED*),

distant	Fr 1391
countries	OF 1275
public	Fr 1484
sturdy	OF 1297
seemed	ON 1200

all of which you will probably agree may be classified as core vocabulary.

10.1.1.2 THE ORDER OF THE WORDS
The unmarked order of a declarative clause is SPCA, with some variation in the placing of certain kinds of adverb. If we label the clause constituents to see how far the grammar is marked, we can then compare it with a rewritten version in unmarked order:

SPCA order (unmarked)

A   *P= S=P*
In distant countries have I been,   I have been in distant countries,

cj cj S P= A =P
And yet I have not often seen   and yet I have not often seen

O/S1 O/S2
A healthy man, a man full grown,   a healthy man, a man full grown,

P A A
Weep in the public roads, alone.   weep in the public roads, alone.

cj O A1
But such a one, on English ground,   But I met such a one, on English ground,

A2 S P
And in the broad highway I met;   and in the broad highway;

A S P
Along the broad highway he came,   he came along the broad highway

S A P Ci
His cheeks with tears were wet: his cheeks were wet with tears:

Ci	*S* *P*	*cj*	*S* *P*	*Ci*		

Sturdy he seemed, though he was sad;   he seemed sturdy, though he was sad;

cj	*A*	*O*	*S* *P*	

And in his arms a lamb he had.   and he had a lamb in his arms.

The rewritten version is prose, losing almost completely its rhythmic pattern and its rhyme. Only lines 2 to 4 of the poem remain unchanged.

Activity 10.2

Write a prose version of the stanza in language that you might expect to hear in 'natural conversation' today.

Coleridge himself wrote a paraphrase as 'a more faithful copy' of the kind of language a countryman might have used – what Wordsworth called 'the real language of men':

I have been in a many parts, far and near, and I don't know that I ever saw before a man crying by himself in the public road; a grown man I mean, that was neither sick nor hurt, etc. etc.

He then goes on to quote another stanza, this time from the poem 'The Thorn', as a genuine example of the language of poetry matching ordinary language:

> At all times of the day and night
> This wretched woman thither goes;
> And she is known to every star,
> And every wind that blows:
> And there, beside the Thorn, she sits,
> When the blue day-light's in the skies,
> And when the whirlwind's on the hill,
> Or frosty air is keen and still,
> And to herself she cries,
> Oh misery! Oh misery!
> Oh woe is me! Oh misery!

Activity 10.3

Is the word order of this stanza like that of 'ordinary language'?

📖 This Activity is briefly discussed in the *Commentary & Data Book.*

10.2   Poetic diction and word order

10.2.1   *Thomas Gray's* 'On the Death of Richard West'

In deliberately rejecting the 'poetic diction' typical of much eighteenth-century verse, Wordsworth quoted as an example a short elegy by Thomas Gray (1716–71), written in memory of his friend Richard West, who died in 1742.

'On the death of Richard West'

> In vain to me the smiling mornings shine,
>   And reddening Phoebus lifts his golden fire:
> The birds in vain their amorous descant join,
>   Or cheerful fields resume their green attire:
> These ears, alas! for other notes repine,
>   A different object do these eyes require.
> My lonely anguish melts no heart but mine;
>   And in my breast the imperfect joys expire.
> Yet morning smiles the busy race to cheer,
>   And new-born pleasure brings to happier men;
> The fields to all their wonted tribute bear;
>   To warm their little loves the birds complain.
> I fruitless mourn to him that cannot hear,
>   And weep the more because I weep in vain.

Wordsworth's conclusion is,

> except in the rhyme, and in the use of the single word 'fruitless' for 'fruitlessly', which is so far a defect, the language of these lines does in no respect differ from that of prose.

We can print the poem as prose and change *fruitless* to *fruitlessly*, which will help to test Wordsworth's statement:

> In vain to me the smiling mornings shine, and reddening Phoebus lifts his golden fire. The birds in vain their amorous descant join, or cheerful fields resume their green attire. These ears, alas! for other notes repine. A different object do these eyes require. My lonely anguish melts no heart but mine, and in my breast the imperfect joys expire.
>
> Yet morning smiles the busy race to cheer, and new-born pleasure brings to happier men. The fields to all their wonted tribute bear; to warm their little loves the birds complain. I fruitlessly mourn to him that cannot hear, and weep the more because I weep in vain.

Activity 10.4

Do you agree with Wordswroth's statement that 'the language of these lines does in no respect differ from those of prose'?

10.2.2 *Commentary*

Even though the poem is printed as prose, the regular rhythm and rhyme cannot be obscured, and both diction and word order are marked as 'poetic'. Another version can be made, using the same words, but with unmarked word order:

> The smiling mornings shine to me, and reddening Phoebus lifts his golden fire in vain. The birds join their amorous descant or cheerful fields resume their green attire in vain. These ears, alas! repine for other notes. These eyes do require a different object. My lonely anguish melts no heart but mine, and the imperfect joys expire in my breast.
>
> Yet morning smiles to cheer the busy race, and brings new-born pleasure to happier men. The fields bear their wonted tribute to all. The birds complain to warm their little loves. I mourn fruitlessly to him that cannot hear, and weep the more because I weep in vain.

which is clearly still not 'the ordinary language of men' because of the choices of vocabulary, or the **diction**.

10.2.2.1   POETIC DICTION – THE VOCABULARY

The phrase 'poetic diction' refers to sets of words which it was thought proper to use in poetry because of their favourable connotations. 'Low and vulgar language' and 'meanness of expression' were considered unsuitable to express 'propriety of thought'. For example, Dr Samuel Johnson, writing in *The Rambler* in the 1750s, quotes these lines from Shakespeare's *Macbeth*,

> Come thick Night,
> And pall thee in the dunnest smoake of Hell,
> That my keene Knife see not the Wound it makes,
> Nor heauen peepe through the Blanket of the darke,
> To cry, hold, hold.

and then comments,

> This is the utmost extravagance of determined wickedness; yet this is so debased by two unfortunate words, that while I endeavour to impress on my reader the energy of the sentiment, I can scarce check my risibility*, when the expression forces itself upon my mind; for who, without some relaxation of his gravity, can hear of the avengers of guilt *peeping through a blanket?*

> * *Risibility* means *laughter* – taken from Latin and first recorded in 1620.

Activity 10.5

Does Dr Johnson's argument convince you of the need to avoid 'low terms' in poetry?

Returning to Thomas Gray's poem, we find a number of words which are not part of the core vocabulary of everyday usage, and which illustrate his use of words reserved for 'poetic diction'. Most of them derive from French:

amorous	1303	*descant*	1380	*require*	1386
anguish	1220	*expire*	1590	*resume*	1412
attire	1250	*fruitless*	1340	*vain*	1300
complain	1374	*imperfect*	1340		

Two are from Latin, *Phoebus* (the personification of the sun) 1386 and *tribute* c. 1340. *Repine* (meaning *to long discontentedly for something*) is first recorded in 1530, an unusual coinage from re- and an OE verb *pine* (*to torment, trouble*). The origin of *wonted* (meaning *accustomed*) is uncertain. It was first recorded in 1413, and has since dropped out of use except in formal or poetic contexts.

10.2.2.2   THE ORDER OF WORDS – THE GRAMMAR

In order to focus on particular meanings, Gray varies the normal word order within some clauses. Phrases are brought to the beginning of the clause and the line of verse, objects come before the verb, and so are made prominent. The following lines all have marked word order:

			Unmarked word order

A	*S*	*P*	
In vain to me	the smiling mornings	shine	The smiling mornings shine in vain to me

S	*A*	*P*	
These ears, alas!	for other notes	repine	These ears, alas! repine for other notes

O	*P = S*	*=P*	
A different object	do these eyes	require	These eyes (do) require a different object

cj	*A*	*S*	*P*	
And	in my breast	the imperfect joys	expire	And the imperfect joys expire within my breast

cj	*S*	*P*	*O*	*P*	
Yet	morning	smiles	the busy race	to see	Yet morning smiles to see the busy race

cj	*O*	*P*	*A*	
And	new-born pleasure	brings	to happier men	And brings new-born pleasure to happier men

S	*A*	*O*	*P*	
The fields	to all	their wonted tribute	bear	The fields bear their wonted tribute to all

P	*O*	*S*	*P*	
To warm	their little loves	the birds	complain	the birds complain to warm their little loves

There is a good deal of 'artificiality' about the word order in Gray's poem, but it is not just his choice of poetic diction and marked word order that makes up its style. Here is a list of the NPs in the poem, grouped by similarity of structure and vocabulary:

Preposition	*Determiner*	*Modifier*	*Head*
	the	smiling	mornings
	the	imperfect	joys
	the	busy	race
	their	amorous	descant
	their	green	attire
	their	wonted	tribute
	their	little	loves
	a	different	object
	my	lonely	anguish
	his	golden	fire
		reddening	Phoebus
		cheerful	fields
		new-born	pleasure

to		happier	men
	the		birds
	these		ears
	these		eyes
	no		heart
	my		breast
			morning
	the		fields
	the		birds

Both diction and grammar combine in a particular structure of noun phrase, often either *dh* or *dmh* – a determiner (*the, a, their, my, his*, etc.), followed by a head noun, either alone or with a single modifier (all adjectives in this poem). NPs like *the busy race*, referring to men and women in general going about their daily business are especially common in much eighteenth-century verse.

The line *And in my breast the imperfect joys expire* combines two meanings, *I am no longer joyful* and *Joy is imperfect*, which are expressed mainly through the NP *the imperfect joys*. The NP *their amorous descant join* could be simply paraphrased as *sing songs of love*. Gray's words are an **elegant variation** from common words and phrases, using the poetic diction fashionable at the time.

In the poem, only eight nouns are unmodified, and none have more than one modifier.

10.2.3 *George Crabbe's* 'Peter Grimes'

The following short extracts come from the poem 'The Borough' (1810), by George Crabbe (1754–1832), in the section that tells the story of the fisherman Peter Grimes. Crabbe wrote his verse narratives entirely in **heroic couplets** – pairs of rhyming lines of ten syllables in iambic metre ('rising duple'), which had been a favourite verse form in the eighteenth century. They are called *heroic* because they were commonly used in **epic poetry**, that is, verse that narrated the deeds of heroes, for example, Achilles in Homer's *Iliad*, Odysseus in the *Odyssey* and Aeneas in Virgil's *Aeneid*.

Activity 10.6

Find examples of any of the lexical and grammatical features that have been discussed in sections 10.1 and 10.2.

📖 This Activity, with a vocabulary list, is discussed in the *Commentary & Data Book*.

(a) Old Peter Grimes made fishing his employ,
    His wife he cabin'd with him and his boy,
    And seem'd that life laborious to enjoy...
(b) 'It is the word of life,' the parent cried;
    – 'This is the life itself,' the boy replied;
    And while old Peter in amazement stood,
    Gave the hot spirit to his boiling blood: –
    How he, with oath and furious speech, began
    To prove his freedom and assert the man;...

(c) And though stern Peter, with a cruel hand,
     And knotted rope, enforced the rude command,
     Yet he consider'd what he'd lately felt,
     And his vile blows with selfish pity dealt.
(d) Thus by himself compell'd to live each day,
     To wait for certain hours the tide's delay;
     At the same times the same dull views to see,
     The bounding marsh-bank and the blighted tree...
(e) What time the sea-birds to the marsh would come,
     And the loud bittern, from the bulrush home,
     Gave from the salt-ditch side the bellowing boom...
(f) Then as they watch'd him, calmer he became,
     And grew so weak he couldn't move his frame,
     But murmuring spake, – while they could see and hear
     The start of terror and the groan of fear...

The words of these extracts are mostly core vocabulary. The style derives from the formality of the verse form, its balanced rhythm and syntax, and the regular rhyming pattern.

10.2.4 *Samuel Johnson's 'London'*

The verse of Samuel Johnson (1709–1784) typifies the poetic style of the 'Augustan age', a period of English literature which has no exact dates, but which is generally identified with writers like Alexander Pope, Joseph Addison, Jonathan Swift and Johnson, in the early and middle eighteenth century.

Here is part of Johnson's poem 'London' (1738). It is written in heroic couplets.

> By numbers here from shame or censure free,
> All crimes are safe, but hated poverty.
> This, only this, the rigid law pursues,
> This, only this, provokes the snarling muse.
> The sober trader at a tattered cloak,
> Wakes from his dream, and labours for a joke;
> With brisker air the silken courtiers gaze,
> And turn the varied taunt a thousand ways.
> Of all the griefs that harass the distressed,
> Sure the most bitter is a scornful jest;
> Fate never wounds more deep the gen'rous heart,
> Than when a blockhead's insult points the dart.
> Has heaven reserved, in pity to the poor,
> No pathless waste, or undiscovered shore;
> No secret island in the boundless main?
> No peaceful desert yet unclaimed by Spain?
> Quick let us rise, the happy seats explore,
> And bear oppression's insolence no more.
> This mournful truth is ev'rywhere confessed,
> SLOW RISES WORTH, BY POVERTY DEPRESSED:
> But here more slow, where all are slaves to gold,
> Where looks are merchandise, and smiles are sold;
> Where won by bribes, by flatteries implored,
> The groom retails the favours of his lord.

Activity 10.7

10.2.4.1 COMMENTARY

Making the syntax 'regular' is a useful procedure because we can return to the poem itself with a much clearer understanding of its structure, and of how that structure is an essential part of the poem's style and meaning.

All crimes but hated poverty are safe here, free from shame or censure by numbers.
The rigid law pursues only this, only this provokes the snarling muse.
The sober trader wakes from his dream at a tattered cloak, and labours for a joke;
the silken courtiers gaze with brisker air, and turn the varied taunt a thousand ways.
A scornful jest is sure the most bitter of all the griefs that harass the distressed;
Fate never wounds the gen'rous heart more deep, than when a blockhead's insult points the dart.
Has heaven reserved no pathless waste, or undiscovered shore, no secret island in the boundless main, no peaceful desert yet unclaimed by Spain, in pity to the poor?
Let us rise quick (to) explore the happy seats, and bear oppression's insolence no more.
This mournful truth is confessed ev'rywhere, Worth rises slow, depressed by poverty:
but here more slow, where all are slaves to gold, where looks are merchandise, and smiles are sold;
where the groom, won by bribes, implored by flatteries, retails the favours of his lord.

The extract has a significant number of examples of the NP patterns discussed in Gray's poem in section 10.2.1 — definite article *the* + modifier + head, and the frequent pre-modification of the head noun. These structures **generalise** the descriptions rather than describe individual people and places:

> By numbers here from shame or censure free,
> All crimes are safe, but ⟦**hated** poverty⟧.
> This, only this, ⟦the **rigid** law⟧ pursues,
> This, only this, provokes ⟦the **snarling** muse⟧.
> ⟦The **sober** trader⟧ at a ⟦**tattered** cloak⟧,
> Wakes from his dream, and labours for a joke;
> With **brisker** air ⟦the **silken** courtiers⟧ gaze,
> And turn ⟦the **varied** taunt⟧ a **thousand** ways.
> Of all the griefs that harass the distressed,
> Sure the most bitter is ⟦a **scornful** jest⟧;
> Fate never wounds more deep ⟦the **gen'rous** heart⟧,
> Than when ⟦a **blockhead's**⟧ insult points the dart.
> Has heaven reserved, in pity to the poor,
> ⟦No **pathless** waste⟧, or ⟦**undiscovered** shore⟧;
> ⟦No **secret** island⟧ in ⟦the **boundless** main⟧?
> ⟦No **peaceful** desert⟧ yet unclaimed by Spain?

Quick let us rise, the **happy** seats explore,
And bear **oppression's** insolence no more.
This **mournful** truth is ev'rywhere confessed,
SLOW RISES WORTH, BY POVERTY DEPRESSED:
But here more slow, where all are slaves to gold,
Where looks are merchandise, and smiles are sold;
Where won by bribes, by flatteries implored,
The groom retails the favours of his lord.

The lines,

Where looks are merchandise, and smiles are sold;
Where won by bribes, by flatteries implored,

show two very common **rhetorical** patterns of language. *Looks are merchandise* and *smiles are sold* show structural **parallelism** (see section 7.1.1.1, where it was a feature of Johnson's prose). If the second line had been written *where won by bribes, implored by flatteries*, it would also have shown parallelism –verb + -PrepP – but in fact the pattern is reversed in the second phrase –PrepP + verb – which makes the crossed pattern called **chiasmus** in traditional rhetoric (see section 6.2.2.2):

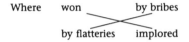

10.2.5 *'Propriety' in language use*

In the eighteenth century there were strongly held views about the proper use of language. A typical statement can be found in the Preface to *A Liberal Translation of the New Testament*, published in 1768 by E. Harwood:

> I begun and pursued the undertaking upon this plan, viz. . . . to cloathe the genuine ideas and doctrines of the Apostles with that propriety* and perspicuity*, in which they themselves, I apprehend, would have exhibited them had they *now* lived and written in our language. The true meaning and design of each author hath been strictly and impartially explored...
>
> So that my *first view* always was with impartiality and critical attention to discover the true sense of my author; my *next* view, to cloathe his ideas in the vest of modern elegance*. Elegance of diction, therefore, hath ever been consulted, but never at the expence of that truth and fidelity*, which ought ever to be sacred and inviolable in the interpreter of Scripture.
>
> It is pleasing to observe, how much our language, within these very few years, hath been refined* and polished, and what infinite improvements it hath lately received.

The meaning and derivation of his 'key words' are,

propriety	fitness, rightness; f. OF *propriété* property (1456)
perspicuity	clearly expressed; f. *perspicuous*, easily understood; ME, = transparent f. L *perspicuus* (1477)
elegance	graceful in appearance or manner, tasteful, refined; f. F *élégant* or L *elegant* (1510)
fidelity	faithfulness, loyalty, strict conformity to truth or fact; f. F *fidélité* or L *fidelitas* (1494)
refined	characterised by polish or elegance or subtlety f. Fr (1574)

Harwood's views on the King James Bible of 1611 are interesting too:

> The author was conscious that the bald and barbarous language of the old vulgar version hath acquired a venerable sacredness from length of time and custom...

You can compare Harwood's translations with some from the King James Bible and others in chapter 11, but what is interesting in this chapter are his beliefs about style and language:

- that ideas are 'cloathed' with language
- that 'true sense' can be discovered and stated with 'modern elegance'
- that the language of the King James Bible was 'bald and barbarous'

'Elegance of diction' is clearly the aim of Samuel Johnson in his poem, and this helps to justify its stylistic features, whatever may be our personal response to it. These conventions of diction and word order are more obvious in comic verse, parodies or poems on commonplace topics.

Activity 10.8

The following texts on less serious topics are extracts from eighteenth-century poems. Not all of them are written in heroic couplets, but they follow the 'elegant' conventions of diction and word order.

(i) Identify any of the stylistic features that have been discussed in this chapter.

(ii) What is the 'true sense' of the texts? Write a paraphrase in present-day language.

📖 This Activity is discussed in the *Commentary & Data Book.*

1. From 'The Bowling-Green' by William Somerville (1675–1742)

> Where fair Sabrina's* wand'ring currents flow,
> A large smooth plain extends its verdant brow;
> Here ev'ry morn, while fruitful vapours feed
> The swelling blade and bless the smoking mead,
> A cruel tyrant reigns: like Time, the swain
> Whets his unrighteous scythe, and shaves the plain.
> Beneath each stroke the peeping flow'rs decay,
> And all th'unripened crop is swept away.
> The heavy roller next he tugs along,
> Whiffs his short pipe, or rears a rural song;
> With curious eyes then the pressed turf he views,
> And ev'ry rising prominence subdues.
>
> * *the River Severn*

2. From 'The Country Man' by George Farewell (*c.* 1733)

> Let us moreover view the poultry tribe,
> And the plumed leaders of the comb-crowned race;
> Whose clapping wings the stars do not abide,
> Whose watchful crowings summon up the day.

3. From 'The Goff. An Heroi-Comical Poem' by Thomas Mathison (1743)

> To free the ball the chief now turns his mind,
> Flies to the bank where lay the orb confined;
> The pond'rous club upon the ball descends,
> Involved in dust th'exulting orb ascends;
> Their loud applause the pleased spectators raise;
> The hollow bank resounds Castalio's praise.

4. From 'The Gymnasiad, or Boxing Match' by Paul Whitehead (1744)

> As when two monarchs of the brindled breed
> Dispute the proud dominion of the mead,
> They fight, they foam, then wearied in the fray,
> Aloof retreat, and low'ring stand at bay:
> So stood the heroe, and indignant glared,
> While grim with blood their rueful fronts were smeared,
> Till with returning strength new rage returns,
> Again their arms are steeled, again each bosom burns.
> Incessant now their hollow sides they pound
> Loud on each breast the bounding bangs resound;
> Their flying fists around the temples glow,
> And the jaws crackle with the massy blow

Though these examples are typical of a particular style adopted in eighteenth-century verse writing, there is much more variety than this suggests – you can find many poems using mainly everyday words and (mainly) unmarked word order, like Christopher Smart's 'For Saturday' (1770):

> Now's the time for mirth and play,
> Saturday's an holiday;
> Praise to heav'n unceasing yield,
> I've found a lark's nest in the field.
> A lark's nest, then your playmate begs
> You'd spare herself and speckled eggs;
> Soon she shall ascend and sing
> Your praises to th'eternal King.

10.2.6 *John Milton's* Paradise Lost

John Milton (1608–74) published his epic poem *Paradise Lost* in 1667. Its subject is not the wars and conquests of heroes of history and myth, but the Fall of the Angels, the Creation of the earth and the story of Adam and Eve's expulsion from the Garden of Eden. The original of the poem is in the Book of Genesis, chapters 2, 3 and 4.

Milton describes it in the 'Argument', or synopsis, at the beginning of the first of the twelve books of the poem:

This first Book proposes first in brief the whole Subject, *Mans disobedience, and the loss thereupon of Paradise wherein he was plac't* and the poem begins with these lines:

> Of Mans first Disobedience, and the Fruit
> Of that Forbidden Tree, whose mortal tast
> Brought Death into the World, and all our woe,
> With loss of Eden, till one greater Man
> Restore us, and regain the blissful Seat,
> Sing Heav'nly Muse, that on the secret top
> Of Oreb, or of Sinai, didst inspire
> That Shepherd, who first taught the chosen Seed,
> In the beginning how the Heav'ns and Earth
> Rose out of Chaos:

The difficulties of understanding this opening sentence lie partly in the assumed knowledge that a reader should have and partly in the rhetoric of the grammar.

10.2.6.1   THE OPENING SENTENCE OF *PARADISE LOST*

Reference and meaning

● *Disobedience* refers to Adam's sin in eating *the Fruit of that Forbidden Tree*,

And the Lord God commanded the man, saying, Of every tree of the garden thou mayest freely eat, but of the tree of the knowledge of good and evil thou shalt not eat of it: for in the day that thou eatest thereof thou shalt surely die.

The *Fruit* of the tree (often said to be an apple, though this is not in the text of Genesis) has a double meaning both as the literal *fruit* and the *result* or *outcome* of the act of eating – the loss of innocence. The text also explains the *mortal tast* – 'taste bringing death' – of the fruit.

● *One greater Man* points to the incarnation of Christ and *Paradise Regained*.
● The *Heav'nly Muse* is one of nine sister-goddesses, the Muses in Greek mythology, who were the offspring of Zeus, and regarded as the inspirers of learning and the arts, especially of poetry and music. Milton invokes Urania (literally 'the heavenly') as the true celestial source of inspiration.
● *That Shepherd* is Moses, who brought the Israelites out of Egypt into the promised land, and who received the Ten Commandments on Mount Sinai,

And the Lord came down upon mount Sinai, on the top of the mount: and the Lord called Moses up to the top of the mount; and Moses went up

● *Chaos* refers to the earth 'without form, and void', before its transformation in the Genesis account:

In the beginning God created the heaven and the earth.
And the earth was without form, and void; and darkness was upon the face of the deep

Vocabulary

All the lexical words (apart from proper nouns) are core vocabulary, and derived from OE or OF, with the possible exception of *disobedience*, though this is a familiar enough word, derived from OF and in the language since before 1400.

But Milton is well-known for using 'Latinate vocabulary', that is, words derived from Latin and sometimes used by him with their original Latin meanings, and not with those that had developed in English. Milton was a Latin scholar, writing verses and documents in Latin, and therefore much influenced by Latin meanings. Because these opening lines of *Paradise Lost* have no examples, Latinate vocabulary is discussed in section 10.2.6.2.

📖 A complete list of the words of the opening lines and their derivations is in the *Commentary & Data Book*.

Structure

But even though the vocabulary is simple, you may find this opening rhetorical **apostrophe** or address to the Muse difficult because of its unusual structure. It is one sentence, whose main clause is,

> *C*   *P*   *Voc*
> Of Mans first Disobedience and the Fruit of that Forbidden Tree... sing Heav'nly Muse

which in an unmarked normal word order would be,

> *Voc*   *P*   *C*
> Heav'nly Muse, sing of Mans first Disobedience and the Fruit of that Forbidden Tree...

The main verb *sing* is an **imperative** making a request to the Muse – the **vocative**, or person addressed – but it does not appear until the sixth line of the poem, which begins with the complement *Of mans first Disobedience* .... But this basic structure is made complex by the addition of other dependent structures, relative and adverbial clauses:

> [*MCl* **Of ⟨Mans first Disobedience, and the Fruit of that Forbidden Tree⟩**,
> [*RelCl* whose mortal tast Brought ⟨Death into the World, and all our woe⟩, with loss of Eden,
> [*AdvCl* till one greater Man ⟨restore us, and regain the blissful Seat⟩]],
> **Sing Heav'nly Muse,**
> [*RelCl* that on the secret top ⟨Of Oreb, or of Sinai⟩, didst inspire That Shepherd, [*RelCl* who first taught the chosen Seed, in the beginning how the Heav'ns and Earth Rose out of Chaos]]]:

Rhetoric

We can diagram the text to show the rhetorical patterning of pairs of words or phrases (put into boxes):

```
┌──────────────────────────────────────┐
│     of Mans' First Disobedience,      │
│                  and                  │
│  (of) the Fruit of that Forbidden Tree│
└──────────────────────────────────────┘


                              ┌──────────────┐
                              │   Death      │
of the whose mortal tast brought│   and      │ into the World
                              │ all our woe, │
                              └──────────────┘

with loss of Eden,
```

till one greater Man | restore us / and / regain the blissful Seat,

Sing Heav'nly Muse,

that on the secret top | or Oreb, / or / of Sinai | didst inspire that Shepherd –

who first taught the chosen Seed in the Beginning

how the | Heav'ns / and / Earth | rose out of Chaos,

Of Mans first Disobedience . . . the blissful Seat is brought to the front as the grammatical **theme** of the sentence. It also states the subject of the whole poem. If the sentence is rewritten in normal unmarked word order, the grammatical complexity remains unchanged, but the rhetorical placing of *Mans first Disobedience* as the theme is lost:

Heav'nly Muse, that didst inspire that Shepherd on the secret top of Oreb, or of Sinai, (and) who first taught the chosen Seed how the Heav'ns and Earth rose out of Chaos in the beginning, sing of Mans first Disobedience, and the Fruit Of that Forbidden Tree, whose mortal tast Brought Death into the World, and all our woe, with loss of Eden, till one greater Man restore us, and regain the blissful Seat.

The verse
Milton describes it in this way,

The measure is *English* Heroic Verse without Rime, as that of *Homer* in *Greek*, and of *Virgil* in *Latin*; Rime being no necessary Adjunct or true Ornament of Poem or good Verse, in longer Works especially

The lines are in 5-stress rising duple rhythm, or iambic pentameter, commonly called **blank verse** when not rhymed (*rising* and *duple* are explained in section 12.2.1 and *iambic pentameter* in 12.2.5.1).

```
Of Mans first Dis o be   dience, and the Fruit
x  /  |   x   /  | x /  | x      /  | x  /  |
  1       2     3        4      5
```

The movement of the lines we are studying comes partly from the six lines that are 'run on' (marked with ⇒) rather than 'end-stopped' by punctuation,

Of Mans first Disobedience, and the Fruit ⇒
Of that Forbidden Tree, whose mortal tast ⇒
Brought Death into the World, and all our woe,
With loss of Eden, till one greater Man ⇒
Restore us, and regain the blissful Seat,
Sing Heav'nly Muse, that on the secret top ⇒
Of Oreb, or of Sinai, didst inspire ⇒
That Shepherd, who first taught the chosen Seed,
In the beginning how the Heav'ns and Earth ⇒
Rose out of Chaos:

(This topic is discussed in more detail in chapter 12, 'Rhyme, rhythm and sound I'.)

Activity 10.9

Study the style of the following extract from *Paradise Lost* (Book I, lines 44–9). It describes how Satan fell from heaven to hell.

(i) Comment on the vocabulary.

(ii) Rewrite the sentence in normal unmarked word order and discuss its structure.

📖 A list of the words and derivations and a syntactic analysis are in the *Commentary & Data Book*.

> Him the Almighty Power
> Hurld headlong flaming from th'Ethereal Skie
> With hideous ruine and combustion down
> To bottomless perdition, there to dwell
> In adamantine Chains and penal Fire,
> Who durst defie th'Omnipotent to Arms

10.2.6.2 'LATINATE' VOCABULARY

Here are some examples of words from *Paradise Lost* that are derived from Latin and used in their Latin sense:

	Latin meaning	*Developed meaning*
Th'undaunted Fiend what this might be **admir'd, Admir'd**, not fear'd...	*admira-ri* to wonder at	regard with approval
art thou hee who **Conjur'd** against the highest...?	*conjurare* to swear, conspire	perform tricks, cause to appear or disappear
Unjustly thou **deprav'st** it with the name Of *Servitude* to serve whom God ordains...	*depravare* to distort	pervert or corrupt morally
The great Seraphic Lords and Cherubim In close recess and secret conclave sat... **Frequent** and full	*frequent-em* crowded	occurring often or in close succession; habitual, constant
Advanc't in view they stand, a **horrid** Front Of dreadful length and dazling Arms...	*horrid-us* bristling	horrible, revolting; unpleasant, disagreeable
...close the Serpent sly **Insinuating**, wove with Gordian twine His beaded train...	*insinuare* to bend in windings, to curve	convey indirectly or obliquely; hint
Not yet in horrid Shade or dismal Den, Not **nocent** yet.	*nocens* harmful	*now an archaic word*
...part **incentive** reed Provide, **pernicious** with one touch to fire.	*incendere* to kindle, set on fire	serving to motivate
	pernicios-us destructive, ruinous	destructive; ruinous; fatal
...lest that too heav'nly form, **pretended** To hellish falshood, snare them.	*pretend-ere* to stretch forth	claimed or asserted falsely

There are many other examples of words derived from Latin in Milton's verse, but more often than not in the sense that had developed in English by the mid-seventeenth century. Here is an extract from Book VI of *Paradise Lost* describing how the fallen angels in hell find the ingredients for gunpowder:

> Forthwith from Councel to the work they flew,
> None arguing stood, innumerable hands
> Were ready, in a moment up they turnd
> Wide the Celestial soile, and saw beneath
> Th'originals of Nature in thir crude
> Conception; Sulphurous and Nitrous Foame
> They found, they mingl'd, and with suttle Art,
> Concocted and adusted they reduc'd
> To blackest grain, and into store conveyd:
> Part hidd'n veins diggd up (nor hath this Earth
> Entrails unlike) of Mineral and Stone,
> Whereof to found thir Engins and thir Balls
> Of missive ruin; part incentive reed
> Provide, pernicious with one touch to fire.
> So all ere day-spring, under conscious Night
> Secret they finish'd, and in order set,
> With silent circumspection unespi'd.

Activity 10.10

(i) Use the list below to discuss Milton's use of words of Latin derivation in this extract.

(ii) Describe its structure.

📖 A structural analysis is in the *Commentary & Data Book*.

Word	Derivation	Meaning in the extract
originals	Fr *original* f. L *originalis*	origins, source
crude	L *crudus* raw	natural, raw state
Conception	L *conceptionem*, f. verb *concipere*, to conceive	the generation or production of plants and minerals
Nitrous Foame	L *nitrosus*	= saltpetre (an ingredient of gunpowder), called 'foam of nitre'
Concocted	L. *concoctus*, the literal sense was to boil together	prepared or brought to perfection by heat
adusted	L. *adustus* f. *adurere* to burn, scorch – scorched, seared; burnt up	scorched, burnt up and dried
to found	L *fundus* bottom, foundation	to mould, create (cp. *foundry*)
missive	L *missive* f. *mittere* to send	missile, as in *missile weapon* = weapon capable of being thrown
ruin	OF f. L *ruina*, f. *ruere* to fall	destruction, devastation
incentive	L *incentivus*, inciting (confused with *incensive*, f. L *incendere* to kindle, set on fire)	capable of kindling, setting alight;
incentive reed		match
pernicious	L *perniciosus* destructive	destructive, fatal
conscious	L *conscius* knowing something with others	knowing, or sharing the knowledge of anything, together with another
circumspection	OF f. L *circumspectionem* looking around	careful looking around, caution

10.2.6.3 POETIC RHETORIC

The lexical and structural complexity of the extract we have just read contrasts with other examples of Milton's verse. In the following extract from Book IV of *Paradise Lost* Adam is speaking to Eve.

Activity 10.11

What do you notice about the structure of these lines?

> Sweet is the breath of morn, her rising sweet,
> With charm of earliest Birds; pleasant the Sun
> When first on this delightful Land he spreads
> His orient Beams, on herb, tree, fruit, and flour,
> Glistring with dew; fragrant the fertil earth
> After soft showers; and sweet the coming on
> Of grateful Eevning milde, then silent Night
> With this her solemn Bird and this fair Moon,
> And these the Gemms of Heav'n, her starrie train:
> But neither breath of Morn when she ascends
> With charm of earliest Birds, nor rising Sun
> On this delightful land, nor herb, fruit, floure,
> Glistring with dew, nor fragrance after showers,
> Nor grateful Evening mild, nor silent Night
> With this her solemn Bird, nor walk by Moon,
> Or glittering Starr-light without thee is sweet.

Commentary

The lines divide into two balancing sections, in which Adam first describes the beauty of the garden, and then affirms his dependence on Eve. He does not affirm this directly, but by repeating the description negatively – *but neither . . . nor*. The key opening word *sweet* is echoed in its repetition as the final word. The balance can be more easily observed if the extract is divided into its two sections, side by side. The repetition is not exact, but varied.

SWEET is *the breath of morn,* her rising sweet,	But neither *breath of Morn* when she ascends
With charm of earliest Birds; pleasant the *Sun*	*With charm of earliest Birds,* nor rising *Sun*
When first *on this delightful Land* he spreads	*On this delightful land,*
His orient Beams, on *herb, tree, fruit,* and *flour,*	nor *herb, fruit, floure*
Glistring with dew; fragrant the fertil earth	*Glistring with dew,* nor *fragrance*
After soft *showers;* and sweet the coming on	*after showers*
Of *grateful Eevning milde,* then *silent Night*	Nor *grateful Evening mild,* nor *silent Night*
With this her solemn Bird and this fair *Moon,*	*With this her solemn Bird,* nor walk by *Moon*
And these the Gemms of Heav'n, her *starrie* train:	Or glittering *Starr*-light without thee is SWEET

10.3 'Linguistic creativity' in Gerard Manley Hopkins's poetry

10.3.1 *Words and grammar in 'Harry Ploughman'*

The poetry of Gerard Manley Hopkins is, like much of Milton's, 'difficult', but for quite different reasons. 'Harry Ploughman' is one of these. It is a sonnet of fourteen lines, with short added 'burden-lines' (*burden* in the sense of a *refrain* or *chorus*). Hopkins called it 'a direct picture of a ploughman, without afterthought'.

Activity 10.12

Read the poem and work at its meaning. You must read it aloud, or at least hear the sound and rhythm in your mind. What problems of understanding do you find?

	'Harry Ploughman'
1.	Hard as hurdle arms, with a broth of goldish flue
2.	Breathed round; the rack of ribs; the scooped flank; lank
3.	Rope-over thigh; knee-nave; and barrelled shank –
4.	Head and foot, shoulder and shank –
5.	By a grey eye's heed steered well, one crew, fall to;
6.	Stand at stress. Each limb's barrowy brawn, his thew
7.	That onewhere curded, onewhere sucked or sank –
8.	Soared or sank – ,
9.	Though as a beechbole firm, finds his, as at a rollcall, rank
10.	And features, in flesh, what deed he each must do –
11.	His sinew-service where do.
12.	He leans to it, Harry bends, look. Back, elbow, and liquid waist
13.	In him, all quail to the wallowing o' the plough: 's cheek crimsons; curls
14.	Wag or crossbridle, in a wind lifted, windlaced –
15.	See his wind lilylocks laced;
16.	Churlsgrace too, child of Amansstrength, how it hangs or hurls
17.	Them – broad in bluff hide his frowning feet lashed! raced
18.	With, along them, cragiron under and cold furls –
19.	With-a-fountain's shining-shot furls.

10.3.1.1 WORDS

Hopkins's vocabulary is deliberately drawn from words of Old English derivation, including many dialectal words. They are usually short, of one or two syllables, but he uses some of them in unfamiliar senses, either because the word is dialectal, or because he is drawing on an archaic meaning. The following words are examples; ? means that the derivation has not been traced and is not known:

barrowy	like a mound	OE beorg, *hill, mound*
beechbole	beech trunk	ON bolr *tree trunk*
bluff	broad, rounded	? Dutch blaf – 17th C
brawn	muscle	OF braon
churlsgrace	elegant movement of a labourer	OE ceorl; OF grace
cragiron	ploughshare	?
curded	knotted	ME crud/curd
fall to	set to work	OE
flank	side (of the body)	OF flanc
flue	down, fluff	?
furls	furrows	?
heed	attention, look	OE hedan
hide	leather	OE hyd
hurl	impel, whirl ?	?
hurdle	wooden frame, fence	OE hyrdel
knee-nave	knee-cap (*nave* meaning *wheel hub*)	OE nafu

lank	lean, spare	OE hlanc
quail	give way to, bend with	?
rack	frame	Dutch rec
scooped	hollowed	Dutch schoppe
shank	leg	OE scanca
shining	shining and changing in tint	OE scinan
shot	like shot silk	OE sceotan
thew	sinew, muscle	OE þeow

A number of the words in the poem are compounds, most of them newly minted by the poet – *rope-over, knee-nave, beechbole, rollcall, sinew-service, crossbridle, windlaced, lilylocks, churlsgrace, Amansstrength, cragiron, with-a-fountain's, shining-shot. Onewhere* is coined on the **analogy** of *somewhere, nowhere*. These compounds carry a double stress, which, together with the single-syllable lexical words that each carries primary stress, has an important effect on the sound and rhythm.

📖 A complete vocabulary list in the *Commentary & Data Book*.

10.3.1.2   DEVIANCE IN GRAMMAR

Hopkins wrote in a letter, 'The difficulties are of syntax no doubt', which you will certainly have found true. Much of the grammar of the poem is **deviant** – that is, it diverges or deviates from the expected forms of English, whether standard or dialectal. There are, for example, very few function words in proportion to the lexical words:

- *The* occurs four times as a determiner in NPs or PrepPs, *a* five times and *his* five times, yet there are nearly fifty noun heads of NPs in the poem.
- Almost all the VPs contain single verbs, either past participles like *steered, laced* or past tenses like *curded, sucked, sank* etc. That is, there is only one auxiliary verb, the modal *must*. A clause like,

His head, foot, shoulder and shank fall to *like* one crew

is compressed into

Head and foot, shoulder and shank – ... one crew, fall to

- The description of the physical characteristics of Harry the ploughman is projected in a series of NPs, all images in words, *the rack of ribs, the scooped flank, lank rope-over thigh* and so on.
- Just as the large number of compounds compress two meanings into one word, so the syntax is also compressed. The meaning of a prosaic statement like,

All his limbs work together like a disciplined group

becomes more vividly expressed as,

Head and foot, shoulder and shank ... fall to; stand at stress.

and the military connotations of *fall to* are continued in,

Each limb's barrowy brawn, his thew ... finds his ... rank, as at a rollcall.

- This last example is also one of the rhetorical **parentheses** (see section 6.2.2.2) in the poem, with phrases and whole clauses inserted into other syntactic structures, sometimes in an unusual way:

Each limb's barrowy brawn, his thew	
That onewhere curded, onewhere sucked or sank –	*RelCl*
Soared or sank –	
Though as a beechbole firm, finds his, **as at a rollcall**, rank	*Verbless Cl*

The long RelCl *That onewhere...beechbole firm* divides the subject NPs *Each limb's...his thew* from the main verbs *finds*, and the PrepP *as at a rollcall* splits the determiner *his* from head noun *rank* of the NP *his rank*.

Head and foot, shoulder and shank –	
By a grey eye's heed steered well, one crew, fall to	*NonfCl*

Probably the most unusual example is *wind lilylocks laced*, in which an underlying clause – *his locks are as white as a lily and laced by the wind* – is first compressed to *see his windlaced lilylocks*. Then the head noun *lilylocks* splits the compound *wind-laced*. (Hopkins himself referred to this structure as 'a desperate deed' and did not think it was 'an unquestionable success'!)

As a final example, the last burden is another compressed line,

With-a-fountain's shining-shot furls

which means, *furrows that sparkle and shine like shot silk, like the water in a fountain*, perhaps?

- The poem is the speaking voice of the poet, which is made clear in the clause *'s cheek crimsons*, the reduced spoken form of *his cheek crimsons*.

Rhythm and sound
The choice of particular words is often determined by their sound as much as their meaning, so the sounds and rhythm of 'Harry Ploughman' and its 'elaborate metrical notation' are discussed in chapter 13, 'Rhyme, rhythm and sound II', section 13.4.

II. Prose translations

II.I *The Swiss Family Robinson*

The Swiss Family Robinson is one of a number of 'children's classic stories'. It was written by a Swiss pastor, Johann David Wyss (1743–1818) and first published in German in 1812. The story tells of a family wrecked on a desert island. The first English translation was published in 1814, and others in 1849 and 1878. These nineteenth-century translations have been described as 'ponderous' in style.

Activity II.I

Read the following paragraph from a nineteenth-century English version of the story. What are your first impressions of the style?

On the following day, my wife and the boys importuned me to begin my manufactory of candles: I therefore set myself to recollect all I had read on the subject. I soon perceived that I should be at a loss for a little fat to mix with the wax I had procured from the berries, for making the light burn clearer; but I was compelled to proceed without. I put as many berries into a vessel as it would contain, and set it on a moderate fire; my wife in the meantime employed herself in making some wicks with the threads of sail cloth. When we saw an oily matter, of a pleasing smell and light green colour, rise to the top of the liquid the berries had yielded, we carefully skimmed it off and put it into a separate vessel, taking care to keep it warm. We continued this process till the berries were exhausted, and had produced a considerable quantity of wax; we next dipped the wicks one by one into it, while it remained liquid, and then hung them on the bushes to harden: in a short time we dipped them again, and repeated the operation till the candles were increased to the proper size, and they were then put in a place and kept till sufficiently hardened for use. We, however, were all eager to judge of our success that very evening, by burning one of the candles, with which we were well satisfied.

Readability – standard.

II.I.I *Commentary*

The style is decidedly 'old-fashioned', and reflects the conventions expected of literary writing in the nineteenth century. Some words belong to the category

formal, and are usually used in contexts other than children's books. Some of the words combine or **collocate** with others to form phrases that we no longer use, and phrases and clauses combine to form complex grammatical structures. Therefore we need to look at these different aspects of the style of *The Swiss Family Robinson* in order to try to discover what is old-fashioned about it.

One way to begin is to write our own version in a style we could call 'present-day English narrative'.

Activity 11.2

Rewrite the paragraph in a narrative style suitable for present-day readers. Make changes that are going to eliminate words and phrases that you think are too formal or out of date, but do not paraphrase or rewrite unnecessarily.

Activity 11.3

(i) Having written your new version, list the changes you made:

  (a) to single words,
  (b) to phrases,
  (c) to sentence structure and punctuation.

(ii) Discuss and explain these changes.

You can then compare your version with those produced in the following discussions of words, phrases and sentences in the original.

11.1.1.1 WORDS

Here is the text with the 'old-fashioned' words marked in boxes:

On the following day, my wife and the boys [importuned] me to begin my [manufactory] of candles: I therefore set myself to [recollect] all I had read on the subject. I soon [perceived] that I should be at a loss for a little fat to mix with the wax I had [procured] from the berries, for making the light burn clearer; but I was [compelled] to [proceed] without. I put as many berries into a [vessel] as it would [contain], and set it on a [moderate] fire; my wife in the meantime [employed] herself in making some wicks with the threads of sail cloth. When we saw an oily [matter], of a pleasing smell and light green colour, rise to the top of the liquid the berries had [yielded], we carefully skimmed it off and put it into a separate [vessel], taking care to keep it warm. We [continued] this process till the berries were [exhausted], and had produced a [considerable] [quantity] of wax; we next dipped the wicks one by one into it, while it remained liquid, and then hung them on the bushes to harden: in a short time we dipped them again, and repeated the [operation] till the candles were [increased] to the proper size, and they were then put in a place and kept till [sufficiently] hardened for use. We, however, were all eager to judge of our success that very evening, by burning one of the candles, with which we were [well satisfied].

As we have seen in previous chapters, words that have been in the language longest are derived from Old English (OE) and Old Norse (ON) up to *c.* 1150, and Middle English (ME), which includes many borrowed words from Old French

(OF). The OF words have long since been fully assimilated and they are inflected with English prefixes and suffixes. These familiar, common words that everyone knows and uses belong to the core vocabulary of English. Words used in more formal contexts, written rather than spoken – the non-core vocabulary – tend to be among those that entered the language after the fourteenth century.

Here is a list of the formal boxed words and their derivations. For Early Modern English words, adopted from the late fifteenth century onwards, the date of the writing in which the first occurrence of the word has been recorded is given.

Word	Derivation and date	Word	Derivation and date
importune	F importuner 1530	*matter*	OF matiere 1340
manufactory	L manu facere 1618	*yielded*	OE g(i)eldan
recollect	L recolligere 1513	*continue*	OF continuer 1340
perceive	OF perçoivre c. 1300	*exhausted*	L exhaurire 1533
procured	OF procurer c. 1300	*considerable*	L considerabilis 1449
compelled	OF compeller c. 1380	*quantity*	OF quantité 1387
proceed	OF proceder c. 1430	*operation*	OF operation c. 1386
vessel	OF vaissel(le) c. 1300	*increased*	OF encreiss- c. 1315
contain	OF contenir 1382	*sufficiently*	OF sufficient + -ly 1375
moderate	L moderatus c. 1412	*satisfied*	OF satisfier 1430
employed	OF employer 1483		

Activity 11.4

(i) Compare the list with the words that you changed in your rewritten version.

(ii) Find synonyms for each word and look up the period or date of their adoption into the language. Classify them as core or non-core words.

(iii) Do you find a correlation between non-core vocabulary and later adoption – occasionally, often, always?

📖 A list of suggested synonyms with their derivations is in the *Commentary & Data Book*, together with some comments.

A first rewriting of the text follows. Single words or lexical units like phrasal verbs have been substituted for the marked words:

Activity 11.5

(i) Is the style of this rewritten version noticeably different from the original?

(ii) Are there any remaining parts of the text that you think need to be brought up to date?

First rewritten version
On the following day, my wife and the boys [asked] me to begin my [making] of candles: I therefore set myself to [remember] all I had read on the subject. I soon [saw] that I should be at a loss for a little fat to mix with the wax I had [got] from the berries, for making the light burn clearer; but I was [forced] to [go on] without. I put as many berries into a [pot] as it would [hold],

and set it on a fairly low fire; my wife in the meantime kept herself busy in making some wicks with the threads of sail cloth. When we saw an oily stuff, of a pleasing smell and light green colour, rise to the top of the liquid the berries had given up, we carefully skimmed it off and put it into a separate dish, taking care to keep it warm. We kept up the process till the berries were used up, and had produced a large amount of wax; we next dipped the wicks one by one into it, while it remained liquid, and then hung them on the bushes to harden: in a short time we dipped them again, and repeated the process till the candles were grown to the proper size, and they were then put in a place and kept till hardened enough for use. We, however, were all eager to judge our work that very evening, by burning one of the candles, with which we were very happy.

Readability – easy.

11.1.1.2 PHRASES

Parts of the rewritten text still remain unsatisfactory as modern English, not single words, but phrases which are not **idiomatic** as informal narrative:

Activity 11.6

Do you agree that the following boxed phrases in the first rewritten version are not idiomatic in present-day English? Are there any other phrases that you would mark?

On the following day, my wife and the boys asked me to begin my making of candles: I therefore set myself to remember all I had read on the subject. I soon saw that I should be at a loss for a little fat to mix with the wax I had got from the berries, for making the light burn clearer; but I was forced to go on without. I put as many berries into a pot as it would hold, and set it on a fairly low fire; my wife in the meantime kept herself busy in making some wicks with the threads of sail cloth. When we saw an oily stuff, of a pleasing smell and light green colour, rise to the top of the liquid the berries had given up, we carefully skimmed it off and put it into a separate dish, taking care to keep it warm. We kept up the process till the berries were used up, and had produced a large amount of wax; we next dipped the wicks one by one into it, while it remained liquid, and then hung them on the bushes to harden: in a short time we dipped them again, and repeated the process till the candles were grown to the proper size, and they were then put in a place and kept till hardened enough for use. We, however, were all eager to judge our work that very evening, by burning one of the candles, with which we were very happy.

Discussion

making of candles	If the phrase is transformed into a compound noun *candle-making*, it seems quite acceptable. *My making of candles* is fully grammatical, but the structure using the *-ing* participle *making* as a 'verbal noun' or gerund, with the possessive pronoun *my*, is somewhat dated in use. *The boys asked me to begin making candles* sounds quite idiomatic, however.
set myself to remember	The vocabulary is simple but the phrase *set myself to* ... does not sound idiomatic to me. Perhaps *set myself the task of...*?
should be at a loss for	Another phrase consisting of simple words, but not what we would now say. *I soon saw that I should need* or *that I lacked*?
of a pleasing smell	A small change of preposition, *with* for *of*, sounds better – there is no grammatical reason for this.
were grown	The use of *be* to form the **perfective** was formerly quite usual with some intransitive verbs, e.g. *he is come, they are got in, it is happened unto thee, after you was gone out*, but this usage is now archaic; *the candles had grown...*

in a place	The phrase sounds too indefinite for current use, either *put away* or *put in a safe place* etc.
with which	*with which we were very happy* is fully grammatical, and keeps the old proscriptive rule of not ending a sentence with a preposition, as in *which we were very happy with*. However, the construction is now used only in formal contexts, and the 'rule' was artificially imposed in the first place.

If we apply these changes of phrase, and eliminate any passive verb phrases, the text then reads:

Second rewritten version
On the following day, my wife and the boys asked me to begin my candle-making: I therefore set myself the task of remembering all I had read on the subject. I soon saw that I should need a little fat to mix with the wax I had got from the berries, for making the light burn clearer; but I had to go on without. I put as many berries into a pot as it would hold, and set it on a fairly low fire; my wife in the meantime kept herself busy in making some wicks with the threads of sail cloth. When we saw an oily stuff, with a pleasing smell and light green colour, rise to the top of the liquid the berries had given up, we carefully skimmed it off and put it into a separate dish, taking care to keep it warm. We kept up the process till the berries were used up, and had produced a large amount of wax; we next dipped the wicks one by one into it, while it remained liquid, and then hung them on the bushes to harden: in a short time we dipped them again, and repeated the process till the candles had grown to the proper size, and we then put them away and kept them till they had hardened enough for use. We, however, were all eager to judge our work that very evening, by burning one of the candles, which we were very happy with.

Readability – fairly easy.

You will have noticed how substituting words and phrases alters the style of a text very quickly. The more changes you make, the further away from the original style the text goes, until it is something quite different.

11.1.1.3 SENTENCE STRUCTURE

If you refer to the original text at the beginning of the chapter, you will see that there are six sentences in the paragraph, identified by the capital letters and full stops. The basic units of grammatical meaning, however, are the clauses. There are 38 clauses, making an average of 6.3 clauses per written sentence.

You will notice also that there are several colons and semi-colons, most of which mark off structures that could have been punctuated as sentences. Colons are used to mark a following explanation or list of items. Semi-colons mark off two main clauses which are closely related in meaning. These two punctuation marks are the most rarely used, and the most difficult to learn to use. As written sentences are clearly marked by full stops, punctuation will affect the kinds of sentence that occur in a text, classified according to the kind and number of clauses they contain:

- Simple – one main clause only
- Complex – main clause and one or more subordinate clauses
- Compound – two or more coordinated main clauses, no subordinate clauses
- Compound-complex – two or more coordinated main clauses with one or more subordinate clauses

We can therefore punctuate the text differently, changing the colons and semi-colons to either full stops or commas:

Original version re-punctuated

1. On the following day, my wife and the boys importuned me to begin my manufactory of candles.
2. I therefore set myself to recollect all I had read on the subject.
3. I soon perceived that I should be at a loss for a little fat to mix with the wax I had procured from the berries, for making the light burn clearer, but I was compelled to proceed without.
4. I put as many berries into a vessel as it would contain, and set it on a moderate fire.
5. My wife in the meantime employed herself in making some wicks with the threads of sail cloth.
6. When we saw an oily matter, of a pleasing smell and light green colour, rise to the top of the liquid the berries had yielded, we carefully skimmed it off and put it into a separate vessel, taking care to keep it warm.
7. We continued this process till the berries were exhausted, and had produced a considerable quantity of wax.
8. We next dipped the wicks one by one into it, while it remained liquid, and then hung them on the bushes to harden.
9. In a short time we dipped them again, and repeated the operation till the candles were increased to the proper size, and they were then put in a place and kept till sufficiently hardened for use.
10. We, however, were all eager to judge of our success that very evening, by burning one of the candles, with which we were well satisfied.

Activity II.7

(i) Say whether each sentence in this repunctuated version is **simple** (one main clause only), **complex** (main clause and one or more subordinate clauses), **compound** (two or more main clauses, no subordinate clauses) or **compound-complex** (two or more main clauses with one or more complex clauses).

(ii) Identify the different clauses within each sentence.

Discussion

There are now ten sentences in the repunctuated version, and the average number of clauses per sentence is 3.8. The sentence structures contained in this version are:

Simple	0
Complex	5
Compound	0
Compound-complex	5

A complete diagrammed analysis is in the *Commentary & Data Book*.

The traditional classification of sentence structure needs to be extended by a brief look at the degree of complexity in any complex, compound and compound-complex clause. This is measured by the number of clauses within a sentence, ranging in this text from seven down to two. There are no simple (one-clause) sentences or compound sentences.

Sentence no.	Type	No. of clauses
6	compound-complex	7
3	compound-complex	6
9	compound-complex	6
8	compound-complex	4
4	compound-complex	3
7	complex	3
10	complex	3
1	complex	2
2	complex	2
5	complex	2

Sentence 6 is the only 'left-branching' sentence with its complex adverbial clause fronted as theme. A reader has to hold this clause in mind while waiting for the two main clauses that follow, which produces a certain degree of difficulty for some readers. But all the other sentences start with their main clause, and as the order of the following clauses generally matches the order of the 'events' being described, the difficulty of reading is minimised. Thus the computer's assessment of the text as *standard* in readability, between *fairly easy* on one hand, and *fairly difficult* on the other, seems to be confirmed by our description of the vocabulary and grammatical structure.

A later twentieth-century translation of the book set out to modify the traditional nineteenth-century style we have been studying, in order to 'recapture the mood and clarity of the original tale in German'. The corresponding extract in this later version follows.

Activity 11.8

(i) Compare the vocabulary and structure of this later version with the nineteenth-century version we have discussed.

(ii) Is the later version easier to read, or more difficult?

Twentieth-century translation

I need scarcely say that the following morning I could get no peace, either from my wife or my children, until I agreed to start making some candles, so I tried to remember what I had previously read on the subject. I knew that if only I had a little animal fat to mix with the wax my candles would burn much more easily; but as there was no means of getting any, I was forced to make do without it, and to hope that the result would be at any rate reasonably satisfactory.

We filled one of our largest saucepans with the wax berries, and warmed them over a slow fire. In this way we obtained a considerable quantity of really excellent wax, which I skimmed off the top and then poured into a second pan.

While I was doing this my wife made some wicks by drawing a number of threads from a piece of canvas. These I steeped carefully in the wax until they were coated with it; then I exposed them to the air until they were dry and hard. I repeated this operation two or three times, until the candles were the thickness we required.

We hung them up in a shady place to harden. It is true that they were not particularly elegant, not so round or so shapely as European candles generally are; but when we tried them out that night they gave us a strong, clear light, and we were more than satisfied with them.

Readability – fairly easy.

Activity 11.9

(i) Compare the lexical words in the later translation with those of the original, for example, the proportion of core to non-core vocabulary.

(ii) Is the structure of the later translation less or more complex than that of the original?

📖 A list of the lexical words and a diagrammed analysis of the grammatical structure of this version are in the *Commentary & Data Book*.

11.2 Translations of the Bible

Books of the Bible have been translated into English since the Old English versions of the end of the ninth century through to the present day, and they offer interesting stylistic variations on the same underlying texts. The earliest translations were from the Vulgate, the Latin translation of St Jerome completed about 404. Later translators used newly discovered manuscripts in the original languages, Hebrew for the Old Testament or Greek for the New Testament.

The translation published in 1611 was authorised by King James I, and has since been known as the King James Bible or the Authorized Version, and was used in the Church of England for over 300 years. During the second half of the twentieth century several new translations into 'modern English' have been made, and their publication has aroused controversy between those for whom the language of the King James Bible is unsurpassable, and others who regard its language as archaic and difficult to understand. Similar changes have taken place in the replacement of the Book of Common Prayer of 1662 by the Alternative Service Book of 1980. Whichever view you take, the stylistic differences provide a good source of data for students of language.

11.2.1 *From the Sermon on the Mount*

As an additional source of comparison and contrast, we shall look at a translation of the New Testament made in the middle of the eighteenth century by Edward Harwood, whose views on language were mentioned in section 10.2.5. He regarded the language of the 1611 King James Bible as 'bald and barbarous'. Here are three versions of the opening sentence of the Sermon on the Mount, from St Matthew's Gospel 5: 3:

Activity 11.10

Discuss the differences of style — words, grammar and meaning — between the three translations.

Early Modern English 1611	18th C literary English 1768	Modern English 1961
King James Bible	*A Liberal Translation of the New Testament* by E. Harwood	*New English Bible*
Blessed are the poor in spirit: for theirs is the kingdom of heaven.	Happy are those who are endowed with true humility – for such are properly disposed for the reception of the gospel.	How blest are those who know they are poor; the kingdom of heaven is theirs.

11.2.1.1 VOCABULARY

1611 King James Bible: 13 words	1768 Edward Harwood: 20 words	1961 New English Bible: 15 words
Lexical words	**Lexical words**	**Lexical words**
blessed OE bledsian	*disposed* OF disposser *c.*1380	*blest* OE bledsian
heaven OE heofon	*endowed* en- + Fr douer 1460	*know* OE cnawan
kingdom OE cyningdom	*gospel* OE godspel	*poor* OF poure *c.*1200
poor OF poure *c.*1200	*happy* ON happ + -y 1375	*kingdom* OE cyningdom
	humility OF humilité *c.*1315	*heaven* OE heofon
	properly OF propre + -ly 1380	
	reception OF reception 1380	
	true OE treowe	

Edward Harwood's intention, quoted in chapter 10, was to 'cloathe his ideas in the vest of modern elegance of diction'. Elegance of diction clearly meant using words that had no 'vulgar' connotations, so he avoids the 'barbarity' of core vocabulary like *blest*, *heaven* and *poor*, preferring the literary *disposed*, *endowed*, *humility* and *reception*.

11.2.1.2 STRUCTURE

The King James Bible verse has two parallel simple clauses, and the second clause has regular metrical rhythm, /xx/xx/,

```
    C    P S             C    P S
[Blessed are the poor in spirit:] for [theirs is the kingdom of heaven]
```

The New English Bible is more complex structurally, its first clause containing a relative clause with an embedded reported noun clause. The order of the words in the second clause, *the kingdom of heaven is theirs*, changes the metrical rhythm of the King James Bible,

```
    C         P  S                        S                P C
         m      q = RelCl
                S    P    NCI
                S    P   Ci
[How blest are those [who know [they are poor]]; [the kingdom of heaven is theirs]
```

and Edward Harwood's translation has a structural complexity to match the style of the vocabulary,

```
    C      P  S
         h      q = RelCl
                S    P           Ca
[Happy are those [who are endowed with true humility] –

    S    P  Ci
         m       h          q
for [such are properly disposed (for the reception of the gospel)]
```

II.2.2   St John's Gospel – 'In the beginning...'

Activity II.II

(i) Read the following extracts from the beginning of St John's Gospel in the same three translations.

(ii) Use the statistics of the derivations of the lexical words and the structural diagrams to discuss the differences in vocabulary and structure between the three texts.

Early Modern English 1611	*18th C literary English 1768*	*Modern English 1961*
1. In the beginning was the Word, and the Word was with God, and the Word was God.	1. Before the origin of this world existed the LOGOS – who was then with the Supreme God – and was himself a divine person.	1. When all things began, the Word already was. The Word dwelt with God, and what God was, the Word was.
2. The same was in the beginning with God.	2. He existed with the Supreme Being, before the foundation of the earth was laid:	2. The Word, then, was with God at the beginning,
3. All things were made by him; and without him was not any thing made that was made.	3. For this most eminent personage did the Deity solely employ in the formation of this world, and of everything it contains.	3. And through him all things came to be; no single thing was created without him.
4. In him was life; and the life was the light of men.	4. This exalted spirit assumed. human life – and from his incarnation the most pure and sacred emanations of light were derived to illuminate mankind:	4. All that came to be was alive with his life, and that life was the light of men.
5. And the light shineth in darkness; and the darkness comprehended it not.	5. This light shot its beams into a benighted world – and conquered and dispelled that gloomy darkness, in which it was inveloped.	5. The light shines on in the dark, and the darkness has never mastered it.
6. There was a man sent from God, whose name was John.	6. To usher this divine personage into the world, and to prepare men for his reception, God previously commissioned and sent John the Baptist.	6. There appeared a man named John, sent from God.

Vocabulary

The derivations of the lexical word types used in the three translations are distributed as follows:

1611 King James Bible	18 types: 16 OE, 1 ON, 1 Latin
1768 *Liberal Translation*	50 types: (to 14th C) 15 OE, 12 OF
	(15th C or after) 9 Fr, 11 Latin, 2 English, 1 Greek
1961 New English Bible	24 types: 20 OE/ME, 3 OF, 1 Latin

which are when expressed in percentages:

	Up to 14th C		15th C and after			
	OE/ON	OF	English	French	Latin	Greek
1611 King James Bible	95%	–	–	–	5%	–
1768 *Liberal Translation*	30%	24%	4%	18%	22%	2%
1961 New English Bible	83.5%	12.5%	–	–	4%	–

📖 A complete list of lexical words and derivations is in the *Commentary & Data Book*.

Structure

	ccj	*scj*	*clause*

King James Bible 1611

1.   [*MCl* In the beginning was the Word],
and   [*MCl* the Word was with God],
and   [*MCl* the Word was God].   *3-clause compound sentence*
2.   [*MCl* The same was in the beginning with God].   *simple sentence*
3.   [*MCl* All things were made by him]; and
   [*MCl* without him was not any thing made [*RelCl* that was made]].
   3-clause compound-complex sentence
4.   [*MCl* In him was life];
and   [*MCl* the life was the light of men].   *2-clause compound sentence*
5. And   [*MCl* the light shineth in darkness];
and   [*MCl* the darkness comprehended it not]. *2-clause compound sentence*
6.   [*MCl* There was a man sent from God],
   [*RelCl* whose name was John]   *2-clause complex sentence*

Liberal Translation 1768

1.   [*MCl* Before the origin of this world existed the LOGOS –
   [*RelCl* who was then with the Supreme God] –
and   [*RelCl* ∅ was himself a divine person].   *3-clause complex sentence*
2.   [*MCl* He existed with the Supreme Being,
   [*AdvCl* before   the foundation of the earth was laid]]:   *2-clause complex sentence*
3. For   [*MCl* this most eminent personage did the Deity solely imploy
   in the formation of this world, and of everything [*RelCl* it contains]].
   complex sentence
4.   [*MCl* This exalted spirit assumed human life] –
and   [*MCl* from his incarnation the most pure and sacred emanations of
   light were derived
   [*NonfCl* to illuminate mankind]]:
   3-clause compound-complex sentence
5.   [*MCl* This light shot its beams into a benighted world] –
and   [*MCl* ∅ ⟨conquered and dispelled⟩ that gloomy darkness],
   [*RelCl* in which it was inveloped].
   3-clause compound-complex sentence
6.   [[*NonfCl 1* To usher this divine personage into the world],
and   [*NonfCl 2* to prepare men for his reception],
   God previously ⟨commissioned and sent⟩ John the Baptist]
   3-clause complex sentence

New English Bible 1961

1.   [[*AdvCl* When   all things began],
   MCl the Word already was].   *2-clause complex sentence*
   [*MCl* The Word dwelt with God],
and   [[*NCI* what God was], *MCl* the Word was].
   3-clause compound-complex sentence
2.   [*MCl* The Word, then, was with God at the beginning],
3. and   [*MCl* through him all things came to be];
   [*MCl* no single thing was created without him].
   3-clause compound sentence

4.	[*MCl* All [*RelCl* that came to be] was alive with his life],
and	[*MCl* that life was the light of men].
	3-clause compound-complex sentence
5.	[*MCl* The light shines on in the dark],
and	[*MCl* the darkness has never mastered it].
	2-clause compound sentence
6.	[*MCl* There appeared a man [*q* named John],
	[*NonfCl* sent from God]] *3-clause complex sentence*

11.2.2.1 COMMENTARY – VOCABULARY

Edward Harwood's translation is markedly different from the others. He draws on a learned non-core vocabulary and phraseology, avoiding the core lexis which is so distinctively used in the seventeenth-century translation. He uses more words in order to expound the theology of the Incarnation by **glossing** the original words – that is, commenting and explaining – and loses the direct simplicity of the King James Bible, which is also partly lost in the 1961 version.

11.2.2.2 COMMENTARY – STRUCTURE

The King James Bible translation is a series of plain, simple main clauses, with just two short relative clauses. Structure and words are matched together in clarity and simplicity. The 1961 translation loses something of this simple structure, the first verse for example becoming two sentences, presumably to try to make explicit the theological meaning of statements like *In the beginning was the Word and the Word was with God*.

Edward Harwood matches his learned vocabulary with a much more complex structure, for example, the following sentence has complexity at clause level, with inversion of subject and object, OPS, and an adverbial complement containing three PrepPs and relative clause:

cj   O   P = S   A   = P
For (this most eminent personage) did the Deity solely imploy

Ca
in the formation ⟨(of this world), and (of everything [it contains])⟩.
PrepP   PrepP   PrepP   RelCl

11.2.3 *Peter's denial*

Activity 11.12

Here is the well-known story from St Matthew's Gospel of how Peter, after the trial and condemnation of Jesus, denied knowing him, but was given away by his Galilean dialectal accent.
   Analyse and discuss the style of these extracts.

Early Modern English 1611	*18th C literary English 1768*	*Modern English 1961*
King James Bible	A Liberal Translation of the New Testament *by Edward Harwood*	*New English Bible*

'for thy speech bewrayeth thee'	'your dialect is a plain demonstration, that you are a Galilean'	'your accent gives you away!'
69. Now Peter sate without in the palace: and a damosell came vnto him, saying, Thou also wast with Iesus of Galilee.	69. Peter, as hath been mentioned above, was now in the hall – where as he was sitting, one of the servant maids came to him and said – I believe you was one of the companions of this Jesus of Nazareth.	69. Meanwhile Peter was sitting outside in the courtyard when a serving-maid accosted him and said,'You were there too with Jesus the Galilean.'
70. But hee denied before them all, saying, I know not what thou saiest.	70. You mistake the person, he replied – I never had the least acquaintance with him – I do not know what you mean.	70. Peter denied it in face of them all. 'I do not know what you mean', he said.
71. And when he was gone out into the porch, another maide saw him, and saide vnto them that were there, This fellow was also with Iesus of Nazareth.	71. He was no sooner gone into the passage, but another maid servant saw him, and said to the people that stood around her – That person there was one of Jesus' particular friends.	71. He then went out to the gateway, where another girl, seeing him, said to the people there, 'This fellow was with Jesus of Nazareth.'
72. And againe hee denied with an oath, I doe not know the man.	72. But he answered with a solemn oath, That he did not so much as know him.	72. Once again he denied it, saying with an oath, 'I do not know the man.'
73 And after a while came vnto him they that stood by, and saide to Peter, Surely thou also art one of them, for thy speech bewrayeth thee.	73. A little after, some of those who stood there said to Peter – you certainly are one of his disciples – for your dialect is a plain demonstration, that you are a Galilean.	73. Shortly afterwards the bystanders came up and said to Peter, 'Surely you are another of them; your accent gives you away!'
74. Then beganne hee to curse and to sweare, saying, I know not the man. And immediatly the cocke crew.	74. Upon this he began to utter the most dreadful oaths and imprecations, making the most solemn appeals to God, that he never had any connection with him – when he heard the cock crow.	74. At this he broke into curses and declared with an oath: 'I do not know the man.'
75. And Peter remembred the words of Iesus, which said vnto him, Before the cocke crow, thou shalt denie mee thrice. And hee went out, and wept bitterly.	75. He then instantly recollected what Jesus had told him – that before the cock crew, he would three several times utter the strongest asseverations that he had never known him – this rushing into his mind struck him with a painful sense of his weakness and wickedness, and he went out and burst into a flood of bitter tears.	75. At that moment a cock crew; and Peter remembered how Jesus had said, 'Before the cock crows you will disown me three times.' He went outside, and wept bitterly.

📖 Complete lists of vocabulary and derivations, and a structural analysis, are in the *Commentary & Data Book*. (A more comprehensive set of translations of this text, to illustrate historical changes in the language, is in Dennis Freeborn's *From Old English to Standard English*, with versions in Old English, Middle English, sixteenth-century Early Modern English, contemporary Scots and Bislama, a pidgin version.)

12. Rhyme, rhythm and sound I – patterns of stress and rhythm

12.1 Patterns of stress and rhythm in everyday speech

12.1.1 Stress patterns in words

The pronunciation of ordinary speech in English is marked by patterns of **stressed** and **unstressed** syllables. One syllable in words of two or three syllables will be relatively stressed and the others unstressed, e.g.:

'lit-tle	fa-'tigue	'beau-ti-ful	u-'pon	a-'bove	'still-ness
'mo-dern	sug-'gest	des-'crip-tion	con-'cern	'pos-si-ble	lin-'guis-tic

Activity 12.1

Mark the stressed syllable in these words.

innocence	glitter	lily	sympathy	aside	function
ribbon	away	begin	forgotten	multiply	language
connection	blackbird	degraded	narrative	however	distort

Sometimes, the placing of the stressed syllable affects the grammatical meaning of a word. There is a set of two-syllable words whose first syllables are stressed when they are used as nouns, and second syllables when used as verbs, for example:

a 'contest/to con'test   a 'permit/to per'mit   a 'protest/to pro'test

In words of four or more syllables, one syllable will carry **primary stress** and one of the others will have **secondary stress** (marked with ⟨ˌ⟩):

be-'ne-vol-ˌence	ˌcor-di-'al-i-ty	ˌin-de-'fi-na-ble	per-'pe-tu-al-ˌly
ex-'em-pli-ˌfy	ˌor-ga-ni-'sa-tion	dis-'tin-gui-ˌshing	'i-ma-ge-ˌry

139

Activity 12.2

Mark primary and secondary stress in these words.

indignantly	indignation	reasonably	circumstances
triangular	inconsistency	accompany	intoxication

📖 Activities 12.1 and 12.2 are discussed in the *Commentary & Data Book*.

12.1.2   *Stress patterns in sequences of words*

A spoken series of words will therefore be marked by rhythmic patterns produced by the stressed and unstressed syllables within the words.

But there is another pattern of rhythm as well. We mark important words using **tonic stress** within the 'units of information' called **tone-units** which make up the sequences of ordinary speech, and this produces another rhythmic pattern which combines with that of the individual words. For example, if we assume that the question *Where were you last night?* was asking for information about *last night*, the word *night* would carry the tonic stress,

> |where were you last '**night**|

The question consists of one-syllable words, so there is no pattern of stressed and unstressed syllables <u>within</u> the words. We tend to reserve stress for lexical words (nouns, verbs, adjectives and adverbs). If, however, you wanted to focus on a different aspect of the question, you could put **contrastive stress** on function words like *where* or *you* as well as on verbs like *were* or adjectives like *last*:

> |'**I** was at home – |where were '**you** last night|
> |I've forgotten the '**place** – |'**where** were you last night|
> |I thought you'd be at the '**club**| – where '**were** you last night|
> |I know where you were on·'**Monday** night – |but where were you '**last** night|

If tonic stress falls on a word of two or more syllables, then it is the syllable with primary stress that carries the tonic stress in the tone-unit.

12.1.2.1   FALLING AND RISING RHYTHM

Stress within words and tonic or constrastive stress within the tone-unit therefore combine to produce distinctive rhythms in speech. If stressed syllables (written $\langle / \rangle$) are separated by single unstressed syllables (marked $\langle x \rangle$), then an 'alternating' pattern is produced. For example, in this part of a sentence from Dickens's *Martin Chuzzlewit*,

> **Tom** could **not** re-**sist** the **cap**-ti-**va**-ting **sense** of **ra**-pid **mo**-tion

the sequence of stressed and unstressed syllables can be marked,

> /   x   /   x/   x   /   x / x   /   x / x   /   x
> **Tom** could **not** resist the **cap** ti **va** ting **sense** of **ra** pid **mo** tion

and because the movement is from stressed to unstressed syllables, a **falling rhythm** is produced. If, however, the rhythm moves from unstressed to stressed,

```
The  four grey hor ses skimmed a long
x  /  x  /  x  /     x /
```

a **rising rhythm** is produced.

But a simple **duple** (two-syllable) pattern does not occur consistently in ordinary speech, and two, three or more unstressed syllables regularly separate stressed syllables. If you read aloud this sentence from *Martin Chuzzlewit*,

Mr Pecksniff sat upon the hassock pulling up his shirt-collar, while Tom, touched to the quick, delivered his apostrophe.

you would perhaps produce this pattern of stressed and unstressed syllables:

```
/  x /   x   /  x x  x  /   x   /  x  x x  /   x  x
M  r Peck sniff sat u pon the has sock pul ling up his shirt col llar,

x    /   /    x x  /   x / x   x  x /  x  x
while Tom, touched to the quick, de li vered his a pos tro phe
```

with from one to three unstressed syllables between the stressed syllables, or none.

12.1.3 *Equal-timed stress – isochrony*

There is a tendency in all speech to produce the series of stressed syllables at more or less regular intervals, and to 'squeeze' the unstressed syllables into the same length of time. This has the linguistic name of **isochrony** – *iso-* (equal) and *-chrony* (time) are derived from Greek – and the stressed syllables are **isochronous**. Try reading any prose sentence aloud while beating your hand regularly to coincide with the stresses.

The point to which this is leading is that this isochronous pattern of spoken English is the basis of verse which has a definite and deliberately produced regularity of rhythm. And if the number of unstressed syllables between each stress is the same, for example, one syllable in a rising rhythm (brackets ( ) indicate 'silent' syllables which complete a line with an odd number of spoken stresses)

```
x  /  x  /  x  /  x  /  x  /  (x /)
The Cur few tolls the knell of par ting day ⇒  ⇒

x  /  x  /  x  /  x  /  x  /  (x /)
The low ing herd wind slow ly o'er the lea ⇒  ⇒
```

or one in a falling rhythm,

```
On ward led the road a gain ⇒
/  x   /  x  /  x /  (x)

Through the sad un co loured plain ⇒
/    x  /  x  / x   /   (x)
```

or two in a rising rhythm,

```
x /     x  x  / x  x  / x  x  / (x)
I sprang to the stir rup and Jo ris and he ⇒

x / x    x   / x   x / x    x /    (x) (x)
I gal loped Dirck gal loped we gal loped all three ⇒ ⇒
```

or two in a falling rhythm,

```
/    x   x  / (x) x  / (x) x  / . x  x  / x  x/    (x) (x)
Would that the struc ture brave the ma ni fold mu sic I build ⇒ ⇒

/  x   x  / x   x/  (x) (x) / x   x  / x  x  /    (x) (x)
Bid ding my or gan o bey ⇒ ⇒ cal ling its keys to their work ⇒ ⇒
```

then we have regularity called **metre**, and the basis of a line of **metrical verse** is a set number of syllables.

12.1.4 Reading a poem

Lines in the writing and printing of prose are arbitrary and not significant. The line in verse is a significant unit of the syntax, and affects the way we read and hear the poem, otherwise all poems would be printed like prose.

Activity 12.3

(i) Read the following text aloud as if it were ordinary prose, and note where you place normal stresses and pauses.

(ii) Now work out the verse form and write the text, a sonnet, in 14 lines of verse — the rhyme pattern is *abba abba cdd ece*.

'Remember' by Christina Rossetti

Remember me when I am gone away,
gone far away into the silent land;
when you can no more hold me by the hand,
nor I half turn to go yet turning stay.
Remember me when no more day by day you tell me of our future that you planned:
only remember me;
you understand it will be late to counsel then or pray.
Yet if you should forget me for a while and afterwards remember,
do not grieve:
for if the darkness and corruption leave a vestige of the thoughts that once I had,
better by far you should forget and smile than that you should remember and be sad.

12.1.4.1 COMMENTARY

You probably found that the first four lines were easy to put into verse, because the grammatical units of the text matched the metrical regularity, x/x/x/x/x/, of these four lines:

> Remember me when I am gone away,
> Gone far away into the silent land;
> When you can no more hold me by the hand,
> Nor I half turn to go yet turning stay.

Because of this, the remaining lines can be fitted into the same metre, so that when you read the text as a poem, you will match the rhythm, its stresses and pauses, to this pattern. You will not read the next sentence without a break,

Remember me when no more day by day you tell me of our future that you planned:

but as two lines,

```
x  /   x  /  x   /  x   /   x  /  (x  x)
Re mem ber me when no more day by day ⇒ ⇒

x  /  x  /  x  /  x  /  x  /    (x  x)
You tell me of our fu ture that you planned ⇒ ⇒
```

and in the next you will not make the pause after *me* so long that the rhythm of the line is broken, nor run on *you understand it* as if there were no line break:

```
/  x  x  /   x  /  x  /  x  /   (x  x)
On ly re mem ber me; you un der stand ⇒ ⇒

x  /  x  /  x  /   x  /   x  /  (x  x)
It will be late to coun sel then or pray. ⇒ ⇒
```

The poem is a sonnet of 14 lines, and has a rhythmic 'shape' that you must discover, which is as much a part of its meaning as the words themselves:

> Remember me when I am gone away ,
>   Gone far away into the silent land;
>   When you can no more hold me by the hand,
> Nor I half turn to go yet turning stay.
> Remember me when no more day by day
>   You tell me of our future that you planned:
>   Only remember me; you understand
> It will be late to counsel then or pray.
> Yet if you should forget me for a while
>   And afterwards remember, do not grieve:
>   For if the darkness and corruption leave
>   A vestige of the thoughts that once I had,
> Better by far you should forget and smile
> Than that you should remember and be sad.

12.2 Patterns of stress and rhythm in verse

12.2.1 *Nursery rhymes*

The fascination of traditional nursery rhymes for young children lies in the strongly marked rhythms and rhymes. The first one,

> Tinker, tailor,
> Soldier, sailor,
> Rich man, poor man,
> Beggarman,
> Thief.

has a regular **falling duple** rhythm, /x (in traditional terms a **trochaic** metre), into which *beggarman* easily fits its three syllables. There is rhyme, *tailor, sailor,* the repetition of *-man*, alliteration in *tinker, tailor* and *soldier, sailor*, and the final 'thump' on the final word *thief*. A *falling* rhythm moves from stressed to unstressed syllables; *duple* refers to a unit of two syllables.

The second,

> When clouds appear
> Like rocks and towers
> The earth's refreshed
> By frequent showers.

has a **rising duple** rhythm, x/ (**iambic**), rhythmically two eight-stress rhyming lines – a **couplet**:

> When clouds appear like rocks and towers
> The earth's refreshed by frequent showers.

A *rising* rhythm moves from unstressed to stressed syllables.

The next rhyme,

```
(x)x   /    x  x  /   x  x /    x   x  /
The world is so full of a num ber of things, ⇒

(x)x   /    x   x    /  x  x /   x   x  /
I'm sure we should all be as hap py as kings.
```

has a **rising triple** rhythm, xx/ (**anapaestic**) – each line begins with two off-beats, or unstressed syllables (one of them 'silent'), whereas 'Ride a cock-horse', though very similar in its rhythm, has a **falling triple** rhythm (three lines out of the four determine this):

```
/    x  x    /   (x)x  /   x   x  /     (x)
Ride a cock- horse   to Ban bu ry Cross, ⇒

x  /  x x  /  x  x /   x  x   /     (x) (x)
To see a fine la dy u pon a white horse; ⇒ ⇒

/    x   x  /  x   x   /   x  x  /    (x) (x)
Rings on her fin gers and bells on her toes, ⇒ ⇒

/   x   x   /   x  x   / x  x  /    (x) (x)
She shall have mu sic wher e ver she goes. ⇒ ⇒
```

The metre of the fifth rhyme,

> Three grey geese in a green field grazing,
> Grey were the geese and green was the grazing.

is basically falling duple (trochaic /x) in a four-stress line, but readily accommodates double off-beats (xx) for *in a, were the* and *was the*. Its alliteration on [g] and [gr] and assonance on [i:] – *three, geese, green, field* – and [ɛɪ] – *grey, grazing* are obvious features of the sound pattern.

The final rhyme

> What a wonderful bird the frog are –
> When he stand he sit almost;
> When he hop he fly almost.
> He ain't got no sense hardly;
> He ain't got no tail hardly either.
> When he sit, he sit on what he ain't got almost.

makes its effect by being an 'anti-rhyme' – by what it does <u>not</u> do. It does not rhyme and its metre is irregular. Its semantics are nonsensical (birds are not frogs, standing is not sitting, and so on), and its grammar is nonstandard. It is funny because our expectations are thwarted in every aspect of what a nursery rhyme is expected to be.

12.2.2 *Alliterative verse, stress-timed*

Metrical verse is not, however, the basis of the oldest English verse, which belongs to the Anglo-Saxon period of history, a thousand years ago. Here is a short example of Old English verse from an epic poem called *The Battle of Maldon*, that tells how the English were defeated by Danish raiders in a skirmish in 991.

Old English	Word-for-word translation
Byrhtwold maþelode, bord hafenode	*Byrhtwold spoke, shield held (up)*
se wæs eald geneat, æsc acwehte	*he was old companion, ash(-spear) shook*
he ful baldlice beornas lærde:	*he full boldly warriors exhorted:*
'Hige sceal þe mare, heorte þe cenre	*'Heart shall the more, heart the keener*
mod sceal þe mare þe ure mægen lytlaþ	*courage shall the more as our strength littles*
Her liþ ure ealdor eall forheawan	*here lies our lord all hewn (down)*
god on greote; a mæg gnornian	*good (man) in dirt; ever may regret*
se þe nu fram þis wigplegan wendan þenceþ'	*he that now from this warplay (to) go thinks'*

The word-for-word translation gives you a very poor impression of the original, which has to be heard rather than read silently. Each line of the Old English has four stresses, and because the stress fell on the first syllable in most OE words (unless it was a prefix), a falling rhythm is typically heard, /x. But you can see that the number of syllables varies from one line to another, so the rhythm is produced by the isochronous stressed syllables, not by a regular alternation of stressed and unstressed syllables. This kind of verse writing is **stress-timed**:

```
 /    x   /   x  x  x /   /  x  x  x
'Byrht wold 'ma þe lod e 'bord  'ha fe no de         11 syllables

 x  x   /   x  /   /   x  /   x
se wæs 'eald ge 'neat æsc ac 'weh te                  9 syllables
'he ful 'bald-li-ce 'beorn-as 'lær-de:                       9
'Hi-ge sceal þe 'ma-re 'heort-e þe 'cen-re                  11
```

'mod sceal þe 'ma-re þe ur-e 'mæ-gen 'lyt-laþ	12
Her liþ ur-e 'eald-or 'eall for-heaw-an	10
'god on 'greo-te a mæg 'gnorn-ian	8
se þe nu fram þis 'wig-ple-gan 'wen-dan þen-ceþ	12

Each line falls into two halves that are linked by **alliteration**. At least one stressed word in each half-line has the same initial consonant, or begins with a vowel (all vowels alliterated with each other). There are often two alliterating words in the first half-line.

Byrhtwold	bord	mod	mare	mægen
eald	æsc	ealdor	eall	
baldlice	beornas	god	greote	gnornian
hige	heorte	wigplegan	wendan	

There are very few function words, so that the meaning is packed into the mainly lexical vocabulary. The words *the* and *a/an* of later English had not yet developed their full function, and many nouns occur without them. At the same time, there is a strong falling rhythm from stressed to unstressed syllables.

But the important fact that explains why OE verse is 'stress-timed' and not metrical is that any number of unstressed syllables, or none, may occur between the stressed syllables:

```
        1            3          0      3
  /     x    /   x   x   x   /      /  x   x   x
 'Byrht wold 'ma þe lod e   bord   'hafe no de

    2          1        0      1       1
  x  x   /    x   /     /   x   /    x
  se wæs 'eald ge 'neat  æsc ac 'weh te
```

This kind of verse matches the rhythms of English speech in the way that it allows a variable number of unstressed syllables, and **foregrounds** alliteration for its own sake as part of the 'music' of the verse.

Activity 12.4

The following extract is from the famous OE poem *Beowulf*. The stressed syllables in each line are marked in bold type.

(i) Identify the words which alliterate in each line.

(ii) How many unstressed syllables occur between the stressed syllables of each line?

(The first consonant of many words beginning with ⟨sc-⟩ was pronounced [ʃ], like MnE ⟨sh-⟩ – *scip* = *ship*, *scinu* = *shin*, *scort* = *short*.)

📖 This Activity is discussed in the *Commentary & Data Book*.

reste hine þa **rum**heort **re**ced **hliu**ade	*rested him(self) then (the) great-hearted (man) (the) hall towered (up)*
geap ond **gold**fah **gæst** inne **swæf**	*gabled and gold-adorned (the) guest within (it) slept*
oþþæt **hrefn bla**ca **heofon**es **wyn**ne	*until raven black heaven's joy*

bliþheort **bo**dode þa com **beorht sca**can	*blithe-heart announced then came brightness moving*
scima æfter **scead**we **sca**þan onetton	*light after shadows (the) warriors hastened*
wæron æþelingas **eft** to **leo**dum,	*were (the) heroes back to (their) people*
fuse to **far**enne wolde **feor þa**non	*eager to journey wished far thence*
cuma **coll**enferhþ **ceol**es **neo**san	*(the) stranger bold (his) ship seek*

The tradition of writing alliterative verse survived the Norman conquest in the eleventh century in some parts of the country, into the fifteenthth century. Some of the best-known medieval poems were written in this tradition, for example William Langland's late fourteenth-century '*Piers Plowman*',

Ac on a **May morn**yng on **Mal**uerne **hull**es	*But on a May morning on Malvern hills*
Me bi**ful f**or to **slep**e for **wery**nesse of-**walk**ed	*(It) me befell for to sleep for weariness of-walked**
And in a **launde** as y **lay, len**ed y and **slep**te	*And in a field as I lay reclined I and slept*
And **mer**ueylousliche me **met**te as y **may tel**le	*And marvellously (it to) me dreamed as I may tell*

* *of-walked = tired out with walking*

12.2.3 Metrical verse

If you compare Langland's verse with that of his contemporary Geoffrey Chaucer, you find a great difference in its rhythmic pattern as well as in its subject matter and dialectal features. Chaucer's verse is **metrical**, that is, the rhythm of its lines is counted in syllables. Most of the *Canterbury Tales* are written in ten-syllable lines in **rising duple** rhythm, and conform to a pattern of alternating unstressed and stressed syllables – x/x/x/x/x/ – with the lines rhyming in pairs, or **couplets**:

```
x  /   x   /  x  / x / x /
A good man was ther of re li gi oun

x  /  x /  x /  x  / x /
And was a pour e per son* of a toun
```

* *parson*

with an occasional extra unstressed syllable,

```
x  /  x  /  x /  x  /  x  /  x
With hym ther was a plow man was his bro ther

x  /   x /  x  /   x  /   x  /  x
That hadde y lad* of donge ful many a foo ther
```

* loaded

Marking the rhythmic pattern of verse is called **scansion**. We **scan** the lines to find out how they sound. In scanning Chaucer's verse you will need to mark some final ⟨e⟩ letters as syllables; *sette* has two syllables in

```
x  /  x /   x  / x / x /
He set te noght his be ne fice to hyre
```

and suffixes such as ⟨-ed⟩ and ⟨-es⟩ are usually separate syllables, like *maked* and *spyced* in

```
x  /   x  /   x /   x  /   x  /
Ne mak ed hym a spyc ed con sci ence
```

and *defautes*,

> Ye **god** a **mande** de **faut** es **sir** quod **she**
> (*Yes, God amend faults sir, said she*)

Notice that *dwelte* in the following line is one syllable, because a final ⟨-e⟩ is always elided before a vowel, whereas *kepte* is two syllables:

```
x   /    x  /   x  /   x /   x  /
But dwelte at hoom and kept e wel his foolde
```

Activity 12.5

Mark the stressed and unstressed syllables in these ten-syllable metrical lines from the *Prologue* to the *Canterbury Tales*.

📖 This Activity is discussed in the *Commentary & Data Book*.

> He wolde thresshe and therto dyke and delue
> For Cristes sake for euery poure wight*
> Withouten hyre if it laye in his myght.
> His tythes payde he ful faire and wel
> Bothe of his propre swynk* and his catel*
>
> * *wight = person; swynk = labour; catel = goods*

The writing of alliterative verse in the older tradition did not continue, and the many varied patterns of metrical verse, with and without rhyme, have become the basis of most English poetry since the early sixteenth century. Metrical verse was originally in imitation of a French tradition, and is to be found as early as the twelfth century in a poem called 'The Owl and the Nightingale', written in eight-syllable rhyming couplets:

þe niȝtingale bigon þe speche	*the nightingale began the speech*
in one hurne of one breche	*in a corner of a clearing*
an sat up one vaire boȝe	*and sat upon a fair bough*
þar were abute blosme inȝe	*where were about (it) blossoms enough*

```
x  /   x  /   x  /   x  /
þe niȝt in gale bi gon þe speche

(x)/ x   /    x  /  x /
   in one hurne of on e breche

x  /   x  /   x /   x  /
an sat up on e vair e boȝe

x  /   x /   x /     x  /
þar were a but e blosme in oȝe
```

But because stress-timed, isochronous rhythm and alliteration are fundamental to ordinary speech, both are to be found within the more regular patterns of metrical verse. One more example from Middle English can illustrate this.

12.2.4 *Alliterative metrical verse*

The York pageant plays, which were first performed in the late fourteenth century, are recorded in a mid-fifteenth-century manuscript. They contain a great variety of metrical verse forms, but at the same time are full of alliterative lines. Here is a stanza from the *Pentecost Play*, spoken by the apostle Peter after the descent of the Holy Spirit:

Activity 12.6

Discuss the features in the stanza which are typical of (a) metrical verse and (b) alliterative verse.

All mys to mende nowe haue we myght	*All sin to mend now have we power*
þis is the mirthe oure maistir of mente	*This is the mirth our master spoke of*
I myght not loke, so was it light	*I could not look, so bright it was*
A loued be þat lorde þat itt vs lente	*Ah loved be the Lord that granted it us*
Nowe hase he holden þat he vs highte	*Now has he fulfilled what he promised us*
His holy goste here haue we hente	*His holy spirit here have we received*
Like to þe sonne itt semed in sight	*Like to the sun it seemed in sight*
And sodenly þanne was itt sente	*And suddenly then was it sent.*

12.2.4.1 COMMENTARY ON THE YORK *PENTECOST PLAY* VERSE

Metre

The stanza has eight lines, each with an underlying metre of eight syllables in rising duple rhythm – x/x/x/x/. Some lines have nine syllables if you count them separately, but the regular rhythm is maintained by speaking two unstressed syllables as one, between stressed syllables:

```
x  /   x  /    x     /    x  /    (x)
All mys to mende nowe haue we myght  ⇒

/   x     /     x   /    x     /
þis is↔the mirthe oure mais tir↔of mente
```

Rhyme

The stanza has only two rhymes, on *-ight* and *-ente*, but in an eight-line pattern *abababab*.

Alliteration

At the same time, each line is strongly alliterated on the stressed words,

```
All mys to mende nowe haue we myght
þis is the mirthe oure maistir of mente
I myght noȝt loke, so was it light
A loued be þat lorde þat itt vs lente
Nowe hase he holden þat he vs highte
His holy goste here haue we hente
Like to þe sonne itt semed in sight
And sodenly þanne was itt sente
```

This highlighting of the alliterating words shows how ingenious and complex the stanza pattern is. Each pair of lines has the same alliterating sound – [m], [l], [h] and then [s], in addition to the regular syllabic metre and rhyme. And this is only one of several different stanza patterns to be found in the plays.

Activity 12.7

Identify the metre, rhyme and alliteration in the following stanza from the York play of *The Flood*, spoken by Noah when he sees the dove returning to the ark with an olive branch.

📖 This Activity is discussed in the *Commentary & Data Book*.

Now barnes we may be blithe and gladde	*Now children we may be blithe and glad*
And lowe oure lord of hevenes kyng;	*And praise our lord king of the heavens*
My birde has done as I hym badde	*My bird has done as I him bade*
An olyve braunche I se hym brynge.	*An olive branch I see him bring*
Blyste beþou fewle þat nevere was fayd,	*Blest be thou bird that never was untrustworthy,*
That in thy force makis no faylyng;	*That in thy strength has not failed,*
Mare joie in herte never are I hadde	*More joy in heart never before I had*
We mone be saved, now may we synge.	*We must be saved, now may we sing.*
Come hedir my sonnes in hye	*Come hither my sons in haste*
Oure woo away is wente	*Our woe away is gone*
I se here certaynely	*I see here certainly*
Þe hillis of Hermonye.	*The hills of Armenia.*
Lovyd be þat lord forthy	*Loved be that lord therefore*
That us oure lyffes hase lente.	*That us our lives has granted.*

12.2.5   Rhythm and metre

In order to distinguish between the stress-timed rhythm of ordinary speech and the more regular metre of verse, it is helpful to call stressed syllables in verse **beats** (B) and unstressed syllables **off-beats** (o). If we hear the sentence *The four grey horses skimmed along* as a line of verse, there is only one off-beat between each beat of the rhythm. This produces a duple pattern of two syllables, off-beat and beat (o B):

```
o   B   o   B   o   B       o B
The four grey hor ses skimmed a long
```

If there are two unstressed syllables between beats, then we talk of a **double off-beat** (o^2); three make up a **triple off-beat** (o^3). As these take up approximately the same time as a single off-beat, because the beats are isochronous, we can then say that all English metrical verse is written on a pattern of alternating beats and off-beats.

📖 This description of rhythm and metre in verse is based on Derek Attridge's *The Rhythms of English Poetry* (1983).

A syllable which would normally be stressed in ordinary speech may be 'demoted' in a verse line to an off-beat, e.g. *trees* in this line,

```
o       B    o   B   o B   o   B
And the dark trees lean un moving arms
```

or a normally unstressed syllable 'promoted' to a beat, as in,

```
o   B    o [B] o B   o B
The world is [as] it used to be
```

The metre of verse is an **underlying** regularity, and the rhythm of many lines will vary from the pattern.

12.2.5.1 THE METRICAL FOOT

This method of analysis of rhythm, identifying beats and off-beats, contrasts with a more traditional way of analysing the metre of verse, in which the unit of rhythm is called a **foot**, an arrangement of stressed and unstressed syllables, named according to the number of unstressed syllables, and whether the stressed or unstressed syllable(s) comes first. It is derived from Latin and Greek verse, which was based upon length of syllable, not stress (there is an example in section 16.1), and therefore has never been a really satisfactory way of analysis. However, its terminology is applied to the stress patterns of English verse and has been widely used since the sixteenth century.

Foot	*Pattern of unstressed* (x) *and stressed* (/) *syllables*
iamb (iambic)	x /
trochee (trochaic)	/ x
anapaest (anapaestic)	x x /
dactyl (dactylic)	/ x x
paeon (paeonic)	/ x x x
spondee (spondaic)	/ /

There are then a number of **feet** to a line of verse. Five feet make up a **pentameter** line, and the **iambic pentameter** – x/x/x/x/x/ – is a common line used by Chaucer, Shakespeare, Milton, Dryden, Pope, Wordsworth and many other poets.

In the following chapters I shall refer to both conventions, so that an iambic pentameter in traditional **prosody** may be represented as a series of five feet.

```
x / | x / | x / | x / | x / |
```

or as series of five alternating single off-beats and beats,

```
o B o B o B o B o B
```

and an **iambic foot**, |x/|, may be called a **rising duple** pattern, and so on.

13. Rhyme, rhythm and sound II – heightening and foregrounding

Verse has been called a **heightened** form of ordinary language, in the sense that it does nothing that is not done in ordinary speech, but what it does is **foregrounded** and focused on <u>for its own sake</u>. So natural rhythms are made more regular, and 'sound effects' like alliteration, assonance and rhyme, which occur in ordinary language but usually in a random way, are made a deliberate part of the sound patterns.

13.1 Foregrounding rhythm

Metrical verse is set out in lines which have underlying patterns of rhythm (beats and off-beats) – the **metre** of the verse. Once you have discovered what the metre is, then you 'fit' the words to the pattern in a way which is different from the natural rhythms of ordinary speech – 'heightening' these rhythms. The line of verse is also a rhythmical unit, and we tend to hear lines in *even* stress patterns, so that a line of five syllable beats (a very common metre in English verse) will have an additional sixth 'silent beat':

> December, and the closing of the year;
>
> o B o B o   B o   B o B   (o B)
> De cember and the closing of the year ⇒

If the end of the line is not the end of a grammatical unit and is unpunctuated, it is 'run on' to the next line (the French term *enjambement* is often used to describe this):

> The momentary carolers complete ⇒
> Their Christmas Eves, and quickly disappear ⇒
> Into their houses on each lighted street. ⇒

If you read this first stanza of 'Christmas Eve in Whitneyville, 1955', by Donald Hall, as prose,

> |The momentary carolers complete their Christmas 'Eves| and quickly disappear into their 'houses |on each lighted 'street|

all sense of the rhythmic ten-syllable lines is lost. Therefore you have to make a slight pause on the words *complete* and *disappear*, lengthening the final syllables into a final sixth beat just enough to keep the underlying rhythm:

```
o   B   o B o B o B   o   B   (o B)
The mom en ta ry ca ro lers com plete ⇒

o   B   o   B   o   B   o B o B   (o B)
Their Christ mas Eves, and quick ly dis ap pear ⇒

?o ?B o   B   o B o   B   o B   (o B)
In to  their hous es on each light ed street ⇒
```

The underlying unit of the metre of these lines moves from a single off-beat to a beat, and is therefore **rising** and **duple** (two syllables) in a ten-syllable line.

13.2 Foregrounding the final syllables of lines – rhyme

You will have noticed that the four lines also rhyme – *year/disappear* and *complete/street*. If the final syllable is on a beat (stressed), the vowels and any following consonants must be identical. Therefore *around/sound, fall/call, sigh/ eye/I, gear/steer/cavalier/sincere* and *can/span/man* are rhymes. If the final syllable is unstressed, then its preceding stressed syllable determines the rhyme, as in *waver/quaver, dimmer/glimmer, winging/singing, investigations/excavations*.

To describe the patterning of the 'rhyme-scheme' of verse, we label the first rhyme *a*, the second *b*, the third *c* and so on. So the four lines we have been discussing are said to rhyme *abab*. But rhyme is not essential to verse.

Poems may be written in **stanzas**, like paragraphs of prose, but each normally having the same number of lines, with the same metrical and rhyming patterns. On the other hand, the lines of a poem may be continuous from beginning to end. Here are a few examples of common patterns of metre and rhyme.

The first is the four-line stanza which has just been discussed:

1. *Rising duple, 10 syllables, 5 beats, rhyming* **abab**

```
o B o B o B o B o B (o B)
```
Rhyming words

December, and the closing of the year;	⇒ year *a*
The momentary carolers complete	⇒ complete *b*
Their Christmas Eves, and quickly disappear	⇒ disappear *a*
Into their houses on each lighted street.	⇒ street *b*

The fourth line is an example of one of the commonest variations in a metre of rising rhythm. In traditional terms it is a 'reversed foot' (/x).

```
/  x  x   /   x / x   /   x /   (x /)
In to their hous es on each light ed street ⇒
```

Using the terms *beat* and *off-beat*, we explain it by using the concept of a 'silent beat' (ô) at the beginning of the line:

```
ô  B   ǒ   B   o B o   B   o B    (o B)
In to their hous es on each light ed street ⇒
```

The concepts of silent, single and double off-beats (unstressed syllables) enable us to justify the simple description of English metrical verse as a succession of alternate beats and off-beats. It takes into account the fact we have already discussed – that English is *isochronous* in rhythm (stresses/beats at regular intervals), and allows more than one unstressed syllable/off-beat between the beats.

2. *Rising duple, 10 syllables, 5 beats, not rhyming*

o B o B o B o B o B (o B)

When I see birches bend to left and right ⇒
Across the lines of straighter darker trees, ⇒
I like to think some boy's been swinging them. ⇒
But swinging doesn't bend them down to stay. ⇒
Ice storms do that.

This metre is called 'blank verse', and has been used by many poets since the early sixteenth century, especially for epic poetry and drama – Shakespeare's plays, Milton's *Paradise Lost*, Wordsworth's 'The Prelude' and many others.

3. *Rising duple, 10 syllables, 5 beats, rhyming in couplets* **aabbcc,** *etc.*

o B o B o B o B o B (o B)

Where'er you walk, cool gales shall fan the glade,   ⇒   glade *a*
Trees, where you sit, shall crowd into a shade: ⇒   shade *a*
Where'er you tread, the blushing flowers shall rise,   ⇒   rise *b*
And all things flourish where you turn your eyes   ⇒   eyes *b*

The pairs of rhyming lines in this metrical and rhyming pattern are called 'heroic couplets'. It was used by Chaucer in his *Canterbury Tales*, and especially in the late seventeenth and the eighteenth centuries by, for example, John Dryden, Alexander Pope and Samuel Johnson.

4. *Rising duple, 8 syllables, 4 beats, rhyming* **abab**

o B o B o B o B

In every cry of every man,   man *a*
In every infant's cry of fear,   fear *b*
In every voice; in every ban,   ban *a*
The mind-forged manacles I hear: hear *b*

5. *Falling duple, 7 syllables, 4 beats, rhyming* **aabb:**

B o B o B o B (o)

In the deserts of the heart   heart *a*
Let the healing fountains start   start *a*
In the prison of his days   days *b*
Teach the free man how to praise   praise *b*

6. *Rising duple, 8 syllables, 4 beats, rhyming* aabb *etc. ('rhyming couplets')*

o B o B o B o B

Had we but world enough, and time	time *a*
This coyness, Lady, were no crime	crime *a*
We would sit down and think which way	way *b*
To walk and pass our love's long day.	day *b*

7. *Rising triple, 14 syllables ('fourteener' lines), 5 beats, rhyming* abab

(Having an odd number of beats (5), this line will have an additional 'silent' beat.)

o^2 B o^2 B o^2 B o^2 B o^2 B o^2 B – x /xx/xx/xx/xx/ (xx/)

o   B o^2 B o^2 B o^2 B o^2 B (o^2 B)

Could **such** be the **haun** tings of **men** of to **day**, at the **cease** ⇒	cease *a*
Of pur**suit**, at the **dusk**-hour, ere **slumber** their **senses** could **seal**!	⇒	seal *b*
En**ghosted** seers, **kings** – one on **horse**back who **asked** 'Is it **peace**?'	⇒	peace *a*
Yea, **strange** things and **spectral** may **men** have be**held** in Jezreel!	⇒	Jezreel *b*

8. *Alternating lines of 8 and 6 syllables (making 'fourteeners'), rhyming* abab – *'ballad metre':*

(The second and fourth lines of 3 (odd) beats will have an additional 'silent' beat.)

o B o B o B o B

o B o B o B (o B)

A slumber did my spirit seal;	seal *a*
I had no human fears – ⇒	fears *b*
She seemed a thing that could not feel	feel *a*
The touch of human years. – ⇒	years *b*

Activity 13.1

Describe the metrical and rhyming pattern of each of the following verses in terms of

(i) duple or triple syllables,

(ii) rising or falling rhythm,

(iii) number of syllables and beats in the lines, and

(iv) the rhyming pattern

📖 This Activity is discussed in the *Commentary & Data Book*.

(i) 'How pleasant to know Mr Lear!'
    Who has written such volumes of stuff!
Some think him ill-tempered and queer,
    But a few think him pleasant enough.

(ii) When midnight comes a host of boys and men
    Go out and track the badger to his den,
And put a sack within the hole, and lie
    Till the old grunting badger passes by.

(iii)   Lives of great men all remind us
       We can make our lives sublime,
    And, departing, leave behind us
       Footprints on the sands of time.

(iv)   The buzz-saw snarled and rattled in the yard
    And made dust and dropped stove-length sticks of wood,
    Sweet-scented stuff when the breeze drew across it.
    And from there those that lifted eyes could count
    Five mountain ranges one behind the other
    Under the sunset far into Vermont.

(v)   He clasps the crag with crooked hands;
    Close to the sun in lonely lands,
    Ring'd with the azure worls, he stands.
    The wrinkled sea beneath him crawls;
    He watches from his mountain walls,
    And like a thunderbolt he falls.

13.3   Foregrounding consonants and vowels – alliteration, assonance, consonance

We have seen how important alliteration was in Old English and some Middle English poetry (see section 12.2.2). It was part of the structure of the verse, and two or three words at least, in every line, had the same initial consonant, or began with a vowel. Alliteration crops up by accident in everything we say. You could check this by looking at newspaper reports for example. The following quotations are taken at random from reports on the day that this section was being written:

Will [C]arling, [c]aptain in [s]ix of [C]ooke's [s]even [s]easons	[k] and [s]
looking after his [b]odyguards and [b]elongings	[b]
the [f]lamboyant [f]ormer chairman	[f]
[ai]d and [ar]ms were linked	vowels
the [S]ecretary of [S]tate for Defence [s]igned a protocol	[s]

In just the same way, we can find words with the same final consonants,

the topi[c] of conversation all wee[k]	[k]
it often happen[s] to other team[s]	[z]
the Fren[ch] coa[ch]	[tʃ]

which is a type of foregrounding called **consonance**, and words with the same vowel sounds,

br[ea]king off rel[a]tions	[ɛɪ]
[a]ll this t[al]k of money	[ɔ]
he is [u]nder en[ou]gh pressure	[ʌ]

which is called **assonance**. Rhyme will occur sometimes,

they are happy to ⌐harp⌐ and ⌐carp⌐ unsolicited

but it is most unlikely that any of these examples is deliberate. We have to be careful, therefore, when attributing 'literary value' to features like alliteration and assonance in verse, or suggesting that such features have any particular 'effect'. A poet may use them 'for their own sake', and this was especially so in the poetry of Gerard Manley Hopkins (1844–89). We shall find examples of the rhythmic and aural effects we have been discussing in his poem 'Harry Ploughman'.

13.4   Gerard Manley Hopkins's 'Harry Ploughman'

We have looked at the role of the vocabulary and grammar of Hopkins's 'Harry Ploughman' in determining its style (section 10.3), but its rhythm and sound patterns are inseparable from the meaning conveyed by the words.

13.4.1   *Rhythm and metrical patterns*

Hopkins referred to the rhythm of the poem in a letter in this way,

> The rhythm of this sonnet, which is altogether for recital, and not for perusal (as by nature verse should be), is very highly studied.

and he included a detailed, annotated copy of the poem to show how he wanted the poem to be read and heard. In section 12.2.2 we noted that Old English and some Middle English poetry was not syllabic – that is, it did not assign a metre (a regular number of syllables) to a line of verse – but was stress-timed. Any number of unstressed syllables, from none to three or four, could occur between the stressed syllables.

Hopkins developed this kind of rhythmic freedom and called it **Sprung Rhythm**, 'the rhythm of common speech and of written prose, when rhythm is perceived in them'.

> Sprung Rhythm is measured by feet of from one to four syllables, regularly, and for particular effects any number of weak or slack syllables may be used. It has one stress...and so gives rise to four sorts of feet.

He used traditional terms from classical verse to label the 'four sorts of feet' which then occur:

1.	one stressed syllable	/	monosyllable
2.	stressed + one unstressed	/ x	trochee
3.	stressed + two unstressed	/ x x	dactyl
4.	stressed + three unstressed	/ x x x	paeon

In addition to these 'falling' rhythmic units, he used what he called **outrides** or **hangers**,

one, two, or three slack syllables added to a foot and not counting in the scanning.

which gives a lot of flexibility to the reading.

Here is a reproduction of Hopkins's annotated copy of the poem. He uses various markings, as in a musical score, and describes some of them in this way:

slurs – 'that is, loops over syllables, to tie them together into the time of one',
outrides or **hangers** – 'marked by a loop underneath them',
accents – '/∧ where the reader might be in doubt which syllable should have the stress',
pauses – ∩ 'to show that the syllable should be dwelt on',
twirls – ∼ 'to mark reversed rhythm'.

Hopkins also wrote, 'each of the basic 14 lines has five metrical stresses', so with this detailed information, we should be able to read the poem in a way that gets

Harry Ploughman

Hard as hurdle arms, with a broth of goldish flue
Breathed round; the rack of ribs; the scooped flank; lank
Rope-over thigh; knee-nave; and barrelled shank —
Head and foot, shoulder and shank —
By a grey eye's heed steered well, one crew, fall to;
Stand at stress. Each limb's barrowy-brawned thew
That onewhere curded, onewhere sucked or sank —
Soared or sank —,
Though as a beechbole firm, finds his, as at a rollcall, rank
And features, in flesh, what deed he each must do —
His sinew-service where do.
He leans to it, Harry bends, look. Back, elbow, and liquid waist
In him, all quail to the wallowing o' the plough. 'S cheek
Wag or crossbridle, in a wind lifted, windlaced —
See his wind- lilylocks -laced;
Churlsgrace too, child of Amansstrength, how it hangs or hurls
Them — broad in bluff hide his frowning feet lashed! raced
With, along them, cragiron under and cold furls —
With-a-wet-sheen-shot furls.

Dromore Sept 1887

near to his intentions. Using the distinction between metrical beats (B) and off-beats (o) briefly described in section 12.2.5, one reading of the rhythm of the poem, taking Hopkins's markings into account, is printed below. The five beats will be roughly isochronous. The <u>metrical</u> rhythm is placed above the line in beats and off-beats, with the normal spoken stress pattern underneath. You will see that some normally stressed syllables have to be **demoted** to metrical off-beats, and some normally unstressed syllables **promoted** to beats. This produces a **counterpoint** between the expected speech rhythms and the metrical rhythm that the five-beat line demands.

The following symbols are used in the diagram of the rhythm and metre of 'Harry Ploughman' that follows.

o	= off-beat
o^2	= double off-beat
o^3	= triple off-beat
ô	= silent off-beat
(x)	= silent stress
$\boxed{/} \Rightarrow \boxed{o}$	= stressed syllable demoted to an off-beat
$\boxed{x} \Rightarrow \boxed{B}$	= unstressed syllable promoted to a beat

5-stress line	|B1	|B2	|B3	|B4	|B5

1.

ô	B	o	B	o^2	B	o	B	o	B	
	|**Hard** as hurdle		|**arms** with a		|**broth** of		|**goldish**		|**flue**	⇒
(x)	/	x $\boxed{/}$	/	x x	/	x	/	x	/	

2.

$\boxed{o}$	B	o	B	o	B	o	B	$\boxed{o}$	B	ô
Breathed	|**round**; the		|**rack** of		|**ribs**; the		|**scooped** flank;		|**lank**	→
$\boxed{/}$	/	x	/	x	/	x	/	$\boxed{/}$	/	(x)

3.

ô	B	o^2	B	ô	B	o^2	B	o	B
	|**Rope**-over		|**thigh**;		|**knee**-nave; and	|**barrelled**		|**shánk**-	
(x)	/	xx	/	x	/ $\boxed{/}$ x	/	x	/	

4.

ô	B	o	B	ô	B	o^2	B
	|**Head** and		|**foot**,		|**shoul** der and	|**shank**-	
(x)	/	x	/	(x)	/	x x	/́

```
       ŏ      B    [o]    B    [o]    B     o     B    [o]    B
5.    By a   |grey eye's  |heed steered  |well, one   |crew, fall   |to;
      x x    /    [/]    /    [/]    /     x     /    [/]    /
```

```
       ô      B   [o²]    B    [o]    B    o²     B     o     B
                         ∩
6.           |Stand at stress. |Each limb's  |barrowy      |brawn, his   |thew ⇒
      (x)    /     x    [/]    /    [/]    /    x x   /     x     /
```

```
       o      B     o     B     o     B     o     B     o     B
7.    That   |one   where  |curd  ed,   |one   where  |sucked  or   |sank-
       x     /     x     /     x     /     x     /     x     /
```

```
                                              ô      B     o     B
8.                                          |Soared ór   |sánk-,
                                            (x)    /     x     /
```

```
       o      B     o     B     ô     B     o     B     o     B
                               ∩
9. Though as as |beech bole  |firm,      |finds his, as a |roll  call  |rank
   outride   /     x     /    (x)    /   outride   /     x     /
```

```
       o      B    o²     B     ô     B    o²     B     o     B
10.   And    |fea tures, ín  |flesh,     |whát  deed he |each  must  |do-
       x     /    x x    /    (x)    /    [/] x   /     x     /
```

```
              o      B     o     B     o     B     o     B     ô     B
11.          His    |sin   ew-   |ser   vice   |where      |do.
              x     /     x     /     x     /     x     /    (x)    /
```

```
       o      B     o     B    [o]    B     ô     B    [o]    B
12.   He    |leans to it, Harry |bends, look. |Back,      |elbow, and liquid |waist ⇒
       x     /   outride   /    [/]    /    (x)    /   outride   /
```

	o	B	o²	B	o	B	⊡o	B o	B
13. (In him), all	**|quail**	to the	**|wal** lowing o' the	**|plough:** 's cheek	**|crim** sons;	**|curls**
outride	/	x x	/ *outride*	/	⃝	/	x	/

	ô	B	o	B	ŏ̌	B	ô	B	o	B	o
14.	**|Wag** or	**|crossbridle, in a |wind**	**|lif** ted,	**|wind** laced-
(x)	/	x	/ ⃝ x x x /	(x)	/	x	/ ⃝ b
				outride						

	o²	B	ô	B	o²	B
15.	See his	**|wind-**	**|li** lylocks-	**|laced,**
	x x	/	(x)	/	x x	/

	ô	B	o²	B	o²	B	o
16.	**|Churls** grace too,	**|child** of A	**|mans** strength, how it
(x)	/	⃝ x /	x x	/	x	*outride*

	B	o	B
	|hangs or	**|hurls** ⇒
	/	x	/

	o	B	o	B	o	B	o	B	o	B
17. (Them)-broad	**|in** bluff	**|hide** his	**|frówn** ing	**|féet**	lashed!**|r á c e-**
d→	/	/	/	/	⃝

	o²	B	o	B	o	B	o²	B	ô	B
18.	With, a	**|long** them,	**|crag** iron	**|un** der and	**|cold**	**|furls-**
	x x	/	x	/	x	/	x x	/	(x)	/

	o²	B	o	B	o²	B
19.	With-a-	**|foun** tain's	**|shin** ing-shot	**|furls**
	x x	/	x	/	x x	/

13.4.2 *Alliteration*

Alliteration, assonance and rhyme must, of course, be <u>heard</u>, and marking the features on the printed page is only a way of drawing attention to the complexity of Hopkins's deliberate patterning of sounds 'for their own sake':

1. [H]ard as [h]urdle arms, with a [br]oth of goldish [fl]ue

2. [Br]eathed [r]ound; the [r]ack of [r]ibs; the scooped [fl]ank; [l]ank

3. [R]ope-over thigh; [kn]ee- [n]ave; and barrelled [sh]ank –

    Head and foot, [sh]oulder and [sh]ank –

4. By a grey eye's heed [st]eered [w]ell, [o]ne crew, fall to;

5. [St]and at [st]ress. Each limb's [b]arrowy [b]rawn, his thew

6. That onewhere curded, onewhere [s]ucked or [s]ank –

    [S]oared or [s]ank – ,

7. Though as a [b]eech [b]ole [f]irm, [f]inds his, as at a [r]ollcall, [r]ank

8. And [f]eatures, in [f]lesh, what [d]eed he each must [d]o –

    His [s]inew- [s]ervice where [d]o.

9. [H]e leans to it, [H]arry [b]ends, [l]ook. [B]ack, e[lb]ow, and [l]i[qu]id [w]aist

10. In him, all [qu]ail to the [w]allowing o' the plough: 's cheek [c]rimsons; [c]urls

11. [W]ag or [c]rossbridle, in a [w]ind [l]ifted, [w]ind [l]aced –

    See his [w]ind- [l]ily [l]ocks - [l]aced;

12. [Ch]urlsgrace too, [ch]ild of Amansstrength, [h]ow it [h]angs or [h]urls

13. Them – [b]road in [b]luff hide his [f]rowning [f]eet lashed! raced

14. With, along them, [c]ragiron under and [c]old [f]urls –

    With-a- [f]ountain's [sh]ining- [sh]ot [f]urls.

13.4.3 *Assonance and rhyme*

	Assonance	*Rhyme*
1. H[ar]d as hurdle [ar]ms, with a broth of goldish **flue**	[ɑː]	[uː]
2. Breathed round; the r[a]ck of ribs; the scooped fl[a]nk; l[a]nk	[æ]	[æŋk]
3. Rope-over thigh; knee-nave; and b[a]rrelled sh[a]nk –	[æ]	[æŋk]
Head and foot, shoulder and sh[a]nk –	[æ]	[æŋk]
4. By a grey eye's h[ee]d st[ee]red well, one cr[ew], fall t[o];	[iː] [uː]	[uː]
5. St[a]nd at stress. Each limb's b[a]rrowy brawn, his **thew**	[æ]	[uː]
6. That [o]newhere curded, [o]newhere s[u]cked or **sank** –	[ʌ]	[æŋk]
S[oar]ed [or] **sank** – ,	[ɔː]	[æŋk]

7.	Though as a b|ee|chbole firm, finds his, as at a rollcall, **rank**	[iː]	[æŋk]
8.	And f|ea|tures, in flesh, what d|ee|d he |ea|ch must **do** –	[iː]	[uː]
	His sinew-service where **do.**		[uː]
9.	He leans to it, Harry b|e|nds, look. Back, |e|lbow, and liquid w|ai|st	[ɛ] [ɛɪ]	[ɛɪst]
10.	In him, all qu|ai|l to the wallowing o' the		
	plough: 's cheek crimsons; **curls**	[ɛɪ]	[ɜːlz]
11.	Wag or crossbridle, in a w|i|nd l|i|fted, w|i|nd **laced** –	[ɪ]	[ɛɪst]
	See his w|i|nd- l|i|lylocks -l|ace|d;	[ɪ]	[ɛɪst]
12.	Ch|urls| gr|ace| too, child of Am|a|nsstrength, how it h|a|ngs or h|urls|	[æ]	[ɜːlz]
13.	Them – broad in bluff hide his frowning feet l|a|shed! **raced**	[æ]	[ɛɪst]
14.	With, along them, cr|a|giron under and cold **furls** –	[æ]	[ɜːlz]
	With-a-fountain's shining-shot **furls.**		[ɜːlz]

📖 A phonetic transcription of the poem in the *Commentary & Data Book*.

13.5 Gerard Manley Hopkins's 'Pied Beauty'

Hopkins gives us three useful bits of information about his poem 'Pied Beauty':

(i) It is what he calls a **curtal sonnet**. *Curtal* was a French word and referred to 'anything docked, or cut short'; *curtail* is a later pronunciation of the same word. *Curtal-sonnet* is Hopkins's name for a poem of ten lines – 'that is they are constructed in proportions resembling those of the sonnet proper, namely 6 + 4 instead of 8 + 6, with however a halfline tailpiece'.

(ii) It is in **sprung rhythm**, Hopkins's term for the kind of traditional English metre discussed in section 13.4.1 – stress-timed beats, with any number of unstressed off-beats between the beats.

(iii) It is **paeonic**, that is, its underlying rhythmic unit is / x x x – a stressed beat followed by three unstressed off-beats.

Activity 13.2

(i) Read the poem aloud and see if you can discover the way to bring out its 'sprung paeonic rhythm'.

(ii) Using the previous analysis of 'Harry Ploughman' as a guide, discuss the rhythm and metre, and the sound patterns of the poem.

The accent marks (e.g. áll), are Hopkins's own notations to indicate words that should carry some stress.

Pied Beauty

Glory be to God for dappled things –
　For skies of couple-colour as a brinded cow;
　　For rose-moles all in stipple upon trout that swim;
Fresh-firecoal chestnut-falls; finches' wings;
　Landscape plotted and pieced – fold, fallow, and plough;
　And áll trádes, their gear and tackle and trim.
All things counter, original, spare, strange;
　Whatever is fickle, freckled (who knows how?)
　　With swift, slow; sweet, sour; adazzle, dim;
He fathers-forth whose beauty is past change:
　　　　　　　　　　　　　　Praise him.

📖　A detailed analysis of 'Pied Beauty' is in the *Commentary & Data Book*.

13.6　Sound and rhythm in Dylan Thomas's *Under Milk Wood*

Under Milk Wood (1954) was written for radio and called 'A Play for Voices'. It portrays a day and night in the life of Thomas's fictional Welsh town of Llaregyb. Examples of simile and metaphor from the play were quoted in chapter 6, but it is equally rich as a source of 'sound effects' in language. Here is a typical sentence:

There's the clip clop of horses on the sunhoneyed cobbles of the humming streets, hammering of horse-shoes, gobble quack and cackle, tomtit twitter from the bird-ounced boughs, braying on Donkey Down.

which provides examples of the poetic sound patterns discussed in section 13.3:

Alliteration

clip clop	kl-	klɪp klɒp
humming – hammering – horseshoes	h-m-	hʌmɪŋ – hæmərɪŋ – hɔsʃuːz
quack – cackle	k-	kwæk – kækl̩
tomtit twitter	t-	tɒmtɪt twɪtə
bird-ounced boughs – braying	b-	bɜdaʊnst baʊz – breɪŋ
Donkey Down	d-	dɒŋki daʊn

Assonance

sunhoneyed – humming	ʌ	sʌnhʌnʌd – hʌmɪŋ
clop – cobbles	ɒ	klɒp – kɒblz
quack – cackle	æ	kwæk – kækl
tomtit twitter	ɪ	tɒmtɪt twɪtə
bird-ounced boughs – Down	aʊ	bɜdaʊnst baʊz – daʊn

Consonance

clip clop	-p	klɪp klɒp

There is also the consonance of the [s] or [z] of plural endings and medial consonants:

there's – horses – cobbles – streets – horse-shoes – ounced – boughs

If you say the sentence aloud, you will hear marked rhythms also.

Activity 13.3

Describe the rhythmic and sound features of the rest of the same paragraph from the play.

📖 This Activity is discussed in the *Commentary & Data Book*.

Bread is baking, pigs are grunting, chop goes the butcher, milk-churns bell, tills ring, sheep cough, dogs shout, saws sing. Oh, the Spring whinny and morning moo from the clog dancing farms, the gulls' gab and rabble on the boat-bobbing river and sea and the cockles bubbling in the sand, scamper of sanderlings, curlew cry, crow caw, pigeon coo, clock strike, bull bellow, and the ragged gabble of the beargarden school as the women scratch and babble in Mrs Organ Morgan's general shop where everything is sold: custard, buckets, henna, rat-traps, shrimp-nets, sugar, stamps, confetti, paraffin, hatchets, whistles.

14. Rhyme, rhythm and sound III

14.1 Free verse

Poetry written without a regular metre, and unrhymed, is called *free verse*. It is recognised visually on the page because it adopts the convention of the verse line. If this paragraph,

> This is just to say I have eaten the plums that were in the icebox and which you were probably saving for breakfast. Forgive me, they were delicious, so sweet and so cold.

in the form of a note, perhaps left on the kitchen table, is printed in the linear form of verse, without conventional punctuation and with a title, it is to be read as a poem. It is by an American poet, William Carlos Williams,

> *THIS IS JUST TO SAY*
>
> I have eaten
> the plums
> that were in
> the icebox
>
> and which
> you were probably
> saving
> for breakfast
>
> Forgive me
> they were delicious
> so sweet
> and so cold

Activity 14.1

What is the effect of setting out the words of the 'note' in lines as verse?

14.1.1 *Commentary*

As a **speech act**, the note has a limited practical function and the paper will be thrown into the waste bin soon after it is read. As a **poem**, however, the event is given permanence and significance. At the same time, its division into short lines makes us read it rhythmically, with subtle differences in speed and rhythm. It is someone speaking – not a scribbled note.

Activity 14.2

Discuss the difference between the following prose paragraph and its proper form as a poem by D. H. Lawrence.

Whatever man makes and makes it live, lives because of the life put into it. A yard of India muslin is alive with Hindu life, and a Navajo woman, weaving her rug in the pattern of her dream, must run the pattern out in a little break at the end so that her soul can come out, back to her. But in the odd pattern, like snake-marks on the sand, it leaves it trail.

'Whatever Man Makes – '

Whatever man makes and makes it live
lives because of the life put into it.
A yard of India muslin is alive with Hindu life.
And a Navajo woman, weaving her rug in the pattern of her dream
must run the pattern out in a little break at the end
so that her soul can come out, back to her.
But in the odd pattern, like snake-marks on the sand
It leaves its trail.

14.2 Doggerel

Doggerel is a word whose origin is not known but which means,

An epithet applied to comic or burlesque verse, usually of irregular rhythm; or to mean, trivial, or undignified verse.

The following description of William McGonagall (1830–1902) comes from the *Oxford Companion to English Literature*:

... the son of an Irish weaver, attracted a certain following in Edinburgh with his readings in public houses and his broadsheets of topical verse. His naïve and **unscanned doggerel** continues to entertain, and he now enjoys a reputation as the world's worst poet.

Activity 14.3

Read the following poem by William McGonagall and discuss why it should be called 'doggerel verse'.

'An Address to the Rev George Gilfillan'

All hail to the Rev George Gilfillan of Dundee,
He is the greatest preacher I did ever hear or see.
He is a man of genius bright,
And in him his congregation does delight,
Because they find him to be honest and plain,

Affable in temper, and seldom known to complain.
He preaches in a plain straightforward way,
The people flock to hear him night and day,
And hundreds from the doors are often turn'd away,
Because he is the greatest preacher of the present day.
He has written the life of Sir Walter Scott,
And while he lives he will never be forgot,
Nor when he is dead,
Because by his admirers it will be often read;
And fill their minds with wonder and delight,
And while away the tedious hours on a cold winter's night.
He has also written about the Bards of the Bible,
Which occupied nearly three years in which he was not idle,
Because when he sits down to write he does it with might and main,
And to get an interview with him it would be almost vain,
And in that he is always right,
For the Bible tells us whatever your hands findeth to do,
Do it with all your might.
Rev George Gilfillan of Dundee, I must conclude my muse,
And to write in praise of thee my pen does not refuse,
Nor does it give me pain to tell the world fearlessly, that when
You are dead they shall not look upon your like again.

14.2.1 Commentary

When you have to explain a joke to someone, the joke somehow stops being funny, and we have a similar problem in taking McGonagall's verse seriously enough to analyse why it is so bad. So we need not spend much time on it, but look at just three aspects of it.

Rhyme
The verse is written mainly in couplets, mostly rhyming *aabbcc* etc., except for the four lines rhyming on *way – day – away – day*, which is economical, if not very effective. The rhymes have been called 'unremitting'. The metrical rhythm is undefined and there are no run-on lines, so each line ends with a strong stress and a pause on the rhyming word. The need to find a rhyme may cause an artificial inversion like *a man of genius bright* or the redundant *does* in *his congregation does delight*. The imperfect rhyme on *Bible* and *idle* draws attention to itself.

Rhythm and metre
There is no regular metre, so each line reads like a line of prose, yet the lines do not have the enhanced rhythm of lines of free verse that we have just briefly looked at in section 14.1. They vary in length from *Nor when he is dead* to *For the Bible tells us whatever your hands findeth to do, do it with all your might* (printed as two lines but clearly one because *might* has to rhyme with *right*).

Content
McGonagall's intention to praise the reputation and life of the Reverend Gilfillan is a good one, but so much of the poem consists of **clichés** (hackneyed expressions) or commonplace expressions, *when he sits down to write he does it with might and main*, or has little real meaning, *to get an interview with him it would be almost vain*.

14.3 'Energetic rhythms and grisly rhymes'

The reference to the 'energetic rhythms' and 'the occasional grisly rhyme' of Browning's verse was part of a literary review quoted in section 1.2.2 of the introductory chapter.

14.3.1 'Energetic rhythms'?

This well-known poem will illustrate what the reviewer probably meant:

> Kentish Sir Byng stood for his King,
> Bidding the crop-headed Parliament swing:
> And, pressing a troop unable to stoop
> And see the rogues flourish and honest folk droop,
> Marched them along, fifty-score strong,
> Great-hearted gentlemen, singing this song.

> (*Cavalier Tunes*, 1, 'Marching Along')

Activity 14.4

Describe the rhythm and metre of the verse in the terms used in chapter 13.

📖 This Activity is discussed in the *Commentary & Data Book.*

14.3.1.1 COMMENTARY

The title 'Marching Along' describes Browning's intention – the beats in the lines are in time with men marching, and will be strongly emphasised. At the same time, the words require a falling triple rhythm, / x x , regular and marked:

```
Kentish Sir Byng ⇒   stood for his King ⇒,
/   x    x   /   (xx) /   x    x   /   (xx)

Bid ding the crop- hea ded Par lia ment swing  ⇒:
/   x    x   /    x   x   /  x   x    /    (x)

And, pres sing a troop ⇒   un a ble to stoop ⇒
x    /   x   x /   x    x   / x x  /    (x)

And see the rogues flou rish and ho nest folk droop ⇒,
x   /   x   x    /   x   x   / x   x    /   (xx)

Marched them a long ⇒,   fif ty-score strong ⇒,
/       x    x /   (xx) / x x    /    (xx)

Great- hear ted gen tle men, sing ing this song ⇒.
/       x    x   /   x   x   /   x   x   /   (xx)
```

The stressed words/syllables *Byng, King, swing, troop, stoop, droop, -long, strong, song* dominate the rhythm, which is reinforced by the rhymes. The poem might well have been printed as,

> Kentish Sir Byng
> Stood for his King,
> Bidding the crop-headed Parliament swing:
> And, pressing a troop
> Unable to stoop...

which would have further marked the rhythm and rhyme.

Activity 14.5

Describe the rhythmic and rhyming patterns in the two following verses from another poem by Robert Browning.

📖 This Activity is discussed in the *Commentary & Data Book*.

> Boot, saddle, to horse, and away!
> Rescue my Castle, before the hot day
> Brightens to blue from its silvery gray.
> *Boot, saddle, to horse, and away!*
> Ride past the suburbs, asleep as you'd say;
> Many's the friend there, will listen and pray
> 'God's luck to gallants that strike up the lay,
> *Boot, saddle, to horse, and away!'*
>
> (*Cavalier Tunes*, III, 'Boot and Saddle')

14.3.2 'Grisly rhyme'?

We have to guess a little in finding rhymes that are *grisly*. The dictionary definition of the modern use of the word is,

Causing uncanny or unpleasant feelings; forbidding; grim, ghastly.

so we can only appeal to the subjective impression that some rhymes cause in our response. Try these rhymes:

> And when fresh gypsies have paid us a **visit, I've**
> Noticed the couple were never **inquisitive**,
> But told them they're folks the Duke don't **want here**,
> And bade them make haste and cross the **frontier**.
>
> ('The Flight of the Duchess')

14.3.2.1 COMMENTARY

First, there is a mismatch between the pronunciation of the two rhyming words of each couplet, presuming that *inquisitive* was pronounced by Browning as we pronounce it now – [ɪnkwɪzɪtɪv], not [ɪnkwɪzɪtaɪv] to rhyme with *I've*, and [frʌntɪə], not [frɒntɪə] to rhyme with *want 'ere*. Second, it is rare in more serious verse for two words to rhyme with one. The incongruity is more often exploited in comic or light verse.

Activity 14.6

Discuss the rhymes in the following couplets from Browning's 'The Pied Piper of Hamelin'.

📖 This Activity is discussed in the *Commentary & Data Book*.

> You hope, because you're old and **obese**,
> To find in the furry civic **robe ease**?

An hour they sate in **council**,
At length the Mayor broke **silence**:
'For a guilder I'd my ermine **gown sell**
I wish I were a **mile hence**!'
And, whether they pipe us free from rats or **fróm mice**,
If we've promised them aught, let us keep our **promise**.

14.4 'Thumping'

In section 1.2.3 of chapter 1, the critic's view of W. B. Yeats's poetry was that he did <u>not</u> 'thump' like the three poets contemporary with him – Henley, Chesterton and Kipling. Here are two examples of each poet's verse, one of which is chosen as a probable example of 'thumping', and the other not.

Activity 14.7

Which of these verses can be said to *thump*? What, more precisely, is meant by 'thumping'?

William Butler Yeats (1865–1939)

1. From 'Three Songs to the Same Tune'

Justify all those renowned generations;
They left their bodies to fatten the wolves,
They left their homesteads to
    fatten the foxes,
Fled to far countries, or sheltered themselves
In cavern, crevice, hole,
Defending Ireland's soul.
*'Drown all the dogs,' said
    the fierce young woman,
'They killed my goose and a cat.
Drown, drown in the water-butt,
Drown all the dogs,' said
    the fierce young woman,*

2. 'Girl's Song'

I went out alone
To sing a song or two,
My fancy on a man,
And you know who.

Another came in sight
That on a stick relied
To hold himself upright;
I sat and cried.

And that was all my song –
When everything is told,
Saw I an old man young
Or young man old?

William Ernest Henley (1849–1903)

1. From 'Margaritæ Sorori'

A late lark twitters from the quiet skies:
And from the west,
Where the sun, his day's work ended,
Lingers as in content,
There falls on the old, gray city
An influence luminous and serene,
A shining peace.

2. From 'Invictus'

Out of the night that covers me,
Black as the pit from pole to pole,
I thank whatever gods may be
For my unconquerable soul.

In the fell clutch of circumstance
I have not winced nor cried aloud.
Under the bludgeonings of chance
My head is bloody, but unbow'd

Gilbert Keith Chesterton (1872-1936)

1. From 'The Rolling English Road'

Before the Roman came to Rye or out to Severn strode,
The rolling English drunkard made the rolling English road.
A reeling road, a rolling road, that rambles round the shire,
And after him the parson ran, the sexton and the squire;
A merry road, a mazy road, and such as we did tread
The night we went to Birmingham by way of Beachy Head.

2. The Donkey

When fishes flew and forests walk'd
And figs grew upon thorn,
Some moment when the moon was blood
Then surely I was born;

With monstrous head and sickening cry
And ears like errant wings,
The devil's walking parody
Of all four-footed things.

The tatter'd outlaw of the earth,
Of ancient crooked will;
Starve, scourge, deride me: I am dumb,
I keep my secret still.

Fools! For I also had my hour;
One far fierce hour and sweet:
There was a shout about my ears,
And palms before my feet.

Rudyard Kipling (1865–1936)

1. From 'Cities and Thrones and Powers'

Cities and Thrones and Powers
Stand in Time's eye,
Almost as long as flowers,
Which daily die:
But, as new buds put forth
To glad new men,
Out of the spent and unconsidered Earth
The Cities rise again...

2. From 'Boots – (Infantry Columns)'

We're foot – slog – slog – slog – sloggin' over Africa –
Foot – foot – foot – foot – sloggin' over Africa
(Boots – boots – boots – boots – movin' up and down again!
There's no discharge in the war!

Seven – six – eleven – five – nine-an'-twenty miles today –
Four – eleven – seventeen – thirty-two the day before
(Boots – boots – boots – boots – movin' up and down again!
There's no discharge in the war!...

14.4.1 Commentary

The pairs of poems were chosen because they seemed to me to provide one 'thumping' rhythm and one 'non-thumping' rhythm for each of the four poets, including Yeats. Any poem with a strong regular rhythmic beat to match its meaning can be said to thump.

14.4.1.1 W. B. YEATS

The poem 'Justify all those renowned generations' has a strong falling triple rhythm in its first four lines and chorus,

```
B   o²  B   o²  B         o² B      o²
Jus ti  fy  all those renowned ge ne ra ⇒  tions;...
/   x  x  /  x    x /     x  x  /  (x) x

B        o²  B       o²  B      o²     B    o²
'Drown all the dogs,' said the fierce ⇒  young wo man,
/        x  x  /    x   x  /   (x) x   /  x  (x)
```

and so qualifies as thumping verse, whereas 'Girl's Song', in a more slowly moving rising duple rhythm, does not.

14.4.1.2 W. E. HENLEY

'Invictus' is the best-known poem by W. E. Henley, whose reputation has declined in the twentieth century. Its underlying metrical line has four beats in a rising duple rhythm, but the 'reversal' of the beat at the beginning of the first two lines adds to the poem's distinctively strong rhythm.

```
ô  B   o²   B    o   B o   B
Out of the night that co vers me,
/   x  x  /    x  /  x   /

ô  B    o²   B  o   B   o  B
Black as the pit from pole to pole,
/    x  x  /  x   /   x  /

o  B    o   B  o  B   o   B
I thank what e ver gods may be
x  /    x   /  x  /   x   /

o   B   o  B  o   B o   B
For my un con quer a ble soul.
x   /  x  /  x   /  x  /
```

It was written in 1875, and expresses his defiance in undergoing the ordeal of a whole year in hospital in Edinburgh. It is perhaps not representative of the patriotic verses he wrote later which can be said to 'thump' more obviously. But the other poem printed above shows him quite capable of writing in a different style.

14.4.1.3 G. K. CHESTERTON

'The Rolling English Road' is a 'fourteener' – a rhyming couplet of 14 syllables in rising duple rhythm:

```
o  B   o  B  o   B   o B  o B  o B o   B    (o B)
Be fore the Ro man came to Rye or out to Se vern strode ⇒,
x  /   x  /  x   /    x /  x /  x / x   /    (x /)

o   B  o   B  o   B    o  B   o  B o  B  o  B    (o B)
The rol ling Eng lish drunk ard made the rol ling Eng lish road. ⇒
x   /  x  /  x   /    x  /   x  /  x / x  /    (x x)
```

This metre is generally associated with lighter narrative verse, and its regularity and final 'thump' on the rhyming word give it a distinctive rhythm.

'The Donkey' is, in fact, in the same metre, but printed in four-line stanzas of eight and six syllables alternately, so that you pause a little on the final syllable of each line. It is 'the same, but different', and its subject matter also causes us to read it differently.

14.4.1.4 RUDYARD KIPLING

The 'thumping' of Kipling's 'Boots' is clear. Its underlying metre has to be an 8-beat falling triple rhythm, even though most of the words have only one or two syllables:

```
o     B  (o²)  B   (o²)  B   (o²)  B   (o²)  B    o²  B o²  B   o²  B (o²)
We're foot       slog      slog      slog      slog gin' o ver Af ri ca ⇒
x      /  (x x) /  (x x)  /  (x x) /  (x x) /  (x)x  /  (x)x / (x)x  /  (x x)
```

and even the shorter last line can be 'stretched' to the same musical rhythm:

```
o       B (o²) B (o²) B      (o²) B (o²) B  (o²   B o² B o² B o²)
There's no ⇒  dis ⇒ charge   ⇒  in  the  war! ⇒   ⇒   ⇒   ⇒
x        /  (x x)/  (x x)/   (x x)/(x)x   /   (x x) (/x x)(/x x)(/x x)
```

'Cities and Thrones and Powers' is also in a falling triple rhythm, but reads quite differently from 'Boots'. Each pair of lines, 3 + 2, forms a metrical unit of 5 beats,

```
B     o²  B      o²    B     (o²)
Ci ties and Thrones ⇒ and Powers ⇒
/  x   x   /     (x) x   /    (x x)
```

```
B    o²     B   (o²)
Stand in Time's eye, ⇒
/     x   x   /  (x x)
```

```
B    o²  B     o²  B      (o)
Al most as long ⇒ as flowers, ⇒
/  x   x   /  (x)x  /      (x)
```

```
o     B     o²  B  (o²)
Which dai   ly die ⇒
x      /  (x) x  /  (xx)
```

A falling triple rhythm does not, therefore, necessarily 'thump'. Its rhythmic movement depends upon how the beats are distributed within and across the lines of the verse, and equally upon the subject matter, which prepares a particular mood for the reading.

14.5 Verse and music – Edith Sitwell's *Façade*

The poet Edith Sitwell (1887–1964) published a set of poems called *Façade*, some of which were set to music for speaker and small orchestra by William Walton in 1922. The first performance caused a public scandal, with one headline reporting 'DRIVEL THEY PAID TO HEAR', but the piece has since become a popular favourite with audiences.

Edith Sitwell wrote this about the poems of *Façade*:

> The poems in *Façade* are *abstract poems* – that is they are patterns in sound. They are, too, in many cases, virtuoso exercises in technique of an extreme difficulty, in the same sense as that in which certain studies by Liszt are studies in transcendental technique in music.
>
> My experiments in *Façade* consist of enquiries into the effect on rhythm and speed of the use of rhymes, assonances, and dissonances, placed at the beginning and in the middle of lines, as well as at the end, and in most elaborate patterns.
>
> (from 'Some Notes on my own Poetry' by Edith Sitwell)

Here for example are the opening lines of a poem from *Façade* called 'Waltz'. A waltz is a dance in triple time, so you count a regular 1 2 3, 1 2 3, 1 2 3 as the basic rhythm.

Activity 14.8

(i) Can you fit the lines of the poem to a regular waltz rhythm?

(ii) Identify the rhymes and assonances.

'Waltz'

Daisy and Lily,
Lazy and silly,
Walk by the shore of the wan grassy sea, –
Talking once more 'neath a swan-bosomed tree.
Rose castles,
Tourelles*,
Those bustles
Where swells
Each foam-bell of ermine,
They roam and determine
What fashions have been and what fashions will be, –

* *tourelle* derives from an OF word meaning *turret*, a diminutive of *tour* (*tower*)

14.5.1 The words set to music

14.5.1.1 'WALTZ'

The composer William Walton set the words so that the performing speaker declaims in this waltz rhythm,

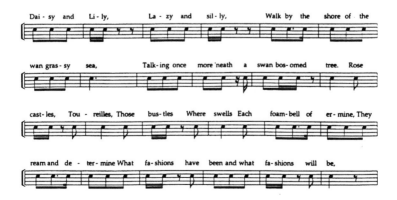

The rhymes and assonances are marked in the following diagram:

Rhymes and assonances

Daisy and Lily,   Daisy – lazy
⇑   ⇑   ⇑   Lily – silly
Lazy and silly,

Walk by the shore of the   wan grassy   sea, –   walk – talk(ing); shore – more; wan – swan; sea – tree
⇑   ⇑   ⇑   ⇑   walk – shore; talk(ing) – more (*assonance*)
Talking once more 'neath a swan-bosomed tree.

Rose castles,   Rose – those; (tour)elles – swells
⇑   ⇑   Tour elles,   castles – bustles (*consonance*)
Those bustles   ⇑
             Where swells

Each   foam-bell of ermine,   foam – roam; ermine – (de)termine
         ⇑   ⇑
They   roam and de termine

What fashions have been and what fashions will be,   been – be (*assonance*)

14.5.1.2 'FOX TROT'

A foxtrot was a ballroom dance popular from the 1920s onwards in a quick four-in-a-bar tempo and, like music derived from jazz, the tune is syncopated over the ground beat. Here is the beginning of Edith Sitwell's poem, whose rhythm fits the pattern of a foxtrot, and the rhythm of the musical setting by William Walton:

'Fox Trot'

         OLD
           Sir
             Faulk,
Tall as a stork,
Before the honeyed fruits of dawn were ripe, would walk,
And stalk with a gun
The reynard-coloured sun,
Among the pheasant-feathered corn the unicorn has torn,
        forlorn the
Smock-faced sheep
Sit
   And
      Sleep;
Periwigged as William and Mary, weep . . .

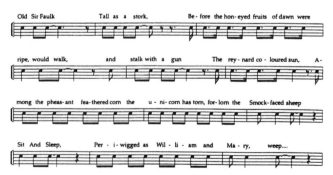

Activity 14.9

Read the poem 'Fox Trot' and Edith Sitwell's notes printed below. Can you identify and follow her technical description of the rhythm and sound patterns?

Edith Sitwell on 'Fox Trot' (from 'Some Notes on my own Poetry')

'Fox Trot' is an experiment in the effect, on rhythm and on speed, of certain arrangements of assonances and dissonance, and of a certain arrangement of intertwining one-syllabled, two-syllabled, and three-syllabled words.

The ground rhythm of the beginning of this poem is partly the result of the drone sounds in the first lines, the dissonances, so subtle, they might almost be assonances, of 'Faulk', 'tall', 'stork', 'before', 'walk' – each having a different depth of darkness ('tall' and the second syllable of 'before', for instance), while the sounds differ (though with an almost incredible faintness both in darkness and in length), dip much deeper in both cases than 'Faulk' or 'stork', while the sound of 'stork' is slightly darker than 'Faulk'. All these drone sounds seem pleasant country shadows, varying slightly in depth, in warmth, in length. In the fifth and seventh lines, the words 'honeyed' and 'reynard' are a little rounder than 'pheasant-feathered' and each casts a little dipping, reversed shadow, because the light fleeting character of the second syllable of 'honeyed' suddenly grows dark in its dissonance, the second syllable of 'reynard', while the first syllable 'honeyed' is a faintly darker dissonance of the 'rey' of 'reynard'. The shadows, therefore, fall in opposite directions.

The fact that in the line:

the reynard-coloured sun

the words ending in 'd' are placed so close together, makes, in this particular case, a slight leap into the air, while, some lines farther on, the three-syllabled words of:

Periwigged as William and Mary, weep...

twirl round on themselves;

* I understand Edith Sitwell to use 'dissonance' to mean the effect produced by vowels which are different from each other.

I have included part of Edith Sitwell's notes to show that some poets take great care over the sound of their verse, and may make distinctions which are difficult for others to hear. Do you find that the 'dissonances' *Faulk, tall, stork, before* and *walk* are different? They would all be transcribed broadly as having the same vowel [ɔː] in RP, though a phonetician would be able to identify differences of length and quality, which will depend upon the preceding and following sounds. Edith Sitwell describes these differences in metaphorical terms – *dark, depth, warmth* as well as *length.*

14.6 Games with words – 'concrete poetry'

In section 1.3, we looked at some of Raymond Queneau's *Exercises in Style*, which were described as *games with language.* We could use the same phrase to label a kind of verse which came to be known in the 1960s as 'concrete poetry'. Writers exploited what a poem looked like on the page, using the typography of print in an unusual way, sometimes creating visual shapes in words. Some of the poems of the Scottish poet Edwin Morgan (b. 1920) fall into this category.

The word *buzzing* is pronounced *bizzin* in Scots. The Scots word *byke* or *bike*, which has not survived in Standard English, means *beehive*. It was recorded in writing as early as *c.* 1300, for example in the long poem *Cursor Mundi*, *Suetter on hony o bike – Sweeter than honey from the hive*. Edwin Morgan uses these two words, with *busy*, *bloody* and *bees*, to create the poem called 'Bees' Nest'. A single syllable ⟨o⟩ is added to *byke* to make it a two-syllable word and maintain the steady falling duple rhythm. Each word begins with [b] and contains three voiced [z] consonants which roughly imitate the sound of bees, so we have both **alliteration** and **onomatopeia** (when words imitate the sound of the thing or action that they signify).

busybykeobloodybizzinbees
bloodybusybykeobizzinbees
bizzinbloodybykeobusybees
busybloodybykeobizzinbees
bloodybykeobusybizzinbees
bizzinbykeobusybloodybees
busybykeobizzinbloodybees
bloodybykeobizzinbusybees
bizzinbusybykeobloodybees
busybizzinbykeobloodybees
bloodybizzinbykeobusybees
bizzinbusybloodybykeobees

Activity 14.10

Read the poem aloud in a regular rhythm, making bees a long syllable,

| / | x | / | x | / | x | / | x | / | ⇒⇒ |
| bu | sy | byke | o | blood | y | biz | zin | bees | |

IPA bɪ zi baɪ ko blʌ di bɪ zɪn biːz ⇒ etc.

Is it genuinely onomatopeic?

Activity 14.11

Can you explain the title and shape of the following two poems?

SIESTA OF A HUNGARIAN SNAKE

s sz sz SZ sz SZ sz ZS zs ZS zs zs z

```
                    MESSAGE  CLEAR
        am              i
                                    if
    i am                        he
        he r        o
        h     ur   t
        the re              and
        he     re      and
        he re
      a               n    d
        the r                   e
    i am     r                      ife
                    i  n
                s       ion and
    i                       d    i e
      am  e  res   ect
      am  e  res   ection
                        o           f
          the                      life
                        o           f
        m   e           n
            sur e
          the                 d    i e
    i         s
              s   e t    and
    i am the   sur        d
      a   t   res    t
                        o       life
    i am he r                      e
    i a           c t
    i         r  u      n
    i  m   e  e     t
    i             t       i  e
    i         s   t    and
    i am th          o     th
    i am   r         a
    i am the  su     n
    i am the  s      on
    i am the  e  rect on      e  if
    i am     re      n     t
    i am       s      a         fe
    i am       s   e  n    t
    i    he e              d
    i    te  s    t
    i        re          a  d
      a  th re           a  d
      a         s   t on      e
      a   t  re          a  d
      a   th r     on         e
    i          resurrect
                          a       life
    i am              i  n       life
    i am     resurrection
    i am the resurrection and
    i am
    i am the resurrection and the life
```

14.6.1 *Commentary*

'Siesta of a Hungarian Snake' uses the fact that the digraph ⟨sz⟩ resembles the spelling *zzz*, which we use to represent the sound of someone snoring, and that ⟨sz⟩, unlike other European languages, occurs frequently in Hungarian writing. Hence the title word *siesta* – an afternoon nap. The typography of the letters produces a long snake-like line, and ⟨sz⟩ is reversed to ⟨zs⟩ in the second half of the line.

The second poem uses only the letters of the final line, *I am the resurrection and the life*, to create the poem's text, by omitting the unwanted letters in each line, but keeping the spaces to create the unique patterning that is produced.

If we write the separate lines as words and phrases, we have the following list,

am I	Sion and	I am the surd	I am the Son	I resurrect
if	I die	at rest	I am the erect one if	a life
I am he	a mere sect	O life	I am rent	I am in life
hero	a mere section	I am here	I am safe	I am resurrection
hurt	of	I act	I am sent	I am the resurrection and
there and	the life	I run	I heed	I am
here and	of	I meet	I test	**I am the resurrection and the life**
here	men	I tie	I read	
and	sure	I stand	a thread	
there	the die	I am Thoth	a stone	
I am rife	is	I am Ra	a tread	
in	set and	I am the sun	a throne	

and we can turn this into a coherent message by adding punctuation,

Am I? If I am he, hero, hurt, there and here and here and there. I am rife in Sion and I die a mere sect, a mere section of the life of men. Sure the die is set and I am the surd at rest. O life! I am here. I act, I run, I meet, I tie, I stand. I am Thoth. I am Ra. I am the sun. I am the Son. I am the erect one. If I am rent, I am safe. I am sent, I heed, I test, I read. A thread, a stone, a tread, a throne. I resurrect a life. I am in life. I am resurrection. I am the resurrection and I am. I am the resurrection and the life.

This way of making a serious statement by 'playing a game with words' is rather different from the established ways of writing poetry and 'making a personal response' to it when we read it.

Another poem by Edwin Morgan based on a similar principle is called 'Seven Headlines'. The headlines which are produced, if printed in conventional form, are,

```
OLD SOLEMN ODE SOLD FOR FENDER IRON
BOLD TREND IN LETTER TO SOLO READER
ARSON IN BOLT FROM BLUE
ABSENT FOOD BUD FOUND
UTTER FERMENT IN REASON
TEAM FEED AT MODERN LODE
NO FETTER FOR ABSOLUTE MODERN MEN
```

and the final line, from which all the letters are taken in order, is the French sentence *il faut être absolument moderne* – 'one has to be absolutely modern'.

Activity 14.12

Can you recreate Edwin Morgan's poem?

📖 This Activity is discussed in the *Commentary & Data Book*.

14.7 Six poems

Activity 14.13

Discuss the differences of technique — rhythm, metre and sound patterns — used in the following six contrasting poems.

📖 This Activity is discussed in the *Commentary & Data Book*.

A

'O where are you going?' said reader to rider,
'That valley is fatal when furnaces burn,
Yonder's the midden whose odours will madden,
That gap is the grave where the tall return.'
'O do you imagine,' said fearer to farer,
'That dusk will delay on your path to the pass,
Your diligent looking discover the lacking
Your footsteps feel from granite to grass?'

(W. H. Auden (1907–73), from 'O Where are you Going?')

B

Let God arise, and let his enemies be scattered:
let them also that hate him flee before him.
Like as the smoke vanisheth, so shalt thou drive them away:
and like as wax melteth at the fire, so let the ungodly perish at the presence of God.
But let the righteous be glad and rejoice before God:
let them also be merry and joyful.

(Psalm 68, from the Book of Common Prayer, 1662)

C

The fair breeze blew, the white foam flew,
The furrow followed free;
We were the first that ever burst
Into that silent sea.

Down dropt the breeze, the sails dropt down,
'Twas sad as sad could be;
And we did speak only to break
The silence of the sea!

(Samuel Taylor Coleridge (1772–1834), from 'The Rime of the Ancient Mariner')

D

Summer Haiku

P o o l.
P e o p l
e   p l o p!
C o o l.

(Edwin Morgan (b. 1920))

E

Between Walls

the back wings
of the

hospital where
nothing

will grow lie
cinders

in which shine
the broken

pieces of a green
bottle

(William Carlos Williams (1883-1962))

F

Jailbird

His plumage is dun,
Talons long but blunt.
His appetite is indiscriminate.
He has no mate and sleeps alone
In a high nest built of brick and steel.
He sings at night
A long song, sad and silent.
He cannot fly.

(Vernon Scannell (b. 1922))

15. Poetic prose

Prose and verse

Some of the ways in which patterns of sound in language are created have been described in chapters 12, 13 and 14, 'Rhyme, rhythm and sound'. You will find these patterns not only in verse and poetry, but also in everyday uses of language. They are exploited in advertising, for example, and in public speaking, perhaps especially in political oratory. If we focus on writing that is considered to be **literary**, we will often find patterning in the language of **prose.**

The novelist and critic Anthony Burgess, discussing the writings of James Joyce, suggested a useful distinction between two kinds of novel. First, those in which the language is 'transparent'. For example, when you read George Orwell's *Animal Farm*, you are aware of a prose style which has been variously described as *vigorous, clear, concise,* and *unpretentious*, but which does not vary or perceptibly change and develop within the novel. Second, those novels whose language draws attention to itself, in which we are aware of the language as part of the meaning, apart from plot, character, theme, setting and so on. The definition of the second kind of novel has particular relevance to James Joyce, but applies equally to the novels of Charles Dickens. Reading any Dickens novel, you find his style changing with the scene he is describing and the feelings he is expressing, so that we have to speak of Dickens's *styles*, in the plural.

15.1 Poetry and rhetoric in The Old Curiosity Shop – 'The death of Little Nell'

15.1.1 Why little Nell?

A famous scene from chapter 51 in *The Old Curiosity Shop* (1841) portrays the death of Little Nell, the idealised heroine of the story. The adjective *little* had important connotations for Dickens, who uses the word frequently to describe other characters like, for example, Ruth Pinch in *Martin Chuzzlewit* and Paul Dombey in *Dombey and Son*. If you were asked to name another word with the same meaning as *little*, you would probably say *small*, but the two words are not interchangeable. What is your reaction to a heroine called *Small Nell*?

Dickens himself comments indirectly on this question in a paragraph from *The Old Curiosity Shop* describing 'Little Bethel', an often used name for a nonconformist chapel:

> It was not badly named in one respect, being in truth a particularly little Bethel – a Bethel of the smallest dimensions – with a small number of small pews, and a small pulpit, in which a small gentleman (by trade a Shoemaker, and by calling a Divine) was delivering in a by no means small voice, a by no means small sermon, judging of its dimensions by the condition of his audience, which, if their gross amount were but small, comprised a still smaller number of hearers, as the majority were slumbering.

If we substitute *little* for *small*, the text reads differently:

> It was not badly named in one respect, being in truth a particularly **little** Bethel – a Bethel of the **littlest** dimensions – with a **little** number of **little** pews, and a **little** pulpit, in which a **little** gentleman (by trade a Shoemaker, and by calling a Divine) was delivering in a by no means **little** voice, a by no means **little** sermon, judging of its dimensions by the condition of his audience, which, if their gross amount were but **little**, comprised a still **littler** number of hearers, as the majority were slumbering.

Activity 15.1

Comment on the stylistic effect of the changes.

Activity 15.2

(i) Read the following short extracts describing the character Ruth Pinch in *Martin Chuzzlewit*. Substitute *small* for *little* and discuss any differences in meaning or effect.

(ii) Do any other words used to describe the character produce similar effects?

[Ruth Pinch – 'a blooming little busy creature']

Well! she was a cheerful little thing; and had a quaint, bright quietness about her that was infinitely pleasant. Surely she was the best sauce for chops that was ever invented....
Pleasant little Ruth! Cheerful, tidy, bustling, quiet little Ruth! No doll's house ever yielded greater delight to its young mistress, than little Ruth derived from her glorious dominion over the triangular parlour and the two small bedrooms.
Oh, heaven, what a wicked little stomacher!... and she had a little ring to pull off her finger, which wouldn't come off (foolish little ring!)...
Such a busy little woman as she was!...(she) burst out heartily into such a charming little laugh of triumph...
...still laughing merrily,...that brave little sister...hovering lightly about and about him...in the light of her quaint, little, old-fashioned tidiness...
So light was the touch of the coy little hand, that he glanced down to assure himself he had it on his arm.

Attitudes and responses to characters like little Ruth Pinch and Little Nell have changed since Dickens's time. The scene of the death of Little Nell was very popular and emotionally convincing to Dickens's readers. His intention was to evoke pity and sadness, a quality which is called **pathos**, but successive generations of readers react differently to pathos, and many would now call the writing **sentimental** in a *pejorative* sense, that is, a word that *belittles*, *disparages* or *depreciates*. The word **bathos**, 'the descent from the sublime to the ridiculous' might be applied. But whatever your personal reaction to it may be, we can study its language objectively.

Activity 15.3

Read the following extract that describes the scene after Little Nell's death, and listen especially to the rhythm and movement of the language – it is best to read it aloud, but you must at least 'hear' it in your mind if you read silently. What do you notice?

For she was dead. There, upon her little bed, she lay at rest. The solemn stillness was no marvel now.

She was dead. No sleep so beautiful and calm, so free from trace of pain, so fair to look upon. She seemed a creature fresh from the hand of God, and waiting for the breath of life; not one who had lived and suffered death.

Her couch was dressed with here and there some winter berries and green leaves, gathered in a spot she had been used to favour. 'When I die, put me near something that has loved the light, and had the sky above it always.' Those were her words.

She was dead. Dear, gentle, patient, noble Nell, was dead. Her little bird – a poor slight thing the pressure of a finger would have crushed – was stirring nimbly in its cage; and the strong heart of its child-mistress was mute and motionless for ever.

Where were the traces of her early cares, her sufferings, and fatigues? All gone. Sorrow was dead indeed in her, but peace and perfect happiness were born; imaged in her tranquil beauty and profound repose.

And still her former self lay there, unaltered in this change. Yes. The old fireside had smiled upon that same sweet face; it had passed like a dream through haunts of misery and care; at the door of the poor schoolmaster on the summer evening, before the furnace fire upon the cold wet night, at the still bedside of the dying boy, there had been the same mild lovely look. So shall we know the angels in their majesty, after death.

The old man held one languid arm in his, and had the small hand folded to his breast, for warmth. It was the hand she had stretched out to him with her last smile – the hand that had led him on through all their wanderings. Ever and anon he pressed it to his lips; then hugged it to his breast again, murmuring that it was warmer now; and as he said it he looked, in agony, to those who stood around, as if imploring them to help her.

She was dead and past all help, or need of it. The ancient rooms she had seemed to fill with life, even while her own was waning fast – the garden she had tended – the eyes she had gladdened – the noiseless haunts of many a thoughtful hour – the paths she had trodden as it were but yesterday – could know her no more.

'It is not,' said the schoolmaster, as he bent down to kiss her on the cheek, and gave his tears free vent, 'it is not on earth that Heaven's justice ends. Think what it is compared with the World to which her young spirit has winged its early flight, and say, if one deliberate wish expressed in solemn terms above this bed could call her back to life, which of us would utter it!'

Readability – very easy.

15.1.2 *Verse rhythms in prose*

It has often been pointed out in the literary studies of Dickens's novels that one of his styles, expressing tragic or pathetic feeling, tends to fall into the rhythms of verse, and the scene of the death of Little Nell illustrates this very clearly.

We usually read a story without conscious attention to the sound of the language, but the extract portraying the death of Little Nell is different. Writing which has alternating stressed and unstressed syllables may come to sound like the regular beats and off-beats of metrical verse. If this regularity falls into grammatical units which contain three, four or five stressed syllables, then we have units which correspond to lines of verse. Much of the extract can be written in the form of verse. For example, after the first sentence *For she was dead*, which recurs several times, the next two form a perfect pair of lines of 'blank verse', or **iambic pentameters** – 5-stress rising duple verse:

5-stress lines – o B o B o B o B o B (o B)
Upon her little bed she lay at rest.
The solemn stillness was no marvel now.

Line 6 of the extract forms a pair of 4-stress lines of verse,

4-stress lines – o B o B o B o B
Her couch was dressed with here and there,
Some winter berries and green leaves.

and part of lines 3 and 4 a pair of 3-stress lines,

3-stress lines – o B o B o B (o B)
So free from trace of pain,
So fair to look upon.

If you are reading poetry in metrical form, then you look for an underlying rhythmic pattern into which you fit the words in ways which you would not necessarily do if you were reading prose. So, once you feel that the episode is charged with such emotion that its rhythmic quality is 'heightened', then you will find many more lines of verse in it. For example, the eleven syllables of *She seemed a creature fresh from the hand of God* can easily be accommodated to a 5-stress verse line,

She **seemed** a **crea** ture **fresh** from the **hand** of **God**
o   B   o B   o   B o^2 B   o B

in which you read *from the* as a double off-beat, like a single syllable.

The first sentence of the paragraph beginning on line 15 falls into 'ballad metre', a 14-syllable line divided into 8 and 6 syllables, 4 and 3 beats,

And **still** her **former self** lay **there,**   o B o B o B o B
Unaltered in this **change.**   o B o B o B

Much of the extract falls into a rising duple rhythm – x/ – from off-beat to beat, in which unstressed and stressed syllables alternate, and so can easily be read as if it were verse. Where this regularity does not occur, it is often easy to fit the words in ways that are quite usual in verse writing. For example, *Sorrow was dead indeed in her* has the rhythm: /xx/x/. You can describe the rhythm of *Sorrow* as 'inverted' from the expected x/; or you could say that the line begins with a 'silent off-beat', with a double off-beat following the first beat:

```
Sor row was dead in deed in her
ô B      o²  B  o B  o B
```

This pattern at the beginning of a line is very common in English verse:

```
Join ing them selves in fa tal har mo ny        (Marvell)
ô B      o²    B   o B o B  o  B
```

```
Holl low of cheek as though it drank the wind   (Yeats)
ô B     o² B    o B     o B    o  B
```

The clause *as he bent down to kiss her on the cheek* spoken normally would not sound verse-like,

```
|as he 'bent down to 'kiss her on the 'cheek|
```

but with an underlying rhythm in mind, we could turn it into an acceptable line,

```
As he bent  down to kiss her on the cheek
o²  B  ôB   o  B  o  B  o  B
```

beginning with a double off-beat, and with a silent beat between *bent* and *down*, which means that we lengthen the word *bent* when speaking, to maintain the metre of the line.

Most of the text can in fact be pressed into verse form, and though it does not become a poem, it may clearly be called **poetic prose**, with the rhythms of metrical verse.

15.1.3 Prose or verse?

In the transcription of the first three paragraphs of the extract following, units that sound like lines of verse are printed in ***bold italics***, with the figure for the number of beats or stressed syllables on the right. The convention of starting a printed line of verse with a capital letter has also been adopted. Parts of the text which show the rhetorical feature of **parallelism** are bracketed [ ].

For

[*she was dead.*]

There,
Upon her little bed she lay at rest.   5
The solemn stillness was no marvel now   5

[*She was dead.*]

No sleep

[*So beautiful and calm*   3]
[*So free from trace of pain* 3]
[*So fair to look upon*   3]

She seemed a creature fresh from the hand of God	5
And waiting for the breath of life,	4
Not one who had lived and suffered death.	4
Her couch was dressed with here and there,	4
Some winter berries and green leaves.	4
gathered in a spot she had been used to favour.	
'When I die,	2
Put me near something that has loved the light,	5
And had the sky above it always.'	4
Those were her words.	2

Activity 15.4

(i) Write the rest of the text marking any lines that seem to you to fall into the metre of verse. Say how many stresses (beats) each line has, and state their rhythm in terms of beats and off-beats.

(ii) Mark any parallelism in the text.

📖 The activity is set out in the *Commentary & Data Book*.

Activity 15.5

Read the following short extracts from the same chapter of *The Old Curiosity Shop*.

(i) Can you turn them, or parts of them, into verse lines?

(ii) Identify the metres and write them as verse.

   (i)   'Why dost thou lie so idle there, dear Nell,' he murmured, 'when there are bright red berries out of doors waiting for thee to pluck them!

  (ii) 'Her little homely dress – her favourite!' cried the old man...

 (iii) ...but yet she had my hand in hers, and seemed to lead me still.'

 (iv) 'I will hear any voice she liked to hear,' cried the old man.

  (v) 'I should be glad to see her eyes again, and to see her smile. There is a smile upon her young face now, but it is fixed and changeless. I would have had it come and go.'

 (vi) 'To be to you what you were once to him,' cried the younger, falling on his knee before him;...'

(vii) 'to call to witness his unchanging truth and mindfulness of bygone days, whole years of desolation.'

(viii) 'And even,' he added in an altered voice, 'even if what I dread to name has come to pass – even if that be so, or is to be (which heaven forbid and spare us!) – still, dear brother, we are not apart, and have that comfort in our great affliction.'

15.1.4 *The vocabulary*

A short text like this extract from *The Old Curiosity Shop* cannot provide results which are 'statistically significant', but a look at the choice of words may provide one of the clues towards an understanding of its style. There are 256 word 'types' in the text out of a total word count of 499 'tokens', a number of them occurring several times, especially function words like *the, and, of*. They are distributed as follows (the percentage figures are approximations):

Early vocabulary: OE 179 (**70%**); ON 10 (**4%**); OF 25 (10%); ME and ME *f*. French 29 (11.3%): 243 words (*c*. 95%)

Later vocabulary: French 9 (3.5%); Latin 4 (1.5%): 13 words (*c*. 5%)

1 syllable		*2 syllables*		*3 syllables*		*4 syllables*	
174 words =	68%	67 words =	26%	14 words =	5.5%	1 word =	0.4%
OE 140 55%		OE 35	13.7%	OE 4	1.6%	Latin 1	0.4%
ME/ME f. Fr 18	7%	OF 16	6.2%	OF 4	1.6%		
ON 9	3.5%	ME/ME f. Fr 10	3.9%	Fr 3	1.2%		
OF 5	2%	Fr 4	1.6%	Latin 2	0.8%		
Fr 2	0.8%	ON 1	0.4%	ME f. Fr 1	0.4%		
Latin 0		Latin 1	0.4%	ON 0			

📖 A complete list of the words by derivation is in the *Commentary & Data Book*.

The use of core vocabulary words that are mostly short and familiar affects the style of a piece of writing, not only in the way it may fall relatively easily into a regular rhythmic pattern, but in the directness of its meaning. About 95% of the vocabulary has been in the language for more than 500 years. The words that you might decide are not in 'everyday' use – e.g. *vent, languid, agony, fatigues, tranquil* – are all relatively late adoptions, and the phrase *ever and anon* is now archaic, though the words are simple enough.

But vocabulary is only one aspect of the style of a text. Whether it is simple to read and understand, or complex, depends equally upon its grammatical structure.

15.1.5   *Structure, rhetoric and style*

Activity 15.6

Examine the structure of the text (or a paragraph or two).

(i) Look at the length of the sentences, the number of subordinate clauses and what sorts of clauses they are.

(ii) Describe the examples of **parallelism** — sequences which repeat the same grammatical structure but with different vocabulary.

📖 A complete analysis of the structure is in the *Commentary & Data Book*.

15.1.5.1   GRAMMATICAL STRUCTURE

The scene of the death of Little Nell is told using relatively simple grammar as well as mostly core vocabulary. Just over half the clauses are main clauses. Of these, ten are simple sentences, like,

- [She was dead].
- [The solemn stillness was no marvel now].
- [All gone].
- [So shall we know the angels in their majesty, after death].

Most subordinate clauses are relative or nonfinite clauses qualifying noun phrases, for example,

- not one[***RelCl*** who had lived] and [***RelCl*** suffered death].
- a poor slight thing [***RelCl*Ø** the pressure of a finger would have crushed]
- [he looked, in agony, to those [***RelCl*** who stood around,]
- [peace and perfect happiness were born; [***NonfCl*** imaged in her tranquil beauty and profound repose.]]

15.1.5.2 RHETORIC – PARALLELISM
Complexity is found only in the rhetorical sequences of **parallelism**, which consist of repetitions of a similar structure in sequence:

so + *adj*	
so beautiful	and calm
so free	from trace of pain
so fair	to look upon

Adverbial ***preposition***	*complement*
at	the door of the poor schoolmaster on the summer evening,
before	the furnace fire upon the cold wet night,
at	the still bedside of the dying boy,

It was		
	NP	*relative clause*
	the hand	she had stretched out to him with her last smile,
	the hand	that had led him on through all their wanderings.

noun phrase	*qualifying relative clause or prepositonal phrase*
The ancient rooms	she had seemed to fill with life, even while her own was waning fast
the garden	she had tended
the eyes	she had gladdened
the noiseless haunts	of many a thoughtful hour
the paths	she had trodden as it were but yesterday

It contrasts with another style that Dickens frequently used, and which has been called **mock-elevated**.

15.2 Mock-elevated style in *Pickwick Papers*

'Elevated style' belongs to literary works marked by vocabulary and grammar reserved for serious or epic subjects, but if such a style is used for vulgar, common objects or stories, then it is a 'mock' style – the style does not suit the sense or the topic. The **connotation** or **association** of words and structures to their normal function is important, and words and structures usually associated with serious subjects seem out of place, sometimes pretentious, sometimes comic.

Here is a paragraph from *Pickwick Papers*, chapter 20, in a style very different from that of 'the death of Little Nell'. Dickens is describing a pub, the Magpie and Stump, where a minor character called Lowten and his friends go every evening.

The Magpie and Stump

This favoured tavern, sacred to the evening orgies of Mr Lowten and his companions, was what ordinary people would designate a public-house. That the landlord was a man of a money-making turn, was sufficiently testified by the fact of a small bulk-head beneath the tap-room window, in size and shape not unlike a sedan-chair, being underlet to a mender of shoes: and that he was a being of a philanthropic mind, was evident from the protection he afforded to a pieman, who vended his delicacies without fear of interruption on the very door-step. In the lower windows, which were decorated with curtains of a saffron hue, dangled two or three printed cards, bearing reference to Devonshire cyder and Dantzic spruce*, while a large black board, announcing in white letters to an enlightened public that there were 500,000 barrels of double stout in the cellars of the establishment, left the mind in a state of not unpleasing doubt and uncertainty as to the precise direction in the bowels of the earth, in which this mighty cavern might be supposed to extend. When we add, that the weather-beaten sign-board bore the half-obliterated semblance of a magpie intently eyeing a crooked streak of brown paint, which the neighbours had been taught from infancy to consider as the 'stump', we have said all that need be said of the exterior of the edifice.

Dantzic spruce – a variety of beer

Readability – very difficult.

Activity 15.7

Identify the features of Dickens's mock-elevated style by discussing the vocabulary and grammar in some detail. Look especially at the following words and phrases, and rewrite them in 'ordinary English'. What difference does this make to the style?

Separate core vocabulary from non-core vocabulary (lexical words).

favoured tavern	bearing reference to
sacred to the evening orgies	an enlightened public
companions	barrels of double stout
designate a public-house	cellars of the establishment
money-making turn	left the mind in a state of not unpleasing doubt and uncertainty
sufficiently testified	precise direction in the bowels of the earth
not unlike a sedan-chair	mighty cavern
mender of shoes	might be supposed to extend
a being of a philanthropic mind	half-obliterated semblance
evident from the protestion he afforded	intently eyeing
vended his delicacies	neighbours
decorated with curtains of a saffron hue	taught from infancy
dangled	the exterior of the edifice

The following paragraph is a paraphrase of Dickens's text. The 'literal' meaning is similar to that of the original – they both say 'the same thing', but only in a restricted sense. The real meaning of Dickens's original lies in its detached, ironic use of language. The vocabulary and grammatical structures he uses are usually associated with serious subjects, and the whole point is missed if you are not aware of this mismatch between 'form' and 'content' when reading.

Mr Lowten and his friends spent their evenings drinking in their favourite pub, the Magpie and Stump. The landlord added to his income by letting out a tiny compartment under the tap-room window to a cobbler, and kindly allowed a pieman to sell his pies freely on the doorstep. Two or three printed cards advertising Devonshire cyder and Dantzic spruce hung in the lower windows, which had yellow curtains, and the notice '500,000 barrels of double stout in the cellars', written on a large black board, left you wondering whereabouts such large cellars might be. The weather-beaten sign-board had a worn-out picture of a magpie looking at a crooked streak of brown paint, which the neighbours all assumed to be the 'stump'. And that is all that need be said about the outside of the building.

15.2.1 Commentary

15.2.1.1 VOCABULARY

In contrast to the description of the death of Little Nell, in which most of the words belong to the core vocabulary of English and derive from Old English, the vocabulary of the *Pickwick Papers* paragraph shows a clear difference. Of 94 lexical words, 28% are from OE, 40% from ME and 32% came into the language after 1480. Much of this 32% is non-core vocabulary, like *establishment, obliterated, philanthropic*.

📖 A complete list of the derivation of the words is in the *Commentary & Data Book*.

15.2.1.2 GRAMMATICAL STRUCTURE

The structure is also in contrast with that of the first text from *The Old Curiosity Shop*. It is much more complex. There are only six main clauses, but each contains a number of embedded subordinate clauses. It is also complex at the level of the phrase. For example the first sentence has a simple underlying structure, *X was Y*, but the subject has a complex qualifying AdjP, and the complement is a rank-shifted clause:

> *MCl 1*   *S[NCl* This favoured tavern, *q* (sacred to the evening orgies of Mr Lowten and his companions),
> *P* was
> *C [NCl* what ordinary people would designate a public-house.]

There are no simple sentences, and this formality of both structure and vocabulary produces a comic effect – language and subject do not match.

📖 A complete structural analysis is in the *Commentary & Data Book.*

15.3 Satire in *Dombey and Son*

Activity 15.8

Here is a sentence from Charles Dickens's *Dombey and Son* in which he is satirising popular evangelical religion.

(i) List any words which you judge not to belong to the core vocabulary of English. Look up their derivations in a dictionary.

(ii) Comment on the grammatical structure of the sentence; is it simple or complex?

(iii) Which style does it resemble – that of 'the death of Little Nell' or 'the Magpie and Stump'? What is your evidence?

📖 The derivations of the lexical words and a structural analysis are in the *Commentary & Data Book.*

The Reverend Melchisedech Howler

It was not unpleasant to remember, on the way thither, that Mrs MacStinger resorted to a great distance every Sunday morning, to attend the ministry of the Reverend Melchisedech Howler, who, having been one day discharged from the West India Docks on a false suspicion (got up expressly against him by the general enemy) of screwing gimlets into puncheons, and applying his lips to the orifice, had announced the destruction of the world for that day two years, at ten in the morning, and opened a front parlour for the reception of ladies and gentlemen of the Ranting persuasion, upon whom, on the first occasion of their assemblage, the admonitions of the Reverend Melchisedech had produced so powerful an effect, that, in their rapturous performance of a sacred jig, which closed the service, the whole flock broke through into a kitchen below, and disabled a mangle belonging to one of the fold.

Readability – fairly easy.

15.4 Poetry and rhetoric in *The Rainbow*

This is the extract from D. H. Lawrence's novel *The Rainbow* (1915) quoted by the literary critic F. R. Leavis – 'Words here are used in the way, not of eloquence, but of creative poetry' (see chapter 1, section 1.2.1).

Activity 15.9 _____

(i) Can you identify the 'creative poetry' in the extract?

(ii) Do you agree that the extract is not 'eloquent'?

(A dictionary definition of eloquence is, 'fluent and effective use of language; rhetoric'.)

The Brangwens had lived for generations on the Marsh Farm, in the meadows where the Erewash twisted sluggishly through alder trees, separating Derbyshire from Nottinghamshire. . . .

So the Brangwens came and went without fear of necessity, working hard because of the life that was in them, not for want of the money. Neither were they thriftless. They were aware of the last halfpenny, and instinct made them not waste the peeling of their apple, for it would help to feed the cattle. But heaven and earth was teeming around them, and how should this cease? They felt the rush of the sap in spring, they knew the wave which cannot halt, but every year throws forward the seed to begetting, and, falling back leaves the young-born on the earth. They knew the intercourse between heaven and earth, sunshine drawn into the breast and bowels, the rain sucked up in the daytime, nakedness that comes under the wind in autumn, showing the birds' nests no longer worth hiding. Their life and interrelations were such; feeling the pulse and body of the soil, that opened to their furrow for the grain, and became smooth and supple after their ploughing, and clung to their feet with a weight that pulled like desire, lying hard and unresponsive, when the crops were to be shorn away. The young corn waved and was silken, and the lustre slid along the limbs of the men who saw it. They took the udder of the cows, the cows yielded milk and pulse against the hands of the men, the pulse of the blood of the teats of the cows beat into the pulse of the hands of the men. They mounted their horses, and held life between the grip of their knees, they harnessed their horses at the wagon, and, with hand on the bridle-rings, drew the heaving of the horses after their will.

In autumn the partridges whirred up, birds in flocks blew like spray across the fallow, rooks appeared on the grey, watery heavens, and flew cawing into the winter. Then the men sat by the fire in the house where the women moved about with surety, and the limbs and the body of the men were impregnated with the day, cattle and earth and vegetation and the sky, the men sat by the fire and their brains were inert, as their blood flowed heavy with the accumulation from the living day.

Readability – fairly easy.

15.4.1 *Is the extract poetic?*

15.4.1.1 RHYTHM, METRE AND SOUND

Metrical rhythm

Like Dickens's description of the 'death of Little Nell' discussed in section 15.1, parts of the extract (though by no means all of it) can be set out in lines which have the rhythms of poetic metre. Much depends on *how* you read the text aloud, but the following lines in this Lawrence text can be scanned as verse. The stressed syllables (beats) are in bold type and the number of stresses in each line is marked:

But **heaven** and **earth** was **teeming around** them,	4
And **how** should this **cease**?	2
They **felt** the **rush** of the **sap** in **spring**,	4
They **knew** the **wave** which **cannot halt**,	4
But every **year** throws **forward** the **seed** to **begetting**,	5
And, **falling** back **leaves** the **young**-born **on** the **earth**.	5
And **clung** to their **feet** with a **weight** that **pulled** like **desire**,	5
The **young** corn **waved** and was **silken**,	3
And the **lustre slid** along the **limbs** of the **men** who **saw** it.	6
They **took** the **udder** of the **cows**,	3
The **cows** yielded **milk** and **pulse against** the **hands** of the **men**,	6
The **pulse** of the **blood** of the **teats** of the **cows**	4
Beat into the **pulse** of the **hands** of the **men**.	4
Drew the **heaving** of the **horses** after their **will**.	5

Repetition and parallelism

The rhythm of the extract is like Lawrence's free verse. which has no regular metrical pattern, but a heightened sense of movement, using rhetorical figures like **repetition** and **parallelism** to achieve this, although the syntactic parallels are seldom exact. For example,

They	felt	the rush of the sap	in spring,
they	**knew**	the wave	which cannot halt,...
They	**knew**	the intercourse	between heaven and earth,
		sunshine	drawn into the breast and bowels,
		the rain	sucked up in the daytime,
		nakedness	that comes under the wind in autumn...

They took the udder of the **cows**
the **cows** yielded **milk** and **pulse against** the **hands** of the **men**,
         the **pulse**   of the **blood**   of the **teats**   of the **cows**
beat into   the **pulse**   of the **hands**   of the **men**.
They   mounted their **horses**,   and held life between the grip of their knees,
they   harnessed their **horses** at the wagon, and, with hand on the bridle-rings,
     drew the heaving of the **horses** after their will.

Assonance, alliteration and vowel harmony

We must be careful not to look mechanically for sound patterns, because these will occur at random in any text. There is some **alliteration**,

> They felt the ru[sh] of the [s]ap in [s]pring, ...
> ... sunshine drawn into the [b]reast and [b]owels,
> and became [s]mooth and [s]upple after their ploughing,
> The young corn waved and was [s]ilken, and the lu[s]tre [s]lid along the limbs of the men who [s]aw it.
> They mounted their [h]orses, and [h]eld life between the grip of their knees, they [h]arnessed their [h]orses at the wagon, and, with [h]and on the bridle-rings, drew the [h]eaving of the [h]orses after their will.
> In autumn the partridges whirred up, [b]irds in [f]locks [b]lew like spray across the [f]allow, ...

and examples of **assonance** are,

> But heaven and earth was t[ee]ming around them, and how should this c[ea]se?
> the r[ai]n s[u]cked [u]p in the d[ay]time, n[a]kedness that c[o]mes [u]nder the wind in autumn showing the b[ir]ds' nests no longer w[or]th hiding.
> The y[ou]ng c[or]n waved and was s[i]lken, and the l[u]stre sl[i]d along the l[i]mbs of the men who s[aw] it ...
> They took the [u]dder of the cows,
> the cows yielded milk and p[u]lse against the hands of the men,
> the p[u]lse of the bl[oo]d of the t[ea]ts of the cows
> b[ea]t into the p[u]lse of the hands of the men

15.4.1.2 VOCABULARY – LEXICAL WORDS

The distribution of the lexical words is as follows:

Adjectives: 15 types/tokens, all from OE except *inert* (Latin 1647) and *unresponsive* (French 1668); one or two syllables except *unresponsive* (4)

Adverbs: 7 types, 8 tokens, all from OE, one or two syllables.

Nouns: 73 types, 99 tokens – the repeated nouns are *men* (6), *earth* (4), *pulse* (4), *cows* (3), *horses* (3), *life* (3), *heaven* (2)/*heavens*, *autumn* (2), *birds*/*birds'*, *blood* (2), *body* (2), *cattle* (2), *day* (2), *fire* (2), *hand*/*hands* (2). Most from OE or early ME from OF, except *accumulation*, *instinct*, *intercourse*, *interrelations*, *lustre*, *vegetation*, which include the only words of more than two syllables (apart from compounds or plurals and *nakedness*).

Verbs: 43 types, 48 tokens. The only late word of Latin derivation is *impregnated* (1605), otherwise all the verbs are one or two-syllable words of OE or early OF derivation

A complete list of the lexical vocabulary and derivations is in the *Commentary & Data Book*.

There is a large number of nouns, with the repetition of several which provide a key to the topic of the extract in describing the natural world, and all from the core vocabulary of the language – *men, earth, pulse, cows, horses, life, heaven/heavens, autumn, birds/birds', blood, body, cattle, day, fire, hand/hands.*

15.4.1.3 GRAMMATICAL STRUCTURE

The prose rhythm of the extract builds up in what is mainly a series of main clauses in a **paratactic** sequence (clauses following each other without any linking word, or linked only by coordination). For example,

[*MCI* In autumn the partridges whirred up], [*MCI* birds in flocks blew like spray across the fallow], [*MCI* rooks appeared on the grey, watery heavens], and [*MCI*Ø flew cawing into the winter].

There are only two adverbial clauses, *when the crops*... and *as their blood*.... The other subordinate clauses are either relative or nonfinite clauses which mostly function as reduced relative clauses – that is, qualifying and describing the nouns that mark the natural world Lawrence is portraying, for example,

[*MCI* They felt the rush of the sap in spring], [*MCI* they knew the wave [*RelCl* which cannot halt], but [*RelCl* Ø every year throws forward the seed to begetting], and, [*NonfCl* falling back] [*RelCl* Ø leaves the young-born on the earth]].

📖 A complete lisnear analysis is in the *Commentary & Data Book*.

16. Verse translation

No two translations of a text from a foreign language into English will be identical. This is especially true of poetic texts. Poetry is the most difficult to translate, because so much of its meaning lies in the sound and rhythm of the original language, and the connotations of words may be impossible to reproduce exactly in another language. So translators of poetry may try to be faithful to an original text in different ways, either by translating into prose and concentrating on the meaning, or writing in verse to try to match the poetic values of the original more closely.

16.1 Homer's *Iliad*

Homer's *Iliad* is one of the most famous of all **epic poems**. It was written in Greek in the seventh century BC. There is no certainty about who Homer was, or even if the same man wrote both the *Iliad* and the other 'Homeric' epic, the *Odyssey*, but what is certain is that these poems had a central place in ancient Greek culture, and in Medieval European education through to the nineteenth century. The poem tells the story of fifty days in the ten-year siege of Troy by the Greeks. The warrior Achilles, having quarrelled with King Agamemnon, refused to fight, but the death in battle of his close friend Patroclus roused his anger against the Trojans. He fought and killed the Trojan hero Hector, and the poem ends with the funeral rites of Hector. The traditional method of describing verse patterns, based on the metrical **foot**, was briefly discussed in section 12.2.5.1. The rhythms of classical Greek and Latin verse are based upon the length or **weight** of syllables, either long (–) or short (∪). The *Iliad* is written in **hexameters**, lines of six feet, the first four consisting of dactyls (– ∪∪) or spondees (– –), and usually ending with a dactyl and final spondee, (– ∪∪ – –). Here, for example, are the opening lines of Book III in the original Greek:

Αὐτὰρ 'επεὶ κόσμηθεν "αμ' 'ηγεμόνεσσιν "εκαστοι,
Τρῶες μὲν κλαγγῇ τ' 'ενοπῇ τ' ἴσαν, ὄρνιθες ὥς,

and the same lines transliterated into the Roman alphabet with a literal translation of each separate word:

Autar epei kosmethen   am'   egemonessin ekastoi,
Then   when they were arranged along with leaders   each

Troes men   klagge t' enope t' isan,   ornithes os,
Trojans on the one hand shouting both noise   and were equal birds   like

The metre of the first line will illustrate the classical hexameter line with its six feet of dactyls and spondees:

Αὐτὰρ'ε | πεὶ κόσ | μηθεν " αμ' | 'ηγεμό | νεσσι "ε | καστοι,

$- \cup \cup \ | - \ - \ | - \ \cup \ \cup \ | - \ \cup\cup | - \ \cup \ \cup | - \ -$

Autar e | pei kos | methen am'| egemo | nessin e | kastoi,

$- \cup \cup \ | - \ - \ | - \ \cup \ \cup \ | - \ \cup\cup | - \ \cup \ \cup | - \ -$

A translator of classical Greek verse into modern English has, therefore, to make a number of decisions. Is the translation to be in prose or verse? If in verse, is it to try to reproduce the rhythm and metre of the original, or to use one more specifically English in tradition? English is a 'stress-timed language', in contrast with classical Greek and Latin and, for example, a modern Latin-derived language like French. Whether prose or verse, is the translation to be literal – as near word for word as the differences between the two languages allow – or is the translator to be more free to convey the meaning?

16.1.1   *Opening lines of Book III*

Dr Samuel Johnson is reported by James Boswell as saying,

> We must try its effect as an English poem. That is the way to judge of the merit of a translation.

Activity 16.1

Read the following translations of the opening nine lines of Book III of The *Iliad*, and discuss their stylistic differences and their 'effect as an English poem'.

The two opposing armies, Trojan and Greek (Achaean), display their forces:

1

When all were drawn up, each company under its own commander, the Trojans advanced with a shouting and din like that of birds. They filled the air with clamour, like the cranes that fly from the onset of winter and the sudden rains and make for Ocean Stream with raucous cries to bring death and destruction to the Pigmies, launching their wicked onslaught from the morning sky. But the Achaeans moved forward in silence, breathing valour, and filled with the resolve to stand by one another.

2

Thus by their leaders' care each martial band
Moves into ranks, and stretches o'er the land.
With shouts the Trojans, rushing from afar,
Proclaim their motions, and provoke the war:
So when inclement winters vex the plain
With piercing frosts, or thick-descending rain,
To warmer seas the cranes embodied fly,
With noise, and order, through the midway sky;
To pigmy nations wounds and death they bring,
And all the war descends upon the wing,
But silent, breathing rage, resolv'd and skill'd
By mutual aids to fix a doubtful field,
Swift march the Greeks: the rapid dust around
Darkening arises from the labour'd ground.

3

Now when the men of both sides were set in order by their leaders,
the Trojans came on with clamour and shouting, like wildfowl,
as when the clamour of cranes goes high to the heavens,
when the cranes escape the winter time and the rains unceasing
and clamorously wing their way to the streaming Ocean,
bringing to the Pygmaian men bloodshed and destruction:
at daybreak they bring on the baleful battle against them.
But the Achaian men went silently, breathing valour,
stubbornly minded each in his heart to stand by the others.

4

Think of the noise that fills the air
When autumn takes the Dnepr by the arm
And skein on skein of honking geese fly south
To give the stateless rains a miss:
So Hector's moon-horned, shouting dukes
Burst from the tunnels, down the counterslope,
And shout, shout, shout, smashed shouted shout
Backward and forth across the sky,
While pace on pace the Greeks came down
With blank, unyielding imperturbability.

16.1.1.1 COMMENTARY

The first translation is by E. V. Rieu, and was published in 1950. It is the nearest of the four to a literal translation into prose.

The second translation, published in 1720, is by Alexander Pope. Pope says in his Preface,

> It is the first grand duty of an interpreter to give his author entire and unmaimed; and for the rest, the diction and versification only are his proper province, since these must be his own, but the others he is to take as he finds them.

By 'the others', Pope means 'the fable, manners and sentiments...every particular image, description, and simile'. So taking as his 'proper province' the diction and versification, Pope used the established poetic form of the 'Augustan' period in English for serious verse – the **heroic couplet** – pairs of rhyming lines, in the 5-stress rising duple metre traditionally known as **iambic pentameter** (see section 12.2.5.1).

The third translation is by the American poet Richard Lattimore, whose translation of the *Iliad* was published in 1951. In a note on the translation he says,

> My aim has been to give a rendering of the Iliad which will convey the meaning of the Greek in a speed and rhythm analogous to the speed and rhythm I find in the original. The best metre for my purpose is a free six-beat line. My line can hardly be called English hexameter....I have allowed anapaests for dactyls, trochees and even iambs for spondees. The line is to be read with its natural stress, not forced into any system.

The fourth was published in 1994 as *The Husbands* and subtitled *An Account of Books Three and Four of Homer's Iliad,* by Christopher Logue. It follows two other similar volumes, *Kings* (1991), Books One and Two, and his first translation, *War Music*, Books 16 to 19, which was commissioned for broadcasting by the BBC and published in 1981. Christopher Logue knew no Greek, so he began by using earlier English translations, and found that each of them gave him 'a quite dissimilar impression of the work'. His own aim was

> to retain the storyline of the passage chosen, but to cut or amplify or to add to its incidents, to vary certain of its similes, and (mostly) to omit Homer's descriptive epithets, 'ten-second-miler-Achilles', 'thick-as-a-pyramid-Ajax' and so forth.

He soon began to use only a literal word-for-word translation provided for him:

> I would concoct a storyline based on its main incident; and then, knowing the gist of what this or that character said, would try to make their voices come alive and to keep the action on the move.
> I was not, then, making a translation in the accepted sense of the word, but what I hope would turn out to be a poem in English...

Alexander Pope's translation

The constraints of any verse translation into English will depend upon the verse form chosen by the translator. The heroic couplet requires both rhyme and the rising duple rhythm of the iambic pentameter, as well as the English vocabulary and grammar of any translation, so in practice this must lead to a **paraphrase** –

> an expression in different words of the sense of a text;
> a free rendering or amplification of a passage and the inclusion of additional material

If we look more closely at the first few lines, we may take the E. V. Rieu translation as a 'base' for comparison, assuming that as a literal prose translation it matches the Greek in its content.

E. V. Rieu's translation	*Alexander Pope's translation*
When all were drawn up, each company under its own commander,	Thus by their leaders' care each martial band Moves into ranks, and stretches o'er the land.

Martial band is Augustan **poetic diction** (see section 10.2) as a synonym for *company*, while the clause *and stretches o'er the land* which is not in the original fills the couplet

the Trojans advanced with a shouting and din like that of birds.	With shouts the Trojans, rushing from afar, Proclaim their motions, and provoke the war:

Pope omits the direct reference to the simile *like that of birds* and adds his own *Proclaim their motions and provoke the war*, a line typical of the formal, balanced grammar and vocabulary of this period. We noted the prevalence of noun phrases with the definite article *the*, with or without modifiers, as in *provoke the war*, in section 10.2.2.2. The line is also Pope's addition to the original. *Afar* and *war* were true rhymes then.

They filled the air with clamour, like the cranes that fly from the onset of winter and Stream with raucous cries	So when inclement winters vex the plain With piercing frosts, or thick-descending rain To warmer seas the cranes embodied fly, With noise, and order, through the midway sky;

It becomes clear that Pope's translation, though it does not deviate from the narrative of events, is very much a paraphrase,

They filled the air with clamour	⇒	with noise
like the cranes that fly...	⇒	the cranes embodied fly

The participle *embodied* has the sense of *in a body, in a flock*.

from the onset of winter and the	⇒	So when inclement winters vex the plain
sudden rains	⇒	With piercing frosts, or thick-descending rain,

Pope adds *inclement*, the formal diction of poetry, and *vex the plain*, which parallels the previous *provoke the war* in form, and glosses *winter* with the descriptive phrase *with piercing frosts* and the modifier *thick-descending*.

and make for Ocean Stream	⇒	to warmer seas
with raucous cries	⇒	with noise, and order, through the midway sky

Pope's *with noise* makes do for the original's *with clamour* and *with raucous cries*, while he adds *and order, through the midway sky*.

These detailed comments on what is added, omitted or paraphrased show the characteristics of Pope's translation sufficiently. You read it as an English version of its time, and accept the conventions of the heroic couplet without reference to what Homer's Greek sounded like.

Activity 16.2

Discuss the remaining lines of this extract in Pope's translation.

E. V. Rieu's translation	*Alexander Pope's translation*
to bring death and destruction to the Pigmies, launching their wicked onslaught from the morning sky. But the Achaeans moved forward in silence, breathing valour, and filled with the resolve to stand by one another.	To pigmy nations wounds and death they bring, And all the war descends upon the wing, But silent, breathing rage, resolv'd and skill'd By mutual aids to fix a doubtful field, Swift march the Greeks: the rapid dust around Darkening arises from the labour'd ground.

Richard Lattimore's translation
Lattimore tells us that he has tried to match the speed and rhythm of Homer's Greek hexameters by using a free six-beat line, to be read 'with its natural stress'.

E. V. Rieu's translation	*Richard Lattimore's translation*
When all were drawn up, each company under its own commander, the Trojans advanced with a shouting and din like that of birds. They filled the air with clamour, like the cranes that fly from the onset of winter and the sudden rains and make for Ocean Stream with raucous cries to bring death and destruction to the Pigmies, launching their wicked onslaught from the morning sky. But the Achaeans moved forward in silence, breathing valour, and filled with the resolve to stand by one another.	Now when the men of both sides were set in order by their leaders, the Trojans came on with clamour and shouting, like wildfowl, as when the clamour of cranes goes high to the heavens, when the cranes escape the winter time and the rains unceasing and clamorously wing their way to the streaming Ocean, bringing to the Pygmaian men bloodshed and destruction: at daybreak they bring on the baleful battle against them. But the Achaian men went silently, breathing valour, stubbornly minded each in his heart to stand by the others.

The difference between these two versions lies in the rhythm of Lattimore's with its six-beat line, and the alliteration – *sides* – *set, came* – *clamour, clamour* – *cranes, high* – *heavens, wing* – *way, bringing* – *bloodshed, bring* – *baleful* – *battle, stubbornly* – *stand*, which remind us of the central place of alliteration in Old English verse (see section 12.2.2).

Christopher Logue's translation
We know from Logue's introduction that his version will be a free rendering of the gist of the storyline. The simile of the cranes is deliberately made an **anachronism**, that is 'an erroneous reference of an event, circumstance, or custom

to a wrong date'. *Cranes* become *geese*, and the scene of the migration is related to contemporary times by the reference to the river Dnepr in Russia. The rest of the extract is clearly a paraphrase, a reworking of the sense of the original to create a new poem in English, marking the contrast between the two armies.

16.1.2   *Extract from Book XIX*

Here are translations by the same authors of a longer episode, taken from Book XIX.

Activity 16.3

Study the four translations and divide the text into its successive topics, beginning with the description of sunrise.
  Discuss the important differences between the Pope, Lattimore and Logue versions.

📖   A detailed study is in the *Commentary & Data Book.*

Achilles' mother Thetis, a nymph goddess, brings him armour made by the god Vulcan (Hephaestus), while Achilles' soldiers, the Myrmidons, look on:

E. V. Rieu's translation

As Dawn in her saffron mantle rose from the River of Ocean to bring daylight to the immortals and to men, Thetis reached the ships with the god's gifts in her hands. She found her son Achilles prostrate with his arms round Patroclus. He was weeping bitterly, and many of his men stood round him wailing. The gracious goddess went up to them and taking her son's hand in her own she said to him: 'My child, the man who lies here was struck down by the will of heaven. No grief of ours can alter that. So let him be now, and receive this splendid armour I have brought you from Hephaestus, armour more beautiful than any man has ever worn.'
  With this, the goddess laid the arms before him in their elaborate loveliness. They rang aloud and all the Myrmidons were struck with awe. They did not dare to look at them, and backed away. But the more Achilles looked, the more his passion rose, and from underneath their lids his eyes flashed fiercely out like points of flame. He picked up the god's splendid gifts and fondled them with delight. And when he had taken in all their beauty, he turned to Thetis and said: 'Mother, this armour of the god's – this is indeed the workmanship we might expect from Heaven. No mortal could have made it. I will go to battle in it now...'

Alexander Pope's translation

> Soon as Aurora heaved her Orient head
> Above the waves, that blush'd with early red,
> (With new-born day to gladden mortal sight,
> And gild the courts of heaven with sacred light,)
> The immortal arms the goddess-mother bears
> Swift to her son: her son she finds in tears
> Stretch'd o'er Patroclus' corse; while all the rest
> Their sovereign's sorrows in their own express'd.
> A ray divine her heavenly presence shed,
> And thus, his hand soft touching, Thetis said:

'Suppress, my son, this rage of grief, and know
It was not man, but heaven, that gave the blow;
Behold what arms by Vulcan are bestow'd,
Arms worthy thee, or fit to grace a god.'
   Then drops the radiant burden to the ground;
Clang the strong arms, and ring the shores around;
Back shrink the Myrmidons with dread surprise,
And from the broad effulgence turn their eyes.
Unmoved the hero kindles at the show,
And feels with rage divine his bosom glow;
From his fierce eyeballs living flames expire,
And flash incessant like a stream of fire:
He turns the radiant gift: and feeds his mind
On all the immortal artist had design'd.
'Goddess! (he cried,) these glorious arms, that shine
With matchless art, confess the hand divine.
Now to the bloody battle let me bend...'

Richard Lattimore's translation

Now Dawn the yellow-robed arose from the river of Ocean
to carry her light to men and to immortals. And Thetis
came to the ships and carried with her the gifts of Hephaistos.
She found her beloved son lying in the arms of Patroklos
crying shrill, and his companions in their numbers behind him
mourned. She, shining among divinities, stood there beside them.
She clung to her son's hand and called him by name and spoke to him:
'My child, now, though we grieve for him, we must let this man lie
dead, in the way he first was killed through the gods' designing.
Accept rather from me the glorious arms of Hephaistos,
so splendid, and such as no man has ever worn on his shoulders.'
The goddess spoke so, and set down the armour on the ground
before Achilleus, and all its elaboration clashed loudly.
Trembling took hold of all the Myrmidons. None had the courage
to look straight at it. They were afraid of it. Only Achilleus
looked, and as he looked the anger came harder upon him
and his eyes glittered terribly under his lids, like sunflare.
He was glad, holding in his hands the shining gifts of Hephaistos.
But when he had satisfied his heart with looking at the intricate
armour, he spoke to his mother and addressed her in winged words:
'My mother, the god has given me these weapons; they are such
as are the work of immortals. No mortal man could have made them.
Therefore now I shall arm myself in them.

Christopher Logue's translation

Rat.
Pearl.
Onion.
Honey:
These colours came before the sun
   Lifted above the ocean,
Bringing light
   Alike to mortals and immortals.
   And through this falling brightness,

Through the by now:
  Mosque,
  Eucalyptus,
  Utter blue,
Came Thetis,
Gliding across the azimuth,
With armour the colour of moonlight laid on her forearms;
Her palms upturned;
Her hovering above the fleet;
Her skyish face towards her son.
  Achilles,
Gripping the body of Patroclus
Naked and dead against his own,
While Thetis spoke:
  'Son...'
The soldiers looking on;
Looking away from it; remembering their own;
'Grieving will not amend what Heaven has done.
Suppose you throw your hate after Patroclus' soul.
Who besides Troy will gain?
  See what I've brought.'
  And as she laid the moonlit armour on the sand
It chimed;
  And the sound that came from it,
Followed the light that came from it,
Like sighing,
Saying,
  Made in Heaven.
  And those who had the neck to watch Achilles weep
Could not look now.
  Nobody looked. They were afraid.
  Except Achilles: looked,
Lifted a piece of it between his hands;
Turned it; tested the weight of it; and then,
Spun the holy tungsten, like a star between his knees,
Slitting his eyes against the flare, some said,
But others thought the hatred shuttered by his lids
Made him protect the metal.
  His eyes like furnace doors ajar.
  When he had got its weight
And let its industry console his grief a bit:
  'I'll fight.'
He said. Simple as that. 'I'll fight.'
  And so Troy fell.

17. First person narrative

If a novel opens like this,

> The Divisional Commissaire, Monsieur Adrien Richard, had retired six days ago. He could have been six weeks gone, or six months for that matter: it was as though he had never been.
> (Nicholas Freeling, *Cold Iron*, 1986)

we recognise a way of telling a story that seems natural and normal. An unnamed narrator, speaking in the 3rd person and using past tenses, tells the story. Narrators like these are able to give us their characters' thoughts and feelings – they are **omniscient**, knowing everything – and it does not surprise us to hear a character's inner thoughts and feelings.

> Castang, a junior commissaire of the grade called 'adjunct', felt surprised.

Nicholas Freeling the author is distinct from his fictional narrator, who has been called the **implied author**. There are different degrees of involvement by implied authors in the narrative they tell. Furthest away from the omniscient narrator is the kind who uses the 1st person *I*, and who is one of the main characters in the story. Everything is told from his or her **point of view**.

17.1 *The Catcher in the Rye* and *David Copperfield*

A novel by the American author J. D. Salinger (b. 1919), *The Catcher in the Rye* (1951), is narrated by an adolescent boy, Holden Caulfield. In the first paragraph the narrator mentions Charles Dickens's *David Copperfield* (1850) as an example of autobiography that his is not. Here are the openings of the two novels:

The Catcher in the Rye

> If you really want to hear about it, the first thing you'll probably want to know is where I was born, and what my lousy childhood was like, and how my parents were occupied and all before they had me, and all that David Copperfield kind of crap, but I don't feel like going into it. In the first place. that stuff bores me, and in the second place, my parents would have about two

haemorrhages apiece if I told anything pretty personal about them. They're quite touchy about anything like that, especially my father. They're *nice* and all – I'm not saying that – but they're also touchy as hell. Besides I'm not going to tell you my whole goddam autobiography or anything. I'll just tell you about this madman stuff that happened to me around last Christmas before I got pretty run-down and had to come out here and take it easy.

David Copperfield

Whether I shall turn out to be the hero of my own life, or whether that station will be held by anybody else, these pages must show. To begin my life with the beginning of my life, I record that I was born (as I have been informed and believe) on a Friday, at twelve o'clock at night. It was remarked that the clock began to strike, and I began to cry simultaneously.

   In consideration of the day and hour of my birth, it was declared by the nurse, and by some sage women in the neighbourhood who had taken a lively interest in me several months before there was any possibility of our becoming personally acquainted, first, that I was destined to be unlucky in life; and secondly, that I was privileged to see ghosts and spirits; both these gifts inevitably attaching, as they believed, to all unlucky infants of either gender, born towards the small hours on a Friday night.

Activity 17.1

(i) Compare the styles of the two texts.

(ii) What is the linguistic evidence that makes a reader imagine that Holden Caulfield is talking, rather than writing his story?

17.1.1   *Discussion – structure and vocabulary*

17.1.1.1   *THE CATCHER IN THE RYE*

Structure
There is little subordination of one clause to another in the narrative, and one thing follows another, either without any linking word, or linked with *and* or *but*. This is an example of **paratactic** structure and typical of speech.

Vocabulary
There is no non-core vocabulary apart from *autobiography*, and there are a lot of **colloquial** words and phrases – *I don't feel like going into it, that stuff bores me, anything pretty personal, they're quite touchy, this madman stuff, I got pretty run-down* etc., and a few examples of expressive 'taboo' words like *lousy, crap, goddam*. Again, using these words and phrases is usually confined to colloquial speech.

📖 A linear analysis and vocabulary list are in the *Commentary & Data Book*.

17.1.1.2   *DAVID COPPERFIELD*

Structure
A diagrammed analysis would clearly show the relative complexity of the grammatical structure of Dickens's opening paragraph. For example, in the first sentence, the object of the verb *must show* consists of two conjoined clauses, brought to the front of the sentence as its theme. There is a lot of subordination of

one clause to another in a **hypotactic** structure, as well as coordination, and the second sentence contains 17 clauses.

Vocabulary

Like Sir Walter Scott and Fenimore Cooper, Dickens uses non-core, formal words in his narrative that match the style of the complex structure.

Both novels are told in the 1st person. *David Copperfield* is clearly intended to be read as a <u>written</u> autobiography – 'as these pages must show'. On the other hand, in *The Catcher in the Rye* we are meant to imagine ourselves listening to Holden Caulfield as he <u>talks</u> about 'this madman stuff' that happened to him. We know we are reading the story, but we imagine the situation of being talked to.

📖 A diagrammed analysis and vocabulary list are in the *Commentary & Data Book*.

Activity 17.2 _____

Compare the styles of the following extracts from the same two novels. Can you find similar evidence of the differences between them?

📖 A vocabulary list and structural analysis are in the *Commentary & Data Book*.

The Catcher in the Rye, chapter 5

Where I want to start telling is the day I left Pencey Prep. Pencey Prep is this school that's in Agerstown, Pennsylvania. You probably heard of it. You've probably seen the ads anyway. They advertise in about a thousand magazines, always showing some hot-shot guy on a horse jumping over a fence. Like as if all you ever did at Pencey was play polo all the time. I never even once saw a horse anywhere *near* the place. And underneath the guy on the horse's picture it always says: 'Since 1888 we have been moulding boys into splendid, clear-thinking young men.' Strictly for the birds. They didn't do any damn more *moulding* at Pencey than they do at any other school. And I didn't know anybody there that was splendid and clear-thinking and all. Maybe two guys. If that many. And they probably *came* to Pencey that way.

Anyway, it was the Saturday of the football game with Saxon Hall. The game with Saxon Hall was supposed to be a very big deal around Pencey. It was the last game of the year, and you were supposed to commit suicide or something if old Pencey didn't win.

David Copperfield, chapter XVI

Doctor Strong's was an excellent school; as different from Mr Creakle's as good is from evil. It was very gravely and decorously ordered, and on a sound system; with an appeal, in everything, to the honour and good faith of the boys, and an avowed intention to rely on their possession of those qualities unless they proved themselves unworthy of it, which worked wonders. We all felt that we had a part in the management of the place, and in sustaining its character and dignity. Hence, we soon became warmly attached to it – I am sure I did for one, and I never knew, in all my time, of any other boy being otherwise – and learnt with a good will, desiring to do it credit. We had noble games out of hours, and plenty of liberty; but even then, as I remember, we were well spoken of in the town, and rarely did any disgrace, by our appearance or manner, to the reputation of Doctor Strong's boys.

17.2 Joseph Conrad's *Heart of Darkness*

Heart of Darkness is a short novel by Joseph Conrad, published in 1902. Conrad began the story in 1899, when the European colonisation and exploitation of

Africa was at its peak, something referred to in the novel as 'a rapacious and pitiless folly'. The story is spoken by a character called Marlow, a seaman, but his narrative is set in a context: four men – a first narrator, a lawyer, an accountant and Marlow – are on a boat, captained by 'the Director of Companies', waiting for the tide to turn on the Thames before sailing.

> The *Nellie*, a cruising yawl, swung to her anchor without a flutter of the sails, and was at rest. The flood had made, the wind was nearly calm, and being bound down the river, the only thing for it was to come to and wait for the turn of the tide....
>
> Between us there was, as I have already said somewhere, the bond of the sea....The Lawyer – the best of old fellows – had, because of his many years and many virtues, the only cushion on deck, and was lying on the only rug. The Accountant had brought out already a box of dominoes, and was toying architecturally with the bones. Marlow sat cross-legged right aft, leaning against the mizzen-mast. He had sunken cheeks, a yellow complexion, a straight back, an ascetic aspect, and, with his arms dropped, the palms of hands outwards, resembled an idol.... We exchanged a few words lazily. Afterwards there was silence on board the yacht.

This first narrator then describes sunset over the River Thames and evokes 'the spirit of the past' – men who had sailed from there,

> What greatness had not floated on the ebb of that river into the mystery of an unknown earth!...The dreams of men, the seeds of commonwealth, the germs of empires.

In 1902, the nineteenth-century colonisation of Africa by Britain, France, Belgium and Germany was more or less complete. The British Empire was at its peak of size and influence.

> 'And this also,' said Marlow suddenly, 'has been one of the dark places of the earth....I was thinking of very old times, when the Romans first came here, nineteen hundred years ago – the other day....They were men enough to face the darkness...all that mysterious life of the wilderness that stirs in the forest, in the jungles, in the hearts of wild men.'

Marlow compares the Roman occupation of Britain two thousand years ago with the nineteenth-century occupation of Africa,

> 'They were no colonists; their administration was merely a squeeze, and nothing more, I suspect. They were conquerors, and for that you want only brute force....It was just robbery with violence, aggravated murder on a grand scale, and men going at it blind – as is very proper for those who tackle a darkness. The conquest of the earth, which mostly means the taking it away from those who have a different complexion or slightly flatter noses than ourselves, is not a pretty thing when you look into it too much. What redeems it is the idea only....'

Marlow then begins his tale about when he *turned fresh-water sailor for a bit*, as captain of a small steamer on *a mighty big river* – in fact the Congo, though it is not named in the story. The imagery of *darkness* has been present in the previous quotations, and is to pervade the whole novel.

So Marlow's is a spoken tale to an audience of three men (hence the quotation marks at the beginning of each paragraph), and it occupies all the book except the introductory pages and a single final paragraph spoken by the first narrator,

Marlow ceased, and sat apart, indistinct and silent, in the pose of a meditating Buddha. Nobody moved for a time. 'We have lost the first of the ebb,' said the Director, suddenly. I raised my head. The offing was barred by a black bank of clouds, and the tranquil waterway leading to the uttermost ends of the earth flowed sombre under an overcast sky – seemed to lead into the heart of an immense darkness.

Marlow as narrator of the story presents an equivocal, uncertain attitude towards the business of empire-building and, in the extract chosen for close study in this chapter, describes the exploitation of the native African by the European colonisers of the Belgian Congo, as Zaire was then known.

Activity 17.3

Study the text of the extract and discuss your first impressions, then make a more detailed analysis of its style in the following activities.

Activity 17.4 – Vocabulary, theme and imagery

(i) How are the participants named, or **classified**? List the nouns and noun phrases used to refer (a) to the Africans and the white man, (b) to parts of their bodies and (c) to their clothing.

(ii) List the words which have meanings or connotations related to *darkness* and *light*.

(iii) List the words whose meanings related to *death*, *disease* or *pain* and associated meanings.

(iv) List the words whose meaning states or implies the negative, what is *not*.

Activity 17.5 – Participant, process and circumstances (i.e. underlying semantic relationships)

Use the concepts of *actor*, *affected*, *process*, *attribute*, *location*, etc. to establish more precisely what the different participants do:

(a) the narrator (Marlow),
(b) the black men,
(c) the white man.

Activity 17.6 – Syntax and style

(i) Relate the semantic categories (e.g. *transactive/non-transactive*, *actional* or *mental* processes) to the grammatical *transitive/intransitive* clause structures.

(ii) Can you find any marked *repetition*, *parallelism* or other stylistic features in the textual structure?

Activity 17.7 – The narrator and narrative style

The story is told in the first person, using 'I' to a group of listeners. Is this *context of situation* reflected in any other features of the vocabulary or grammar?

In the extract, Marlow has just arrived at the Congo river in West Africa by boat, and is making his way on foot to the nearby trading company station, where he is going to work. His first impressions are of,

mounds of turned-up earth by the shore
this scene of inhabited devastation
an undersized railway-truck lying there on its back with its wheels in the air. One was off.
pieces of decaying machinery, a stack of rusty nails

He then sees,

'To the left a clump of trees made a shady spot, where dark things seemed to stir feebly.... 'A slight clinking behind me made me turn my head. Six black men advanced in a file, toiling up the path. They walked erect and slow, balancing small baskets full of earth on their heads, and the clink kept time with their footsteps. Black rags were wound round their loins, and the short ends waggled to and fro like tails. I could see every rib, the joints of their limbs were like knots in a rope; each had an iron collar on his neck, and all were connected together with a chain whose bights swung between them, rhythmically clanking.... They were called criminals, and the outraged law had come to them, an insoluble mystery from the sea....'

The extract we shall look at more closely then follows:

'...At last I got under the trees. My purpose was to stroll into the shade for a moment; but no sooner within than it seemed to me I had stepped into the gloomy circle of some Inferno. The rapids were near, and an uninterrupted, uniform, headlong, rushing noise filled the mournful stillness of the grove, where not a breath stirred, not a leaf moved, with a mysterious sound – as though the tearing pace of the launched earth had suddenly become audible.

'Black shapes crouched, lay, sat between the trees leaning against the trunks, clinging to the earth, half coming out, half effaced within the dim light, in all the attitudes of pain, abandonment, and despair. Another mine on the cliff went off, followed by a slight shudder of the soil under my feet. The work was going on. The work! And this was the place where some of the helpers had withdrawn to die.

'They were dying slowly – it was very clear. They were not enemies, they were not criminals, they were nothing earthly now, – nothing but black shadows of disease and starvation, lying confusedly in the greenish gloom. Brought from all the recesses of the coast in all the legality of time contracts, lost in uncongenial surroundings, fed on unfamiliar food, they sickened, became inefficient, and were then allowed to crawl away and rest. These moribund shapes were free as air – and nearly as thin. I began to distinguish the gleam of the eyes under the trees. Then, glancing down, I saw a face near my hand. The black bones reclined at full length with one shoulder against the tree, and slowly the eyelids rose and the sunken eyes looked up at me, enormous and vacant, a kind of blind, white flicker in the depths of the orbs, which died out slowly. The man seemed young – almost a boy – but you know with them it's hard to tell. I found nothing else to do but to offer him one of my good Swede's ship's biscuits I had in my pocket. The fingers closed slowly on it and held – there was no other movement and no other glance. He had tied a bit of white worsted round his neck – Why? Where did he get it? Was it a badge – an ornament – a charm – a propitiatory act? Was there any idea at all connected with it? It looked startling round his black neck, this bit of white thread from beyond the seas.

'Near the same tree two more bundles of acute angles sat with their legs drawn up. One, with his chin propped on his knees, stared at nothing, in an intolerable and appalling manner: his brother phantom rested its forehead, as if overcome with a great weariness; and all about others were scattered in every pose of contorted collapse, as in some picture of a massacre or a pestilence. While I stood horror struck, one of these creatures rose to his hands and knees, and went off on all-fours towards the river to drink. He lapped out of his hand, then sat up in the sunlight, crossing his shins in front of him, and after a time let his woolly head fall on his breastbone.

'I didn't want any more loitering in the shade, and I made haste towards the station. When near the buildings I met a white man, in such an unexpected elegance of get-up that in the first moment I took him for a sort of vision. I saw a high starched collar, white cuffs, a light alpaca jacket, snowy trousers, a clean necktie, and varnished boots. No hat. Hair parted, brushed, oiled, under a green-lined parasol held in a big white hand. He was amazing, and had a penholder behind his ear...'

17.2.1 Classification of participants

The different words and phrases we use to name someone are an indication of how we view them. The African natives are not classified as men, but as dehumanized *shapes, shadows, bones, acute angles, phantoms* and *creatures*. There are more references to them as parts of bodies rather than as whole human beings. The white accountant, however, is classified by his elegant 'get-up' – *white, snowy, clean* – and his clothing – *starched, varnished*. The contrast is obvious but incongruous in the context of the trading station and the treatment of the African men.

📖 Lists of the classified participants are in the *Commentary & Data Book*.

17.2.2 Vocabulary

The gloomy circle of some Inferno (line 2) is a reference to a journey into Hell, taken from the *Divine Comedy* by the thirteenth-century Italian poet, Dante Alighieri. The Inferno is a place of despair – 'Abandon hope all ye who enter here' – and the reference sets the whole scene. The dominant imagery throughout the extract (and the book) is of *darkness*, with its contrasted opposite *light*, each of them expressed in a variety of related words with similar connotations.

17.2.3 Themes and imagery

Underlying the narrative, and sometimes explicitly stated, is the theme of the exploitation of blacks by whites. The theme is there in the extract with its contrasting images, by juxtaposition, of the black Africans 'allowed to die' and the immaculate white accountant – the effects of 'civilization' are quite clear, and can be seen, for example, in the ironic and parallel contrast of:

> **black shadows** of disease and starvation, lying confusedly in the **greenish gloom**
> a **white** man,...under a **green-lined** parasol held in a big **white** hand.

and in the symbolic 'bit of white worsted' round the neck of the boy –

> 'It looked startling round his **black** neck, this bit of **white** thread from beyond the seas.'

📖 The vocabulary is sorted into sets in the *Commentary & Data Book*.

17.2.4 Negatives

Negatives are directly stated using *no/not/nothing* or the negative prefixes *un-* and *in-*, e.g. **not a breath stirred**, **unfamiliar food**, or implied as in *half* effaced, and reinforce the themes of the extract.

   📖 A complete list is in the *Commentary & Data Book.*

17.2.5 Participant-process analysis

If we look 'below the surface' of the grammatical structure, we can become more aware of how the narrator sees the action going on and what the participants are actually doing to themselves and to others. We identify the participants who are performing an action as **actors,** what they are said to be doing or not doing as **processes**, and the persons or things that are affected by the processes as either **affected** or **recipients**. If the process is one of a number of **mental processes**, we identify any **attributes** or **locations** or **objectives**.

17.2.5.1 PROCESSES INVOLVING MARLOW

Marlow is the narrator, but his role in the action is mostly as observer. The only action of his which affects the Africans is to *offer a biscuit*. He himself is affected by the white worsted round the boy's neck, and is the objective of the eyes which look up at him. The narrative concentrates on the African men.

   📖 A table showing all the processes involving Marlow is in the *Commentary & Data Book.*

17.2.5.2 PROCESSES INVOLVING THE AFRICAN MEN

The Africans are exploited victims. They are the affected participants in actions already completed beforehand – *abandoned, starved, brought from the coast* and *fed on unfamiliar food*. There is no participant affected by them, except themselves in 'reflexive' actions – *their legs drawn up, his chin propped on his knees, his brother phantom rested its forehead, crossing his shins in front of him, let his woolly head fall on his breastbone.*

Everything else that they 'do' is **non-transactive**, that is, it does not affect a second participant as a transactive process is said to do – *crouch, lie, sit, lean, cling, despair, withdraw to die, sicken, crawl away, recline, look up, stare* etc. The only other actions reported are of the fingers that *close on* and *hold* Marlow's offered biscuit, and the man who *goes off to drink* and *laps water out of his hand.* The choice of *close on* rather than *grasp* or *grab* contributes to the sense of the weakness of the dying man; *to lap* is to *drink like an animal.*

This analysis is inferred from the 'surface' grammar of the text, and an analysis of the structure shows how the underlying process-participant relationships are presented.

   📖 A table showing all the processes involving the African men is in the *Commentary & Data Book.*

17.2.6 Clause structure: transitive/intransitive; focus of information

Complexity within the clauses is produced mainly by **coordination** rather than in sentence structures with subordination. There is a significant number of adverbial constituents, which enlarge on and describe the place and manner of the actions observed, for example, *under the trees, with a mysterious sound, in the greenish gloom, slowly, round his neck, on his breastbone.* There are only three finite subordinate clauses, beginning *as though, as if, while,* and three non-restrictive relative clauses, beginning with *where,* and a few prepositional clauses, e.g. *with their legs drawn up,* and nonfinite clauses, e.g. *leaning against the trunks.*

As we saw in the previous section, almost all the processes are non-transactive actionals, and this is expressed grammatically by **intransitive verbs**, which have no direct object corresponding to an affected participant.

The only **transitive verbs** expressing transactive actional processes are:

- Unnamed white employers *bring* the natives from the coast and *feed* them on unfamiliar food, then *abandon* and *starve* them (n.b. the use of passives in the text – *brought from, fed on, abandoned starved*).
- Marlow *offers* a biscuit.
- The native whose fingers *close on* and *hold* a biscuit, and who had *tied* white worsted round his neck.
- The two men who *draw up* their legs, the man who *props* his chin on his knees, the man who *rests* his forehead, and the man who *laps* water and *crosses* his shins.

but these are, as we have already seen, mostly reflexive actions, none of which affect a second human participant.

There are some non-actional 'mental processes'. Marlow *has a purpose, he distinguishes, startles, is appalled, takes for a vision, sees.* The men *despair, look up at, stare.*

📖 A complete structural analysis of the text in the *Commentary & Data Book.*

17.2.7 *Foregrounded features of style*

The repetition of phrases or clauses with similar structures but different vocabulary produces **parallelism**:

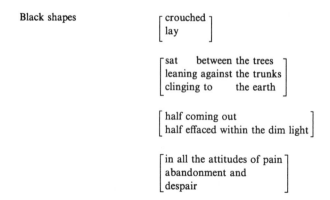

They were not $\begin{bmatrix} \text{enemies} \\ \text{criminals} \end{bmatrix}$

Ø Ø $\begin{bmatrix} \text{nothing early now} \\ \text{nothing but} \quad \text{black shadows of disease and} \\ \text{starvation} \end{bmatrix}$

Brought $\begin{bmatrix} \text{from all the recesses of the coast} \\ \text{in all the legality of time contracts} \end{bmatrix}$

$\begin{bmatrix} \text{lost} & \text{in} & \text{uncongenial surroundings} \\ \text{fed} & \text{on} & \text{unfamiliar food} \end{bmatrix}$

they $\begin{bmatrix} \text{sickened} \\ \text{became inefficient} \end{bmatrix}$

and were then allowed to $\begin{bmatrix} \text{crawl away and} \\ \text{rest} \end{bmatrix}$

These moribund shapes were $\begin{bmatrix} \text{(as)} & \text{free} & \text{as} & \text{air} \\ \text{as} & \text{thin} & \text{(as} & \text{air)} \end{bmatrix}$ and nearly

there was $\begin{bmatrix} \text{no other} & \text{movement and} \\ \text{no other} & \text{glance} \end{bmatrix}$

Was it $\begin{bmatrix} \text{a badge} \\ \text{an ornament} \\ \text{a charm} \\ \text{a propitiatory act?} \end{bmatrix}$

I saw $\begin{bmatrix} \text{a high starched collar} \\ \text{white cuffs} \\ \text{a light alpaca jacket} \\ \text{snowy trousers} \\ \text{a clean nectie and} \\ \text{varnished boots} \end{bmatrix}$

Hair $\begin{bmatrix} \text{parted} \\ \text{brushed} \\ \text{oiled} \end{bmatrix}$

$\begin{bmatrix} \text{under a green-lined parasol} \\ \text{held in a big white hand} \end{bmatrix}$

17.2.8 Narration and the spoken voice

Marlow's narrative is a spoken tale to an audience, and this is consistently indicated from time to time throughout the novel. It explains the occasional representation of features of **spoken narrative**. The following examples are taken from the extract and also from other parts of the novel.

17.2.8.1   MINOR SENTENCES

Minor sentences lack one of the essential constituents of a complete sentence, but convey their meaning fully in their context.

> No hat.
> Hair parted, brushed, oiled, . . .
> No use telling you much about that.
> A great silence around and above.

17.2.8.2   INTRODUCTORY WORDS AND INITIAL *AND* OR *BUT*

To begin a sentence with *and* or *but* is not ungrammatical, but it tends to be avoided in written prose. However, it is extremely common in spoken narrative, like other 'introductory' words and phrases such as *Well, You know,*

> **And** this was the place . . .
> **Yes,** I respected . . .
> **But** at the moment it presented itself as a confounded nuisance.
> **Well,** never mind.
> **Anyways,** it could not be found there.

17.2.8.3   USE OF 1ST AND 2ND PERSON

Using 1st person narrative does not necessarily convey the sense of an audience unless there is from time to time a reminder that listeners are present, which can be done by addressing them by name or with the pronoun *you*:

> but **you know** with them it's hard to tell
> I wouldn't have mentioned the fellow to **you**
> Annoying, **you know,** to hold your own coat like a parasol over a man's head
> **You** have no idea how effective such a . . . faculty can be.
> **You see** the thing had gone off like a box of matches.

17.2.8.4   QUESTIONS AND EXCLAMATIONS

'Rhetorical questions', which do not expect an answer, and exclamations are used in conversation to make a point,

> The work!
> Why? Where did he get it? Was it a badge – an ornament – a charm – a propitiatory act? Was there any idea at all connected with it?
> His position had come to him – why?
> By Jove! I've never seen anything so unreal in my life.
> Oh, these months!

17.2.8.5   REDUCTION IN INFORMAL SPEECH

> **There's** something pathetically childish in the ruins of grass walls . . .
> **Can't** say I saw any road or any upkeep.
> I **wouldn't** have mentioned the fellow to you . . .
> **That's** backbone.

17.2.8.6 INFORMAL VOCABULARY

I had a white companion too, **not a bad chap**...
But at the moment it presented itself as **a confounded nuisance**.
I went to work the next day, turning, **so to speak**, my back on that station.
Very soon I became **awfully** curious to see what he would find out from me.

These and similar examples constantly serve to produce the effect of 'Marlow talking', not 'Conrad writing'.

17.2.9 LINGUISTIC DESCRIPTION AND LITERARY CRITICISM

This analysis of part of *Heart of Darkness* is not intended to be a 'literary appreciation' of the extract, but tries to show that linguistic description can help in focusing on how literary effects are achieved. It is an objective study, and can be either verified or shown to be wrong. Literary criticism tends to include subjective comment describing 'personal response' to a text. Phrases like 'sensuous prose', 'subtle command of the tone of voice', 'affirmative eloquence' and 'discomposing astringency' are used to describe the style of *Heart of Darkness*, but they are not verifiable in the way that linguistic analysis is. Neither approach is an end in itself, but they are complementary in trying to make the reading of a text more fully informed – to make us want to read it and enjoy it.

18. The spoken voice

18.1 Dialogue

18.1.1 *Direct speech and free direct speech*

Conversation in a novel or short story resembles authentic conversation, but never copies it. You do not, for a start, reproduce typical non-fluency features, except for the occasional hesitation or incomplete sentence. And from the literary point of view, conversation in a novel has to do much more than sound like real-life talk. It advances the action and adds to our knowledge about a character. Here are some examples. The first is from the American writer Ernest Hemingway's *The Sun Also Rises* (1926). Hemingway's style created a fashion which was copied by many other writers. In structural terms it is **paratactic**, both its narrative and dialogue, consisting largely of simple sentences or short clauses linked by *and* or *but*.

> We walked across the square. It was dark and all around the square were the lights from the cafés under the arcades. We walked across the gravel under the trees to the hotel.
> They went upstairs and I stopped to speak with Montoya.
> 'Well, how did you like the bulls?' he asked.
> 'Good. They were nice bulls.'
> 'They're all right' – Montoya shook his head – 'but they're not too good.'
> 'What didn't you like about them?'
> 'I don't know. They just didn't give me the feeling that they were so good.'
> 'I know what you mean.'
> 'They're all right.'
> 'Yes. They're all right.'
> 'How did your friends like them?'
> 'Fine.'
> 'Good,' Montoya said.
> I went upstairs. Bill was in his room standing on the balcony looking out at the square. I stood beside him.

We can contrast this with almost any other novel writer, but here for example is a short sequence from Henry James's *The Europeans* (1878):

'Thank me for telling you,' Felix rejoined. 'It's a good thing to know.'

'I am not sure of that,' said Mr Brand.

'Ah, don't let her languish!' Felix murmured, lightly and softly.

'You *do* advise me, then?' And Mr Brand looked up.

'I congratulate you!' said Felix, smiling....

Mr Brand kept gazing, over his hat. 'She has always been a lucid, limpid nature,' he said solemnly.

'She has always been a dormant nature. She was waiting for a touchstone. But now she is beginning to awaken.'

'Don't praise her to me!' said Mr Brand, with a little quaver in his voice.

The expression of the speakers' voices is implied in verbs like *rejoined, murmured, smiling* and adverbs like *lightly, softly, solemnly,* as well as direct statements – *with a little quaver in his voice.* Here is a similar short example from Jane Austen's *Mansfield Park,*

'Then she had better come to us,' said Lady Bertram with the utmost composure. After a short pause, Sir Thomas added with dignity, 'Yes, let her home be in this house....

This kind of presentation is called **direct speech**. The words are **quoted** directly, exactly as they were spoken, and introduced or followed by a **quoting clause** – *she said, he replied* and so on, with many variations in detail. Once a conversation is set going, then the spoken words may be presented without introduction. When you read, you have to keep in mind who is speaking or replying, for example, in this section of **free direct speech** from the first text above,

'What didn't you like about them?'

'I don't know. They just didn't give me the feeling that they were so good.'

'I know what you mean.'

'They're all right.'

'Yes. They're all right.'

'How did your friends like them?'

'Fine.'

Free direct speech is direct speech without any introductory or concluding *she said* etc. Both forms are usually clearly marked with inverted commas, or speech marks. There are, however, other ways of presenting dialogue and conversation.

18.1.2 *Indirect, or reported speech*

The next quotation from *Mansfield Park* also records speech, but does not quote it. A sentence that might have been written,

Mrs Norris was often observing to the others, 'I cannot get my poor sister and her family out of my head. As much as we have done for her, I seem to be wanting to do more...'

is in fact written,

Mrs Norris was often observing to the others, that she could not get her poor sister and her family out of her head, and that much as they had all done for her, she seemed to be wanting to do more...

This way of presenting speech is **reported** indirectly rather than quoted, so it is called either **reported** or **indirect speech**, and there are some grammatical changes to the words spoken.

18.1.2.1 DECLARATIVE CLAUSES

• The reported clause is marked by *that*,

> To this, Kit's mother replied, **that** certainly it was quite true, and quite right, and quite proper

which may, however, be deleted,

> They said ∅ this came of cherishing such creatures as the Pinches.

and does not occur at all if the reporting clause splits the reported clause,

> This came, they said, of cherishing such creatures as the Pinches.

• Tense in reported speech is *backshifted* – present tense in direct speech,

> To this, Kit's mother replied, 'Certainly it **is** quite true, and quite right, ...'

becomes past:

> To this, Kit's mother replied, that certainly it **was** quite true, and quite right ...

• 1st and 2nd person pronouns are changed to 3rd person, unless the person is present at the utterance:

> The two girls said, '**We** have predicted it to Mrs Todgers...'
> The two girls said **they** had predicted it to Mrs Todgers...
>
> '**I** assure **you**, my good lady,' said the mild schoolmaster, 'that **I** have told **you** the plain truth.'
> The mild schoolmaster said that **he** assured **her** that **he** had told **her** the plain truth.

• Demonstrative pronouns *this/these* become *that/those*:

> Hari said, "I have no money to pay for all **this** food you are giving me. Will you let me work in your kitchen instead?'
> 'You can start by washing **these** pots.'
>
> Hari said he had no money to pay for all **that** food he was giving him. Would he let him work in his kitchen instead?
> He was told he could start by washing **those** pots.

• References to time and place are modified:

> 'Ruth has **now** two pupils to attend to.'
> She said that Ruth had **then** two pupils to attend to.
>
> 'You will have to hold a sort of levee, sir, while you're **here**.'
> He said that Martin would have to hold a sort of levee while he was **there**.

18.1.2.2 IN INTERROGATIVE CLAUSES
In addition,

- Changes in word order are necessary:

  'Dear, dear!' cried Tom, 'what **have I** done?'
  Tom asked what **he had** done.

- A *wh*-word is inserted in the report of a yes/no question.

  Oh Tom, dear Tom, will *this* be set right too?
  Ruth asked **whether** that would be set right too.

Activity 18.1

Rewrite the following paragraph from Charles Dickens's *The Old Curiosity Shop* in direct speech

To this, Kit's mother replied, that certainly it was quite true, and quite right, and quite proper, and Heaven forbid that she should shrink, or have cause to shrink, from any inquiry into her character or that of her son, who was a very good son though she was his mother, in which respect, she was bold to say, he took after his father, who was not only a good son to *his* mother, but the best of husbands and the best of fathers besides, which Kit could and would corroborate she knew, and so would little Jacob and the baby likewise if they were old enough, which unfortunately they were not, though as they didn't know what a loss they had had, perhaps it was a great deal better that they should be as young as they were; and so Kit's mother wound up a long story by wiping her eyes with her apron, and patting little Jacob's head, who was rocking the cradle and staring with all his might at the strange lady and gentleman.

Activity 18.2

Restore the following paragraph from Charles Dickens's *Martin Chuzzlewit* to its original form in reported speech.

But his daughters, less tranquil-minded, burst into a torrent of indignation. 'This comes,' they said, 'of cherishing such creatures as the Pinches. This comes of lowering ourselves to their level. This comes of putting ourselves in the humiliating position of seeming to know such bold, audacious, cunning, dreadful girls as this. We have expected this. We have predicted it to Mrs Todgers, as she can depone*, this very morning.' To this, they added, 'The owner of the house, supposing us to be Miss Pinch's friends, has acted, in our opinion, quite correctly, and has done no more than, under such circumstances, might reasonably have been expected.' To that they added (with a trifling inconsistency), 'He is a brute and a bear,' and then they emerged into a flood of tears, which swept away all wandering epithets before it.

* *depone = to state or declare upon oath; testify*

📖 Activities 18.1 and 18.2 are discussed in the *Commentary & Data Book*.

18.1.3 FREE INDIRECT SPEECH

Activity 18.3

Read the next extract from *Mansfield Park*. Is all the speech quoted directly?

[Fanny] was found one morning by her cousin Edmund, the youngest of the sons, sitting crying on the attic stairs.

'My dear little cousin,' said he with all the gentleness of an excellent nature, 'what can be the matter?' And sitting down by her, was at great pains to overcome her shame in being so surprised, and persuade her to speak openly. 'Was she ill? or was any body angry with her? or had she quarrelled with Maria and Julia? or was she puzzled about any thing in her lesson that he could explain? Did she, in short, want any thing he could possibly get her, or do for her?' For a long while no answer could be obtained beyond a 'no, no – not at all – no, thank you;' but he still persevered, and no sooner had he begun to revert to her own home, than her increased sobs explained to him where the grievance lay. He tried to console her.

'You are sorry to leave Mamma, my dear little Fanny,' said he, 'which shows you to be a very good girl; but you must remember that you are with relations and friends, who all love you, and wish to make you happy....'

If we write out the dialogue only,

'My dear little cousin, what can be the matter?'

'Was she ill? or was any body angry with her? or had she quarrelled with Maria and Julia? or was she puzzled about any thing in her lesson that he could explain? Did she, in short, want any thing he could possibly get her, or do for her?'

'No, no – not at all – no, thank you.'

'You are sorry to leave Mamma, my dear little Fanny, which shows you to be a very good girl; but you must remember that you are with relations and friends, who all love you, and wish to make you happy....'

the second paragraph is clearly not what Edmund actually said, which would have been something like,

'**Are you** ill? or **is** any body angry with **you**? or **have you** quarrelled with Maria and Julia? or **are you** puzzled about any thing in **your** lesson that **I can** explain? **Do you**, (in short), want any thing **I can** possibly get **you**, or do for **you**?'

Jane Austen wrote this in indirect speech, but placed the passage within speech marks – it reads like something between direct and indirect speech, and is called **free indirect speech**. It is not necessarily marked with inverted commas, and so may look at first like the plain narrative of the author,

Her eldest was a boy of ten years old, a fine spirited fellow who longed to be out in the world; but what could she do? Was there any chance of his being hereafter useful to Sir Thomas in the concerns of his West Indian property? No situation would be beneath him – or what did Sir Thomas think of Woolwich? or how could a boy be sent out to the East?

but we can hear the original words of the speaker in this free indirect speech,

'What **can I** do? **Is** there any chance of his being useful...how **can** a boy be sent out to the East?'

Activity 18.4

The following paragraph from *The Old Curiosity Shop* is partly in direct and partly in free indirect speech. Rewrite it in direct speech.

'Barbara,' said Kit, 'you're not cross with me?'

Oh dear no! Why should Barbara be cross? And what right had she to be cross? And what did it matter whether she was cross or no? Who minded *her*!

'Why, *I* do,' said Kit. 'Of course I do.'

Barbara didn't see why it was of course, at all.

Kit was sure she must. Would she think again?

Certainly Barbara would think again. No, she didn't see why it was of course. She didn't understand what Christopher meant. And besides she was sure they wanted her up-stairs by this time, and she must go, indeed...

📖 The rewritten paragraph is in the *Commentary & Data Book.*

18.1.4 *Speech acts referred to in the narrative*

Not all speech and dialogue is quoted or reported, but it may be summarised or paraphrased as part of the author's narrative:

> Mr Rushworth was eager to **assure** her ladyship of his aquiescence, and **tried to make out** something complimentary; but between his submission to *her* taste, and his having always intended the same himself, with the super-added objects of professing attention to the comfort of ladies in general, and of **insinuating**, that there was one only whom he was anxious to please, he grew puzzled; and Edmund was glad to put an end to his speech by a **proposal** of wine. Mr Rushworth, however, though not usually a great talker, had still more to say on the subject next his heart....

It is clear that Mr Rushworth has been talking, but none of his words appear. The narrator interprets what he has been saying as *assurance*, *insinuation*. Edmund might have said, 'Will you take a glass of wine?', but this is summarised as a *proposal of wine*. This has been called **narrative report of speech acts** (see G. N. Leech and M. H. Short, *Style in Fiction*, 1981). Each of these ways of reporting speech may be used for the reporting of a character's thoughts and feelings – the unheard 'inner voice'.

Activity 18.5

Identify and discuss the different presentations of speech or thought in the following extracts from *Mansfield Park.*

📖 This Activity is discussed in the *Commentary & Data Book.*

[*This continues the episode between Edmund and Fanny in the extract above.*]

> '...Let us walk out in the park, and you shall tell me all about your brothers and sisters.'
>
> On pursuing the subject, he found that dear as all these brothers and sisters generally were, there was one among them who ran more in her thoughts than the rest. It was William whom she talked of most and wanted most to see. William, the eldest, a year older than herself, her constant companion and friend; her advocate with her mother (of whom he was the darling) in every distress. 'William did not like she should come away – he had told her he should miss her very much indeed.' 'But William will write to you, I dare say.' 'Yes, he had promised he would, but he had told *her* to write first.' 'And when shall you do it?' She hung her head and answered, hesitatingly, 'she did not know; she had not any paper.'
>
> 'If that be all your difficulty, I will furnish you with paper and every other material, and you may write your letter whenever you choose. Would it make you happy to write to William?'
>
> 'Yes, very.'

[*Fanny's brother William has visited Fanny before going to sea.*]

Luckily the visit happened in the Christmas holidays, when she could directly look for comfort to her cousin Edmund; and he told her such charming things of what William was to do, and be hereafter, in consequence of his profession, as made her gradually admit that the separation might have some use.

[*Tom is Edmund's elder brother. Sir Thomas has had to pay off Tom's debts and so cannot afford to present Edmund with the vacant church living that he controls.*]

Tom listened with some shame and some sorrow; but escaping as quickly as possible, could soon with cheerful selfishness reflect, 1st, that he had not been half so much in debt as some of his friends; 2dly, that his father had made a most tiresome piece of work of it; and 3dly, that the future incumbent, whoever he might be, would, in all probability, die very soon.

A different aspect of fictional dialogue is the way that **dialectal speech** is presented.

18.2   Dialectal speech in novels

We distinguish the vocabulary and structure of non-standard or regional English from its pronunciation by referring to **dialect** for the former and **dialectal accent**, or just **accent**, for the latter. When writers want us to hear the speech of a working-class or rural character, they give us a variety of clues, usually without trying to reproduce the dialect completely. Their problem in reproducing pronunciation lies in the fact that the letters of the alphabet are inadequate for matching pronunciation precisely, especially the vowels. There are five vowel letters, *a*, *e*, *i*, *o*, *u* plus *y*, to stand for twenty or more vowel sounds, and the combinations of vowel letters like *ai*, *ea*, *ee*, *ie*, *oo*, *ou*, *ue* and so on do not do the job properly. Some letters and digraphs (two letters for one sound) represent more than one sound, and the same sound may be represented by more than one letter. An ideal alphabet would contain one letter for one sound, so English would require about 45 letters for Received Pronunciation (RP), with a few spare for dialectal vowel or consonant sounds which do not occur in RP. But writers have to make do with the 26 letters of the Roman alphabet.

Activity 18.6

Read the following extract from *Absolute Beginners* by Colin MacInnes (1959) and,

(i) Mark all words which are 'misspelt'.

(ii) Rewrite them in standard spelling

(iii) What difference does this make to your impression when you read the text?

'Arve moved,' he said, 'Darn ear.'
'And all the click?' I asked him. 'All the notorious Dockhead boys?'
'Not v'click,' said Ed-Ted. 'Jus me.'...
'And why, Ed,' I said, 'have you moved darn ear?'

'Cos me Ma as,' he said. 'She's bin re-owsed.'

'So you still live with Momma?' I enquired.

'Course,' he said.

'Big boy like you hasn't got his own little hidey-hole?' I asked.

'Lissen,' he said. 'I respeck my Mar.'

'Cool, man,' I said. 'Now, tell me. What about the mob, the click? Have they been re-owsed as well?'

'Ner,' he said.

'Ner? What, then?'

'The click's split up.'

'You mean,' I said, 'that bunch of tearaways have thrown you out?'

'Eh-y?' he cried.

'You heard, Ed. You've been expelled from the Ted college?'

'Naher! Me? Espel me? Wot? Lissen! Me, R lef *them*, see? You fink I'm sof, or sumfink?'

18.2.1 Discussion

This writer has respelt many more words than most writers do, and they are all intended to indicate a London Cockney accent.

'Arve moved,' he said, 'Darn ear .'

'And all the click ?' I asked him. 'All the notorious Dockhead boys?'

'Not v', click ,' said Ed-Ted. 'Jus me.' ...

'And why, Ed,' I said, 'have you moved darn ear ?'

'Cos me Ma as ,' he said. 'She's bin re-owsed .'

'So you still live with Momma?' I enquired.

'Course,' he said.

'Big boy like you hasn't got his own little hidey-hole?' I asked.

'Lissen ,' he said. 'I respeck my Mar .'

'Cool, man,' I said. 'Now, tell me. What about the mob, the click ? Have they been re-owsed as well?'

'Ner ,' he said.

'Ner ? What, then?'

'The click 's split up.'

'You mean,' I said, 'that bunch of tearaways have thrown you out?'

'Eh-y ?' he cried.

'You heard, Ed. You've been expelled from the Ted college?'

'Naher ! Me? Espel me? Wot ? Lissen ! Me, R lef *them*, see? You fink I'm sof , or sumfink?'

A version of the text in normal spelling removes all traces of Ed's accent, because a text in normal spelling tends to sound like RP, even if we know that the speaker would have a regional accent. There is no nonstandard grammar.

Activity 18.7

Are any respellings unnecessary?

'I've moved,' he said, 'down here.'

'And all the clique?' I asked him. 'All the notorious Dockhead boys?'

'Not the clique,' said Ed-Ted. 'Just me.' ...

'And why, Ed,' I said, 'have you moved down here?'

'Because my Ma has,' he said. 'She's been re-housed.'

'So you still live with Momma?' I enquired.

'Course,' he said.

'Big boy like you hasn't got his own little hidey-hole?' I asked.

'Listen,' he said. 'I respect my Ma.'

'Cool, man,' I said. 'Now, tell me. What about the mob, the clique? Have they been re-housed as well?'

'No,' he said.

'No? What, then?'

'The clique's split up.'

'You mean,' I said, 'that bunch of tearaways have thrown you out?'

'Eh?' he cried.

'You heard, Ed. You've been expelled from the Ted college?'

'No! Me? Expel me? What? Listen! Me, I left *them*, see? You think I'm soft, or something?'

18.2.2 Commentary

Some respellings do not in fact alter the pronunciation of the word, but give the impression of an uneducated or dialect speaker simply because of the misspelling. This is called **eye-dialect**:

	Normal spelling	Pronunciation
bin	been	[bɪn]
lissen	listen	[lɪsən]
Mar	Ma	[mɑ]
wot	what	[wɒt]

(i)   [bɪn] is the normal unaccented pronunciation of *been*.

(ii)   *listen* has a 'silent' ⟨t⟩ in all dialects, [lɪsən].

(iii)   The spelling *Mar* is presumably intended to suggest a long low back vowel [mɑː], but this relies on the convention that the ⟨r⟩ in the spelling ⟨ar⟩ is not pronounced, and indicates the sound of the vowel. But there are several dialects in England that are still **rhotic** and pronounce the ⟨r⟩ after a vowel, as well as the Scots and the Americans.

(iv)   [wɒt] is the pronunciation of *what* in most dialects. In Scots, and in some careful pronunciations, the ⟨w⟩ is aspirated, ⟨hw⟩ – [ʍɒt].

	Normal spelling	Pronunciation
mɪ	my	[mɪ]

The spelling of *me* is intended to represent the normal reduced unaccented form of *my* – [mɪ], not the object pronoun *me* pronounced [miː].

The other respellings roughly indicate dialectal accent, and may be grouped into sets showing similar features:

Sound changes

RP	⇔ Dialectal	RP spelling		Respelling	
[aɪ]	⇔ [ɑ]	I've	⇔	arve	
		I	⇔	R	(an unusual use of a capital letter to show pronunciation)
[aʊ]	⇔ [æː]	down	⇔	darn	

[iː]	⇔	[ɪ]	clique	⇔	click
[ð]	⇔	[v]	the	⇔	v'
[θ]	⇔	[f]	think	⇔	fink
			something	⇔	sumfink
[ʊ]	⇔	[ɜː]	no	⇔	ner/naher
final [ŋ]	⇔	[ŋk]	something	⇔	sumfink

(⟨ng⟩ is still pronounced [ŋg], the original pronunciation, in some dialects, so the Cockney has simply devoiced the final [g] ⇒ [k])

cluster	⇔	single consonant	just	⇔	jus
			respect	⇔	respeck
			expel	⇔	espel
			left	⇔	lef
			soft	⇔	sof
loss of initial [h]			here	⇔	ear
			has	⇔	as
			housed	⇔	owsed

Activity 18.8

Discuss the presentation of dialect and accent in one or more of the following extracts from novels.

📖 This activity is discussed in the *Commentary & Data Book*.

1

'What 'ave you gotten stopped for?'

'For nowt, just nowt,' he began. 'Or, if you like, for bein' a man and not a damned monkey.... This morning I hadn't a waggon in, and so were doin' nowt for a bit. Simpson, t'under-manager, comes up and ses, "What are you on with Oakroyd?" and I tells him, "Nowt, just now." They're putting up a temporary shed for t'waggons, and so Simpson ses, "Well, help wi' t'shed. You can start by getting this into shape." And he points to a beam they pulled out o' t'old shed, and he finds measurements for me.'

(J. B. Priestley, *The Good Companions*, 1929)

2

'What are those?' she asked old Jerry.

'Love-apples, me dear. Love-apples, they be; though some hignorant folks be a callin' 'em tommytoes. But you don't want any o' they – nasty sour things, they be, as only gentry can eat...Don't 'ee go tryin' to eat it now. It'll only make 'ee sick.'

(Flora Thompson, *Lark Rise to Candleford*, 1939)

3

'Now, Master Poorgrass, your song!' said Coggan.

'I be all but in liquor, and the gift is wanting in me,' said Joseph, diminishing himself.

'Nonsense; wou'st never be so ungrateful, Joseph – never!' said Coggan, expressing hurt feelings by an inflection of voice. 'And mistress is looking hard at ye, as much as to say, "Sing at once, Joseph Poorgrass".'

'Faith, so she is; well, I must suffer it!...Just eye my features, and see if the tell-tale blood overheats me much, neighbours?'

'No, yer blushes be quite reasonable,' said Coggan.

'I always tries to keep my colours from rising when a beauty's eyes get fixed on me,' said Joseph, diffidently; 'but if so be 'tus willed they do, they must.'

(Thomas Hardy, *Far from the Madding Crowd*, 1874)

4

'Do you know what I ain't?' he said.

'What?' I said.

'I ain't a nigger any more. I done been abolished.' Then I asked him what he was, if he wasn't a nigger any more and he showed me what he had in his hand. It was a new scrip dollar; it was drawn on the United States Resident Treasurer, Yoknapatawpha County, Mississippi, and signed, 'Cassius Q Benbow, Acting Marshal' in a neat clerk's hand, with a big sprawling X under it.

'Cassius Q Benbow?' I said.

'Co-rect,' Ringo said. 'Uncle Cash that druv the Benbow carriage twell he run off with the Yankees two years ago. He back now and he gonter be elected Marshal of Jefferson. That's what Marse John and the other white folks is so busy about.'

'A nigger?' I said. 'A nigger?'

'No,' Ringo said. 'They ain't no more niggers in Jefferson nor nowhere else. Naw, suh, this war ain't over. Hit just started good. Used to be when you seed a Yankee you knowed him because he never had nothing but a gun or a mule halter or a handful of hen feathers. Now you don't even know him and stid of the gun he got a clutch of this stuff in one hand and a clutch of nigger voting tickets in the yuther.'

(William Faulkner, *The Unvanquished*, 1934)

We can now look at an extract from Sir Walter Scott's *The Bride of Lammermoor* from the point of view of its representation of Scots dialect.

18.2.2 *Scottish dialectal speech in* The Bride of Lammermoor

The impression of the narrator that we get when reading the novel is of an educated person of upper rank, speaking Standard English in a formal style. There is nothing specifically Scottish about it. The style is unchanged in the speech and dialogue of his upper-class characters, as you will see in the speech of the Master of Ravenswood in the extract below. But the speech of the many characters below the rank of lords, ladies and gentlemen is reproduced authentically, and we hear the genuine Scots dialect of the eighteenth and early nineteenth centuries.

This dialogue from *The Bride of Lammermoor* is an exchange between Ravenswood and Johnie Mortsheugh, one of his tenants and the church sexton, who is explaining how he lost his original place as trumpeter to the Ravenswood family.

Johnie's Scots dialectal accent is reproduced, in part, by Scott's respelling of numbers of words. There are some dialectal words also, which are translated into Standard English at the end of the extract.

Activity 18.9

Use the glossary at the end of the extract to study Johnie Mortsheugh's Scots dialect. Discuss the spelling and pronunciation, vocabulary, and the differences in grammatical structure between Johnie's and the Master's spoken dialogue, and the author's style of narrative.

'...But as for the Ravenswoods, I hae seen three generations of them, and deil ane to mend other'.

'I thought they had enjoyed a fair character in the country,' said their descendant.

'Character! Ou, ye see, sir,' said the sexton, 'as for the auld gude-sire body of a lord, I lived on his land when I was a swanking young chield, and could hae blawn the trumpet wi' ony body, for I had wind eneugh then – and touching this trumpeter marine that I have heard play afore the Lords of the Circuit, I wad hae made nae mair o' him than of a bairn and a bawbee whistle – I defy him to hae played "Boot and saddle," or "Horse and away," or "Gallants, come trot," with me – he hadna the tones.'

'But what is all this to old Lord Ravenswood, my friend?' said the Master, who, with an anxiety not unnatural in his circumstances, was desirous of prosecuting the musician's first topic – 'What had his memory to do with the degeneracy of the trumpet music?'

'Just this, sir,' answered the sexton, 'that I lost my wind in his service. Ye see I was trumpeter at the castle, and had allowance for blawing at break of day, and at dinner-time, and other whiles when there was company about, and it pleased my lord; and when he raised his militia to caper awa to Bothwell Brigg against the wrang-headed wastland whigs, I behoved, reason or nane, to munt a horse and caper awa wi'them.'

'And very reasonable,' said Ravenswood; 'you were his servant and vassal.'

'Servitor, say ye?' replied the sexton, 'and so I was – but it was to blaw folk to their warm dinner, or at the warst to a decent kirkyard, and no to skirl them awa to a bluidy brae side, where there was a deil a bedral but the hooded craw. But bide ye – ye shall hear what cam o't, and how far I am bund to be bedesman to the Ravenswoods. – Till't, ye see, we gaed on a braw simmer morning, twenty-fourth of June, saxteen hundred and se'enty-nine, of a' the days of the month and year, – drums beat – guns rattled – horses kicked and trampled. Hackstoun and Rathillet keepit the brigg wi' musket and carabine and pike, sword and scythe for what I ken, and we horsemen were ordered down to cross at the ford, – I hate fords at a' times, let abe when there's thousands of armed men on the other side. There was auld Ravenswood brandishing his Andrew Ferrara at the head, and crying to us to come and buckle to, as if we had been gaun to a fair, – there was Caleb Balderstone, that is living yet, flourishing in the rear, and swearing Gog and Magog, he would put steel through the guts of ony man that turned bridle, – there was young Allan Ravenswood, that was then Master, wi' a bended pistol in his hand, – it was a mercy it gaed na aff, – crying to me, that had scarce as much wind left as serve the necessary purpose of my ain lungs, "Sound, you poltroon! sound, you damned cowardly villain, or I will blow your brains out!" and, to be sure, I blew sic points of war, that the scraugh of a clockin-hen was music to them.'

'Well, sir, cut all this short,' said Ravenswood.

'Short! – I had like to hae been cut short mysell, in the flower of my youth, as Scripture says; and that's the very thing that I compleen o'. – Weel! in to the water we behoved a' to splash, heels ower head, sit or fa' – ae horse driving on anither, as is the way of brute beasts, and riders that hae as little sense, – the very bushes on the ither side were ableeze, wi' the flashes of the whig guns; and my horse had just taen the grund, when a blackavised westland carle – I wad mind the face o' him a hundred years yet – an ee like a wild falcon's, and a beard as broad as my shovel, clapped the end o' his lang black gun within a quarter's length of my lug! – by the grace o' Mercy, the horse swarved round, and I fell aff at the tae side as the ball whistled by at the tither, and the fell auld lord took the whig such a swauk wi' his broadsword that he made twa pieces o' his head, and down fell the lurdane wi' a' his bowk abune me.' 'You were rather obliged to the old lord, I think,' said Ravenswood. 'Was I? my sartie! first for bringing me into jeopardy, would I nould I – and then for whomling a chield on the tap o' me, that dang the very wind out of my body? – I hae been short-breathed ever since, and canna gang twenty yards without peghing like a miller's aiver.' 'You lost, then, your place as trumpeter?' said Ravenswood. 'Lost it? to be sure I lost it,' replied the sexton, 'for I couldna hae played pew upon a dry humlock...'

Scots	English	Scots	English
(let) abe	be	*gude-sire*	grandfather
abune	above	*humlock*	hemlock (stalk)
aiver	carthorse	*ken*	know
bairn	child	*lug*	ear
bawbee	halfpenny	*lurdane*	rogue, rascal
bedesman	pensioner, almsman	*mind (v)*	remember
bedral	beadle	*my ain*	my own
blackavised	dark-complexioned	*peghing*	puffing, gasping
bowk	= bulk	*play pew*	puff
brae	bank, brow of hill	*sartie*	?
braw	fine, splendid	*scraugh*	screech
brigg	bridge	*skirl (v)*	scream, screech
carle	fellow, peasant	*swanking*	active, agile
chield	child, fellow	*swauk (n)*	swipe, blow
dang f. ding	beat, knock	*tae – tither*	the one – the other
deil	devil	*till*	to
ee	eye	*whomling f. whummle*	push, overturn
fell (adj)	fierce		

📖 A complete table with derivations is in the *Commentary & Data Book*.

Activity 18.10

(i) Write out the text in conventional spelling, changing all the dialectal fatures to Standard English.

(ii) Distinguish between the features of **dialect** (vocabulary or structure) and **accent** (pronunciation) that are marked in the text.

(iii) What difference does the change to Standard English vocabulary and conventional spelling make to your impression of the sexton?

📖 A complete rewritten text and commentary is in the *Commentary & Data Book*.

Activity 18.11

(i) Identify the Scots dialectal vocabulary and accent in the following extract from Sir Walter Scott's *The Antiquary*.

(ii) Contrast the language of the speaker with that of the author's narrative style in the second paragraph.

📖 This Activity is discussed in the *Commentary & Data Book*.

[*Edie Ochiltree is the king's bedesman – 'one who prays for the souls of others' – with a licence to beg. He has been wrongly put in prison.*]

'The prison,' he said, 'wasna sae dooms bad a place as it was ca'd. Ye had aye a good roof ower your head to fend off the weather, and, if the windows werena glazed, it was the mair airy and pleasant for the summer season. And there were folk enow to crack wi', and he had bread eneugh to eat, and what need he fash himsell about the rest o't.'

The courage of our philosophical mendicant began, however, to abate, when the sunbeams shone fair on the rusty bars of his grated dungeon, and a miserable linnet, whose cage some poor debtor had obtained permission to attach to the window, began to greet them with his whistle.

'Ye're in better spirits than I am,' said Edie, addressing the bird, 'for I can neither whistle nor sing for thinking of the bonnie burnsides and green shaws that I should hae been dandering beside in weather like this. – But hae, there's some crumbs t'ye, an ye are sae merry; and troth ye hae some reason to sing an ye kent it, for your cage comes by nae faut of your ain, and I may thank mysell that I am closed up in this weary place.'

dooms	very, extremely	*shaws*	woods
crack	talk, gossip	*dandering*	strolling
fash	trouble	*kent*	knew
burn	stream, brook		

18.3 The spoken voice in letters

Samuel Richardson (1689–1761) was one of the most popular novelists of the eighteenth century, though now he is not so widely read. His first novel *Pamela* began as a series of letters on the problems of everyday life. It was published in 1740 and was immediately successful. His long second novel, *Clarissa* or *The History of a Young Lady* (1747–8) was also written as a series of letters – an **epistolary** novel – and so gives us an approximation to the styles of contemporary speech and informal conversation.

Activity 18.12

What stylistic features of the following short extract from *Clarissa* suggest the spoken voice?

This Activity is discussed, with a structural analysis, in the *Commentary & Data Book*.

Miss Clarissa Harlowe, To Miss Howe
[After Clarissa's return from a visit]

Harlowe-Place, Feb. 20.

I beg your excuse for not writing sooner. Alas. my dear, I have sad prospects before me! My Brother and Sister have succeeded in all their views. They have found out another Lover for me; an hideous one! – yet he is encouraged by every-body. No wonder that I was ordered home so suddenly. At an hour's warning! – No other notice, you know, than what was brought with the chariot that was to carry me back. – It was for fear, as I have been informed [an unworthy fear!] that I should have entered into any concert with Mr. Lovelace had I known their motive for commanding me home; apprehending, 'tis evident, that I should dislike the man they had to propose to me. And well might they apprehend so: – For who do you think he is? – No other than that Solmes! – Could you have believed it? – And they are all determined too; my Mother with the rest! – Dear, dear excellence! how could she be thus brought over, when I am assured that on his first being proposed she was pleased to say, That had Mr. Solmes the Indies in possession, and would endow me with them, she should not think him deserving of her Clarissa? ...

...Mr. Solmes came in before we had done Tea. My Uncle Antony presented him to me, as a gentleman he had a particular friendship for. My Uncle Harlowe in terms equally favourable for him. My father said, Mr. Solmes is my friend, Clarissa Harlowe. My Mother looked at him, and looked at me, now-and-then, as he sat near me, I thought with concern. – I at her, with eyes appealing for pity. At him, when I could glance at him, with disgust little short of affrightment. While my Brother and Sister Mr. Solmes'd him, and Sirr'd him up, at every word. So caressed in short, by all; – yet such a wretch! – But I will at present only add, My humble thanks and duty to your honoured Mother (to whom I will particularly write, to express the grateful Sense I have of her goodness to me); and that I am

Your ever obliged,

CL. HARLOWE.

18.4 The unspoken voice – interior monologue

In the first half of the twentieth century some novelists were influenced by contemporary psychological writing and began to represent the unbroken flow of associated ideas, memories and sense impressions of their characters. This kind of **interior monologue** is also called **stream of consciousness**, and is demonstrated at length in the three main characters of James Joyce's novel *Ulysses* (1922), a story set in Dublin on a single day, Thursday 16 June, 1904, now known as *Bloomsday*, after the chief character.

18.4.1 *James Joyce's* Ulysses

The three main characters in a cast of dozens are Leopold Bloom, a Jewish advertising agent, his wife Molly, and Stephen Dedalus, who was the subject of Joyce's earlier autobiographical novel *Portrait of the Artist as a Young Man*. As we follow their activities during the day, we overhear their thoughts and impressions in interior monologues that clearly differentiate the three characters.

18.4.1.1 LEOPOLD BLOOM

In chapter 6 of *Ulysses* Leopold Bloom attends the funeral of a friend and joins others in a horse-drawn carriage taking them to the cemetery. They are passing through the streets of Dublin,

> The carriage halted short.
> —What's wrong?
> —We're stopped.
> —Where are we?
> Mr Bloom put his head out of the window.
> —The grand canal, he said.
> Gasworks. Whooping cough they say it cures. Good job Milly* never got it. Poor children! Doubles them up black and blue in convulsions. Shame really. Got off lightly with illnesses compared. Only measles. Flaxseed tea. Scarlatina, influenza epidemics. Canvassing for death. Don't miss this chance. Dogs' home over there. Poor old Athos*! Be good to Athos, Leopold, is my last wish. Thy will be done. We obey them in the grave. A dying scrawl. He took it to heart, pined away. Quiet brute. Old men's dogs usually are.
> A raindrop spat on his hat. He drew back and saw an instant of shower spray dots over the grey flags. Apart. Curious. Like through a colander. I thought it would. My boots were creaking I remember now.
> —The weather is changing, he said quietly.

* Milly is Bloom's daughter; Athos was Bloom's father's dog.

Joyce does not use any typographical devices to indicate the difference between narrative and interior monologue, nor does he use conventional speech marks to show dialogue, simply a long dash at the beginning of each speaker's contribution. The sense and grammar tell us which is which, so that the narrative content,

> The carriage halted short.
> Mr Bloom put his head out of the window.
> A raindrop spat on his hat. He drew back and saw an instant of shower spray dots over the grey flags.

has the verbs of its short clauses in the simple past tense, whereas the interior monologue consists largely of minor sentences without verbs.

18.4.1.2 MOLLY BLOOM

In the final chapter 18 Molly Bloom is in bed almost asleep, waiting for Leopold to return home. The whole chapter is a long soliloquy, a stream of Molly's consciousness as the events of the past day and her past life go through her mind. Here she is thinking of her husband:

> still I like that in him polite to old women like that and waiters and beggars too hes not proud out of nothing but not always if ever he got anything really serious the matter with him its much better for them to go into a hospital where everything is clean but I suppose Id have to dring it into him for a month yes and then wed have a hospital nurse next thing on the carpet have him staying there till they throw him out or a nun maybe like the smutty photo he has shes as much a nun as Im not yes

18.4.1.3 STEPHEN DEDALUS

Stephen is based on Joyce's own character and is the subject of the earlier autobiographical *Portrait of the Artist as a Young Man*. Just as in the chapters about Bloom, the text moves from narrative to dialogue and interior monologue. This short extract demonstrates the three modes in that order,

> [*Stephen, who intends to be a writer, is living with a medical student, Buck Mulligan, in a martello tower on the coast near Dublin. 'Kinch' is Mulligan's nickname for Stephen. It is early morning.*]
>
> Buck Mulligan suddenly linked his arm in Stephen's and walked with him round the tower, his razor and mirror clacking in the pocket where he had thrust them.
> —It's not fair to tease you like that, Kinch, is it? he said kindly. God knows you have more spirit than any of them.
> Parried again. He fears the lancet of my art as I fear that of his. The cold steel pen.

Activity 18.13

Identify the narrative, dialogue and interior monologue in the following short extracts from *Ulysses*.

📖 This Activity is discussed in the *Commentary & Data Book*.

1. Molly

because theyre so weak and puling when theyre sick they want a woman to get well if his nose bleeds youd think it was O tragic and that dyinglooking one off the south circular when he sprained his foot at the choir party at the sugarloaf Mountain the day I wore that dress Miss

Stack bringing him flowers the worst old ones she could find at the bottom of the basket anything at all to get into a mans bedroom with her old maids voice trying to imagine he was dying on account of her to never see thy face again though he looked more like a man with his beard grown a bit in the bed father was the same

2. Stephen

[*Stephen has a temporary job as a teacher. He is taking a lesson in Roman history.*]

—You, Armstrong. Do you know anything about Pyrrhus?

A bag of figrolls lay snugly in Armstrong's satchel. He curled them between his palms at whiles and swallowed them softly. Crumbs adhered to the tissues of his lips. A sweetened boy's breath. Welloff people, proud that their eldest son was in the navy. Vico Road. Dalkey.

—Pyrrhus, sir? Pyrrhus, a pier.

All laughed. Mirthless high malicious laughter. Armstrong looked round at his classmates, silly glee in profile. In a moment they will laugh more loudly, aware of my lack of rule and of the fees their papas pay.

3. Bloom

[*Bloom is in the carriage going to the cemetery.*]

—Are we late? Mr Power asked.

—Ten minutes, Martin Cunningham said, looking at his watch.

Molly. Milly. Same thing watered down. Her tomboy oaths. O Jumping Jupiter! Ye gods and little fishes! Still, she's a dear girl. Soon be a woman. Mullingar*. Dearest Papli*. Young student. Yes, yes: a woman too. Life.

The carriage heeled over and back, their four trunks swaying.

* Bloom's daughter Milly is living at Mullingar. 'Papli' is a nickname for 'father'.

19. Original and simplified texts

The literature of the past is sometimes difficult to read, either because the language has changed so much that words and structures are unfamiliar, or because the author's style is complex and different from 'ordinary language'. This is a particular problem for pupils learning to read, or for anyone who finds reading difficult, so that they are unable to read and enjoy many worthwhile books.

In order to help learners and slow readers (and also foreign learners of English), 'simplified' versions of novels and stories are published, and it is interesting to compare the differences between originals and simplified versions,

(a) to understand more clearly what differences of style are produced by the use of different choices of language, and
(b) to appreciate the quality of the original as a piece of literary writing.

When we compare two texts with the same underlying narrative (as in an original and a simplified text, or perhaps two translations of the same foreign language text), there are often omissions and changes of content to observe as well.

19.1 Robert Louis Stevenson's *Treasure Island*

On the next pages are two versions of the opening paragraphs of Robert Louis Stevenson's classic *Treasure Island*, which was published in 1883. He had originally started to write the story to amuse his twelve-year-old stepson during the winter months, and used to read it aloud to him. The simplified version was prepared for the use of foreign learners of English as a second language.

Activity 19.1
Read text A (the original) and write a brief commentary on its suitability for 12-year-old readers today.

Activity 19.2

Read text B, and write down your reaction to its style. Has anything been gained or lost?

Text A *Part I: The Old Buccaneer – Chapter I, 'The old sea-dog at the "Admiral Benbow"'*

Squire Trelawney, Dr. Livesey, and the rest of these gentlemen having asked me to write down the whole particulars about Treasure Island, from the beginning to the end, keeping nothing back but the bearings of the island, and that only because there is still treasure not yet lifted, I take up my pen in the year of grace 17–, and go back to the time when my father kept the 'Admiral Benbow' inn, and the brown old seaman, with the sabre-cut, first took up his lodging under our roof.

I remember him as if it were yesterday, as he came plodding to the inn door, his sea-chest following behind him in a hand-barrow; a tall, strong, heavy, nut-brown man; his tarry pigtail falling over the shoulders of his soiled blue coat; his hands ragged and scarred, with black, broken nails; and the sabre-cut across one cheek, a dirty, livid white. I remember him looking round the cove and whistling to himself as he did so, and then breaking out in that old sea-song that he sang so often afterwards:– 'Fifteen men on the dead man's chest– Yo-ho-ho, and a bottle of rum!' in the high, old tottering voice that seemed to have been tuned and broken at the capstan bars. Then he rapped on the door with a bit of stick like a handspike that he carried, and when my father appeared, called roughly for a glass of rum. This, when it was brought to him, he drank slowly, like a connoisseur, lingering on the taste, and still looking about him at the cliffs and up at our signboard.

'This is a handy cove,' says he, at length; 'and a pleasant sittyated grog-shop. – Much company, mate?'

My father told him no, – very little company, the more was the pity.

'Well then,' said he, 'this is the berth for me. Here you, matey,' he cried to the man who trundled the barrow; 'bring up alongside and help up my chest. I'll stay here a bit,' he continued. 'I'm a plain man; rum and bacon and eggs is what I want, and that head up there for to watch ships off. What you mought call me? You mought call me captain. Oh, I see what you're at – there!' and he threw down three or four gold pieces on the threshold. 'You can tell me when I've worked through that,' says he, looking as fierce as a commander.

Readability – easy

Text B *Jim Hawkins tells his story – Chapter one, 'The old seaman at the Benbow Inn'*

I remember him clearly, the brown old seaman, as he came to the inn door, his sea chest following behind him in a handcart; a tall, strong, heavy man in a dirty blue coat; his hands hard and torn; and the sword-cut across one cheek, a dirty, blue-white mark. I remember him looking round the bay and singing that old sea song: 'Fifteen men on the dead man's chest Yo-ho-ho, and a bottle of rum!'. Then he knocked on the door with a bit of stick and, when my father appeared, called roughly for a glass of rum. He drank the rum slowly, still looking about him at the cliffs and up at our signboard.

'This is a nice bay,' he said at last, 'and a pleasantly placed inn. Do many people come here?'

My father told him no – unfortunately.

'Well, then,' the old man said, 'this is the place for me. Here you, young fellow!' he cried to the man with the handcart. 'Bring my chest in. I'll stay here a bit.' And to my father he said, 'You may call me "Captain".' And he threw down three or four gold pieces on the floor. 'You can tell me when I've worked through that,' he said, looking very fierce.

Readability – very easy

19.1.1 *Omission and changing of words*

The writer of the simplified version has done two things:

(i) he has **omitted** a lot of the original text, sometimes a whole paragraph, sometimes phrases or single words, and
(ii) he has **changed** the original wording.

The two texts are next set out side by side, with the corresponding paragraphs opposite each other, so that you can make comparisons more easily. Those parts of the original which are omitted or changed in the simplified version are printed in *bold italic type*. Similarly, the same type is used to mark the parts of the simplified version which differ from the original.

The following activities suggest a way in which you can make a detailed study of the two texts, and they should help you to assess the quality of Robert Louis Stevenson's writing and the value of the simplified version.

Activity 19.3

The whole of the first paragraph of the original is left out in the simplified version.

(i) What is the purpose of the information which is given us in the original opening paragraph?

(ii) Is the paragraph difficult for a 12-year-old reader? If so, what are the difficulties?

Activity 19.4

Discuss each omission and change (or a selected number of them) in the simplified version:

(i) Suggest a reason for the omission and say how far you think it affects the meaning.

(ii) For each change, explain any difference between the choice of wording in the two versions. Is the alteration justified because of the difficulty of the original? Is the original meaning retained?

Chapter I, 'The old sea-*dog* at the "*Admiral* Benbow"'	Chapter one, 'The old sea*man* at the Benbow *Inn*'

Squire Trelawney, Dr. Livesey, and the rest of these gentlemen having asked me to write down the whole particulars about Treasure Island, from the beginning to the end, keeping nothing back but the bearings of the island, and that only because there is still treasure not yet lifted, I take up my pen in the year of grace 17-, and go back to the time when my father kept the 'Admiral Benbow' inn, and the brown old seaman, with the sabre-cut, first took up his lodging under our roof.

I remember him **as if it were yesterday**, as he came **plodding** to the inn door, his seachest following behind him in a **handbarrow**; a tall, strong, heavy, **nut-brown** man; **his tarry pigtail falling over the shoulders** of his **soiled** blue coat; his hands **ragged** and **scarred, with black, broken nails**; and the **sabre**-cut across one cheek, a dirty, **livid** white. I remember him looking round the **cove** and **whistling to himself as he did so, and then breaking out in** that old sea-song **that he sang so often afterwards**:-

'Fifteen men on the dead man's chest– Yo-ho-ho, and a bottle of rum!'

in the high, old tottering voice that seemed to have been tuned and broken at the capstan bars. Then he **rapped** on the door with a bit of stick **like a handspike that he carried**, and when my father appeared, called roughly for a glass of rum. **This, when it was brought to him**, he drank slowly, **like a connoisseur, lingering on the taste**, and still looking about him at the cliffs and up at our signboard.

'This is a **handy cove**,' **says he**, at **length**; 'and a pleasant **sittyated grog-shop**. – **Much company, mate?**'

My father told him no, – **very little company, the more was the pity.**

'Well then,' said he, 'this is the **berth** for me. Here you, **matey**,' he cried to the man **who trundled the barrow**; 'bring **up alongside and help up** my chest. I'll stay here a bit,' **he continued. 'I'm a plain man; rum and bacon and eggs is what I want, and that head up there for to watch ships off. What you mought call me?** You **mought** call me captain. **Oh, I see what you're at – there!**' and he threw down three or four gold pieces on the **threshold**. 'You can tell me when I've worked through that,' **says he**, looking **as** fierce **as a commander.**

I remember him **clearly, the brown old seaman**, as he came to the inn door, his sea chest following behind him in a **handcart**; a tall, strong, heavy man

in a **dirty** blue coat; his hands **hard** and **torn**; and the **sword**-cut across one cheek, a dirty, **blue**-white **mark**. I remember him looking round the **bay** and

singing that old sea song:

'Fifteen men on the dead man's chest Yo-ho-ho, and a bottle of rum!'

Then he **knocked** on the door with a bit of stick and, when my father appeared, called roughly for a glass of rum.

He drank **the rum** slowly, still looking about him at the cliffs and up at our signboard.

'This is a **nice bay**,' **he said** at **last**, 'and a pleasantly **placed inn. Do many people come here?**'

My father told him no – **unfortunately.**

'Well, then,' **the old man** said, 'this is the **place** for me. Here you, **young fellow!**' he cried to the man **with the handcart**. '**Bring my chest in**. I'll stay here a bit.'

And to my father he said, 'You **may** call me "Captain".'

And he threw down three or four gold pieces on the **floor**. 'You can tell me when I've worked through that,' **he said**, looking **very** fierce.

19.1.2 *Grammatical structure – sentence level*

The grammar of text B, the simplified version, is less complex than the original, but it is not oversimplified, however. (Some simplified texts reduce structure to a series of simple one-clause sentences.) For example, the first sentence of B keeps to a pattern similar to A's corresponding second sentence, though it is reduced in length by the omission of detail. B follows the descriptive pattern of the original in a series of **nonfinite clauses** (NonfCl) and noun phrases functioning like clauses but without verbs – **verbless clauses** (Vbless Cl):

Text A

MCl	I remember him
AdvCl	as if it were yesterday,
AdvCl	as he came plodding to the inn door,
NonfCl	his sea-chest following behind him in a hand-barrow;
Vbless Cl	a tall, strong, heavy, nut-brown man;
NonfCl	his tarry pigtail falling over the shoulders of his soiled blue coat;
Vbless Cl	his hands ragged and scarred, with black, broken nails;
Vbless Cl	and the sabre-cut across one cheek, a dirty, livid white.

Text B

MCl	I remember him clearly, the brown old seaman,
AdvCl	as he came to the inn door,
NonfCl	his sea chest following behind him in a handcart;
Vbless Cl	a tall, strong, heavy man in a dirty blue coat;
Vbless Cl	his hands hard and torn;
Vbless Cl	and the sword-cut across one cheek, a dirty, blue-white mark.

The difficulty of paragraph 1 of the original is structural – that is, in the organisation and relationship of its clauses and phrases. It consists of only one sentence, but contains seven clauses. The first three clauses are introductory, non-finite clauses without main verbs, which need to be held 'in suspension' before the main clauses finally appear. This kind of **front-weighted** structure is more difficult to read and process in the mind:

NonfCl	Squire Trelawney, Dr. Livesey, and the rest of these gentlemen having asked me to write down the whole particulars about Treasure Island, from the beginning to the end,
NonfCl	keeping nothing back but the bearings of the island, and that only
AdvCl	because there is still treasure not yet lifted
MCl	**I take up my pen in the year of grace 17–,** and
MCl	**[I] go back to the time**
RelCl	when my father kept the 'Admiral Benbow' inn, and
RelCl	[when] the brown old seaman, with the sabre-cut, first took up his lodging under our roof.

19.1.3 *Grammatical structure – clause level*

There is also complexity at clause level. The structure of a declarative clause is SP(C)(A) – Subject, followed by Predicator (Verb) and, if the sense requires it, one or more Complements (including Objects) and Adverbials. For example,

> *S   P   O   A*
> He drank the rum slowly,

is the simplified version of,

> *O   A = AdvCl   S P   A   A = PrepP*
> This, [when it was brought to him,] he drank slowly, (like a connoisseur),
>
>   *A = NonfCl*
>   [lingering on the taste].

The **object** (O) *This* is brought to the front as **theme**, and the second adverbial *like a connoisseur* is a **prepositional phrase** (PrepP). In addition, the main clause, *This he drank slowly like a connoisseur*, is split by an **adverbial clause** (AdvCl), *when it was brought to him*, and concluded with a second adverbial clause, this time **nonfinite** (NonfCl), *lingering on the taste*. This structure is complex because clauses are embedded within the main clause. A less complex version would have been, for example,

> *A   S P   A   A   A*
> This **then** he drank slowly, **expertly** and **lingeringly**.

There is a similar complexity within the clauses of the opening sentence of the original text:

> *S*   *P*
> *NP*   *NP*   *NP*
> Squire Trelawney, Dr. Livesey, and the rest of these gentlemen having asked
>
> *(O/S) P*   *O*
>   *NP*
>   **d   m   h   q**
> me   to write down the whole particulars about Treasure Island,
>
> *A*   *A*
> *PrepP*   *PrepP*
> from the beginning to the end,

The subject (S) is a complex noun phrase (NP) consisting of three coordinated NPs. The predicator (P) is also complex, an example of **predicators in phase** with two main verbs, and *me* functioning as the object (O) of *having asked* and also as the subject (S) of *to write down*. The object complement (O) is a complex NP, with a qualifier (q) (a post-modifying PrepP *about Treasure Island*) – and there are two more adverbial PrepPs to conclude, *from the beginning* and *to the end*.

This descriptive explanation is more complex than the original clause, but if you follow it closely with the diagram, it should help you to understand the difference between more simple and more complex grammatical structures.

The author of the simplified edition has either omitted or reduced such relatively complex structures. Some other examples are,

> *ccj S P   C*
> as if it were yesterday   ⇒   clearly
> *AdvCl*   ⇒   *Adverb*
>
>   **p   d   h   q**
> his tarry pigtail falling over the shoulders of his soiled blue coat ⇒ in a dirty blue coat
> *NonfCl*   ⇒ *PrepP*
>
> *A* = PrepP with relative clause as qualifier (post-modifier)
> **p   d   m   m   m   h   q**
>   *RelCl*
>   *S   P*   *P   A*
> in the high, old tottering voice that seemed to have been tuned and broken at
> the capstan bars ⇒
> (omitted in simplified version)

But simplifying the text to reduce some of the stuctural complexity transforms Stevenson's art as a writer. For example, the last two extracts just quoted are essential to the vividness of the description of the 'old sea-dog'. They are the means by which we begin to create him as a 'character', seeing him visually and hearing him talk.

19.1.4   The dialogue

The dialogue between the old sea-dog and Jim Hawkins's father is equally important. The Captain talks in an informal style and uses 'nautical' jargon – *handy cove, grog-shop, matey, berth, bring up alongside.* The two words *sittyated* and *mought* are enough for us to hear some kind of dialectal accent in the pronunciation of *situated* and the archaic past tense form *mought* of the verb *may.* His dialect is also heard in the non-standard *that head up there for to* watch ships *off.*

This is one feature of text B that fails to match the original. There is a complete loss of characterisation in the simplified wording of *this is the place for me* and *Here you, young fellow. Bring my chest in,* as well as in the omission of *rum and bacon and eggs is what I want.*

19.1.5   Is a change of words a change of meaning?

Choice of words is really inseparable from structural choice in producing the effectiveness of narrative description and dialogue, and you will have already observed and described the change brought about by, for example, omitting or changing *plodding, nut-brown, tarry pigtail, ragged and scarred, black broken nails, livid, whistling to himself, high old tottering voice, like a connoisseur,* and so on.

A writer commissioned to produce a simplified version of an established novel is in a dilemma. Changing the wording rewrites the novel into something different. The underlying narrative may be retained, but no retelling of it can be Robert Louis Stevenson's *Treasure Island.* So we must judge the success of the new version in terms of its function – to provide a text which foreign learners of English can read more easily than the original.

This is not, however, the point of this chapter, which is focused on the text of the original, in order to understand a little about how Stevenson's style works. Using a simplified version means that we can make a **contrastive analysis** of the two texts. You will find this a very helpful way of studying style.

19.2   Charles Dickens's *David Copperfield*

Here are three versions of an episode in *David Copperfield.* The young David is being sent away to school by his step-father. Pegotty is the housekeeper and David's nurse.

Activity 19.5 _____

(i) Read the three versions. What are your first impressions?

(ii) Text C tells the 'story'. Is the original text A necessary?

Text A

After we had jogged on for some little time, I asked the carrier if he was going all the way.

'All the way where?' inquired the carrier.

'There,' I said.

'Where's there?' inquired the carrier.

'Near London,' I said.

'Why, that horse,' said the carrier, jerking the rein to point him out, 'would be deader than pork afore he got over half the ground.'

'Are you only going to Yarmouth, then?' I asked.

'That's about it,' said the carrier. 'And there I shall take you to the stage-cutch, and the stage-cutch that'll take you to – wherever it is.'

As this was a great deal for the carrier (whose name was Mr Barkis) to say – he being, as I observed in a former chapter, of a phlegmatic temperament, and not at all conversational – I offered him a cake as a mark of attention, which he ate at one gulp, exactly like an elephant, and which made no more impression on his big face than it would have done on an elephant's.

'Did *she* make 'em, now?' said Mr Barkis, always leaning forward, in his slouching way, on the footboard of the cart with an arm on each knee.

'Peggotty, do you mean, sir?'

'Ah!' said Mr Barkis. 'Her.'

'Yes. She makes all our pastry and does all our cooking.'

'Do she though?' said Mr Barkis.

He made up his mouth as if to whistle, but he didn't whistle. He sat looking at the horse's ears, as if he saw something new there; and sat so for a considerable time. By-and-by, he said:

'No sweethearts, I b'lieve?'

'Sweetmeats did you say, Mr Barkis?' For I thought he wanted something else to eat, and had pointedly alluded to that description of refreshment.

'Hearts,' said Mr Barkis. 'Sweethearts; no person walks with her?'

'With Peggotty?'

'Ah!' he said. 'Her.'

'Oh, no. She never had a sweetheart.'

'Didn't she, though?' said Mr Barkis.

Again he made up his mouth to whistle, and again he didn't whistle, but sat looking at the horse's ears.

'So she makes,' said Mr Barkis, after a long interval of reflection, 'all the apple parsties, and she does all the cooking, do she?'

I replied that such was the fact.

'Well, I'll tell you what,' said Mr Barkis. 'P'raps you might be writin' to her?'

'I shall certainly write to her,' I rejoined.

'Ah!' he said, slowly turning his eyes towards me. 'Well! If you was writin' to her, p'raps you'd recollect to say that Barkis was willin'; would you?'

'That Barkis was willing,' I repeated, innocently. 'Is that all the message?'

'Ye-es,' he said, considering. 'Ye-es. Barkis is willin'.'

'But you will be at Blunderstone again tomorrow, Mr Barkis,' I said, faltering a little at the idea of my being far away from it then, 'and could give your own message so much better.'

As he repudiated this suggestion, however, with a jerk of his head, and once more confirmed his previous request by saying, with profound gravity, 'Barkis is willin'. That's the message,' I readily undertook its transmission.

Readability – easy

Text B

I asked the carrier, 'Are we going all the way there?'

'All the way where?' asked the carrier.

'There,' I said.

'Where is "there"?' asked the carrier.

'London,' I asked.

'Why that horse would be dead before he got half that distance. I'm only going to Yarmouth, and the *coach* will take you to London.' This was a long speech for Mr Barkis. (Barkis was the name of the carrier.)

I offered him a cake. He put it in his big mouth and swallowed it whole.

'Did she make that?' he said.

'Do you mean Peggotty, sir? – Yes, she did. She does all the cooking.'

Mr Barkis sat looking at the horse's ears, and thinking for a long time.

Then he said, 'No husband?'

'No, sir. She is not married.'

He sat looking at the horse's ears.

'So she does all the cooking?'

'Yes,' I answered.

'Perhaps you will be writing to her?' he said.

'Yes,' I answered.

'Well,' he answered, slowly turning his eyes towards me, 'if you are writing to her, say that Barkis is willing.'

' "Barkis is willing." – Is that all the message?' said I, not understanding.

'Yes,' he said slowly.

'But you will be passing my home tomorrow, Mr Barkis. Could you not give your own message better?'

' "Barkis is willing." That's the message,' he said.

Readability – very easy

Text C

The cart took me to Yarmouth. Mr Barkis was driving it and he asked me a lot of questions about Peggotty. He wanted to marry her but he was afraid to speak to her. She did not know that he wanted to marry her.

Readability – easy

Activity 19.6

The original text A is printed below with the parts that were omitted in the simplified version B in bold italics.

Discuss the purpose and effect of those parts in Dickens's original. What is lost by leaving them out?

After we had jogged on for some little time, I asked the carrier if he was going all the way.

'All the way where?' inquired the carrier.

'There,' I said.

'Where's there?' inquired the carrier.

'Near London,' I said.

'Why, that horse,' said the carrier, *jerking the rein to point him out*, 'would be deader than pork afore he got over half the ground.'

'Are you only going to Yarmouth, then?' I asked.

'That's about it,' said the carrier. 'And there I shall take you to the stage-cutch, and the stage-cutch that'll take you to – wherever it is.'

As this was a great deal for the carrier (whose name was Mr Barkis) to say - *he being, as I observed in a former chapter, of a phlegmatic temperament, and not at all conversational* – I offered him a cake *as a mark of attention*, which he ate at one gulp, *exactly like an elephant, and which made no more impression on his big face than it would have done on an elephant's.*

'Did *she* make 'em, now?' said Mr Barkis, *always leaning forward, in his slouching way, on the footboard of the cart with an arm on each knee.*

'Peggotty, do you mean, sir?'

'Ah!' said Mr Barkis. 'Her.'

'Yes. She makes all our pastry and does all our cooking.'

'Do she though?' said Mr Barkis.

He made up his mouth as if to whistle, but he didn't whistle. He sat looking at the horse's ears, *as if he saw something new there*; and sat so for a considerable time. By-and-by, he said:

'No sweethearts, I b'lieve?'

'Sweetmeats did you say, Mr Barkis?' For I thought he wanted something else to eat, and had pointedly alluded to that description of refreshment.

'Hearts,' said Mr Barkis. 'Sweethearts; no person walks with her?'

'With Peggotty?'

'Ah!' he said. 'Her.'

'Oh, no. She never had a sweetheart.'

'Didn't she, though?' said Mr Barkis.

Again he made up his mouth to whistle, and again he didn't whistle, but sat looking at the horse's ears.

'So she makes,' said Mr Barkis, after a long interval of reflection, 'all the apple parstles, and she does all the cooking, do she?'

I replied that such was the fact.

'Well, I'll tell you what,' said Mr Barkis. 'P'raps you might be writin' to her?'

'I shall certainly write to her,' I rejoined.

'Ah!' he said, slowly turning his eyes towards me. 'Well! If you was writin' to her, p'raps you'd recollect to say that Barkis was willin'; would you?'

'That Barkis was willing,' *I repeated, innocently.* 'Is that all the message?'

'Ye-es,' he said, considering. 'Ye-es. Barkis is willin'.'

'But you will be at Blunderstone again tomorrow, Mr Barkis,' *I said, faltering a little at the idea of my being far away from it then,* 'and could give your own message so much better.'

As he repudiated this suggestion, however, with a jerk of his head, and once more confirmed his previous request by saying, with profound gravity, 'Barkis is willin'. That's the message,' *I readily undertook its transmission.*

Activity 19.7

Text A and text B are now printed side by side with only those parts of text A that were used in the simplified version. The omitted sections are marked with an asterisk*.

Compare and contrast the language of the two versions.

Text A

I asked the carrier if he was going all the way.

'All the way where?' inquired the carrier.

'There,' I said.

'Where's there?' inquired the carrier.

'Near London,' I said.

Text B

I asked the carrier, 'Are we going all the way there?'

'All the way where?' asked the carrier.

'There,' I said.

'Where is 'there'?' asked the carrier.

'London,' I asked.

'Why, that horse,' said the carrier *, 'would be deader than pork afore he got over half the ground.'

'Are you only going to Yarmouth, then?' I asked.

'And there I shall take you to the stage-cutch, and the stage-cutch that'll take you to – wherever it is.'

As this was a great deal for the carrier (whose name was Mr Barkis) to say – * – I offered him a cake* , which he ate at one gulp, *.

'Did *she* make 'em, now?' said Mr Barkis*.

'Peggotty, do you mean, sir?' *

'Yes. She makes all our pastry and does all our cooking.'

* He sat looking at the horse's ears *; and sat so for a considerable time. By-and-by, he said:

'No sweethearts, I b'lieve?' *.

'Oh, no. She never had a sweetheart.'

*but sat looking at the horse's ears.

'So she * does all the cooking, do she?' I replied that such was the fact.

* said Mr Barkis. 'P'raps you might be writin' to her?'

'I shall certainly write to her,' I rejoined.

'Ah!' he said, slowly turning his eyes towards me. 'Well! If you was writin' to her, p'raps you'd recollect to say that Barkis was willin'; would you?'

'That Barkis was willing,' *. 'Is that all the message?'

'Ye-es,' he said, considering. *.

'But you will be at Blunderstone again tomorrow, Mr Barkis,'* 'and could give your own message so much better.'

* 'Barkis is willin'. That's the message,' *.

'Why that horse would be dead before he got half that distance. I'm only going to Yarmouth, and the *coach* will take you to London.'

This was a long speech for Mr Barkis. (Barkis was the name of the carrier.). I offered him a cake. He put it in his big mouth and swallowed it whole.

'Did she make that?' he said.

Do you mean Peggotty, sir? –
Yes, she did. She does all the cooking.'

Mr Barkis sat looking at the horse's ears, and thinking for a long time. Then he said,

'No husband?'

'No, sir. She is not married.'
He sat looking at the horse's ears.
'So she does all the cooking?'
'Yes,' I answered.
'Perhaps you will be writing to her?' he said.

'Yes,' I answered.

'Well, he answered, slowly turning his eyes towards me, 'if you are writing to her, say that Barkis is willing.'

' "Barkis is willing." – Is that all the message?' said I, not understanding.

'Yes,' he said slowly.

'But you will be passing my home tomorrow, Mr Barkis. Could you not give your own message better?'

' "Barkis is willing." That's the message,' he said.

19.3 Shakespeare's *Macbeth* 'made easy'

There is a series of school textbooks published with the stated object of 'making Shakespeare easy',

> [It] is intended for readers approaching the play for the first time, who find the language of Elizabethen poetic drama an initial obstacle to understanding and enjoyment.

Activity 19.8

Read the following versions of part of Shakespeare's *Macbeth*. Text A is in the original spelling of the First Folio edition of 1623, and text B from *Shakespeare Made Easy*, published in 1984.

(i) What are the present-day meanings of *witness, groom, infirm*? Do these meanings seem to be those of the original text?

(ii) What other difficulties do you find in understanding Shakespeare's language?

(iii) Compare the styles of the two versions.

Text A (Shakespeare's text)

Lady Goe get some Water,
And wash this filthie Witnesse from your Hand.
Why did you bring these Daggers from the place?
They must lye there: goe carry them, and smeare
The sleepie Groomes with blood.
   Macb. Ile goe no more:
I am afraid, to thinke what I haue done:
Looke on't againe, I dare not.
Lady Infirme of purpose:
Giue me the Daggers: the sleeping, and the dead,
Are but as Pictures: 'tis the Eye of Child-hood,
That feares a painted Deuill. If he doe bleed,
Ile guild the Faces of the Groomes withall,
For it must seeme their Guilt.   [*Exit*
                    [*Knocke within*

Text B

Lady Macbeth ...Go and get some water. Wash that filthy evidence off your hands. And why did you bring the daggers with you? They should be up there. Take them back, and smear the sleepy servants with blood.

Macbeth [*Horrified*] I won't go back! I'm afraid to think of what I've done. I daren't look at it again!

Lady Macbeth Coward! Give me the daggers! Sleeping and dead people are like pictures of themselves. Only children fear a picture, even of the devil. If he's still bleeding, I'll smear the faces of the servants so it will look as if they did it.
   [**Lady Macbeth** *goes out. There are sounds of knocking*]

19.3.1 Commentary

Shakespeare's language is said to be an 'initial obstacle to understanding and enjoyment'. This is caused partly by the fact that English has changed since 1600, and partly by Shakespeare's own use of the language of his time.

The spelling of Shakespeare's original text looks unfamiliar, but this is not an intrinsic feature of the style, except in the ambiguity of *guild* and *guilt*, which is discussed below.

19.3.1.1 CHANGES IN THE MEANINGS OF WORDS

Words change their meaning over time, and this may cause problems of understanding. In the short passage of text we are looking at, the following words are worth examining:

- *witnesse* – originally an OE word meaning *knowledge, understanding, wisdom*. This developed into *evidence, testimony*, which is Shakespeare's meaning in this text. It occurs elsewhere in *Macbeth*:

   An euill soule producing holy **witnesse**,
   Is like a villaine with a smiling cheeke.

   The word's current meaning of *one who gives evidence* is a later semantic development.
- *groomes* – in ME *groom* meant *boy*. Its later meanings developed as *man, fellow*, then *serving-man, servant*, as in *The Taming of the Shrew*,

   You logger-headed and vnpollisht **groomes**,
   What? no attendance?

The same word would be used in a context that referred to horses, e.g. in *Richard II*,

> I was a poore **Groome** of thy Stable, King,
> When thou wer't King.

and finally reached its current exclusive meaning of *a servant who attends to horses*. So Macbeth's *groomes* are not stable boys.

- *infirme* – originally meant *weak, unsound, not firm, feeble*, and applied both to things and to arguments, as in Chaucer (1374),

> The sonne ne may nat by the **Infirme** lyht of his beemes, brekyn or percen the inward entrailes of the erthe.

This is Shakespeare's meaning in *infirme of* purpose. The word developed to refer to physical weakness and to old age, as in *King Lear*,

> The vnruly way-wardnesse, that infirme and cholericke yeares bring with them.

- *guild* or *gild, guilt* – both words have their current meanings: (a) *gild*, spelt *guild* in Shakespeare's text, meaning *to cover with a thin layer of gold*; and (b) *guilt* meaning *the state of having wilfully committed crime*. The original spellings, *guild* and *guilt*, make the **pun** on *guilt* clearer – the grooms are gilt, or smeared, with blood, and at the same time criminally guilty.

19.3.1.2 SHAKESPEARE'S USE OF LANGUAGE

Apart from differences between early seventeenth-century and present-day English, the essential contrast lies in the verse-form of most of the text of *Macbeth*. The rhythm of the iambic pentameter line underlies all the dialogue, and 'heightens' the effect.

There is also a more direct use of words in the original. For example, *The sleeping, and the dead, Are but as Pictures* is 'made easy' as *Sleeping and dead people are like pictures of themselves*. The modernised text adds *people* and *of themselves*, which are arguably redundant and less effective than *the sleeping and the dead* and *as Pictures*.

The style of the modernised version is of colloquial conversation, and this reduces the 'high style' of Shakespeare's dialogue to something that sounds more like that of a TV soap opera. Compare the effect of differences of rhythm and vocabulary in these corresponding extracts from the texts:

They should lie there	They should be up there
Go, carry them	Take them back
Ile go no more	I won't go back
Look on't againe I dare not	I daren't look at it again!
If he do bleed	If he's still bleeding
For it must seem their Guilt	so it will look as if they did it

Activity 19.9

Discuss the two versions of the play in the continuation of the scene printed below.

Macb. Whence is that knocking?
How is't with me, when euery noyse appalls me?
What Hands are here? hah: they pluck out mine Eyes.
Will all great *Neptunes* Ocean wash this blood
Cleane from my Hand? no: this my Hand will rather
The multitudinous Seas incarnadine,
Making the Greene one, Red.

[*Enter Lady*
Lady My Hands are of your colour: but I shame
To weare a Heart so white.

[*Knocke*
         I heare a Knocking
At the South entry: retyre we to our Chamber:
A little Water cleares vs of this deed.
How easie is it then? your Constancie
Hath left·you vnattended.
[*Knocke*
         Hearke, more knocking.
Get on your Night-Gowne, least occasion call vs,
And shew vs to be Watchers: be not lost
So poorely in your thoughts.
  Macb. To know my deed, 'twere best not know my selfe.
[*Knocke*
Wake *Duncane* with thy knocking: I would thou could'st.
         [*Exeunt*

Macbeth Where's that knocking? What's happened to me, that every noise scares me? [*Looking down*] Whose hands are these? They're plucking my eyes out! [*Groaning*] Is there enough water in the oceans to wash my hands of this blood? No! More likely my hands will stain the vast green seas blood-red.
  [**Lady Macbeth** *returns. Her hands are red with blood*]

Lady Macbeth My hands are the same colour as yours – but I'd be ashamed to have a heart as white as yours!
[*There is more knocking*]
I can hear someone knocking at the South Gate. Let's return to our bedroom. A little water will wash away all suspicion. Then it will be easy. [*Scornfully*] You've lost your nerve! [*Knocking*]

Listen – more knocking. Put your nightgown on, in case we're called for, and seen to be out of bed. And don't get so lost in thought!

Macbeth Better to be lost in thought than face reality. [*The knocking continues. He shudders*]

Wake Duncan with your knocking! I wish you could!
  [*They leave together*]

📖 There is a discussion of selected vocabulary in the *Commentary & Data Book*.

20. Parody and pastiche

Part I – Parody

The *OED* defines a parody as,

A composition in prose or verse in which the characteristic turns of thought and phrase in an author or class of authors are imitated in such a way as to make them appear ridiculous, especially by applying them to ludicrously inappropriate subjects.

20.1 Guide-books

Guide-books for tourists are published by local councils and tourist associations. Their object is to present an attractive picture of town or countryside so that people will be persuaded to visit and to take their holidays there.

The first of the two following texts consists of extracts from a genuine example of guide-book style dating from the 1930s (except that the names have been changed). The second is a parody from Dylan Thomas's *Under Milk Wood*, written in 1952. There is no direct connection between the two texts, which are unrelated except in subject-matter.

Text 1 *Woolbridge – the centre of the beautiful sunshine-favoured West Leys with its splendid coast-line and unspoilt countryside*

Those who know the West Leys will easily forgive its admirers their enthusiasm for its unspoilt countryside, its splendid sea-coast, its romantic traditions. A curious name this – the West Leys – yet it stands for a region unsurpassed in Britain for smiling beauty, vivid colouring, and generous admixture of moor and seashore, hill and combe, wood and stream, meadow and lane.

It comes nearer to being the ideal climate for most Britons than any other spot in the world! Its characteristic is its equableness – a not-too-hot summer and a mild winter. Beset by the sea on both sides, the influence of the Gulf Stream on this district is marked.

The town has a clean, pleasant appearance, and is built around the one long street – Main Street – which runs up north from the estuary head. Visitors will find that the Woolbridge traders are an alert and courteous body of men and women, ready to supply all requirements at prices that will compare very favourably with any other town.

The West Leys offers abundant facilities for sport and games, pastimes and recreations.

Sea bathing facilities are plentiful. Always to seek advice as to local conditions is a sound rule before bathing on any part of the coast.

Opportunities for the fisherman are legion; excellent sea-fishing may be enjoyed all along the coast, pollock and mackerel being very plentiful during a great portion of the summer season and providing really good sport; trout is abundant in the upper part of the River Alston, and salmon in the lower reaches. The large freshwater Sunning Lake is thronged with pike, perch, rudd and huge eels.

There are many inviting spots for the free-and-easy life associated with camping and caravaning.

For the walker and rambler the West Leys offers great scope: hidden lanes in which one finds wild flowers every month of the year; trout streams and beautiful rivers crossed by quaint bridges; hillsides bright with gorse or heather; field-paths that have existed for centuries; stone-built manor houses; thatched and cobbled cottages.

The Parish Church of St Edmund is of Saxon foundation. Visitors are invited to inspect this fine old church. Space does not permit us to detail the monuments and memorials in the church, which are many.

Text 2 *Llaregyb*

Less than five hundred souls inhabit the three quaint streets and the few narrow by-lanes and scattered farmsteads that constitute this small, decaying watering-place which may, indeed, be called a 'backwater of life' without disrespect to its natives who possess, to this day, a salty individuality of their own.

The main street, Coronation Street, consists, for the most part, of humble, two-storied houses many of which attempt to achieve some measure of gaiety by prinking themselves out in crude colours and by the liberal use of pinkwash, though there are remaining a few eighteenth-century houses of more pretension, if, on the whole, in a sad state of disrepair.

Though there is little to attract the hillclimber, the healthseeker, the sportsman, or the weekending motorist, the contemplative may, if sufficiently attracted to spare it some leisurely hours, find, in its cobbled streets and its little fishing harbour, in its several curious customs, and in the conversation of its local 'characters', some of that picturesque sense of the past so frequently lacking in towns and villages which have kept more abreast of the times.

The River Dewi is said to abound in trout, but is much poached.

The one place of worship, with its neglected graveyard, is of no architectural interest.

Activity 20.1

A parody imitates the style of another text, often to make fun of it.

(i) What evidence have you found to tell you that

 (a) Text 1 is trying to persuade you to take a holiday in Woolbridge and the West Leys, and that

 (b) Text 2 is unlikely to be from a genuine guide-book?

(ii) Comment on the style of text 1.

20.2 Guide-book to Woolbridge and the West Leys

We can verify our first impressions by looking in more detail at the vocabulary and grammar used in the texts which are part of their distinctive style – 'the language of tourist guide-books in the 1930s'.

20.2.1 *Vocabulary*

20.2.1.1 CONNOTATION AND COLLOCATION

Most lexical words have **connotations**, that is, associated meanings, favourable or unfavourable, formal or informal and so on. Two or more words which tend to occur together regularly are said to **collocate**, and particular collocations may have connotations which do not belong to the words individually.

20.2.1.2 DESCRIPTIVE AND EVALUATIVE ADJECTIVES

For example, *thatched* means *roofed with thatch* as against, say, *tiled*. But *thatched cottages* have connotations, for many people, of traditional 'olde worlde' country scenes and nostalgic memories of the past. We can call adjectives like *thatched, stone-built, long, cobbled* **descriptive**, because they provide factual, verifiable attributes of the nouns they modify, whatever other connotations they may have. Other adjectives imply a value judgement; *excellent, good, romantic, unsurpassed* are therefore **evaluative**. You can argue and disagree with the judgement implied – 'I wouldn't call her *generous*, she could afford much more than that!' – whereas you can't argue the fact of a thatched roof.

Activity 20.2

(i) Identify the adjectives in the guide-book text and divide them into sets, (a) descriptive and (b) evaluative, with a third (c) other, for any that do not fit easily into either category.

(ii) Is the number and category of descriptive and evaluative adjectives significant in promoting the intentions of the writer of the guide-book?

📖 A complete list is in the *Commentary & Data Book*.

20.2.1.3 NPs WITH MODIFIERS

More than half of the nouns are modified by adjectives, which makes a repetitive stylistic pattern in noun phrases (NPs) of modifier (adjective) + head (noun) – *splendid coast-line, unspoilt countryside*, and so on.

Activity 20.3

List the NPs consisting of *modifier + head* and discuss their connotations and evaluative judgements.

📖 A complete list is in the *Commentary & Data Book*.

20.2.1.4 NOUNS IN SEMANTIC SETS

If a guide-book is going to attract tourists, then it must describe a region or town in as positive and enthusiastic a way as it can. Everything said about Woolbridge and the West Leys presents the town and countryside attractively.

We can check our first impressions about the 'focus of interest' in the text by grouping the nouns into **semantic sets**, that is, into groups of words, each of which belongs to a general or **superordinate** category of meaning. You find that there are six clearly marked sets, which can be described under the headings,

  (i) rural countryside, places and buildings
 (ii) people
(iii) time and seasons
(iv) recreation
 (v) fish and angling
(vi) qualities

with a seventh marked *other* which you need for nouns that do not easily fit into any of the main categories.

20.2.1.5 UNMODIFIED NOUNS

Not all the nouns have modifiers, but the unmodified nouns fit into the same semantic sets just listed, and so contribute to the topics presented in the text.

The largest sets will give evidence about those topics that the writer of the guide-book believed to be the most important – that is, those which best described the delights of Woolbridge and the West Leys and the kind of holiday and sporting activities which appealed in the 1930s.

Activity 20.4

(i) List the nouns under the seven suggested semantic headings.

(ii) Which are the largest sets?

📖 Complete lists of the nouns in semantic sets are in the *Commentary & Data Book*.

20.2.1.6 Abstract nouns and 'literariness'

The head noun *admixture* of the NP *generous admixture* is an **abstract noun** which belongs to the vocabulary of a formal style of writing. The noun is unfamiliar and not often heard. Abstract nouns of this kind tend to create a 'literary' style, which is less likely to be found in tourist guides of the 1990s. NPs and single nouns of this kind in the text are,

generous **admixture**   abundant/plentiful **facilities**
characteristic   sea-bathing **facilities**
equableness   local **conditions**
the **influence** of the Gulf Stream   **opportunities** (are legion)
clean/pleasant **appearance**   great **scope**
all **requirements**

Activity 20.5

Rewrite these NPs in a more informal style without using the abstract nouns. You may have to paraphrase the meaning and use different constructions. For example, you could rewrite *all requirements* as *all you need* or *everything you want*.

You will probably have noticed the **archaic**, literary word *legion* in the clause *opportunities for the fisherman are legion*. The word is being used as an adjective meaning something like *innumerable*, *very many*, *lots of*, *loads of*, in descending order of formal usage. This unusual meaning of the word derives from its biblical connotations, 'My name is Legion,...there are so many of us' (St Mark's Gospel 5: 9).

20.2.1.7 RELATIONAL AND ACTIONAL VERBS

Verbs are popularly called 'doing words', and in some kinds of narrative writing are important in making the action lively. In certain other kinds of writing, for example, legal language and academic papers, verbs tend to be less central to meaning (even though every clause will have a verb of some kind). In the guide-book text the verbs are mostly **relational** and not **actional**. That is, their main function is grammatical, by linking the subject to the complement or object or adverbial.

The commonest relational verb is *be*, and it occurs throughout the Woolbridge guide-book text. Frequent use of *be* as a main verb reduces any sense of action, of things actually <u>happening</u>. Other verbs in the text *relate* rather than *act*, and so produce an important feature of its style. The writer of the guide-book is telling us that *There are* many things to see and do.

If you use *be* as a main verb with abstract nouns, for example, *Its characteristic is its equableness*, the resulting clause is formal in style, and adds little to the meaning expressed by *a not-too-hot summer and a mild winter*.

Activity 20.6

List the clauses with the verb *be* as their main verb. (It may have any one of eight forms – *be, am, is, are, was, were, been, being*.)

Other verbs are used in ways similar to the 'existential' use of *be*. They do not represent actions in which people do things. The verb *have* in *The town **has** a clean, pleasant appearance* could just as well have been written, *The town **is** clean and pleasant* or *The town **appears** clean and pleasant*. Other examples of verbs used in this way are,

the West Leys	**offers**	facilities
the West Leys	**offers**	great scope
pollock	**provide**	sport
paths that	**have existed**	

We all use verbs in this way and there is nothing wrong with doing so, but it affects the style of a text when many of its verbs are relational.

Activity 20.7

Make a complete list of the verbs in the text. Are any of them active, actional verbs in the context in which they are used, that is, are people <u>doing</u> anything?

📖 A complete list of the verbs is in the *Commentary & Data Book*.

20.2.1.8 ADVERBS

There are only five adverbs – the fourth kind of lexical word – in the text, so they play no significant part in creating its style (*always, around, easily, favourably, really*).

20.2.2 GRAMMAR

Activity 20.8 _____

(i) Is the grammar simple or complex on the whole?

(ii) Has the writer tried to produce the effect of the spoken voice, or does the grammatical style reflect the conventions of written prose – or both?

(iii) The guide-book was published in the 1930s. Can you identify anything in the style which seems 'old-fashioned' to you?

📖 A complete linear analysis of the grammatical structure is in the *Commentary & Data Book*.

20.2.2.1 COMPLEXITY OF STRUCTURE – PARALLELISM

A feature of the style is the amount of repetition in 'parallel' phrases, having the same grammatical structure but with changed vocabulary – parallelism. This often takes the form of a list, for example,

> its unspoilt countryside
> its splendid sea-coast
> its romantic traditions

which consists of three NPs, *its* + modifier + head noun in parallel.

Activity 20.9 _____

Find and describe other examples of parallelism in the text.

Parallelism as a feature of style generally means that there is some complexity of grammatical structure in the constituents which contain it, such as the complex NP following the prepositional verb *stands for* in sentence 3:

> a region [unsurpassed in Britain for ⇒ smiling beauty
> vivid colouring, and
> generous admixture of ⇒ moor and seashore
> hill and combe
> wood and stream
> meadow and lane].

The head word of the NP, *region*, is post-modified by the nonfinite clause beginning *unsurpassed*, with the prepositional phrases *for smiling beauty*, (*for*) *vivid colouring* and (*for*) *generous admixture* forming its adverbial. The third PrepP is itself post-modified by the list of pairs of nouns from *of moor and seashore* to *meadow and lane*.

This kind of grammatical complexity is not, however, difficult to read, because the lists are not embedded one within the other, but follow in a series.

20.2.2.2 COMPLEXITY OF STRUCTURE – FORMAL STYLE

Sentences consist of clauses, and clauses consist of phrases, but we can also use clauses where phrases more normally appear. The most noticeable example in the text is,

> [Always to seek advice as to local conditions]

which is a nonfinite clause functioning as the subject of the sentence, where we usually use a NP. The stylistic effect of this construction is one of formality. We would probably not use it in ordinary conversation, but say something like,

> It's a good idea to find out locally whether it's a safe bathing area before you have a swim.

A clause has a higher rank than a phrase in the 'rank-scale' *sentence – clause – phrase – word*. Using a clause like *always to seek advice as to local conditions* as the subject of another clause is an example of **rankshift**, another grammatical feature which tends to lead to complexity of style. Another term we might use is **embedding** – a clause is embedded inside another one. Other formal stylistic features have been mentioned in previous sections, such as the use of abstract nouns coupled with the verb *be* expressing the existence of something, for example, *Sea bathing facilities are plentiful*, which might have been written *There are plenty of places where you can bathe in the sea*.

The nonfinite clause *Beset by the sea on both sides* is noticeable not only for the rather archaic verb *beset* but for its order in the sentence. The nonfinite clause comes first, so it is marked as the **theme** of the sentence. A more informal version of the sentence might be, *The sea is on both sides of the district, so the Gulf Stream keeps it warm in winter*.

Using the **passive voice** can sometimes affect the style of a text. There are, however, only a few instances, including *beset by*, which cannot be made active without creating a finite clause – *The sea besets the district on both sides* – and so changing its grammatical function in the sentence.

The town is built is a necessary passive, because we cannot supply a suitable subject for *X built the town*. There are two examples of passive constructions which you might judge to be stylistically formal,

> excellent sea-fishing **may be enjoyed** all along the coast
> Visitors **are invited to inspect** this fine old church

which could be written in more informal style, but with some change of focus of information as well. In,

> you can enjoy excellent sea-fishing all along the coast

the theme of the clause is no longer *excellent sea-fishing*, because it does not come first. The more chatty style of,

> you should certainly go and see this fine old church

lacks the polite formality of the *invitation to inspect*. The other passive clause,

> The large freshwater Sunning Lake **is thronged** with pike ...

is not necessarily improved in the active form,

> Pike ... **throng** the large freshwater Sunning Lake

20.2.2.3 THE SPOKEN VOICE

Although the text in its vocabulary and grammar has the style of formal written prose, it does have features which convey a certain impression of speech – speech, however, which is polite and formal.

> A curious name this – the West Leys

lacks a verb, though the words function like a clause,

> The West Leys is a curious name, isn't it?

and the construction is a spoken idiom.

20.2.2.4 'OLD-FASHIONED' STYLE?

To call the style 'old-fashioned' is to make a subjective statement, an impression which will vary with each individual. Some of the stylistic features discussed so far will contribute to this impression. We do not nowadays read tourist guide-books and information which are written in this way, so it is perhaps more of a historical document than an example of contemporary English style.

But because the description of Llaregyb which follows was written in the early 1950s as a parody, poking fun at typical guide-book style, then the guide to Woolbridge is probably more relevant to our study than a guide-book of the 1990s.

20.3 Guide-book to Llaregyb – a parody

A parody has to be both like and unlike its subject text. It must resemble it in style, through its choices of vocabulary and structure, otherwise it cannot be recognised as a parody, but at the same time the meaning of these choices must be **incongruous** – out of keeping or absurd.

20.3.1 *Vocabulary*

20.3.1.1 ADJECTIVE MODIFIERS IN NPs

Activity 20.10

(i) List the NPs with adjective modifiers.

(ii) Compare those NPs in the Llaregyb text with those describing Woolbridge and the West Leys.

(iii) What impressions about the attractiveness of Llaregyb do the descriptive and evaluative adjectives give you?

(iv) Do other words give the same impression?

The only adjectives which appear in both texts are in the NPs *cobbled cottages/cobbled streets*, *curious name/**curious** customs*, *local conditions/local 'characters'* and ***quaint** bridges/**quaint** streets*. *Cobbled* and *local* are both descriptive adjectives, *curious* and *quaint* are subjective and evaluative, and probably typical of guide-book style in suggesting something to attract the visitor.

Several of the adjectives in the parody have connotations that are unfavourable, or, if not unfavourable, that diminish the attractiveness of Llaregyb so that the impression given of the size and life of the 'watering-place' is unattractive on the whole. No authentic guide-book would advertise a ***decaying** watering-place*, ***crude** colours*, *a **few** eighteenth-century houses*, ***sad** state of **disrepair***, or ***neglected** graveyard*. These pejoratively-used adjectives then 'colour' our response to others which take on similar connotations – *three **quaint** streets*, *the few **narrow** by-lanes and **scattered** farmsteads*, and ***humble** two-storied houses* – why bother to visit? The word *salty* describing the 'natives' often collocates with *wit* to mean *sharp, biting, sarcastic*, so this is unlikely to be used in an authentic text.

However, knowing that the text is fictitious, our response to it is already conditioned to be different from the way we read the real guide-book. It is not Llaregyb itself that we attend to – it does not exist – but the language of the parody, <u>how</u> it is described in relation to how we read real guide-books.

20.3.1.2 OTHER VOCABULARY

It is not only the adjectives which make the parody. Referring to people as *souls* and *natives* has something of the 'literariness' noticed in the Woolbridge guide, like *inhabit* rather than *live in*, *farmsteads* for *farms*, *watering-place* for *small town*. The noun *pretension* in the phrase *houses of more pretension* implies that the houses *pretend* to be better than they really are.

If a place *attempts to achieve* something, we infer that it has not succeeded. The verb phrase *is said to abound* (*in trout*) is formal and old-fashioned in style. To *prink out* means *make smarter*, but the verb carries connotations of *showing off*. To say *there is little to attract* a whole series of holiday-makers is to put them all off, and the claim to a *picturesque sense of the past* is ironic in the context of the whole text. Guide-books do not advertise *much poached* rivers or *neglected* graveyards.

NPs with modifiers

The stylistic pattern produced by NPs with modifiers is reproduced in the parody, some with one or two pre-modifiers, e.g. *three quaint streets*, *neglected graveyard* and others with post-modifiers, e.g. *sad state of disrepair*.

📖 A complete list of the NPs with modifiers is in the *Commentary & Data Book*.

Nouns in semantic sets

We can fit the nouns in the text into similar sets with the same superordinate categories as those listed in section 20.2.1.4, but the selection of words is rather different. The only nouns which occur in both texts are *houses, river(s), street(s), town(s), trout, part*. The choice of *place of worship* for *church*, and *watering-place* is in keeping with the parody's deliberate formality of style, like *healthseeker, contemplative, hillclimber*.

Abstract nouns

The shorter text of the parody has fewer abstract nouns, but *disrespect, disrepair, individuality,* and *pretension* help to produce the mock literariness of its style.

Verbs

Like the guide-book, the parody lacks actional verbs – only *is much poached* and *prinking* have this function.

📖 The verbs are listed in the *Commentary & Data Book*.

Adverbs

The two adverbs, *sufficiently* and *so frequently* appear to have no particular stylistic significance.

20.3.2 Grammar

Activity 20.11

Can you find any similarities between the grammatical structures of the guide-book and the parody?

📖 A complete linear analysis is in the *Commentary & Data Book*.

20.3.2.1 PARALLELISM AND LISTS

The shorter parody will not produce the same number of examples, but it contains some lists which have the stylistic effect of parallelism,

the	three quaint streets	
the	few narrow by-lanes and	
	scattered farmsteads	
the hillclimber		
the healthseeker		
the sportsman or		
the weekending motorist		
in	its	cobbled	streets and
		little	fishing harbour
in	its	several curious	customs and
in	the		conversation of
	its	local	'characters'

20.3.2.2 FORMAL STYLE

The structural formality of the parody lies in the complex sentence structures:

1. [*MCl* [that ... *RelCl 1* [which ... *RelCl 2* [who ... *RelCl 3*]]]
2. [*MCl* [many of which ... *RelCl* [by ... *PrepCl*]] [though ... *AdvCl*]]
3. [[Though ... *AdvCl 1*], *MCl* [if ... *AdvCl 2*] *MCl contd* [so ... *NonfCl* [which ... *RelCl*]]]
4. [*MCl 1*] but [*MCl 2*]
5. [*MCl* [with ... *Verbless Cl*] *MCl contd*]

📖 A full diagrammed analysis is in the *Commentary & Data Book*.

The two final sentences are short and relatively simple, and can be said to have the rhetorical function of **anticlimax** – a climax parodied so that it raises a laugh.

20.4   Stella Gibbons's *Cold Comfort Farm*

Cold Comfort Farm was published in 1932. It is described in the *Oxford Companion to English Literature* as,

> a witty and highly successful parody of the earthy primitive school of regional fiction popular at the beginning of the century, e.g. Sheila Kaye-Smith (1887–1956), Mary Webb (1881–1927) and D. H. Lawrence (1885–1930)

She writes a spoof Foreword to an imaginary 'Anthony Pookworthy Esq.', explaining why some passages in the book are starred:

> And it is only because I have in mind all those thousands of persons not unlike myself, who work in the vulgar and meaningless bustle of offices, shops and homes, and who are not always sure whether a sentence is Literature or whether it is just sheer flapdoodle, that I have adopted the method perfected by the late Herr Baedeker*, and firmly marked what I consider the finer passages with one, two or three stars. In such a manner did the good man deal with cathedrals, hotels and paintings by men of genius. There seems no reason why it should not be applied to passages in novels.
>
> It ought to help the reviewers, too.

> * Karl Baedeker (1801–59) was a German publisher who began the issue of tourist guide-books which are still internationally famous.

The definition of parody at the beginning of the chapter refers to *characteristic turns of thought and phrase in an author or class of authors* applied to *ludicrously inappropriate subjects* in order to make them appear ridiculous. The parody of guide-book style in section 20.3 clearly fits this definition when compared with the genuine guide-book. It is not easy to find precisely matching extracts from the authors Stella Gibbons is parodying, but some examples of their writing follow. In any case, *Cold Comfort Farm* is a very amusing book in itself. Even though you may not have read Mary Webb or D. H. Lawrence, it is difficult to take the narrative and the dialogue seriously as a portrait of real country life.

Activity 20.12

One of Stella Gibbons's starred 'finer passages' is printed below, together with part of the extract from D. H. Lawrence's *The Rainbow* discussed in section 15.4

What features of Stella Gibbons's style are evidence of its being a parody and not a serious description of spring in the countryside?

[*The farmhand Adam Lambsbreath is driving a buggy to Beershorn.*]

The reins lay between his knotted fingers, and his face, unseeing, was lifted to the dark sky. *** ... The country for miles, under the blanket of the dark which brought no peace, was in its annual tortured ferment of spring growth; worm jarred with worm and seed with seed. Frond leapt on root and hare on hare. Beetle and finch-fly were not spared. The trout-sperm in the muddy hollow under Nettle Flitch Weir were agitated, and well they might be. The long screams of the hunting owls tore across the night, scarlet lines on black. In the pauses, every ten minutes, they mated. It seemed chaotic, but it was more methodically arranged than you might think. But Adam's deafness and blindness came from within, as well as without; earthy calm seeped up from his sub-conscious and met descending calm in his conscious.

They felt the rush of the sap in spring, they knew the wave which cannot halt, but every year throws forward the seed to begetting, and, falling back leaves the young-born on the earth. They knew the intercourse between heaven and earth, sunshine drawn into the breast and bowels, the rain sucked up in the daytime, nakedness that comes under the wind in autumn, showing the birds' nests no longer worth hiding. Their life and interrelations were such; feeling the pulse and body of the soil, that opened to their furrow for the grain, and became smooth and supple after their ploughing, and clung to their feet with a weight that pulled like desire, lying hard and unresponsive, when the crops were to be shorn away. The young corn waved and was silken, and the lustre slid along the limbs of the men who saw it.

20.4.1 Commentary

Once you have been told that a text is a parody, then you will inevitably read it differently and expect to find it amusing. Spring is a season of renewal and the subject of countless poems and prose descriptions, almost always optimistic and 'smiling'. Stella Gibbons's farm and landscape are portrayed in ways that are quite different from the expected. So *the dark which brought no peace, its annual tortured ferment, jarred, agitated, screams,* are not words or phrases that you usually read in descriptions of springtime.

Satire is like irony in its reliance on a reader's interpretation of its meaning, because there is an incongruous mismatch between what is being said and what a reader conventionally expects. The season and the growth of the natural world, the procreation of birds, animals and fish, are presented in Lawrence with terms like *the rush of the sap, the wave which cannot halt, the young-born on the earth, the young corn waved and was silken.* In Stella Gibbons the 'tortured ferment' of springtime focuses on the *jarring* of worms and seed, hares *leaping* on hares. The odd choice of *beetle and finch-fly* to represent animal life, and phrases like *were not spared, and well they might be,* all combine to comic effect – at least for many readers.

Of course, some people may read *Cold Comfort Farm* as a serious novel in the Mary Webb tradition, and be disappointed. In the end, you cannot prove a book to be satirical.

Activity 20.13

Which of the two in the following pairs of short extracts is the parody? Try to say why in as much detail as you can.

A commentary with the sources of the texts is in the *Commentary & Data Book.*

1a
She looked full into his face, and her blue, inchoate eyes had now a furtive look, and a look of knowledge of evil, dark and indomitable. A flame ran secretly to his heart.

1b
A pair of large blue eyes looked at her steadily above the green hand-woven hood. She pensively noted that they were fine eyes, and that the hood was the wrong green.

2a
His young man's limbs, sleek in their dark male pride, seemed to disdain the covering offered them by the brief shorts and striped jersey. His body might have been naked, like his full, muscled throat, which rose, round and proud as the male organ of a flower, from the neck of his sweater.

2b
In his clear northern flesh and his fair hair was a glisten like sunshine refracted through crystals of ice. And he looked so new, unbroached, pure as an arctic thing. Perhaps he was thirty years old, perhaps more. His gleaming beauty, maleness, like a young, good-humoured, smiling wolf, did not blind her to the significant, sinister stillness in his bearing, the lurking danger of his unsubdued temper.

3a
The man's big body, etched menacingly against the bleak light that stabbed in from the low windows, did not move. His thoughts swirled like a beck in spate behind the sodden grey furrows of his face. A woman...Blast! Blast! Come to wrest away from him the land whose love fermented in his veins like slow yeast. She-woman. Young, soft-coloured, insolent. His gaze was suddenly edged by a fleshy taint. Break her. Break. Keep and hold and hold fast the land. The land, the iron furrows of frosted earth under the rain-lust, the fecund spears of rain, the swelling, slow burst of seed-sheaths, the slow smell of cows and cry of cows, the trampling bride-pride of the bull in his hour. All his, his...
'Will you have some bread and butter?' asked Flora, handing him a cup of tea...
Defeated, Reuben came in.

3b
Still she stared into his face with that slow, full gaze which was so curious and so exciting to him....He felt full of strength, able to give off a sort of electric power. And he was aware of her blue, exposed-looking eyes upon him. She had beautiful eyes, flower-like, fully opened, naked in their looking at him....
She appealed to him strongly. He felt an awful, enjoyable power over her, an instinctive cherishing very near to cruelty. For she was a victim. He felt that she was in his power, and he was generous. The electricity was turgid and voluptuously rich, in his limbs. He would be able to destroy her utterly in the strength of his discharge. But she was waiting in her separation, given.

4a
Gillian's laugh rang out, and Simon, who loved her voice, came purring across the kitchen and leapt into her lap.
'Saving your presence, Miss Gillian, child,' added Mrs Makepeace, 'and excuse me making a game of your A'ntie.'

'Time and agen,' said Gillian, pushing away the plate of raisins, 'I think I'd lief get in the cyart by A'nt Fanteague when she goes back to Sil'erton, and go along of her, beyond the Gwlfas and the mountains, beyond the sea –'

'Wheer then?' queried Mrs. Makepeace practically.

'To the moon-O! maybe.'

'By Leddy! What'd your feyther do?'

'Feyther's forgetful. He wouldna miss me sore.'

'And Robert? My Bob?'...

'Robert Rideout?' she murmured. Then she swung her plaits backwards with a defiant toss, and cried: 'He wouldna miss me neither!'

She flung Simon down and got up.

'It's closing in,' she said. 'I mun see to my coney wires.'

4b

At this moment there came a soft rap at the closed door which led out into the yard; and a second later it was repeated. Adam shuffled across to the door, muttering 'My liddle wennet!' and flung it qide.

A figure which stood outside, wrapped in a long green cloak, rushed across the room and up the stairs so quickly that Flora only had the merest glimpse of it.

She raised her eyebrows. 'Who was that?' she asked, though she was sure that she knew.

'My cowdling – my liddle Elfine,' said Adam, listlessly picking up his thorn twig, which had fallen into the snood of porridge on the hearth.

'Indeed, and does she always charge about like that?' inquired Flora, coldly; she considered her cousin deficient in manners.

'Ay. She's as wild and shy as a Pharisee of the woods, Days she'll be away from home, wanderin' on the hills, wi' only the wild birds and the liddle rabbits an' the spyin' maggies for company.

'Does she go to school?' asked Flora, looking distastefully into a cupboard for a rag with which to dust her shoes. 'How old is she?'

'Seventeen. Nay, niver talk o' school for my wennet. Why, ye might as soon send the white hawthorn or the yellow daffydowndilly to school as my Elfine. She learns from the skies an' the wild marsh-tiggets, not out o' books.'

'How trying,' observed Flora, who was feeling lonely and rather cross.

Part 2 – Pastiche

A literary composition made up from various authors, or in imitation of the style of another author.   (*Oxford Companion to English Literature*)

The difference between a parody and a pastiche lies in the intention of the writer rather than in the style that is produced. There can be no 'parody style' or 'pastiche style', because both depend completely on imitating another style. A pastiche becomes a parody when it is written to poke fun, sometimes gentle, sometimes barbed, rather like satire.

A book that is full of pastiche is James Joyce's *Ulysses*. Joyce's use of interior monologue in this book is discussed in section 18.4.1. Several of its later chapters are pastiches based upon other styles. One chapter is written wholly in pastiches of the styles of great writers of literature, from Old and Middle English through to the end of the nineteenth century – too many to be demonstrated in this chapter, which ends with just one example of a literary pastiche.

20.5 Medieval fantasy

William Morris (1834–96) was an artist of wide interests and immense energy. He was not only a writer of verse, prose stories, political tales, essays and historical romances, but an architect and designer of furniture, textiles, tapestries, wallpapers and stained glass. He was head of the Socialist League and lectured and wrote for this political cause. He founded the Kelmscott Press in 1890 and designed type founts and ornamental letters and borders.

In *The Wood Beyond the World* (1894), one of his prose historical romances, William Morris creates a medieval fantasy world of adventure and courtly love in a pastiche that creates the impression of medieval writing. The first extract is from the beginning of Chapter I, 'Of Golden Walter and his father':

Activity 20.14

(i) Rewrite the paragraph as if you were telling the story in contemporary English.

(ii) Which features of William Morris's writing are 'medieval'?

> A while ago there was a young man dwelling in a great and goodly city by the sea which had to name Langton on Holm. He was but of five and twenty winters, a fair-faced man, yellow-haired, tall and strong; rather wiser than foolisher than young men are mostly wont; a valiant youth, & a kind; not of many words but courteous of speech; no roisterer, nought masterful, but peaceable and knowing how to forbear: in a fray a perilous foe, & a trusty war-fellow. His father, with whom he was dwelling when this tale begins, was a great merchant: he was of the Lineage of the Goldings, therefore was he called Bartholomew Golden, & his son Golden Walter.

20.5.1 Commentary

The narrative of the story itself is a fantasy, and Morris creates a style that borrows from late Middle English and Early Modern English writing without being in any way an authentic reproduction of any one period or writer. Much of the writing depends upon the use of **archaisms**. Archaic language belongs to an earlier period and is no longer in common use, though it is used for special purposes, as in Morris's romance, which echoes the great interest in medieval art of the group of artists and poets in the 1850s who were called the Pre-Raphaelite Brotherhood.

The archaisms in the extract can be simply listed with a paraphrase as lexico-grammatical, that is, either to do with vocabulary (lexical) or grammar. You may prefer to add or omit examples:

A while ago	Once upon a time
dwelling	living, who lived; *dwell* is archaic.
a great and goodly city	a great, splendid city; *goodly* is archaic.
which had to name Langton on Holm	which was called . . .; *to name* resembles the phrase *to one's name* meaning *belonging to.*
He was but of five and twenty winters	*but* meaning *only*; *winters* was used in OE and ME for *years* in describing the passage of time.
a fair-faced man	Meaning either, or both, *handsome* and *light-coloured.*

yellow-haired	We would be more likely to use *fair-haired*. There is no twentieth-century usage, referring to men or women, listed in the *OED*.
rather wiser than foolisher than young men are mostly wont	*foolisher* is a comparative that is not idiomatic in modern English.
a valiant youth & and a kind	An archaic coordinated phrase found in Middle English; MnE requires *a valiant and a kind youth*.
no roisterer	The noun *roister* meant *a swaggering or blustering bully*; *a riotous fellow*; *a rude or noisy reveller*. It was very common from about 1550 to 1700, but *roisterer* was generally used after that until the later nineteenth century.
nought masterful	*nought* for *not*, a 'flavouring' of older usage.
and knowing how to forbear	*forbear* – earlier archaic meanings include *endure*, *tolerate*, *avoid*, later becoming *abstain from cease*, *refrain from*. Any of these meanings would fit Morris's text.
in a fray a perilous foe	*a fray* – the word developed from the original OF *affray*, meaning *a fight* or *an attack*.
& a trusty war-fellow	A coinage with the appearance of an older compound word.
he was of the Lineage of the Goldings therefore was he called Bartholomew Golden	*lineage* meaning *descendants of an ancestor*. Archaic/literary reversal of subject *he* and auxiliary *was*.

Activity 20.15

Identify and discuss the archaic features of the following extract from the same book.

This Activity is discussed in the *Commentary & Data Book*.

The second extract is from Chapter II, 'Golden Walter takes ship to sail the seas':

When Walter went down to the Katherine next morning, there was the skipper Geoffrey, who did him reverence, and made him all cheer, and showed him his room aboard ship, and the plenteous goods which his father had sent down to the quays already, such haste as he had made. Walter thanked his father's love in his heart, but otherwise took little heed to his affairs, but wore away the time about the haven, gazing listlessly on the ships that were making them ready outward, or unlading, & the mariners and aliens coming and going. At last when he had well-nigh come back again to the Katherine, he saw there a tall ship, which had her boats out, and men sitting to the oars thereof ready to tow her outwards when the hawser should be cast off, and by seeming her mariners were but abiding for some one or other to come aboard. So Walter stood idly watching the said ship, and as he looked, lo! folk passing him toward the gangway. These were three; first came a dwarf, dark-brown of hue & hideous, with long arms & ears exceeding great and dog-teeth that stuck out like the fangs of a wild beast.

He was clad in a rich coat of yellow silk, and bare in his hand a crooked bow, and was girt with a broad sax. After him came a maiden, young by seeming, of scarce twenty summers; fair of face as a flower; grey-eyed, brown-haired, with lips full & red, slim and gentle of body. Simple was her array, of a short and strait green gown, so that on her right ankle was clear to see an iron ring. Last of the three was a lady, tall and stately, so radiant of visage & glorious of raiment, that it were hard to say what like she was. They went over the gangway into the ship, and Walter saw them go along the deck till they came to the house on the poop, and entered it, and were gone from his sight.

21. Styles of news reporting

Preliminary – political reporting and ideology

Both the BBC and ITV are required to maintain an unbiased view of political events in the broadcasting of news, but this constraint does not apply to daily newspapers, each of which tends to support one or other of the national political parties.

Most people buy and read a newspaper which suits their political point of view. It informs and reflects their own ideas and opinions – their **ideology**. This is not the only criterion, of course, but an important one. They know what to expect and tend not to read critically. Each of us brings to the reading of news about politics our own beliefs and attitudes, so that the meanings and connotations of certain words will differ according to individual speakers and listeners. For example, the meaning of *progressive* in talking about education may carry either favourable or unfavourable connotations. When naming political parties, it makes a difference whether you use the words *Conservative* or *Tory*, *Labour* or *Socialist*, and the connotations of these terms differ from one individual to another. Provided that we recognise this 'in-built bias' in our own responses to the reporting of political news, we can be reasonably objective when we discuss and evaluate the language used.

However, the study of the ideology of the papers is not the subject of this chapter. Its principal purpose is to show how important are the choices of vocabulary and grammatical structure in producing the distinctive styles of writing that serve to make that ideology clear. These choices lead to different levels of **readability** or 'reading ease', from easy to difficult.

21.1 Tabloid and broadsheet newspapers

Two kinds of daily newspapers are distinguished by their size, the larger **broadsheet** papers (e.g. *The Times, Independent, Daily Telegraph, Guardian*) and the smaller **tabloids** (e.g. the *Sun, Daily Mirror, Daily Mail, Daily Express*). If we go by circulation figures, the tabloids are the more popular variety, while the broadsheets tend to be regarded as more 'serious' reading.

(reference)

All newspapers, broadsheet and tabloid, are printed in columns, and this has affected the conventions of punctuation. Paragraphs typically consist of one or two sentences only. There is also a wide variety of typographical features, such as variation in fonts and font sizes, the use of roman and italic script, and different headline layouts.

The following texts are leading articles from (A) a tabloid and (B) a broadsheet, published in the 1980s, and no longer 'news', but typical of their kind.

Activity 21.1

Read the two reports. Is one of them more difficult to read than the other? What is the evidence for your opinion?

A

METERS, PLEASE!

Local Government Minister Tom King is producing a discussion paper on allowing householders to pay for water by meter.

He should not merely talk about meters. He should have them installed.

The present system of basing water rates on the size of a house is unfair and wasteful.

It means that a woman living alone can pay as much as, or more than, a large family.

It does NOTHING to encourage people to economise with their water.

Who cares about running taps if the bill is going to be the same anyhow?

Scarce

Water is becoming an increasingly expensive and scarce resource.

We should do everything possible to conserve it.

Meters will help.

Let's have them.

B

Inside South Africa

The opportunities for peaceful change in South Africa are steadily diminishing. Black hatred of the apartheid system now runs so deep that moderate black leaders who would prefer to negotiate for political rights with the government fear that they may soon be overtaken by younger men determined to destroy apartheid by violence.

Yet, faced with black unrest and international condemnation, the South African government becomes all the more determined to demonstrate its might and to enforce its control over the black population with greater vigour. The cycle of violence thus continues unresolved, each time taking a heavier toll in the country...

21.1.1 *Readability*

A number of different guides to 'readability' have been devised to help teachers in selecting reading material for their pupils and students. One such guide (called the Fog Index) proposes a formula for producing a 'reading age' – the age of reader for which the text is judged to be appropriate:

1 Select texts or extracts of 100 words each.
2 Count up in each text or extract
   (a) the total number of syllables and
   (b) the total number of sentences.
3 Read off the 'reading age' on a prepared graph, using the two figures you have worked out.

If the method of working out readability is applied to the two texts, the reading age on the graph for the tabloid text (A) is 10.5 years, and for the broadsheet text (B) 17.5 years.

Another method, provided in word-processing applications, has been used in earlier chapters to provide a 'readability' grading from *very easy* to *very difficult*. It is based upon the relation between the number of paragraphs, sentences and words. Longer words and sentences are assumed to be more difficult to read than shorter words and sentences. Here are the figures for the two texts:

A	B
118 words	104 words
4 paragraphs	2 paragraphs
11 sentences	3 sentences
2.75 sentences per paragraph	1.5 sentences per paragraph
10.73 words per paragraph	35 words per paragraph
4.58 characters per word	5.5 characters per word
Readability – standard	Readability – difficult

21.1.1.1 VOCABULARY – LONG AND SHORT WORDS
The length of words is best stated in terms of syllables rather than written letters. The figures for the two texts are (to the nearest whole number):

	Text A – tabloid		Text B – broadsheet	
1-syllable words	75 (49 types)	= 64%	64 (39 types)	= 60%
2-syllable words	27 (21 types)	= 23%	17 (17 types)	= 16%
3-syllable words	13 (13 types)	= 11%	17 (11 types)	= 16%
4-syllable words	2 (2 types)	= 2%	6 (6 types)	= 6%
5-syllable words	0		2 (2 types)	= 2%

13% of the tabloid and 24% of the broadsheet vocabulary is of three or more syllables. If we look at the derivation of the 4- and 5-syllable words in each text we find the following:

	OE	OF before c. 1400	OF/Fr after c. 1400	Latin	Other
Tabloid 'Meters, please'					
3-syllable word types	anyhow becoming everything householders	allowing discussion minister possible	encourage government	expensive family producing	–
4-syllable word types	–	increasingly	–	–	economise (Gk)
Broadsheet 'Inside South Africa'					
3-syllable word types	Africa heavier	continues violence	determined government	demonstrate moderate unresolved	steadily (?MHG/MDu) apartheid (Afrikaans)
4-syllable word types	overtaken	–	diminishing	condemnation negotiate political population	–
5-syllable word types	–	–	international opportunities	–	–

The broadsheet leader has a higher proportion of non-core, longer words derived from Latin.

📖 The complete vocabulary of the texts is listed by syllable length and derivation in the *Commentary & Data Book*.

21.1.1.2 STRUCTURE

Tabloid leader

There are 118 words. Each of the 11 paragraphs of the tabloid report consists of one sentence. Five are one-clause simple sentences. The others are complex sentences whose complexity is limited, however, to two clauses, except for sentence 5, a reporting–reported sequence of three short clauses. Five of the subordinate clauses are post-modifying qualifiers (q) of nouns or adjectives.

The rhetorical effectiveness of the leader is marked by the sequences of short sentences,

> He should not merely talk about meters.
> He should have them installed.
>
> Meters will help.
> Let's have them.

1. 19 words

    MCl   [Local Government Minister Tom King is producing a discussion paper
    PrepCl   [q on allowing householders to pay for water by meter]]. ***complex sentence***

2. 7 words

    MCl   [He should not merely talk about meters].   ***simple sentence***

3. 5 words

   MCl   [He should have them installed].   *simple sentence*

4. 17 words

   MCl   [The present system . . . *q* . . . is unfair and wasteful].
   PrepCl   [*q* of basing water rates on the size of a house]   *complex sentence*

5. 18 words

   MCl reporting [It means that
   NCl reported   [a woman . . . *q* . . . can pay as much as, or more than, a large family].
   NonfCl   [*q* living alone]   *complex sentence*

6. 11 words

   MCl   [It does NOTHING
   NonfCl   [*q* to encourage people to economise with their water]].   *complex sentence*

7. 15 words

   MCl   [Who cares about running taps
   AdvCl   [if the bill is going to be the same anyhow]]?   *complex sentence*

8. 9 words

   MCl   [Water is becoming an increasingly expensive and scarce resource].
                                                simple sentence

9. 8 words

   MCl   [We should do everything possible [*q* to conserve it].   *complex sentence*

10. 3 words

   MCl   [Meters will help].   *simple sentence*

11. 3/4 words

   MCl   [Let's have them].   *simple sentence*

Broadsheet leader

There are 104 words and two paragraphs of two sentences each. One sentence is simple, the others complex, consisting of four, four and two clauses. The comparative difficulty of this leader is caused by the length of the second and third sentences (41 and 33 words) and their more complex structures with four clauses, together with the higher proportion of non-core vocabulary.

Paragraph 1

1. 11 words

   MCl   [The opportunities for peaceful change in South Africa are steadily
                    diminishing].   *simple sentence*

2. 41 words

MCl	[Black hatred of the apartheid system now runs so deep
CompCl	that [moderate black leaders [*RelCl* who would prefer to negotiate for political rights with the government] fear
NCl	that [they may soon be overtaken by younger men [**q** determined to destroy apartheid by violence]]]]. *complex sentence*

paragraph 2

3. 33 words

	Yet,
NonfCl	[faced with black unrest and international condemnation],
MCl	[the South African government becomes all the more determined [**q** to demonstrate its might] and [**q** to enforce its control over the black population with greater vigour]]. *complex sentence*

4. 16 words

MCl	[The cycle of violence thus continues unresolved,
NonfCl	[each time taking a heavier toll in the country]] *complex sentence*

21.2 Tabloid reporting style

The following text is typical of the kind of news reported in the tabloid papers and unlikely to be found in the broadsheets.

Activity 21.2

What are the marked stylistic features of the report?

(i) The vocabulary – length of words in syllables, proportion of core to non-core words, use of colloquial words.

(ii) The structure – number of sentences in each paragraph, proportion of simple and complex sentences.

An analysis of the words and structure is in the *Commentary & Data Book*.

BABY BOUNCER

BOUNCING baby Melissa Collins scared her baby-sitter half to death.

Stacy Maher had settled down to watch TV confident that the toddler was tucked up in bed.

But then there was a knock on the door. And standing on the step was 22-month-old Melissa.

She'd fallen 20 FEET from her bedroom window.

Miraculously, she was none the worse.

Her fall was broken by a rose bush.

Mum Debbie, 30, said yesterday: 'Stacey was hysterical but all Melissa could do was giggle and say "Window".'

The tough toddler was taken to hospital for observation, then released.

Debbie added: 'People say she looks like an angel but they couldn't be more wrong.'

Now Melissa's dad Karl is to put locks and bars on her bedroom window to prevent another escape.

Readability: easy

21.2.1 Commentary

21.2.1.1 NAMING

bouncing baby Melissa Collins	her baby-sitter	Mum Debbie, 30	Melissa's dad Karl
the toddler	Stacy Maher	Debbie	
22-month-old Melissa Stacey			
Melissa			
the tough toddler			

Names tend to be introduced with modifying, descriptive phrases that are an economical way of providing more information. Grammatical **apposition** is used – the placing side by side of the name and an attribute – together with pre- and post-modification of the head word, e.g., *bouncing baby Melissa Collins, 22-month-old Melissa, Melissa's dad Karl, Mum Debbie, 30*. There is one example, *the tough toddler*, of what would be called **elegant variation** in a literary work, that is, the use of a descriptive phrase to avoid the constant repetition of the name, in this case, *Melissa*.

There are also two examples of the 'creative' use of alliteration, which you often find in reports of less serious news – *bouncing baby, tough toddler* and the headline *Baby Bouncer*, which also carries a comic connotation, because a 'baby bouncer' is a piece of apparatus that you put babies in to amuse them at home.

21.2.1.2 COLLOQUIAL VOCABULARY

The style of the piece is set by the use of colloquial vocabulary that is normally used in familiar speech, e.g. *scared her to death, toddler, Mum, Dad, tough*.

The use of capitals – *She'd fallen 20 FEET* – is a typographical feature that you will find in tabloids rather than broadsheets.

21.3 Tabloid vocabulary

21.3.1 'Gnome-napped'

Here is another typical tabloid report in the light-hearted style of *Baby Bouncer*:

Activity 21.3

Identify and discuss the evidence that this report is from a tabloid rather than a broadsheet newspaper.

GNOME-NAPPED!

'Give us a Coke or else' threat

A GANG of kidnappers have demanded a three-part ransom — for the safe return of two gnomes.

The sneaky snatchers swooped in dawn raids leaving notes behind for the startled owners.

The ransom letters read: "Dear Sir or Madam, if you wish to see your garden gnome alive again please deposit the following articles in a yellow carrier bag behind the telephone box at Manor Garage, time 13.15 hours."

They demanded:

- Three cans of Coca-Cola
- 30 Benson and Hedges cigarettes.
- Three walnut whips.

Readability: fairly easy.

They were signed by Porky, Wolfy and Doris.

Gnome-lovers Donald Whittaker and Anthony Holloway, of Horrabridge, near Tavistock, Devon, called in the police as soon as they found the demands pushed through their front doors.

PC Kevin Reed said yesterday: "One of the owners had difficulty stopping laughing, the other was a bit annoyed.

"But after being ridiculed by his neighbours he saw the funny side too."

21.3.1.1 COMMENTARY

The fact that the story appears at all is the first evidence. A practical joke involving the theft and ransom of garden gnomes by three children would not be accepted as 'newsworthy' in a broadsheet, except perhaps in a feature columnist's 'diary' or a similar item devoted to comic or ephemeral news. The report maintains its mock-serious style as a **parody** of a real-life kidnapping, with the incongruous ransom of Coca-Cola, cigarettes and sweets and the names of the 'gang'. The linguistic evidence includes:

- the pun on *gnome-napped* and *kidnapped*
- the vocabulary associated with kidnapping – *threat, gang of kidnappers, ransom, ransom letters*
- the heavily pre-modified NP *'Give us a Coke or else' threat*, and the NPs in apposition in *Gnome-lovers Donald Whittaker and Anthony Holloway, of Horrabridge, near Tavistock, Devon.*
- the alliteration of *sneaky snatchers swooped*, as well as the colloquial connotations of *sneaky* and *snatchers*, with *swooped* an over-used journalistic cliché.

Activity 21.4

Is the following brief report from a tabloid or broadsheet?

21.3.2 'Posh kids'

Posh kids are forced to sweep the streets

CHAPS who misbehave at the toffs' school, Harrow, are being punished with a spell of street sweeping.

Instead of a whacking, they are forced out of bed at 7am. to tidy up the London borough's cobbled streets under the eagle eye of prefects.

One 13-year-old offender, who has been on clean-up duties for a fortnight, said yesterday: 'It's a pain in the backside, old boy.

'I'll be a lot more subtle next time I do something naughty.'

Readability: easy.

21.4 Broadsheet and tabloid vocabulary

21.4.1 'Curried eggs'

Activity 21.5

Study the following extracts from tabloid and broadsheet newspaper reports. They describe an incident that took place in December 1988. The extracts consist of the headlines and first paragraphs of the reports, which conventionally sum up the news item.

(i) Identify the reports as tabloid or broadsheet in style. What evidence do you use to decide?

(ii) What uses of the connotations of *curry* and *egg* does each report make? Are these connotations exploited in each report?

Newspaper A, front page

CURRIE IN EGG PICKLE
'Poison' farms fury

TROUBLE-PRONE Junior **Health Minister Edwina Currie last night faced the threat of being sued for millions.**

Furious farmers are planning to take her to court over her "irresponsible" warning that people eating raw eggs risk food poisoning.

Readability – difficult.

Newspaper B, page 2

Fowl! Farmers' anger at Currie's egg crack

EDWINA Currie has fallen fowl of farmers after her recent outburst over poisoned eggs.

They fear she could cost them a fortune.

And now some Whitehall bosses have joined the attack on the junior health minister.

The row follows Mrs Currie's claim that most of Britain's eggs contain salmonella poisoning.

"She really has got egg on her face this time," Peter Barton, a senior official for egg producers and farmers, said last night.

Readabillity – standard.

Newspaper C, front page

Farmers threaten to sue Minister

AXE EDWINA CALL IN EGG POISON ROW

MRS THATCHER was under intense pressure last night to sack outspoken Edwina Currie in the row over poisoned eggs.

The poultry trade is so incensed that farmers' leaders are threatening to sue the Junior Health Minister for the damage they feel she has done to the egg industry.

Readability – fairly difficult.

Newspaper D, front page

EDWINA EGG ROW

BOILS OVER

THE scare over food poisoning in eggs plunged Edwina Currie into a furious row last night.

The junior Health Minister was accused of deepening the crisis threatening the industry and thousands of farming jobs.

Producers are planning to sue her and demanding she be sacked by Mrs Thatcher.

Readability – fairly difficult.

Newspaper E, front page

Currie provokes storm with salmonella claim

EDWINA CURRIE, the health minister, has started a major inter-departmental argument and risks a libel action after claiming that most of Britain's egg production was infected with salmonella bacteria.

Minister of Agriculture officials were yesterday "extremely angry" at her comments in an interview with ITN at the weekend. There was no research to support Mrs Currie's claims, they said.

Readability – difficult.

An analysis of the vocabulary of these texts is in the *Commentary & Data Book.*

21.4 Choices of vocabulary – what connotations imply

21.4.1 *Degrees of violence*

Activity 21.6

Discuss the different connotations of the following two headlines which report the same incident. Do they imply approval or disapproval? How serious was the action of the policeman?

Constable strikes boy

Teenage yob slapped by PC

21.4.1.1 COMMENTARY

In *Constable strikes boy* the **actor,** the grammatical **subject** and the **theme** of the simple sentence are identical. Everything focuses on the constable in an active clause. The verb *strikes* does not suggest that the action was justified. The noun *boy* has no positive connotations apart from the implication that he is young.

Teenage yob slapped by PC is a passive clause in which the **theme** and **grammatical** subject, *teenage yob* represents the **affected** person. The pejorative connotations of the colloquial *yob* are transferred to *teenage* also. The PC's action of *slapping* implies a mild, probably justified rebuke.

We do not consciously think all this when reading a headline, but I suggest that the implications are registered in our minds and colour our response to the news item, which did in fact report a similar incident in July 1994.

Activity 21.7

Discuss and **classify** the differences of meaning and connotation between the verbs in the following set of short invented headlines.

(i) Grade them from *most to least violent* in their meanings.

(ii) Distinguish *formal* and *informal/colloquial/slang* verbs.

(iii) Are any marked with reference to specific parts of the body?

X assaults boy	X clobbers boy	X pats boy	X spanks boy
X bashes boy	X clouts boy	X pokes boy	X strikes boy
X beats boy	X cuffs boy	X pummels boy	X thrashes boy
X beats up boy	X elbows boy	X punches boy	X thumps boy
X biffs boy	X gives boy a blow	X sends boy flying	X wallops boy
X boxes boy's ears	X hammers boy	X slaps boy	X whacks boy
X butts boy	X hits boy	X smacks boy	
X clips boy's ear	X lashes out at boy	X smites boy	

21.4.2 Classifying participants

To **classify** a word is to put it into a class or set with similar meanings.

Activity 21.8

Classify the following words, which are all used to refer to the police force or to a policeman, from *most affectionate* to *least affectionate* in connotation.

bobby	cop	flatfoot	PC	rozzer	the fuzz
constable	copper	officer	policeman	the force	the law

Activity 21.9

(i) By what names is the police constable referred to in each of the following reports? (Include any relative clauses or appositional phrases which qualify the names.) Do they imply different points of view towards him?

(ii) What impression of the behaviour of the boy is given by each of the reports? Quote the evidence on which you base your conclusion.

Activity 21.10

Identify the words (verbs or nouns) used in the following press reports to refer to *striking* or *hitting*. What effects do the different choices have on your understanding of what took place? Which of them imply that the constable's offence was serious?

The first report appeared the day before the other two, and anticipates the 'crunch decision' to be made on the following day and reported in the second and third reports. (The names of the participants have been changed.)

Newspaper 1

THANKS A BUNDLE!

Letters help so much says cuff cop Dave

EAR-CLIP cop Dave Jarvis saluted his army of backers as he faced today's crunch decision on his job.

PC Dave and wife Jane clutched a huge bundle of mail from around the world supporting his no-nonsense stand on law and order.

And thousands of readers phoned us yesterday to pledge their support for Dave. He said: 'The letters and calls have been overwhelming.'

The 38-year-old constable risks the sack for cuffing a teenage yob who was terrorising an elderly cancer victim. . . .

Magistrates fined the bobby £100 and ordered him to pay compensation to the 14-year-old.

More than 16,000 people have signed a petition calling for PC Dave to keep his job.

The bobby has been on desk duties.

PC Dave, a volunteer lifeboatman, said he planned to take Jane on holiday to Spain after the hearing.

Readability – fairly easy.

Newspaper 2

PC who hit boy wins job reprieve

THE 14-year-old boy who was awarded compensation after being hit by a policeman has gone to live with his father's family in Spain, it emerged yesterday as the officer was told he could keep his job.

The boy's parents might also leave Britain because of a hate campaign.

PC Dave Jarvis, aged 38, was fined £100 and ordered to pay the boy £50 compensation by magistrates last month.

The boy was one of a group taunting pensioners Sarah and George Beaumont by banging on their door and running away. PC Jarvis has admitted clipping him round the ear but denied hitting him on the nose with his elbow.

The solicitor representing the boy's family, who cannot be named for legal reasons, said they had suffered a barrage of threats. The business they had run for more than a decade was close to collapse.

PC Jarvis, who leaves for a holiday in Spain today with his wife Jane, arrived at police headquarters fearing the sack.

The Chief Constable took 30 minutes to reach his decision after the one-hour hearing.

The announcement was greeted with applause at the force headquarters. PC Jarvis said: 'A great shadow has been lifted from my shoulders and I am extremely grateful to the chief constable for his decision.'

But the boy's solicitor said: 'The boy was taken to hospital for treatment for injuries to his nose, which was pouring with blood: how does a slap do that?

The boy is no thug or hooligan, contrary to what some sections of the press have tried to say. He has no criminal record of any sort, and no action was taken against him over this.'

The officer, helmsman on an inshore lifeboat, said that £6,000 in donations he had received would be split between the Royal National Lifeboat Institution and the victim support scheme. He did not know whether he would be able to return to the beat.

Readability – standard.

Newspaper 3

<u>Assault on boy was 'momentary lapse'</u>

Slap case PC reprimanded but allowed to keep job

CONSTABLE Dave Jarvis, the community policeman fined £100 for slapping a 14-year-old boy, was yesterday reprimanded by his Chief Constable. But after the private police disciplinary hearing, PC Jarvis said he was "very relieved" to have kept his job.

After the hearing at the force headquarters, the constable emerged smiling and said: "A great shadow has been lifted from my shoulders and I am extremely grateful to the Chief Constable for his decision. I have remained honest and true to the police service for 20 years and he has given me the opportunity now to complete my service." ...

Shortly afterwards, Chief Inspector James Wright read a statement saying: "The Chief Constable accepted that this was a momentary lapse in an otherwise commendable career and that Constable Jarvis had been completely honest throughout and retained his integrity."

During the court case the boy alleged PC Jarvis struck him twice – an elbow blow to his nose causing bleeding and an open slap to his cheek. The officer, who was looking for youths who had pestered a pensioner, denied the elbow blow, but admitted the slap.

The solicitor for the boy's family said: "I am not surprised by the decision. Both the family and I were expecting it." The case had been a "nightmare" for the family, he said. They had received death threats and feared that their business was on the verge of collapse. "They feel that reporting has been one-sided."

Readability: – standard

21.4.2.1 COMMENTARY

References to the participants are:

The policeman

Newspaper 1	Newspaper 2	Newspaper 3
cuff cop Dave	PC who hit boy	slap case
ear-clip cop Dave Jarvis	a policeman	PC
PC Dave (2)	the officer	Constable Dave Jarvis, the community policeman fined £100 for slapping a 14-year-old boy
Dave	PC Dave Jarvis, aged 38	PC Jarvis (2)
the 38-year-old constable	PC Jarvis (3)	the constable
the bobby (2)	the officer, helmsman of an inshore lifeboat	Constable Jarvis
PC Dave, a volunteer lifeboatman		the officer

The boy

Newspaper 1	Newspaper 2	Newspaper 3
a teenage yob who was terrorising an elderly cancer victim	boy (4)	boy (2)
	the 14-year-old boy who was awarded compensation after being hit by a policeman the boy (is NO thug or hooligan)	a 14-year-old boy

Notice how much information is included by the journalistic use of pre-modification, e.g.

ear-clip cop = policeman who clipped (someone) over the ear

or post-modification, e.g. with a relative clause,

a teenage yob **who was terrorising an elderly cancer victim**

or by apposition, e.g.

PC Dave, a volunteer lifeboatman

Activity 21.11

(i) Discuss the differences of meaning and connotation in the vocabulary used in the different papers:

(a) *terrorising, taunting, pestering*
(b) *teenage yob, a group, youths*
(c) *elderly cancer victim, pensioner(s)*

(ii) What point of view is implied in the phrase *his no-nonsense stand on law and order* in the first newspaper?

(iii) What effect on your reading of the reports has the inclusion of the fact that the constable was a volunteer lifeboat-man?

21.5 Grammar, vocabulary and style

Activity 21.12

Discuss the differences in style in the following two reports, tabloid and broadsheet. The events took place in 1978.

Newspaper 1

CUP FANS RIOT

MOUNTED policemen charged on to the Elland Road ground yesterday in the vital F.A. Cup tie between Leeds United and Manchester City when rioting fans spilled on to the pitch.

Carlisle referee Colin Seel stopped the game in the 76th minute and players stood on the pitch as fans clashed with police.

Readability – standard.

As the violence spread, Mr Seel first appealed for the pitch to be cleared and then – when this failed – he led the players off the field with Manchester City leading 2–0. . . .

Trouble flared just 10 minutes from time when a fan got on to the pitch and clashed with Manchester City goalkeeper Joe Corrigan. . . .

The fringe ask to be fenced in

Manchester City won with conviction, English football lost ignobly, besmirched by yet another sorry example of crowd indiscipline. And for those who still choose to look upon football as a game rather than a cause, the second factor over shadowed the first at Leeds on Saturday. There was no shred of injustice to ferment bitterness and incite hundreds to spill over from the terraces behind the Manchester goal, where Leeds supporters were thickest; only disappointment that Leeds United were about to depart the FA Cup competition at the first hurdle and, among some at least, perhaps a half-formed idea that they might somehow divert the course of events.

A posse of mounted policemen was needed to disabuse them and the match was held up for a quarter of an hour or so – a thoroughly depressing episode and a sad commentary on the mentality of a small segment of modern football followers.

The first hint of the disturbance came 12 minutes from the end of a hard-fought cup tie with Manchester leading 2–0. A solitary intruder headed towards City's goal and it says something for his intelligence that he even considered a confrontation with Corrigan, a goal-keeper against whom Goliath would seem a pigmy. He was quickly hustled away, but others followed, a trickle became a tide, and suddenly a thin line of policemen and yellow coated stewards was struggling to contain a mass of people on the fringe of the pitch.

The players withdrew to a safe distance and were eventually shepherded to the dressing-rooms. It was not until eight mounted policemen trotted their mounts on to the pitch that the retreat began; those so stubborn and brave in numbers suddenly found they did not have the stomach for it after all and scuttled away like startled rabbits to their burrows.

A precise parallel to the scene was difficult to recall on an English football field and there was another unprecedented moment still to come. A microphone lead was run out from beneath the main stand on to the pitch so that the referee, Mr Seel, could tell the crowd personally that he had no intention of abandoning the match, even if it meant staying until midnight. When it did ultimately restart Leeds got a late goal from a penalty, but it was very much an anti-climax; City won 2-1 and deservedly so – just as deservedly as those troublesome supporters will now, surely, be fenced in at Elland Road.

Readability – fairly difficult.

21.5.1   *Commentary – vocabulary*

21.5.1.1   WORD-CLASSES AND LENGTH OF WORDS

First of all, we should compare the kinds of lexical words used in each report and their distribution by word-class and syllable-length, and see if there is any significant difference between them. The tabloid report is rather short, and so will not provide as accurate a set of data as the longer text.

Tabloid

There are 46 lexical word tokens in the tabloid report:

adjectives	5 – 11%
adverbs	4 – 9%
nouns	23 – 50%
verbs	14 – 30%

varying in length by syllables as follows:

1 syllable	29 – 63%
2 syllables	11 – 24%
3 syllables	6 – 13%
4 syllables	0 – 0%
5 syllables	0 – 0%

Broadsheet

The comparable figures for the broadsheet report are:

adjectives	33 – 18%
adverbs	22 – 12%
nouns	90 – 48.5%
verbs	40 – 21.5%
1 syllable	64 – 34.5%
2 syllables	67 – 36%
3 syllables	36 – 18.5%
4 syllables	16 – 9%
5 syllables	2 – 1%

Word-length is only a guide to the relative complexity of two texts, but these figures support everyone's immediate assessment of the broadsheet report as more difficult, with a use of linguistic features we would expect in academic or literary writing.

21.5.1.2 CORE AND NON-CORE VOCABULARY

Tabloid

There appear to be no non-core words in the tabloid report, many of which, as you would expect, belong to a set that could be labelled 'the vocabulary of football', such as *FA Cup, fans, field, game, goalkeeper, ground, pitch, players, referee*, although there are fewer than usual referring to the game itself because of the pitch invasion.

More than half (63%) of the words are of one syllable, and none have more than three.

Broadsheet

In the vocabulary of football *FA Cup, field, game, goalkeeper, pitch, players, referee* all appear, but not *fans* or *ground*. But the vocabulary of the broadsheet is principally marked by its 10% of 4- and 5-syllable words, as well as a number of shorter words that you would not usually expect in a football report like, for example, *besmirched, ferment, pigmy, posse, scuttled, segment, conviction, disabuse, ignobly, intruder*. The writer also refers to the police horses as *mounts*, which although short, is not commonly used.

The derivations of the longer words, with the date of the earliest written record, are,

abandoning	OF 1375	mentality	Fr 1691
anticlimax	Latin and Greek 1727	overshadowed	OE
commentary	Latin 1531	personally	OF 1398
competition	Latin 1608	solitary	Latin 1340
confrontation	Latin 1632	ultimately	Latin 1660
deservedly (2)	OF 1548	yellow-coated	OE + OF
disappointment	Fr 1614	eventually	Fr 1660
indiscipline	Fr 1783	unprecedented	Fr 1623
intelligence	OF 1390		

None of them are rare, and some, like *commentary* or *intelligence*, you might think common enough to be core vocabulary, while *yellow-coated* is a made-up compound of two core words. But 11 of these 17 words came into the language in the sixteenth, seventeenth or eighteenth centuries, and this is supporting evidence for a general impression of the 'literary' nature of the writing. This is reinforced by the writer's comparison of the goalkeeper to Goliath, and the simile that likens the fans to startled rabbits scuttling away to their burrows.

An obvious detail in the contrast between the two reports is how the tabloid says that the mounted police **charged** *on to the field*, while in the broadsheet they **trotted** *their mounts on to the pitch*. This matches the tabloid headline *Cup fans riot*, suggesting extreme crowd violence, whereas the broadsheet sequence *solitary intruder – trickle – tide – mass of people on the fringe of the pitch* implies nothing like a riot. Which do you believe?

21.5.2 Commentary – structure

Tabloid

There are four paragraphs of one sentence each. None of them is a simple one-clause sentence, but their complexity is reduced by the shortness of the individual clauses, for example sentence 3,

AdvCl	[[As the violence spread,
MCl	Mr Seel first appealed
PrepCl	[for the pitch to be cleared] and then –
AdvCl	[when this failed] –
MCl	[he led the players off the field
PrepCl	[with Manchester City leading 2–0]. *Compound-complex sentence*

which is the longest sentence, has six clauses but is easy to read.

Broadsheet

This has five paragraphs and 12 sentences, which contain from two to eight clauses, the most complex of which is the third sentence in paragraph 1,

MCl	[There was no shred of injustice
NonfCl	[to ferment bitterness] and
NonfCl	[∅ incite hundreds to spill over from the terraces behind the Manchester goal],
RelCl	[where Leeds supporters were thickest];
MCl	[∅∅ only disappointment
AppCl	that [Leeds United were about to depart the FA Cup competition at the first hurdle] and,
MCl	[among some at least, ∅∅ perhaps a half-formed idea
NCl	that [they might somehow divert the course of events]].

Six of the 12 sentences are compound-complex, four are complex and two compound.

The combination of formal vocabulary and complex grammatical structures explains the relative difficulty of the broadsheet report in readability. It attempts to do far more than the tabloid, expressing the writer's interpretation of the events in a style that resembles an academic essay more than a sports report.

📖 A complete list of the vocabulary of the two reports and structural analyses are in the *Commentary & Data Book*.

Bibliography

Wales, Katie, *A Dictionary of Stylistics* (Longman, 1989).

Aspects of English Series

Carter, R. (ed.), *Language and Literature* (Allen & Unwin, 1982).
Carter, R., *Vocabulary* (Allen & Unwin, 1987).

Interface Series

Birch, D., *Language, Literature and Critical Practice* (Routledge, 1989).
Nash, W., *Language in Popular Fiction* (Routledge, 1990).
Stephens, J. and Waterhouse, R., *Literature, Language and Change* (Routledge, 1990).
Toolan, M. (ed.), *Language, Text and Context* (Routledge 1992).

Carter, R. and Nash, W., *Seeing Through Language* (Blackwell, 1990).
Cluysenaar, Anne, *Introduction to Literary Stylistics* (Batsford, 1976).
Crystal, D. & Davy, D. *Investigating English Style* (Longman, 1969).
Fowler, R., *Linguistics & the Novel* (Methuen, 1977).
Fowler, R., *Literature as Social Discourse* (Batsford, 1981).
Fowler, R., *Linguistic Criticism* (OUP, 1986).
Fowler, R., *Language in the News* (Routledge, 1991).
Kress, G. and Hodge, R., *Language as Ideology* (Routledge, 1979).
Lakoff, G. and Johnson, M., *Metaphors We Live By* (University of Chicago Press, 1980).
Leech, G., *A Linguistic Guide to English Poetry* (Longman, 1969).
Leech, G. and Short, M., *Style in Fiction* (Longman, 1981).
Nash, W., *Designs in Prose* (Longman, 1980).
Queneau, R., *Exercises in Style* (Calder, 1979).
Widdowson, H. G., *Stylistics and the Teaching of Literature* (Longman, 1975).

Index of texts quoted and used for stylistic analysis

'In the beginning...', St. John's Gospel, Ch 1 vv 1–6, 135

Absolute Beginners, Colin MacInnes, 224

An Address to the Rev George Gilfillan, William McGonagall, 167

Animal Farm, George Orwell, 35, 38, 40, 90

Antiquary, The, Sir Walter Scott, 230

Battle of Maldon, The, 145

Bear, The, William Faulkner, 48, 50

Bees' Nest, Edwin Morgan, 178

Beowulf, 146

Between walls, William Carlos Williams, 182

Biographia Literaria, Samuel Taylor Coleridge, 106

Boot and Saddle, Robert Browning, 170

Boots, Rudyard Kipling, 172

Bowling-Green, The, William Somerville, 115

Bride of Lammermoor, The, Sir Walter Scott, 101, 104, 229

Canterbury Tales, Geoffrey Chaucer, 147–8

Catcher in the Rye, J D Salinger, 206, 208

Cities and Thrones and Powers, Rudyard Kipling, 172

Clarissa, Samuel Richardson, 231

Clockwork Orange, A, Anthony Burgess, 28, 30

Cold Comfort Farm, Stella Gibbons, 260–2

Cold Iron, Nicholas Freeling, 206

Country Man, The, George Farewell, 115

D. H. Lawrence: Novelist, F. R. Leavis, 3

David Copperfield, Charles Dickens, 207–8, 242–3

David Copperfield, simplified version, 243

Dombey & Son, Charles Dickens, 193

Donkey, The, G K Chesterton, 172

Ecclesiastes, 39

Ecclesiastes, Orwell's parody of, 39

Europeans, The, Henry James, 219

Eveline, James Joyce, 54

Exercises in Style, Raymond Queneau: *Asides*, 4; *Botanical*, 5; *Ignorance*, 5; *Notation*, 4; *Official letter*, 5; *Permutations*, 6; *Reported speech*, 5; *Sonnet*, 5

Far from the Madding Crowd, Thomas Hardy, 227

Finnegans Wake, James Joyce, 31

Flight of the Duchess, The, Robert Browning, 170

Flood Play, The (York), 150

For Saturday, Christopher Smart, 116

Fox Trot, Edith Sitwell, 176

Girl's Song, W. B. Yeats, 171

Goff, The, An Heroi-Comical Poem, Thomas Mathison, 116

Good Companions, The, J. B. Priestly, 227

Guide-book to Woolbridge and the West Leys, 249

Gymnasiad, The, or Boxing Match, Paul Whitehead, 116

Hamlet, William Shakespeare, 20

Harry Ploughman, Gerard Manley Hopkins, 123, 157

Heart of Darkness, Joseph Conrad, 209–11

Homage to Switzerland, Ernest Hemingway, 88

Iliad, book III, translated E. V. Rieu, 199; Alexander Pope, 199; Richard Lattimore, 199; Christopher Logue, 199

Iliad, book XIX, translated E. V. Rieu, 203; Alexander Pope, 203; Richard Lattimore, 204; Christopher Logue, 204

Invictus, W. E. Henley, 171

Justify all those renowned generations, W. B. Yeats, 171

Lark Rise to Candleford, Flora Thompson, 227

Last of the Mohicans, The, Fenimore Cooper, 93, 100

Letter to a Young Gentleman in Holy Orders, Jonathan Swift, 33

Letter to James Boswell, Dr Samuel Johnson, 75

Letter to *The Independent*, 15

Liberal Translation of the New Testament, A, Edward Harwood, 114–5

Llaregyb, *Under Milk Wood*, Dylan Thomas, 250

London, Dr Samuel Johnson, 112

Macbeth, William Shakespeare, 109, 246, 248

Macbeth, 'made easy', 246, 248

Mansfield Park, Jane Austen, 219, 222–4

Marching Along, Robert Browning, 169

Margaritæ Sorori, W. E. Henley, 171

Martin Chuzzlewit, Charles Dickens, 184, 221

Message Clear, Edwin Morgan, 179

Newspaper reports, *Meters, please!*, 266; *Inside South Africa*, 266; *Baby Bouncer*, 270; *Gnome-napped!*, 272; *Posh kids are forced to sweep the streets*, 273; *Currie in egg pickle*, 273; *Fowl! Farmers' anger at Currie's egg crack*, 274; *Axe Edwina call in egg poison row*, 274; *Edwina egg row boils over*, 274; *Currie provokes storm with salmonella claim*, 275; *Thanks a bundle!*, 277; *PC who hit boy wins job reprieve*, 277; *Slap case PC reprimanded but allowed to keep job*, 278; *Cup fans riot*, 279; *The fringe ask to be fenced in*, 280

Nursery rhymes: *Tinker, tailor*, 144; *When clouds appear*, 144; *The world is so full*, 144; *Ride a cock-horse*, 144; *Three grey geese*, 144; *What a wonderful bird the frog are*, 145

O Where are you Going?, W. H. Auden, 181

Old Curiosity Shop, The, Charles Dickens, 184, 188, 221, 223

On the Death of Richard West, Thomas Gray, 108

Orwell's parody of *Eccelesiastes*, 39

Outsider, The, Albert Camus, 85

Owl and the Nightingale, The (12th C), 148

Paradise Lost, John Milton, 117, 120–2

Pentecost Play (York), 149

Peter Grimes, George Crabbe, 111

Pickwick Papers, The, ch. XX, Charles Dickens, 191

Pied Beauty, Gerard Manley Hopkins, 164

Pied Piper of Hamelin, The, Robert Browning, 170

Piers Plowman, William Langland, 147

Practical Rhetorick, Joshua Pool, 71

Preface, *Lyrical Ballads*, William Wordsworth, 105

Psalm 68, from *The Book of Common Prayer*, (1662), 181

Rainbow, The, D. H. Lawrence, 19, 260, 261

Rambler, The, Dr Samuel Johnson, No 38, 76, No 49, 80, No 168, 109

Remember, Christina Rossetti, 143

Riddley Walker, Russell Hoban, 20 ff.

Rime of the Ancient Mariner, The, Samuel Taylor Coleridge, 181

Rolling English Road, The, G. K. Chesterton, 172

Sermon on the Mount, The, *St Matthew's Gospel*, 5, 3, 134

Seven for a Secret, Mary Webb, 261

Siesta of a Hungarian Snake, Edwin Morgan, 178

Some Notes on my own Poetry, Edith Sitwell, 175, 177

St Matthew's Gospel, ch 26, 69–75; Peter's denial, 138

Suitable Boy, A, Vikram Seth, 87, 89

Summer Haiku, Edwin Morgan, 182

Sun also Rises, The, Ernest Hemingway, 218

Swiss Family Robinson, The, 19th-C version, 126; 20th-C version, 132

This is just to say, William Carlos Williams, 166

Thorn, The, William Wordsworth, 107

Treasure Island, Robert Louis Stevenson, 236; simplified version, 236

Ulysses, James Joyce, 232–4

Under Milk Wood, Dylan Thomas, 64, 164–5

Unvanquished, The, William Faulkner, 228

Whatever Man Makes, D. H. Lawrence, 167

Wine of Wyoming, Ernest Hemingway, 89

Wood beyond the World, The, William Morris, 263–4

Woodlanders, The, Thomas Hardy, 17–18

Writing Degree Zero, Roland Barthes, 84

General Index

abstract poetry, 175
abstract words or expressions, 8, 52, 92, 96, 98, 253, 255, 258
academic writing and nominalization, **section 4.3**, 40 ff.
accent
    dialectal, 224, 241
    London Cockney, 225
action, reflexive, 213–4
actional verb, 253
active and passive voice, **section 4.1.2.1**, 35 ff.
active voice, 33
actor, participant, 213
adjective
    descriptive, 251, 257
    evaluative, 251
adverb, modal, 85
affected participant, 213
agent deletion, **section 4.1.2.2**, 35 ff.
alliteration, 144–6, 148–9, 152, 156–7, 162, 178, 195, 202
alliteration in *Harry Ploughman*, **section 13.4.2**, 162 ff.
alliterative verse, stress-timed, **section 12.2.2**, 145 ff.
alliterative metrical verse, **section 12.2.4**, 149 ff.
alphabet, Roman, 224
Alternative Service Book, 133
anachronism, 202
analogy, 124
analysis, contrastive, 241
anapaest, 151
anapaestic metre, *see* rising triple rhythm
Anglo-Saxon, 145
Anglo-Saxon place names, 25
Animal Farm, George Orwell, **section 8.3**, 89 ff.
antimetabole (rhetorical figure), *see* chiasmus

antithesis (rhetorical figure), 68
aposiopesis (rhetorical figure), 66, 71
apostrophe (punctuation), 23
apostrophe (rhetorical figure), 62, 68, 71, 118, 141
archaic/archaism, 101, 123, 133, 189, 241, 253, 255, 263
assimilation, 11, 12, 13, 15, 62, 98, 128
assonance, 145, 152, 157, 162, 175–6
assonance and rhyme in *Harry Ploughman*, **section 13.4.3**, 162 ff.
attribute of a participant, 213
Augustan style, 75, 112, 200
author, implied, 206
Authorized Version of the Bible, 133
autobiography, 208

backshifted tense, 220
balance, rhetorical, 70, 74–5, 77–9, 82, 91, 122
ballad metre, 186
barbarous language, 115
bathos, 185
Battle of Maldon, The, 145
be as a main verb, 253
Bear, The, William Faulkner – style and grammar, **section 5.1**, 47 ff.
beat (in verse), 150
beat, silent, 152, 187
Bible translations, **section 11.2**, 133 ff.
Birds of a Feather Flock Together, 13
blank verse, 119, 154, 186
Book of Common Prayer, 133
Boots, Rudyard Kipling, 174
Borough, The, George Crabbe, 111
Bride of Lammermoor, The, Sir Walter Scott (i), **section 9.3**, 100 ff.
Bride of Lammermoor, The, Sir Walter Scott (ii), **section 9.4**, 104 ff.
burden-lines, 123

Canterbury Tales, Geoffrey Chaucer, 147
Catcher in the Rye, The, J. D. Salinger, 206
Chaucer's *Pardoner's Tale*, 14
Chesterton, G. K., **section 14.4.1.3**, 173 ff.
chiasmus (rhetorical figure), 69, 114
choice of words in speaking and writing –
formal and informal, **section 2.2**, 12 ff.
Christmas Eve in Whitneyville, Donald Hall,
152
Cider with Rosie, Laurie Lee, 63
circumlocution, 8–10, 69
Cities and Thrones and Powers, Rudyard
Kipling, 174
Clarissa or *The History of a Young Lady*,
Samuel Richardson, 231
classical Latin, 11
classification of participants in *Heart of
Darkness*, **section 17.2.1**, 212 ff.
classification of sentence structures, 56
clause
descriptive, 51
interrogative, in reported speech, 221
narrative, 51
nonfinite, 238
quoting, 219
verbless, 238
cliché, 15, 89, 91–2, 168
climax (trope), 62, 65, 71, 259
Clockwork Orange, A, Anthony Burgess,
section 3.2, 28 ff.
Cockney accent, 225
coined words, **section 3.2.1**, 29
Cold Comfort Farm, Stella Gibbons, **section
20.4**, 259 ff.
Coleridge, Samuel Taylor, 105
collocation, 127, 251
colloquialism, 5, 55, 87, 207, 247
complex sentence, 56, 90
complex structure, 102
complexity, stylistic, 96
compound noun, 129
sentence, 56
words, 124
compound-complex sentence, 56, 90
compressed syntax, 124
concrete poetry – games with words,
section 14.6, 177 ff.
concrete words or expressions, 8, 9
connotation, 19, 22, 23, 31, 33, 58, 86, 98,
109, 124, 134, 183, 190, 197, 212, 251,
253, 257
Conrad, Joseph, 208
consciousness, 233
consonance, 156
contrastive analysis, 241
stress, 140

conversation in the novel, 218
Cooper, James Fenimore, 93
coordination, 213
core vocabulary, 10, 12, 13, 53, 55, 76, 79,
83, 91, 101, 106, 112, 117, 128, 133–4,
189, 192, 195, 269, 281–2
counterpoint (in verse), 159
couplet, 144, 147
heroic, 111, 154, 200–1
rhyming, 148, 168, 173
curtal sonnet, 163

dactyl, 151, 157, 197
David Copperfield, Charles Dickens, 206,
section 19.2, 241 ff.
'death of Little Nell, the', **section 15.1**,
183 ff.
deconstruction, 52, 53
deletion of *that*, 220
deletion of the agent, **section 4.1.2.2**, 35 ff.
demotion of stressed syllables, 150, 159
derivation (*no further references indexed*), 11
descriptive adjective, 251, 257
clauses, 51
deverbal noun, 96, 99
deviance in grammar (Gerard Manley
Hopkins), **section 10.3.1.2**, 124 ff.
dialect, Scots, 228
dialectal accent, 224, 241
dialectal speech in novels, **section 18.2**,
224 ff.
dialectal speech (Scottish) in *The Bride of
Lammermoor*, **section 18.2.2**, 228 ff.
dialectal words, 123
dialogue, 241
dialogue, **section 18.1**, 218 f.
diction
'elegance' of, 115, 134
poetic, 105, 108, 109, 200–1
diction, poetic and word order, **section 10.2**,
107 ff.
dictionary definitions of style, **section 1.1**, 1
Dictionary, Dr Samuel Johnson's (1755), 72
direct speech and free direct speech, **section
18.1.1**, 218 ff.
Disposition (medieval), 58
dissonance, 175, 177
doggerel verse, **section 14.2**, 167 ff.
Donkey, The, G. K. Chesterton, 174
double negative, 73
double off-beat, 150, 159, 186–7
duple (two-syllable) pattern of speech, 141

elegance of diction, 115, 134
elegant variation, 111
'elevated' style, 190

Elocution (medieval), 58
embedding, 255
end-stopped lines, 119
end-weighting, or right-branching, **section 4.1.2.4**, 37 ff.
end-weighting, 99, 103
'energetic' rhythm, **section 14.3.1**, 169 ff.
epic poetry, 62, 111, 145, 197
epistolary novel, 231
equal-timed stress – isochrony, **section 12.1.3**, 141 ff.
evaluative adjective, 251
Eveline, James Joyce, style and grammar, **section 5.2**, 54 ff.
exclamation (rhetorical figure), 62, 67, 68, 71, 216
Exercises in Style, Raymond Queneau, **section 1.3**, 4 ff.
extended simile, 62
eye-dialect, 226

Façade, Edith Sitwell, verse and music, **section 14.5**, 174 ff.
falling and rising rhythm, **section 12.1.2.1**, 140 ff.
falling duple rhythm, 144, 145, 178
falling rhythm, 141–2, 145–6
falling triple rhythm, 169, 173–4
fantasy, Medieval, **section 20.5**, 263 ff.
Faulkner, William, 47
figurative meaning, 64
figures (rhetorical), **section 6.2.2**, 66 ff.
Finnegans Wake by James Joyce, **section 3.3**, 30 ff.
first person narrative, **ch 17**, 206 ff.
Flood Play, The (York), 150
focus of information, 255
focus of information – end-weighting, or right-branching, **section 4.1.2.4**, 37 ff.
focus of information – theme in the clause, **section 4.1.2.3**, 36 ff.
foot
    metrical, 151, 197
    reversed, 153, 173
foregrounding, 23, 88, 91, 146, 152, 156
foregrounding rhythm, **section 13.1**, 152 ff.
foregrounding the final syllables of lines – rhyme, **section 13.2**, 153 ff.
formal and informal words (*no further references indexed*), 12
formal style, 13, 19, 39, 74–5, 79, 94, 98, 101, 104, 127–8, 201, 208, 228, 252–3, 255–7, 259
fourteener (14 syllable line of verse), 173
Fowler brothers and the King's English, **section 2.1.1**, 8 ff.

Fox Trot, Edith Sitwell, **section 14.5.1.2**, 176 ff.
free direct speech, 219
free indirect speech, **section 18.1.3**, 221 ff.
free verse, **section 14.1**, 166 ff.
Freeling, Nicholas, 206
French, 15
front-weighting, 38, 239

games with words – 'concrete poetry', **section 14.6**, 177 ff.
garage, 14
Germanic, 11
Gibbons, Stella, 259
Girl's Song, W. B. Yeats, 173
grammar
    nonstandard, 22
    prescriptive, 8
grammatical words (*no further references indexed*), 15
Greek, 197
'grisly' rhyme, **section 14.3.2**, 170 ff.
guide-book style, 249

hangers (outrides) in Hopkins' verse, 158
Harry Ploughman, rhythm and metre of, 159
Harry Ploughman, words and grammar, **section 10.3.1**, 122 ff.
Heart of Darkness, Joseph Conrad, **section 17.2**, 208 ff
heightening, 53, 152, 186
Henley, W. E., **section 14.4.1.2**, 173 ff.
heroic couplet, 111, 154, 200–1
    poetry, 119
hexameter verse, 197, 198
high style, 75, 247
Homer's *Iliad*, **section 16.1**, 197 ff.
Hopkins, Gerard Manley, 122
Humpty-Dumpty, 31
hyperbole (trope), 62, 65, 71
hypotactic structure, 208

I am the resurrection and the life, Edwin Morgan, 180
iamb, 151
iambic
    metre, *see* rising duple rhythm
    pentameter, 119, 151, 186, 200, 247
ideology, 265
idiomatic, 129, 256, 264
Iliad, Homer's, **section 16.1**, 197 ff.
imagery, 212
imperative mood, 212
implied author, 206
incongruity, 256

indicative mood, 85
indirect, or reported speech, **section 18.1.2**, 219 ff.
informal style, 19, 24, 101, 216, 231, 241, 255
   vocabulary, 217
information, unit of, 140
interior monologue, 48, 232–3, 262
interrogative clauses in reported speech, 221
intransitive verb, 214
Introduction to Modern English Word-Formation, An, Valerie Adams, 70
'introductory' word, 216
Invention (medieval), 58
Invictus, W. E. Henley, 173
irony, 15, 16, 24, 191, 260
irony (trope), 62, 66, 71
isochrony – equal-timed stress, **section 12.1.3**, 141 ff.
isochrony, 145, 148, 150, 154, 159

jargon, 'nautical', 241
Joyce, James, 232
Justify all those Renowned Generations, W. B. Yeats, 173

King James Bible, 133
King's English, The, 8
Kipling, Rudyard, **section 14.4.1.4**, 174 ff.

language
   'barbarous', 115
   'rustic', 105
   'transparent', 183
language game, 32
Last of the Mohicans, The, Fenimore Cooper, **section 9.1**, 93 ff., **section 92**, 100 ff.
Latin, 9, 11–12, 15
   classical, 11
   teaching of, 15
   words in English, 11–13
Latinate words, 12, 16, 118, 120
Lattimore, Richard, 200
Leavis, F. R., 2–3, 193
left-branching, 132
Letter to Lord Bute, Dr Samuel Johnson, **section 7.1.1**, 72 ff.
lexical words (*no further references indexed*), 15
literal meaning, 64
'literary' style, 252–3, 257
litotes (trope), 62, 66, 71, 73
little, 183
Llaregyb, *Under Milk Wood*, 164
location of a process, 213

Logue, Christopher, 200
London Cockney accent, 225
London, Dr Samuel Johnson, **section 10.2.4**, 112 ff.
Lyrical Ballads, 105

marked order of clauses, 97
marked word order, 106, 108, 110
Marlow (narrator, *Heart of Darkness*), 209
Martin Chuzzlewit, Charles Dickens, 140, 141
McGonagall, William, 167
meaning
   figurative, 64
   literal, 64
Medieval fantasy, **section 20.5**, 263 ff.
mental process, 213–4
metaphor, 5, 57, 62–5, 71, 86, 95, 164, 177
metaphor, **section 6.2.1.2**, 63 ff.
Metaphors We Live By, Lakoff and Johnson, 63
metonymy and synecdoche, **section 6.2.1.3**, 65 ff.
metre, 142, 152
   ballad, 186
   iambic, 111
   paeonic, 163
   poetic, 194
metrical foot, **section 12.2.5.1**, 151 ff. 197
metrical verse, **section 12.2.3**, 147 ff., 142, 152, 186
Middle English, 12
Milton, John, 116
mimsy, 31
minor sentence, 216, 233
mock-elevated style in *Pickwick Papers*, **section 15.2**, 190 ff
modal
   adverb, 85
   verb, 85
monologue, interior, 48, 232–3, 262
monosyllable, 157
mood (grammatical), 85
   imperative, 85, 118
   indicative, 85
   optative, 85
   subjunctive, 85
Morgan, Edwin, 177
Morris, William, 263

narrative report of speech acts, 223
narrative, first person, **ch 17**, 206 ff
   clauses, 51
   spoken, 215
narrator, omniscient, 206

'nautical' jargon, 241
negative, 73
  double, 73
negatives in *Heart of Darkness*, 213
neologism (newly coined word), 30
neutral term, 85
nominalization, 40–1, 78–9, 96, 98–9
nominalization in academic writing, **section 4.3**, 40
non-core vocabulary, 55, 91, 101, 128, 137, 192, 208
non-transactive process, 213–14
nonfinite clause, 238
nonstandard grammar, 22
  punctuation, 22
  spelling, 22
  word-forms, 22
noun phrase structure, 111, 113
noun, compound, 129
  deverbal, 96, 99
novel, epistolary, 231
novels, dialectal speech in, **section 18.2**, 224
nursery rhymes, **section 12.2.1**, 143

objective criteria of judgement, 2, 89, 185, 217, 265
objective of mental process, 213
off-beat (in verse), 150, 159
  double, 150, 159, 186–7
  silent, 159, 187
  triple, 150, 159
Old English, 10–13, 15–16, 156, 192
  derivation (words), 123
  verse, 145, 202
Old French, 11–13
Old Norse, 11
'old-fashioned' style, 126, 256
omniscient narrator, 206
On the Death of Richard West, Thomas Gray, **section 10.1.2**, 107 ff.
onomatopeia (rhetorical figure), 62, 69, 178
optative mood, 85
Orwell on good writing, **section 4.1**, 33 ff.
Orwell's vocabulary and the Fowler's rules, **section 4.2**, 39 ff.
Orwell's use of the passive in *Animal Farm*, **section 4.1.2**, 35 ff.
outrides (hangers) in Hopkins' verse, 158
Outsider, The, Albert Camus, **section 8.1**, 84 ff.
Oxford English Dictionary, 1, 13, 17, 29, 92, 106, 249, 264
oxymoron (trope), 62, 66, 71

paeon, 151, 157, 163
Paradise Lost, John Milton, 62, 63 **section 10.2.6**, 116
parallelism, 70, 74, 78, 82, 114, 187, 190, 194, 201, 214, 254, 258
paraphrase, 200–2
paratactic structure, 195, 207
parenthesis (rhetorical figure), 62, 68, 71, 125
parison (rhetorical figure), 70, 74
  see also parallelism
Parlement of Foules, Chaucer, 59
parody, **ch 20 Part 1**, 249 ff.
parody, 39, 41, 172
paronomasia (rhetorical figure), 67, 75
participant actor, 213
  affected, 213
  recipient, 213
participants, classification of, in *Heart of Darkness*, **section 17.2.1**, 212 ff.
passive and active voice, **section 4.1.2.1**, 35 ff.
passive voice, 33, 40, 74, 255
passive voice – Orwell's use in *Animal Farm*, **section 4.1.2**, 35 ff.
pastiche, **ch 20 Part 2**, 262 ff.
pathos, 185
patterns of stress and rhythm in everyday speech, **section 12.1**, 139 ff.
patterns of stress and rhythm in verse, **section 12.2**, 143 ff.
patterns of verse, 197
pejorative, 91, 257
pentameter, 151
  iambic, 119, 151, 186, 200, 247
Pentecost Play, The (York), 149
periphrasis (rhetorical figure), 10, 69, 71
periphrasis, *see* circumlocution
personification, 64, 109
Peter Grimes, George Crabbe, **section 10.2.3**, 111 ff.
phonotactics, 29
Pied Beauty, Gerard Manley Hopkins, **section 13.5**, 163 ff.
Piers Plowman, William Langland, 147
place names, 25
place names, Anglo-Saxon, 25
poetic diction, 105, 108–9, 200–1
poetic diction and word order, **section 10.2**, 107
poetic metre, 194
poetry
  abstract, 175
  concrete, 177
  epic, 62, 111, 145, 197
  heroic, 119

poetic prose, **ch 15**, 183 ff.
poetry and rhetoric in *The Old Curiosity Shop*, **section 15.1**, 183 ff.
poetry and rhetoric in *The Rainbow*, **section 15.4**, 193 ff.
point of view, 2, 47, 55, 206, 228
polar opposition, 85
Politics and the English Language, George Orwell, 33
Pope, Alexander, 199
portmanteau words, 31
Portrait of the Artist as a Young Man, James Joyce, 233
post-modification, 9, 45, 96, 99
Practical Rhetorick, Joshua Pool, 62
pre-modification, 113
prepositional phrase (*no further references indexed*), 9
prescriptive grammar, 8
primary stress, 139, 140
process
  mental, 213–14
  non-transactive, 213
  non-transactive actional, 214
  transactive, 213
  transactive actional, 214
promotion of unstressed syllables, 151, 159
pronoun changes (1st and 2nd person) in reported speech, 220
pronoun changes (demonstrative) in reported speech, 220
pronunciation of words derived from French, **section 2.2.2**, 14
proposition, 52, 53
propriety in language use (18th-century views), **section 10.2.5**, 114
prose, poetic, **ch 15**, 183
pun (rhetorical figure), 5, 31, 67, 247
punctuation, 48
  nonstandard, 22

qualifier, *see* post-modification
Queneau, Raymond, *Exercises in Style*, 62
question, rhetorical, 216
quoting clause, 219

Rainbow, The, D. H. Lawrence, 193
Rambler, The, and rhetorical style, **section 7.1.3**, 76 ff., **section 7.1.4**, 80 ff.
Rambler, The, Dr Samuel Johnson, 109
rank-shift, 80, 255
readability, 265
Received Pronunciation (RP), 224
recipient participant, 213
recursive structure, 99
reduction in speech, 216

reflexive action, 213, 214
regularity of rhythm, 141
relational verb, 253
Remember, Christina Rossetti, **section 12.1.4**, 142 ff.
Renaissance, 12
repetition (rhetorical), 82, 194, 254
reported, or indirect speech, **section 18.1.2**, 219 ff.
reversed foot, 153, 173
rhetoric, 58–9, 61–4, 66, 68, 76, 90, 117, 118, 259
Rhetoric, the medieval Art of, **section 6.1**, 58 ff.
rhetorical balance, 70, 74–5, 77–9, 82, 91, 122
  figures, in *Tristram Shandy*, **section 6.2.2.1**, 66
  question, 216
rhyme, 119, 152, 153, 162, 175–6, 200
  'grisly', **section 14.3.2**, 170
rhyme-scheme, 153
rhyming couplet, 148, 168, 173
rhythm and metre, **section 12.2.5**, 150 ff.
rhythm
  'energetic', **section 14.3.1**, 169 ff.
  falling, 141–2, 145–6
  falling, duple, 144–5, 178
  falling triple, 144, 169, 173, 174
  regularity of, 141
  rising, 141–2
  rising duple, 144, 147, 149, 153–4, 173, 186, 200
  rising triple, 144
  sprung, 163
  stress-timed, 148
  'thumping', in verse **section 14.4**, 171 ff.
  waltz, 175
Rhythm, Sprung (Hopkins), 157
Richardson, Samuel, 231
Riddley Walker, Russell Hoban, **section 3.1**, 20 ff.
Rieu, E.V., 199
right-branching, **section 4.1.2.4**, 37 ff.
rising duple rhythm, 111, 119, 144, 147, 149, 153–4, 173, 186, 200
rising rhythm, 141–2
rising triple rhythm, 144
Rolling English Road, The, G. K. Chesterton, 173
Roman alphabet, 224
Romance languages, 11, 12, 16
  words, 8, 11, 13
Romanz (Old French), 11
rule of three, 78
rules for choosing words (Fowler brothers), 8

run-on lines, 119
rustic language, 105

satire, 260, 262
satire in *Dombey & Son*, **section 15.3**, 192 ff.
Saxon, 8, 10, 13, 250
  see also Old English
scansion of verse, 147
Scots, 11, 178, 228
Scott, Sir Walter, 100
Scottish dialectal speech in *The Bride of Lammermoor*, **section 18.2.2**, 228 ff.
secondary stress, 139
semantic field, 64
  set, 251, 258
sentence
  complex, 56, 90
  compound, 56, 90
  compound-complex, 56, 90
  minor, 216, 233
  simple, 56, 90
sentence structures, classification of, 56, 130
sentimentality, 185
Seven Headlines, Edwin Morgan, 180
Shakespeare's *Macbeth* 'made easy', **section 19.3**, 245 ff.
Siesta of a Hungarian Snake, Edwin Morgan, 180
silent beat, 152, 154, 187
silent off-beat, 159, 187
silent stress, 159
simile, **section 6.2.1.1**, 62 ff., 57, 71, 84, 164, 200–2
  extended, 62
simple sentence, 56, 90
Sitwell, Edith, 174
slang, 5
slithy, 31
small, 184
soliloquy, 233
sonnet, 122, 143
  curtal, 163
sound symbolism, 70
speaking voice, 86, 125
speech
  direct, 219
  free direct, 219
  free indirect, **section 18.1.3**, 221
  indirect, or reported, **section 18.1.2**, 219
speech act, 166
speech acts, narrative report, **section 18.1.4**, 223 ff.
speech marks, 232
spelling, nonstandard, 22
spoken narrative, 215

spoken voice, the, **ch 18**, 218 ff., 256
spoken voice in letters, **section 18.3**, 231 ff.
spondee, 151, 197
sprung rhythm, 163
Sprung Rhythm (Hopkins), 157
Standard English, 228
stanza, 153
Stevenson, Robert Louis, 235
stream of consciousness, 49, 232
stress
  contrastive, 140
  primary, 139–40
  secondary, 139
  silent, 159
  tonic, 140
stress patterns in sequences of words, **section 12.1.2**, 40 ff.
stress patterns in words, **section 12.1.1**, 139 ff.
stress-timed rhythm, 148
stress-timed verse, 145, 157
structure
  complex, 102
  hypotactic, 208
  noun phrase, 111, 113
  paratactic, 195, 207
  recursive, 99
structure and rhetoric in Dr Johnson's prose, **section 7.1**, 72 ff.
style
  Augustan, 75, 112, 200
  'elevated', 190
  formal, 13, 19, 39, 74–5, 79, 94, 98, 101, 104, 127, 128, 201, 208, 228, 252–3, 255–7, 259
  informal, 19, 24, 101, 216, 231, 241, 255
  'literary', 252–3, 257
  mock-elevated, in *Pickwick Papers*, **section 15.2**, 190 ff.
  'old-fashioned', 126, 256
style in literary criticism and reviews of books, **section 1.2**, 2 ff.
stylistic complexity, 96
subjective criteria of judgement, 2, 9, 55, 89, 170, 217, 256–7
subjunctive mood, 85
Suitable Boy, A, Vikram Seth, **section 8.2**, 87 ff.
superordinate category, 252
Swift, Johnathan, 33
Swiss Family Robinson, The, **section 11.1**, 126 ff.
synedoche, 62, 65
synonym, 12, 19, 95, 201
System of Rhetoric, A, John Stirling, 62

'taboo' words, 207
tenor of a metaphor, 64
tense, backshifted, 220
that, marking a reported clause, 220
theme (grammatical), 87, 97, 119, 207, 255
theme in the clause – focus of information,
   section 4.1.2.3, 36 ff.
theme of exploitation in *Heart of Darkness*,
   212
This is the House that Jack Built, 32
Through the Looking-Glass Lewis Carroll,
   31
'thumping' rhythm in verse, **section 14.4**,
   171
token (words) (*no further references
   indexed*), 15
tone-unit, 140
tonic stress, 140
transactive actional process, 213–14
transformation, 37, 45, 129
transitive verb, 214
translations of the Bible, **section 11.2**, 133 ff.
'transparent' language, 183
Treasure Island, Robert Louis Stevenson,
   section 19.1, 235 ff.
triple off-beat, 150, 159
Trivium, the (Medieval Rhetoric, Grammar
   and Logic), 58
trochaic metre, *see* falling duple rhythm
trochee, 151, 157
tropes, **section 6.2.1**, 62 ff.
tropes and figures, **section 6.2**, 61 ff.
type (words) (*no further references indexed*),
   15

Ulysses, James Joyce, **section 18.4.1**, 232 ff.
Under Milk Wood, Dylan Thomas, 63
   sound and rhythm in, **section 13.6**, 164 ff.
unit of information, 140
unmarked order of words, 106, 110, 119

variation, elegant, 111
vehicle of a metaphor, 64
verb
   actional, 253
   intransitive, 214
   modal, 85
   relational, 253
   transitive, 214

verbless clause, 238
vernacular, 11
verse
   alliterative, 147
   black, 154, 186
   doggerel, 167
   free, **section 14.1**, 166 ff.
   hexameter, 197, 198
   metrical, **section 12.2.3**, 147 ff., 152, 156
   Old English, 145
   scansion of, 147
   stress-timed, 145, 157
verse patterns, 197
verse rhythms in prose, **section 15.1.2**,
   185 ff.
village, 14
vocabulary
   informal, 217
   non-core, 55, 91, 101, 128, 137, 192, 208
vocative, 118
voice
   active and passive, **section 4.1.2.1**, 35 ff.
   passive, 74, 255

Walton, William, 174–6
waltz rhythm, 175
Waltz, Edith Sitwell, **section 14.5.1.1**, 175 ff.
Wood Beyond the World, The, William
   Morris, 263
Woodlanders, The, Thomas Hardy – formal
   words, **section 2.4**, 16 ff.
word form, 29
   function, 29
   order (*no further references are indexed*),
   33
   'introductory', 216
   portmanteau, 31
word-forms, nonstandard, 22
words
   compound, 124
   dialectal, 123
   Old English derivation, 123
   'taboo', 207
Wordsworth, William, 105
Writing Degree Zero, Roland Barthes,
   section 8.1, 84 ff.

Yeats, W. B., **section 14.4.1.1**, 173 ff.
York pageant plays, 149